Capital Market Liberalization an

THE INITIATIVE FOR POLICY DIALOGUE SERIES

The Initiative for Policy Dialogue (IPD) brings together the top voices in development to address some of the most pressing and controversial debates in economic policy today. The IPD book series approaches topics such as capital market liberalization, macroeconomics, environmental economics, and trade policy from a balanced perspective, presenting alternatives and analyzing their consequences on the basis of the best available research. Written in a language accessible to policymakers and civil society, this series will rekindle the debate on economic policy and facilitate a more democratic discussion of development around the world.

OTHER TITLES PUBLISHED BY OXFORD UNIVERSITY PRESS
IN THIS SERIES

Fair Trade for All
Joseph E. Stiglitz and Andrew Charlton

Stability with Growth
Joseph E. Stiglitz, José Antonio Ocampo, Shari Spiegel,
Ricardo Ffrench-Davis, and Deepak Nayyar

Economic Development & Environmental Sustainability
Ramón López and Michael A. Toman

Capital Market Liberalization and Development

Edited by

José Antonio Ocampo and Joseph E. Stiglitz

OXFORD
UNIVERSITY PRESS

OXFORD

UNIVERSITY PRESS

Great Clarendon Street, Oxford OX2 6DP

Oxford University Press is a department of the University of Oxford.
It furthers the University's objective of excellence in research, scholarship,
and education by publishing worldwide in

Oxford New York

Auckland Cape Town Dar es Salaam Hong Kong Karachi
Kuala Lumpur Madrid Melbourne Mexico City Nairobi
New Delhi Shanghai Taipei Toronto

With offices in

Argentina Austria Brazil Chile Czech Republic France Greece
Guatemala Hungary Italy Japan Poland Portugal Singapore
South Korea Switzerland Thailand Turkey Ukraine Vietnam

Published in the United States
by Oxford University Press Inc., New York

First published 2008

British Library Cataloguing in Publication Data
Data available

Library of Congress Cataloging in Publication Data
Data available

Typeset by SPI Publisher Services, Pondicherry, India
Printed in Great Britain
on acid-free paper by
Biddles Ltd., King's Lynn, Norfolk

ISBN 978-0-19-923058-7
      978-0-19-923844-6 (Pbk.)

10 9 8 7 6 5 4 3 2 1

Acknowledgement

This book is based on the work of the Capital Markets Liberalization (CML) task force of the Initiative for Policy Dialogue (IPD). IPD is a global network of over 250 economists, researchers and practitioners committed to furthering understanding of the development process. We would like to thank all task force members, whose participation in provocative and productive dialogues and debates on CML informed the content of this book.

Special thanks goes to Shari Spiegel, who served as Executive Director of IPD during the course of this project.

We would also like to thank IPD staff Sheila Chanani, Sarah Green, Siddhartha Gupta, Ariel Schwartz, Lauren Anderson and Shana Hoftsetter for their work organizing task force meetings and coordinating production of this book. Thanks also to IPD interns Vitaly Bord and Raymond Koytcheff, and to members of Joseph Stiglitz's support staff Jill Blackford and Maria Papadakis. A special thanks to Dan Choate for his work on the glossary.

We thank our editors Sarah Caro and Jennifer Wilkinson and the staff of Oxford University Press for bringing this book into publication.

Finally, we are most grateful to The Ford Foundation, The John D. and Catherine T. MacArthur Foundation and the Canadian International Development Agency for funding the work of the CML task force and supporting IPD activities.

Contents

Contents

List of Figures

List of Figures

List of Tables

List of Tables

1

Capital Market Liberalization and Development

José Antonio Ocampo, Shari Spiegel, and Joseph E. Stiglitz

1.1 Introduction

In the 1980s and 1990s, many countries opened their capital accounts and liberalized their domestic financial markets as part of the wave of liberalization that characterized the period. In 1997, the IMF even proposed changing its charter to include a mandate to promote capital market liberalization. At the time, many other economists warned that open capital accounts would lead to volatility and increased risk without contributing to growth or stability. Yet there was virtually no body of material or survey of the literature that could provide the background for the debate on this issue. This book, along with *Stability with Growth: Macroeconomics, Liberalization, and Development* (Stiglitz et al. 2006) attempts to fill that gap—and go a step further, by providing an analysis of both the risks associated with capital market liberalization and the alternative policy options available to enhance macroeconomic management.

Today, the central intellectual battle over the effects of capital market liberalization (CML) has for the most part ended. In 2003, an IMF paper (Prasad et al. 2003) publicly acknowledged the risks inherent in CML. It has become clear that pro-cyclical capital flows—particularly (but not only) short-term speculative flows—have been at the heart of many of the crises in the developing world since the 1980s. Even when capital flows were not the direct cause of the crises, they played a central role in their propagation. These volatile flows have also made it difficult for policymakers to respond to the crises with traditional economic tools aimed at smoothing business cycles.

It is equally recognized that these flows may result in higher volatility of consumption, implying that there may be direct welfare losses from capital account liberalization, and that the recessions that accompany sharp contractions of external financing have high social costs. In addition, the uncertainties associated with volatile financing and growth may reduce investment and economic growth.

But critical policy debates continue, such as how much government should intervene, and when it does intervene, the best way to do so. Although capital market liberalization might not produce the promised benefits, many economists and policymakers still worry about the costs of intervention. Do these costs exceed the benefits? If so, how can policymakers use capital market interventions? What are the best kinds of interventions, under what circumstances? To answer these questions, we have to understand first why capital market liberalization has failed to enhance growth, why it has resulted in greater instability, why the poor appear to have borne the greatest burden, and why the advocates of capital market liberalization were so wrong.

There is another reason for this book's detailed analysis of capital market liberalization: while a new understanding of the consequences of CML is reshaping many policy discussions among academics and international institutions, ideological and vested interests remain. Principles of capital market liberalization have been included in bilateral trade agreements signed by the US, even with countries such as Chile, Colombia, and Singapore that, as we will see in this book, have made productive use of capital account regulations. Developing countries should be aware of all the consequences when they consider signing such agreements.

In recent years, there have even been some renewed calls for giving the IMF a mandate for capital account convertibility. The authors of the original 2003 IMF paper published another article in 2006 (Kose et al. 2006), asserting that financial globalization has 'collateral benefits' that might be difficult to uncover in econometric analysis. These benefits include financial market and institutional development, better governance, and macroeconomic discipline. However, as we point out in this chapter and elsewhere in this volume, the pro-cyclical nature of capital flows and the volatility associated with CML (which *are evident* in econometric analysis) have often had the *opposite* effect on both financial market and institutional development. Similarly, the market discipline imposed by short-term capital flows is not necessarily a positive force for long-term sustainable growth.

In this volume, the Initiative for Policy Dialogue (IPD) has brought together some of the leading researchers and practitioners from around the world to address these questions and examine the alternative forms of intervention. Although all the authors in this volume recognize the risks of capital market liberalization, they do not provide a simple or single answer to the questions posed above. It is clear to the authors of this introductory chapter, as well as to some others in this volume, that the ability to manage (which means, many times, restrict) capital flows is critical to counter-cyclical macroeconomic management. But others (see, in particular, the contributions of Schmukler and Rojas-Suarez) argue against direct controls, and have an inclination towards more indirect forms of intervention.

This first chapter introduces the arguments and provides a framework for the issues. It is divided into four sections, aside from this introduction. Section 1.2 addresses an important set of market failures—imperfections in markets that are likely to be particularly significant in developing countries. Many of the arguments for capital market liberalization are predicated on the assumption that, but for government intervention, markets would efficiently allocate resources. These market failures, however, provide a rationale for interventions in capital markets; whereas capital market liberalization may exacerbate the consequences of these market failures. Section 1.3 analyzes the effects of capital market liberalization on developing countries. Section 1.4 introduces alternative policy options for interventions in capital markets. The last section provides brief conclusions.

The rest of the chapters in this volume are organized around three major themes. The first part of the volume examines the effects of CML on developing countries. The second part analyzes experiences with different types of capital account management. The third part considers different forms of national and global financial regulations that may be used to manage the risks that capital flows generate on domestic financial systems.

1.2 Implications of Market Failures in Financial Markets

Advocates of capital market liberalization believed that CML would increase economic growth and efficiency and reduce risk. In their view, CML would stabilize consumption and investment. The two main arguments put forward were: (a) that capital would flow from industrial countries, where capital has low marginal returns, to developing countries, where its relative scarcity implies high marginal returns; and (b) that CML would enhance stability by allowing countries to tap into diversified sources of funds.

Today, even the IMF recognizes that capital market liberalization has not led to growth and efficiency, and has not enhanced stability as they had hoped—and predicted. In the well known 2003 study cited earlier (Prasad et al. 2003), they repeatedly emphasize that 'theory' predicts that CML *should* enhance stability. Their 2006 study (Kose et al. 2006) repeats this conclusion but offers alternative interpretations to what seems to them the anomalous finding that CML does not bring the benefits promised. But the basic problem, as Stiglitz argues in his contribution to this volume, is that their 'theory' (i.e., orthodox neoclassical theory) is predicated on *perfect capital markets* (e.g., no credit rationing, no information imperfections, and perfect forecast of future events) and *perfect inter-temporal smoothing* (with individuals living infinitely long or fully integrating their children's welfare with their own).

Yet it has long been recognized that such assumptions are also entirely unrealistic. It should have been obvious to even a casual observer that something was wrong with the standard theory, at least as applied to developing countries. The standard theory predicted that capital flows would be counter-cyclical; yet the underlying concern of critics of capital market liberalization is that the facts suggest otherwise. It is precisely because capital often flows out of a country in times of crisis and during booms that some restrictions are needed. Had the IMF study shown that consumption volatility was lower in liberalized economies, they would have faced a daunting challenge: to explain how, in spite of pro-cyclical capital flows, CML contributed to stability. To our knowledge, no advocate of CML has ever even attempted this task.

As we suggested earlier, underlying many of the arguments for capital market liberalization is a simple theory: free and unfettered markets lead to economic efficiency. But economic science has provided several important caveats to such free market doctrines. For more than seventy five years, economists have realized that, without government intervention, market economies may operate significantly below their potential. Certain types of shocks can lead to unemployment, and this unemployment can, without government intervention, persist. Government policies are required to: (a) change the nature of the shocks the economy confronts; (b) reduce the underperformance of the economy that results when the economy experiences a shock, both with automatic stabilizers and discretionary actions; and (c) create social protection systems to help individuals and firms cope with the consequences of these shocks.

Capital market liberalization is an example of a structural policy that affects both the nature of the shocks the economy experiences and the way the economy responds to these shocks. Hence, an analysis of CML within a model in which the economy is always at full employment ignores what fundamentally is at issue.[1]

Theoretical and empirical research over the past quarter century have helped explain why the market economy often does not function as well as free market advocates had hoped. Many of the problems are related to problems in capital markets.[2] There are several types of market failures: general macroeconomic failures, which together with the information problems inherent to the functioning of capital markets imply that financial markets face waves of euphoria and pessimism; problems with externalities; and problems associated with coordination failures. In addition, risk (or insurance)

---

[1] But, as Stiglitz (this volume) points out, even in a full employment model, their conclusions are flawed.

[2] Most of these market failures are related to problems of information asymmetries. See, e.g., Stiglitz (2002b).

markets are imperfect even in developed countries, but such markets are particularly weak, or absent, in most developing countries.

As a result of these problems, market economies are not self-regulating, and government interventions are necessary to provide regulations that reduce exposure to risks, reduce the extent to which markets amplify the shocks to which they are exposed, and enhance the capacity to quickly restore the economy to health.

1.2.1 *Imperfect Information and General Macroeconomic Failures*

All countries—both developed and developing—confront problems of capital market instability, but, as we shall see, the consequences of CML are greater in developing countries. Even the United States suffered an 'attack' on the dollar in 1971. It intervened in the free flow of capital and was forced to go off the fixed exchange rate system. In the mid-1990s, the United States worried about the fall of the dollar relative to the yen despite no apparent changes in the real economic positions of the two countries, and in 2003–04, Europe worried about the rise of the euro relative to the dollar. This high volatility was not related to sudden changes in trade; rather, capital movements were largely responsible for the exchange rate fluctuations.

IRRATIONAL AND RATIONAL EXUBERANCE AND PESSIMISM

Traditionally, economists argued that rational speculation helps stabilize markets. But, often, markets do not exhibit rationality. Since the late 1990s, economists have noted markets' 'irrational exuberance'.[3] There are macroeconomic consequences of this irrationality. Investor 'herding' is one of the key reasons for the booms and busts that characterize financial markets. When investors flee a country—as they did in Thailand, Korea, and Indonesia in 1997 and in the myriad of other financial panics around the world—innocent bystanders get hurt.

Interestingly, recent research shows that herd behavior *is* consistent with rational expectations when information is imperfect, though the extent of the herd behavior may well be greater than can be explained by these models.[4] The essential reason for volatility in financial markets, as emphasized by Keynes, is that market players respond to *expectations*. The value of any asset today depends on what others are *expected* to be willing to pay for it tomorrow, and that depends in turn (in a never ending chain) on what others

[3] The phrase was made famous by Alan Greenspan. See Greenspan (1996). See the classic study by Kindleberger (2000, first published 1978); and the more recent work of Shiller (2000).

[4] See Banerjee (1992); Bikhchandani et al. (1992). For an application to portfolio allocations on international stock markets, see Calvo and Mendoza (2000); for other applications see Chamley (2004); Caplin and Lehay (1994).

are expected to be willing to pay the day after.[5] These expectations are based on information about current conditions. Such information is inherently incomplete and costly to process. This makes it rational for everyone to glean information about the desirability of investing from the opinions and actions of others. In addition, the major market players—investment banks, rating agencies, international financial institutions—use the same sources of information and tend to reinforce each other's interpretations. Since these market players have better access to relevant information and are better able to process it, others are likely to follow their lead, resulting in herd behavior (See Ocampo 2002b).

These characteristics of financial markets give rise to risks of 'correlated mistakes': unexpected news that simultaneously contradicts the general opinion is reported, and all market players realize that they were wrong and pull their funds out of certain asset classes. This type of correlated mistake has triggered numerous panics and crises. For example, the realization that Thailand's reserves were close to zero was one of the culminating factors that triggered the Asian crisis in 1997.[6]

This 'contagion' of opinions and expectations can lead to euphoria or panic, as has been reflected through history in successive waves of irrational exuberance and unwarranted pessimism—or, to use the terminology of financial markets, of phases of 'appetite for risk' (underestimation of risks) followed by phases of 'flight to quality' (risk aversion). Herding behavior by investors takes place even in normal times but can be particularly devastating in periods of high uncertainty when 'information' becomes unreliable and expectations become highly volatile. Indeed, when views converge, the information that underlies panics and crises may be factually imprecise or incorrect, but it may still prevail in the functioning of the market, generating what the literature has come to call 'self-fulfilling prophesies'.[7]

---

[5] These expectations may, of course, be related to expectations of underlying variables, like dividends, interest rates, etc. The only way that prices today would not depend on expectations would be if there were futures markets extending infinitely out into the future, i.e. one could buy and sell securities at any date no matter how far away. Arrow and Debreu, in their classic studies of the idealized market economy, assumed that such markets existed. See, e.g., Arrow and Debreu (1954).

[6] While the discovery of the foreign exchange position of the Thai central bank triggered the crisis, even if the Thai central bank had not been taking the positions it had, it is likely that there would eventually have been a crisis. The puzzle is why the market did not seem to recognize this. The stock and real estate markets had boomed in the mid-1990s, the exchange rate had appreciated, and imports had surged, generating an increase in the external deficit, and financing—as recognized only ex post by the IMF and financial markets—was dangerously short-term.

[7] That is, if everyone hears a rumor that the stock is going to crash, they all sell, and the stock does in fact fall in price, as expected. There is a somewhat more difficult question: whether there are multiple rational expectations that are precisely correct (rather than *roughly* correct, in the sense that the stock is going down). Forty years ago, Hahn (1966), Shell and Stiglitz (1967), and Stiglitz (1973) provided the affirmative answer—see footnote 8 below.

Standard compensation packages for investment managers, which often measure performance relative to a benchmark index, may exacerbate the problem of herding. Latin America, for instance, is heavily weighted in the major emerging market indices. The investment manager that stays close to the index (and/or follows the herd) will not underperform the index (and/or their competitors) when Latin America has disappointing returns, but if they do underweight Latin America and Latin America performs exceptionally well, they will underperform and their pay will most likely be adjusted accordingly (see Nalebuff and Stiglitz 1983).

BUBBLES AND CONTAGION

These theories of herding are part of a growing literature that demonstrates how investor behavior easily leads to bubbles (see, e.g., Shiller 2000). Bubbles even appear (and burst) in developed countries with well functioning markets and the best available standards of prudential regulation and supervision. Much of this work is a development of the analysis of the instability of the *real* dynamics, for example of Hahn (1966) and Shell and Stiglitz (1967),[8] and the even more relevant analysis by Minsky (1982) of the endogenous unstable dynamics of financial markets. Minsky showed how financial booms generate excessive risk taking by market agents, eventually leading to crises. A similar explanation has been suggested by White (2005), who underscores how the 'search for yield' characteristic of low interest rate environments generates incentives for credit creation, carry trade, and leverage that easily build up asset bubbles.[9] In developing countries with thin or small markets, a short-term bias (as discussed below), and weaker prudential regulation and supervision, bubbles are easier to create, and their effects are more devastating.[10]

The problems of bubbles are exacerbated by contagion—when a bubble breaks in one economy, the downturn quickly spreads elsewhere. Contagion is clearly visible in the dynamics of international capital markets vis-à-vis developing countries. Indeed, some empirical studies have argued that many, perhaps most, of the shocks (both positive and negative) experienced by

[8] Hahn (1966) and Shell and Stiglitz (1967) showed that there could be multiple paths consistent with rational behavior in the short run. Without capital markets extending infinitely far into the future, the economy will not necessarily converge to the long run equilibrium. There are paths which are dynamically consistent with rational expectations in the short run. While herding behavior is often attributed to investor myopia, these results suggest that bubbles may arise so long as investors do not look infinitely far into the future. However, even when investors look infinitely far into the future, it may not be possible for them to predict (on the basis of rational expectations alone) how the economy will evolve, if, for instance, there are multiple paths consistent with rational expectations. See Stiglitz (1973).

[9] In the words of the BIS in reference to world financial conditions in 2005: 'the main risks to the financial sector could stem from financial excesses linked to a generalized complacency towards risk reinforced by a benign short-term outlook' (BIS 2005: 120).

[10] In addition, as we will see, capital market liberalization also makes it more difficult for governments to respond to booms and busts in effective ways.

developing countries involve *contagion*—of both optimism and pessimism. During the boom in international capital markets in the 1990s, capital even flooded countries that had major macroeconomic problems, such as Moldova (which defaulted on its debt shortly thereafter) (see Spiegel forthcoming). After the 1997 East Asian crisis, external financing even dropped in countries that seemed to have good 'macroeconomic fundamentals', such as Hong Kong and Chile.

ALTERNATIVE EXPLANATIONS OF CONTAGION

Information problems are particularly important in international capital markets, where investors face not only greater information asymmetries, but also different legal systems, and much weaker (or absent) regulation. As discussed above, expectations may be largely derived from the actions of others. In a world in which prices are determined by expectations, 'contagion' of optimism and pessimism among market agents can result in a crisis in one country spreading elsewhere. (There may or may not be a 'rational' basis of such shared optimism or pessimism. There may be little reason that good news about East Asia would portend well for Latin America.) When investors see capital fleeing one country, they may well worry that something is wrong with other similar countries and pull their money out of those countries as well.

But 'contagion of expectations' is only one of several explanations of the spread of crises from one country to another.[11] Financial linkages that characterize a globalized financial world can spread problems from one area to another. Financial agents that incur losses in some markets are often forced to sell their assets in other markets to recover liquidity (or pay their short-term obligations, including margin calls). Similarly, in periods of euphoria, access to finance in one part of the world economy can facilitate investments in others, and gains in one country can lead to investments elsewhere, often involving greater risk.

An important aspect of behavior in financial markets—which can exacerbate fluctuations—is their short-term focus. Market-sensitive risk management practices (Persaud 2000), evaluation of investment funds (and managers' bonuses) by short-term criteria, benchmarking against indices, bank regulations requiring less capital for purposes of capital adequacy standards for short-term debt,[12] the behavior of credit-rating agencies, and investment rules for certain categories of fiduciaries,[13] and, more recently, the practice

[11] The IMF often seemed to emphasize this source of contagion in the East Asia crisis.

[12] While such rules might make sense for any single bank, when all banks are subjected to such rules, typically they all cannot easily pull out their short-term money quickly. Moreover, bank regulators tend to ignore the systemic consequences of these rules.

[13] These are restricted to put their money in investment grade securities. In the East Asia crisis, credit-rating agencies, who failed to anticipate the crisis, quickly downgraded the bonds of the affected countries to below investment grade, forcing quick sales, which further depressed bond prices. See Ferri et al. (1999).

of requiring firms, even in advanced financial markets, to announce short-term profit forecasts (which are inherently uncertain) all contribute to the short-term bias that characterizes the behavior of financial agents. Standard operating procedures of financial markets also contribute to this volatility. Countries (as well as firms) tend to be clustered in certain risk categories by analysts; this clustering leads to contagion. While these practices contribute to herding behavior and market volatility in all markets, their consequences are especially serious in the thin markets that characterize developing countries.

Finally, trade linkages can play an important role in contagion—as a downturn in one country reduces the demand for the products produced by countries that export to it.[14] Standard analyses of East Asia before the crisis underestimated the importance of these linkages and the role that they might play in spreading the downturn in one country to its trading partners.

1.2.2 *Externalities and Coordination Failures*

The presence of contagion implies the existence of an externality—what goes on in one country has effects on others. Herding behavior itself reflects an externality: the actions of one individual convey information to others. Whenever there are externalities, markets are not likely to work well. This section traces through the nature and consequences of these externalities.

The bail-outs of the mid- and late 1990s recognized the presence of this externality: 'contagion' justified the interventions. Discussions on the need for more information about the quantity of capital flows also implicitly recognize externalities—in well functioning markets, prices convey all the relevant information; such quantitative information would be irrelevant. Yet if there are externalities, and it is desirable to intervene in markets to deal with the *consequences* of capital flows, it should be desirable to intervene in markets before the problems arise; if government has a role in treating a disease, it also has a role in preventing the disease.

These externalities take on a variety of forms. *Price externalities* arise both during periods of capital inflows and outflows. During waves of inflows, the exchange rate often appreciates, harming exporters and those attempting to compete with imports.[15] During outflows the exchange rate often weakens,

---

[14] These trade interdependencies played a large role in the 'contagion' in the East Asia crisis. By contrast, the contagion of the Russia crisis to Brazil had little to do either with trade or information but with specific institutional features of the market. Such trade linkages are, of course, standard fare in Keynesian style macroeconomic models, where output is limited by aggregate demand. Keynes' concern about these trade linkages provided part of the underlying motivation for the creation of the IMF. It was thus ironic that these linkages seem to have been underestimated in that crisis.

[15] Classical microeconomic theory suggested that pecuniary externalities did not matter—at least for the standard welfare theorems—but when there are market imperfections, including imperfections of information, they do. See Greenwald and Stiglitz (1986).

and the domestic value of foreign-denominated debt (in terms of domestic currency) rises. Central banks often raise interest rates to limit the extent of currency depreciation. The exchange rate depreciation and interest rate increases can force firms into bankruptcy, destroying jobs. As we will explain below, the magnitude of the volatility depends on the amount and form of borrowing. Since the volatility itself exerts an externality, the borrowing that can give rise to it generates an externality as well.[16]

Quantity externalities are particularly acute when capital outflows lead to credit rationing: when capital leaves the country, banks may be forced to reduce credit availability. Another quantity externality arises when a country's creditors look at the total short-term debt of the country and the ratio of outstanding short-term debt to reserves and, believing that that higher ratio indicates a higher probability of a crisis, cut commercial credit lines. More generally, the greater the amount of outstanding debt (relative to a country's reserves) the higher the likelihood of a crisis.[17] The IMF implicitly recognized the importance of this externality during the East Asia crisis, when it urged greater information about the total supply of outstanding short-term debt (see Rodrik and Velasco 2000). In a standard competitive equilibrium model, such quantitative information would be of no relevance.[18]

There are then two related externalities: if a country does not increase reserves when its domestic firms increase short-term foreign currency borrowing, it faces a greater risk of a crisis. But several countries (even those with flexible exchange rates) chose not only to keep significant international reserves, but also to increase their reserves as foreign-denominated short-term liabilities increase. This is a basic reason why, after the costly crises that took place between 1997 and 2002, many developing countries have opted to accumulate large volumes of international reserves as 'self-insurance' against future capital account crises.

---

[16] All of this assumes that individuals or firms do not fully insure themselves against these risks. In many cases, such insurance is not available. Individuals who borrow in foreign currency (with incomes denominated in local currencies) will see their wealth plummet as the exchange rates fall. But as their wealth plummets, they may retrench investment and consumption. The resulting fall in GDP may simultaneously reduce confidence in the country and its currency, leading to further falls in the exchange rate. These are another set of external costs which individuals do not take into account in making their borrowing decisions. See Korinek (2007) for a fuller discussion of these externalities.

[17] Whether this is inherently so is a question of some debate; but if market participants believe that is the case, their actions may lead to self-fulfilling behavior, as they pull their money out of the country when foreign denominated indebtedness rises above a critical level. See Furman and Stiglitz (1998).

[18] Standard economic theory argues that all relevant information is contained in prices. Modern information economics has helped explained what is wrong with this standard result of competitive equilibrium analysis. (For a discussion in the context of insurance markets, see, for instance, Arnott and Stiglitz 1990, 1991.)

But there are high opportunity costs of these reserves. Reserves are usually held in US Treasury bills or bonds or other liquid assets denominated in 'hard currencies', which have relatively low rates of return. These social costs (the difference between the return on the US Treasury bills and what the funds could have yielded if invested elsewhere as well as the increased likelihood of a crisis) are not incorporated in the decisions of private domestic firms to borrow short-term funds abroad. (These costs might be mitigated if there were adequate 'collective insurance' against financial crises.)

An interrelated set of market failures involves creditor or investor coordination problems. This is especially relevant during periods of capital flight. It pays investors to remain in a country as long as other investors also remain. But if some investors start to believe that the country will face a crisis and begin to remove their money, it will be in the interest of others to do the same. Investors and creditors can get caught in the rush to pull out their funds, causing the markets to collapse. The currency, interest rate, and stock market weaken and tend to overshoot substantially.[19] The economy enters into recession, weakening the tax base and making it more difficult for the government to repay its loans. Since the markets usually rebound afterwards, investors would have been better off collectively if they had left their funds in the country. This is true even though it was in each individual investor's interest—given their expectations about what others would do—to exit at the time.

The behavior of short-term capital during the Asian crisis provides an example of these types of coordination problems. If all lenders had agreed to roll over their loans to Korea, Korea would have been able to meet its debt obligations relatively easily (as the country clearly demonstrated over the next few years). But none of the lenders wanted to take the risk. When each refused to roll over outstanding loans, the country faced a crisis.[20] Capital flight in Russia during the 1990s provides another example. Arguably, it was in most people's interest to reinvest in the country and build a stronger legal and regulatory environment.[21] But if each believed that others were going to

---

[19] When a currency weakens excessively, by say 30%, and then strengthens so that the total devaluation is only around 20%, the currency is said to overshoot. For example, according to a poll of the Citibank trading floor in 1989, traders believed that interest rate and currency markets react to bad news by overshooting by an average of 50%. Sometimes, overshooting is part of a dynamically consistent path with rational expectations, but typically, it reflects an overreaction of market expectations.

[20] In the end, in 1998, some months after the massive bail-out that failed to stabilize the exchange rate, the US Treasury helped coordinate a rollover of Korean loans.

[21] There were probably some oligarchs—those who were much better at asset stripping than at wealth creation—who benefited from the lack of the rule of law and open capital markets. Conceivably, had there not been open capital markets, even though GDP might have been higher, there might have been a greater demand for the rule of law; and if a rule of law had been quickly instituted, they would not have been able to 'steal' as much as they did. These policies had both adverse efficiency and distributive consequences.

take their money out of the country and that the country would plummet into a recession, it would pay each to pull their capital out. Russia's open capital markets provided an opportunity for investors to remove substantial amounts of money from the country. Open capital markets also increased the incentive of Russian entrepreneurs to 'asset strip', that is, to engage in transactions that allowed them to convert their assets into dollars that could be deposited in foreign banks.[22] Russia's plight worsened as they did so. Because of the capital flight, those who stripped assets did in fact do better than those who attempted to create wealth inside the country by investing more. But the country as a whole was worse off.

The essential rationale for restrictions on capital outflows in the face of externalities and coordination failures is that they can eliminate a 'bad equilibrium' and ensure that an economy coordinates on the 'good equilibrium', where the costs of externalities are taken into account. The interesting aspect of this intervention is that there are no additional costs (e.g., of enforcement) of bringing about the 'good equilibrium'. When all players invest in the country, it pays each individual investor to do just that.[23]

1.2.3 The Effect of Incomplete Domestic Financial Markets in Developing Countries

One of the reasons that CML has such a large negative effect on developing countries is because capital markets are thin[24] and financial instruments are generally short-term or non-existent.[25] Higher risks are, in turn, a characteristic of thin markets. Market resource allocations are typically inefficient, *even taking into account the absence of the risk market*, and are clearly so when the markets for insuring against risks are absent (i.e., the market is not constrained Pareto efficient).[26] There are, therefore, government interventions which would constitute a welfare improvement. In these circumstances,

---

[22] The problem was exacerbated by the political illegitimacy of the privatization, which meant that there might be long-run pressures to renationalize. Only by taking money out of the country could the oligarchs truly protect their ill-gotten wealth.

[23] There are many examples of this kind of multiple equilibria, and such models have played an increasing role in explaining crisis. Among the early examples was that of Diamond and Dybvig (1983), explaining bank runs.

[24] Later, we shall discuss another effect of thin markets—the possibility of manipulation.

[25] Standard economic theory (Arrow-Debreu) requires that there be a complete set of risk and futures markets if the competitive market equilibrium is to be (Pareto) efficient. The absence of these markets is a *market failure*. Modern economic theories (based on imperfect and asymmetric information) have helped to explain why, for instance, risk markets are often absent.

[26] There are externality like effects. Actions by individuals can affect the probability distribution (e.g., of exchange rates), in ways which can increase risk and lower welfare. See Stiglitz (1982) and Greenwald and Stiglitz (1986).

capital market liberalization can lead to a *worsening* of market efficiency, and appropriately designed capital market interventions can increase welfare.

Developing country financial markets are, for instance, often characterized by maturity mismatches, with long-term investments partly, or largely, financed by short-term loans. During a crisis, there is a risk that creditors might not roll over short-term liabilities, generating a liquidity crunch as borrowers are unable to repay their loans. Even when short-term debts are rolled over, domestic borrowers still bear the cost of interest rate fluctuations.[27]

To overcome the short-term bias of domestic financial markets, agents that have access to foreign credit often borrow from abroad. Those firms that do not sell in external markets, and thus have no revenues in foreign currencies, then incur currency mismatches. (The fact that the opportunity to borrow abroad is available only to the larger economic agents also generates distributive issues, as it implies that smaller firms have no way of covering their maturity mismatch.)[28] When domestic banks use foreign funds to finance domestic currency loans, they incur a currency mismatch between their assets and liabilities that can lead to a financial meltdown if and when the currency depreciates. (If banks lend those funds domestically in foreign currencies to avoid currency mismatches in their portfolio, they merely transfer the risk to those firms that do not have foreign exchange revenues. This can lead to capital losses for those non-financial firms during crises, generating credit risks for the banks that lend to them.)

Until quite recently, the external debt of most developing countries was issued in foreign currencies, a phenomenon that has come to be called the 'original sin'. Indeed, international creditors often have been unwilling to take local market risks (or they have demanded such high compensation to bear that risk that local borrowers would prefer to bear it themselves), so they lend to developing countries in hard currencies, with the domestic borrowers assuming the currency risk. Even domestic financial assets and liabilities are sometimes denominated in such currencies. This domestic financial dollar/euroization generates great risks for developing countries. Furthermore, what matters is not the average or total exposure, but the exposure of each market participant. The net worth of every participant that has a currency mismatch between assets and liabilities is exposed to the risks of exchange rate volatility.

---

[27] Historically, long-term finance was slow to develop. In several countries, direct government intervention was required. Asymmetries of information (and especially monitoring costs) explain the prevalence of short-term contracts. See, e.g., Rey and Stiglitz (1993).

[28] These distributive issues came to the fore during the East Asia crisis, where the IMF put rescuing foreign lenders above the interests of local borrowers.

Mismatches would cause less concern if the corporations or banks involved purchased insurance ('cover'). In developing countries, however, the insurance premia for currency risk are excessive and, when available,[29] insurance typically provides only short-term coverage.[30] The result is that developing countries bear the brunt of the currency risk, even though lenders in developed countries are better placed to take on this risk since they have the ability to diversify their portfolios.[31] Furthermore the major instruments to cover risks, derivatives, may become an additional source of instability: those purportedly providing 'cover' default precisely in those times (i.e., crises) when the insurance is most needed.

The problems just discussed are a manifestation of a fundamental market failure: in international capital markets, developing countries bear the brunt of exchange rate and interest rate risk even when the source of the fluctuations lies outside the country.[32] This bears no resemblance to an optimal international arrangement, as the developed countries are better able to bear these risks.

One of the reasons that financial market volatility takes such a toll on developing countries is because equity markets are weak, so firms have to rely more on debt. When firms make decisions about how much to borrow, they need to take into account the size of fluctuations in output, prices, and interest rates. The greater volatility of these variables under CML means that firms make less use of debt financing. But the alternative—raising new capital by issuing equity—is difficult in developing countries. (This is also true in developed countries because information asymmetries make raising funds by

---

[29] The economics of information has provided explanations for the absence of insurance markets, associated particularly with the existence of information asymmetries.

[30] The problem is related perhaps to the 'irrationality' of market participants. They consider the implicit insurance premium excessive, given their view of the low probability of a devaluation of the currency. But why borrowers should believe that their estimate of the probability is more accurate than the market's is not clear. There is a further difficulty: even when cover is obtained, there is a risk that the insurer will not be able to honor his commitment. The cost of ascertaining whether an insurance firm will honor its commitment to provide insurance is another explanation of the absence of insurance.

[31] See Dodd and Spiegel (2005) for an analysis of risk diversification in developing country currency markets.

[32] That is, if the source of the instability was in the behavior of the country itself, one might worry that more complete 'insurance' would alter incentives to engage in risk-reducing activities. If, for instance, the reason for the risk associated with domestic debt is volatile monetary policies, giving rise to instability in the inflation rate, providing insurance against this volatility would reduce incentives to have more responsible monetary policies. When there is 'moral hazard' (with insurances affecting behavior), there will only be partial insurance.

issuing new equity costly.)[33] In effect, CML has forced firms to rely more on self-financing. The result is that capital is allocated less efficiently. This failure is particularly ironic because the major argument in favor of capital market liberalization has been that it increases efficiency in the allocation of capital.[34]

Moreover, with CML, the scope for countercyclical monetary policy is restricted. (This is an example of the broader problem of reduced policy autonomy.) To avoid a rush of capital out of the country in a crisis, governments usually raise interest rates, depressing the economy further. Even firms with moderate levels of debt equity ratios flounder and are sometimes forced into bankruptcy. There is an enormous economic cost to bankruptcy in these cases. It is not just inefficient firms that are forced out of business; even well managed firms that borrowed too much, because conditions prevailing before the crisis seemed to justify more investment, are forced into bankruptcy. The destruction of organizational and informational capital can set back growth for years.[35]

1.2.4 *The Effect of Institutional Weaknesses*

The supporters of the 1997 effort to change the IMF charter to institute an agenda of capital account liberalization did, appropriately, add several caveats. They recognized that liberalization requires sufficiently strong and stable financial institutions, which in turn means that a strong regulatory framework needs to be in place before liberalization takes place (a recommendation that, in any case, reflects that CML was initiated in countries without strong regulatory frameworks in the previous quarter century, when much of the liberalization processes took place). Still, it was clear that they thought most developing countries should liberalize their capital markets.

Today, recognition of the importance of those caveats has grown, as the contributions of Schmukler and Rojas-Suarez to this volume indicate. But

---

[33] See Greenwald and Stiglitz (2003) and the references cited there; or Majluf and Myers (1984). In developing countries, there are additional reasons for the lack of use of equity markets, such as the absence of a legal framework to ensure the rights of shareholders, including minority shareholders.

[34] See, e.g., Shapiro and Stiglitz (1984).

[35] Typically, it is argued, bankruptcy does not result in the destruction of physical capital, but only its reorganization in more productive ways. But when there is systemic bankruptcy associated with high interest rates and/or a major economic slowdown, the prospects for efficient reorganization are diminished, and the chances of a delayed reorganization are enhanced. Without adequate oversight, there is a real risk of asset stripping during the extended period of reorganization.

even economically advanced countries have found it difficult to establish sufficiently effective regulatory structures to avoid crises, as the financial crises in Scandinavia in the early 1990s and the savings and loan scandals in the United States in the 1980s demonstrate. These examples show that crises can easily occur in countries with relatively strong regulation, high degree of transparency, and limited crony capitalism. The financial crisis of Japan from the early 1990s to the mid-2000s also indicates that crises (or significant slowdowns) can be long-lasting, even in industrial countries.

The institutional framework in which financial institutions operate in developing countries is generally weaker, and thus less able to withstand shocks—despite the fact that these countries face more frequent and larger shocks. The issues that the institutional framework must address are also different, due to shallower financial markets and widespread presence of maturity and currency mismatches. Therefore, the induced volatility arising from capital market liberalization can easily lead to systemic problems that may persist for years, and which may far outweigh any benefits that capital market liberalization may have brought in the pre-crisis years.

The growing use of derivatives has made the formulation of appropriate regulations more complex, as Dodd argues in his contribution to this volume. Indeed, this demonstrates that the caveats about the need for stronger financial regulation generally leave aside this important (and the most dynamic) segment of financial markets, which is under-regulated even in industrial countries. The US government-engineered, privately financed bail-out of Long Term Capital Management (LTCM) in October 1998 and recent debates on the need to regulate hedge funds in advanced countries demonstrate this. Even proponents of CML argued that the collapse of this single hedge fund, with an estimated exposure of a trillion dollars, could have global repercussions so great that government intervention was required.[36] If this is true, the argument that speculative activity associated with capital market liberalization in developing countries could have devastating effects is all the more compelling. Moreover, much of the money put at risk by LTCM came from supposedly well regulated banks, so improving regulation by itself will not suffice.

1.2.5 Productivity Shocks

We have seen how, regardless of the source of a disturbance to the economy, capital market liberalization may amplify the effects and reduce

[36] Those who defended the role of the government in the bail-out (and who resisted allegations that underlying the publicly orchestrated, privately financed bail-out was crony capitalism and corporate mis-governance, American, rather than East Asian, style) did so because they believed LTCM posed a global threat. For a discussion of the LTCM bail-out see Edwards (1999); Jorion (2000); Stiglitz (2002a, 2003).

the scope of government stabilization. Capital market liberalization short-circuits some of the mechanisms that would naturally (and over time) smooth out the impact of disturbances (see Stiglitz 2004).[37] For instance, with capital market regulations in place, higher incomes during a positive productivity shock lead to more savings as earnings are re-invested in the local economy. This drives down interest rates and boosts wages in subsequent periods. Some of the benefits of the productivity shock are saved for the future. With full capital market liberalization, this does not occur because the (temporarily) higher earnings are often invested abroad.

Consider an economy with an open capital market. An economy experiencing a period of unusually high productivity (a productivity shock) has an increased ability and desire to borrow (as the United States did in the 1990s). Capital flows into the country, and workers' incomes rise during the boom, both because of the productivity shock *and* because of the capital inflow. When productivity returns to more normal levels, incomes shrink as capital flows out of the country. The open capital market amplifies the effects of productivity fluctuations at home.

1.3 Effects of Capital Market Liberalization on Developing Countries

The previous section explained, in general, why markets often fail to lead to efficient resource allocations, providing a rationale for government interventions in markets. We focused our attention on market failures in financial markets and showed that capital market liberalization might exacerbate the market inefficiencies, increasing volatility and reducing the efficiency with which resources are allocated.

In this section, we focus more directly on the problems of developing countries. As the contribution of Schmukler to this volume indicates, there is now a fairly general recognition that capital market liberalization has generated risks and has made it more difficult for developing countries to achieve real macroeconomic stability. There is also relatively broad recognition that it has also failed to help these countries achieve faster rates of economic growth.

Higher risks mean, first, that the marginal returns to capital adjusted for risk are often less in these countries than in developed countries.[38] So, capital does not necessarily flow in the direction expected by defenders of CML in many cases, it flows in the opposite direction ('water flowing uphill'). More

---

[37] One should contrast this analysis with that of the IMF study by Prasad et al. (2003).

[38] For an elaboration of this point, see Stiglitz (1989); and Lucas (1990).

generally, higher risks imply that integration of developing countries into international financial markets is necessarily a *segmented integration*, and that the persistence of high risk premia (at least for long periods of time) is a structural effect of financial globalization, as Frenkel argues in his contribution to this volume.

In the paragraphs below, we trace the evidence on the relationship between capital market liberalization and capital account instability, between capital account instability—and, more broadly CML—and macroeconomic instability, and between CML and growth.

1.3.1 *Capital Account Volatility and Developing Countries*

The worst crises in developing countries have been characterized by the shrinking availability of capital—foreign lenders cut new lending sharply and refuse to roll over loans. As we have already noted, banks' unwillingness to roll over trade and other short-term credit lines played a central role in the Asian crisis and other episodes. But domestic investors are also important. Domestic capital flight (based on speculation that the currency was going to depreciate) played a central role in several crises, such as the 1994 Mexican crisis.

While short-term speculative flows are particularly unstable, the volatility of other capital flows is also important. Instability is, for instance, also a feature of longer term portfolio investments. Even though most bond issues are medium to long-term, bond financing is strongly pro-cyclical. This may reflect the short-term bias of many institutional investors who are active in the emerging bond market. The same is true of investments (also by institutional investors) in developing country equities. When stock markets are doing well, additional funds flow in, reinforcing the boom; but when stock markets crash, the opposite occurs. Since exchange rate fluctuations are pro-cyclical, investors in bonds and stocks denominated in developing country currencies buy when there are expectations of appreciation and sell when there are expectations of depreciation.

More broadly, capital flows to developing countries are subject not only to short-term volatility but also to *medium* term fluctuations, which reflect the successive waves of optimism and pessimism that characterize financial markets (see Figure 1.1 in relation to the evolution of spreads since 1994). These fluctuations are reflected in the pro-cyclical pattern of spreads (narrowing during booms and widening during crises), variations in the availability of financing (absence or presence of credit rationing), and in maturities (shorter maturity of financing during crises, or the use of options that have a similar effect).

Interestingly, as Figure 1.1 indicates, the large fluctuations in risk premia for emerging markets tend to correlate with spreads of US high-yield bonds.

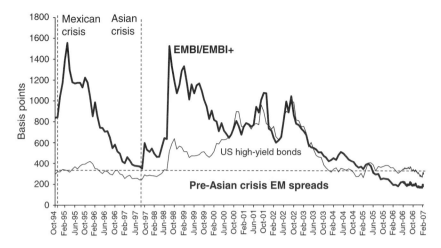

Figure 1.1 Spreads on JP Morgan EMBI+ and US high-yield bonds (October 1994 to 2007 YTD)

Source: ECLAC, on the basis of data from Merrill Lynch's US High-Yield Master II Index (H0A0), and JP Morgan's EMBI (until February 1996), and EMBI+ (from March 1996 to 2007 YTD).

Thus, pro-cyclicality of financial markets is a characteristic that affects all types of assets considered risky by market agents. (Correlations between spreads of different assets are, of course, imperfect, reflecting the specific factors associated with the different asset classes.)

Not all forms of capital flows contribute, or at least contribute equally, to instability. In this regard, it is important to distinguish between foreign direct investment (FDI) and financial flows. Foreign direct investors to a larger extent place their funds in fixed illiquid assets and are thus interested in the stability and the long-term performance of the domestic economy. FDI is also often accompanied by access to foreign markets, new technology, and training. The new investments in plant and equipment associated with FDI generate jobs and real growth; by contrast, long-term investment can hardly be financed by volatile capital, which is more likely to be used to finance consumption (see below).

As the policies of several countries illustrate, a country can restrict flows of volatile capital and still invite significant amounts of foreign direct investment, undermining the claim that capital market liberalization is necessary for countries to attract FDI. China retained capital controls and still attracted more FDI than any other developing country. In other countries that imposed capital controls, such as Malaysia, Chile, and Colombia, FDI continued to flow when controls were in place.[39] Similarly, in the early to mid-1990s,

---

[39] The issue of whether the imposition of capital controls discourages FDI remains mired in econometric and statistical difficulties. The literature is accordingly inconclusive. See, e.g.,

Hungary attracted the greatest amount of FDI in Eastern Europe, even though it retained restrictions on short-term capital.

However, it is worth noting that FDI also moves pro-cyclically (although not to the same extent as more volatile capital flows) (see World Bank 1999). There are four primary reasons for this. First, FDI will be correlated with global fluctuations. The global financial crisis of 1998 led to a reduction of FDI everywhere. Second, much of what is classified as FDI is sometimes really 'finance'. For instance, privatizations and mergers and acquisitions are categorized as FDI, even though they often represent an ownership transfer rather than new investment. It is therefore important to distinguish between new 'greenfield' investments and mergers and acquisitions. Third, to the extent that FDI is geared toward the domestic market, it responds to economic booms and downturn in much the same way domestic investment does. Fourth, foreign direct investors know that it might be difficult to sell their assets during a crisis, so they often use derivative products, such as currency forwards and options, to sell the local currency short as a hedge of their investment, adding to a run on the currency during a crisis.

The increasing use of derivative products is, in fact, an additional source of instability, as the contribution of Dodd to this volume indicates.[40] Although the accelerated growth of derivative markets has helped to reduce 'micro-instability' by creating new hedging techniques that allow individual agents to cover their microeconomic risks, it might have increased 'macro-instability'. In the words of Dodd, if short-term capital flows are 'hot' money, under critical conditions derivatives can turn into 'microwave' money, speeding up market responses to sudden changes in opinion and expectations. Derivatives have also reduced transparency by allowing large off-balance-sheet positions that are difficult to regulate.

Some critics of capital market liberalization go further: they argue that the thinness of markets in developing countries exposes them to market manipulation. The Central Bank of Malaysia has contended that international hedge funds manipulated the Malaysian financial markets in the 1990s. Similarly, Hong Kong's market came under attack by speculators in August 1998.[41]

1.3.2 *Macroeconomic Instability and Management*

There are three distinct but related reasons why CML has increased macroeconomic stability.

Montiel and Reinhart (1999); Hernandez et al. (2001); Carlson and Hernandez (2002); Mody and Murshid (2002).

[40] Some economists and practitioners argue that derivatives will further decrease the effectiveness of capital controls.

[41] For more information, see Stiglitz et al. (2006).

First, as we have just shown, there is ample evidence that macroeconomic policies in developing countries, especially those that have liberalized, are pro-cyclical and thus exacerbate rather than dampen both economic booms and recessions. Indeed, they have become one of the major—and for many countries the major—source of business cycles. The basic reason is that capital inflows and outflows have mostly pro-cyclical effects on major macroeconomic variables: they directly affect exchange rates, interest rates, domestic credit, and stock market values—and these variables, in turn, impact investment, savings, and consumption decisions.

Second, CML restricts the ability of economic actors to respond to booms and busts. There is ample evidence that macroeconomic policies in developing countries are pro-cyclical (see Kaminsky et al. 2001) and that pro-cyclical macroeconomic policies often reflect pro-cyclical capital flows.

Third, as we have seen, both the private and public sector are often dependent on short-term finance due to incomplete domestic financial markets. This means that the refinancing needs of domestic debtors tend to be high. We have also seen that balance sheets in developing countries are characterized by maturity mismatches (See Furman and Stiglitz 1998; Krugman 2000; Aghion et al. 2001; Eichengreen et al. 2003), so that public and private sector debts are more susceptible to short-term fluctuations in interest rates. This can be avoided by borrowing abroad at longer maturities, but when there is a resulting currency mismatch, the borrower is exposed to exchange rate fluctuations. This can be critical during recessions in sectors, such as real estate, where these risks become evident at the same time asset values are strongly depressed.

A major implication of the exchange rate fluctuations generated by capital account fluctuations (appreciation during capital account booms, depreciation during crises) is that they generate major pro-cyclical wealth effects in countries that have net liabilities denominated in foreign currencies. These pro-cyclical wealth effects reinforce those generated directly by fluctuations in the cost and availability of financing. They have impacts on consumption and investment and can even result in bankruptcy and financial disruption, which have brutal effects that are not quickly self-correcting. Also, pro-cyclical fluctuations in domestic interest and exchange rates imply that evaluation of debt ratios is subject to significant uncertainties. Debt that looks—and in fact, is—sustainable at given interest and exchange rates, may become entirely unsustainable when external financing conditions change and domestic interest and exchange rates adjust abruptly.

Standard recipes for dealing with a crisis call for central banks to reduce interest rates and for governments to stimulate the economy by increasing expenditures and/or cutting taxes. But countries that have opened their capital market often find it difficult to do either. Rather than lowering interest rates in a downturn, countries with open capital markets are typically forced to raise interest rates to stop capital outflows. The high interest rates have adverse effects on fiscal policy, particularly in countries where the government has high levels of short-term debt or, more generally, high levels of debt that matures and needs to be refinanced during a crisis. Even when the country can borrow larger amounts in the short term, it might be feeding unsustainable debt dynamics (Frenkel 2005).

Even worse, as we have noted, countries dependent on borrowing face the problem that foreign creditors may demand repayment of their loans: even at a higher interest rate, creditors may refuse to make credit available.[42] Credit rationing will exist when creditors perceive that debt dynamics are unsustainable. If governments cannot fully finance the increased interest costs, they will be forced to increase primary *surpluses*.[43] Their actual level of spending on goods and services contracts, making the economic downturn more severe.

When the exchange rate has become overvalued due to capital inflows during booms, markets press for exchange rate devaluation during the succeeding crises. This is a positive feature from the point of view of the adjustment of the current account but, as we have noted, it generates negative wealth effects that feed the downturn in economies with net external liabilities. It could also generate inflationary pressures. If monetary authorities respond with a narrow 'inflation targeting' view of their mandate, they would feed into the downturn by increasing interest rates.

What is true of crises is, in a converse way, valid for booms. During periods of financial euphoria, economic authorities have limited room to undertake policies to cool down the economy. This is particularly true of monetary policy, as booming capital inflows tend to reduce interest rates and increase credit and the money supply, restricting the capacity of monetary authorities to adopt contractionary monetary policies. Alternatively, if they try to dampen the economy in the standard way by increasing interest rates, there will be a further inflow of capital, exacerbating the underlying problems. With flexible exchange rates, some argue that authorities still have the capacity to raise interest rates but that the exchange rate would appreciate, generating expansionary wealth effects. Appreciation may also have long-run costs on tradable sectors in open economies (Dutch disease effects).

Fiscal policy can always be used under these conditions to help taper the boom, but it faces two sources of problems. First, it is not as flexible an instrument as monetary or exchange rate policy. Second, it faces strong political economy pressures, particularly when markets and international institutions

---

[42] The problem could, of course, occur even if governments borrow domestically, but governments typically have far more control over domestic financial markets. In general, they may be forced to borrow at high market rates during crises, which lead to an unsustainable debt dynamic.

[43] The primary balance (which can be either in deficit or surplus) is defined as the fiscal balance (total income minus expenditures), other than interest payments.

forced authorities to adopt austerity policies during the preceding crisis. Under these conditions, the public's perception of austerity policies is so negative that it can be very hard for governments to justify them during the boom.

As this discussion indicates, in the face of pro-cyclical capital flows, the capacity of authorities to maintain policy autonomy to undertake counter-cyclical macroeconomic policies is limited (Ocampo 2002a, 2005). The exchange rate policy is perhaps the most critical issue in this regard, as the exchange rate plays the central role of linking the external and the domestic macroeconomic dynamics. As Frenkel argues in his contribution to this volume, avoiding exchange rate overvaluation during booms is critical to avoiding a destabilizing trajectory of the external debt and the traumatic balance sheet effects associated with sharp devaluations during crises. But the capacity to manage the real exchange rate is tied to the broader capacity to maintain certain degrees of policy autonomy, which generally implies choosing a form of integration into international financial markets that avoids full deregulation—that is, limiting capital market liberalization.

1.3.3 *Growth*

Proponents of capital market liberalization maintained that open capital markets would stimulate growth because of improvements in economic efficiency and increased investment, including investment in technology.[44] The expansion of aggregate income would then further increase domestic savings and investment, thereby creating a virtuous circle of sustained economic expansion. This 'virtuous circle' (Devlin et al. 1995) would contribute to converging levels of economic development among countries.

An examination of the data, both over time and across countries, shows that CML is not associated with faster economic growth or higher levels of investment (see, e.g., Rodrik 1998).[45] After the Second World War, global GDP growth per capita was high, although, except for the US, capital markets were not liberalized. More recently, as CML has become more widespread, the pace of world growth has been falling: GDP per capita rose 1.8 percent in the 1970s, 1.4 percent in the 1980s, and only 1.1 percent between 1990 and 2003 (Maddison 2001). It is only in the mid-2000s that we have seen performance comparable to the post-war boom. These global trends are reflected in growth trends in Europe where liberalization occurred some three decades ago and in Latin America where it occurred more recently.

[44] In the standard growth models, the long-term rate of growth in income per capita is determined solely by the rate of technological progress; growth in the short term is also affected by the rate of savings/investment.

[45] Two surveys of the contrasting results in the literature are Eichengreen (2001); and Edison et al. (2002). For a discussion on identification problems focused on Latin American countries, see Ffrench-Davis and Reisen (1998) and Frenkel (1998). Ocampo and Taylor (1998) give a theoretical perspective on the effects of liberalizing both trade and capital markets.

When analyzing the effects of CML on growth it is important to recognize that capital inflows can have a positive effect in the short run during periods of booming capital inflows, but a negative effect in the long run. On the positive side, when capital flows into an economy that has unutilized productive factors, the added capital and aggregate demand can stimulate a recovery. It is important, however, not to confuse rising output and productivity based on the utilization of previously idle labor and capital with a structural increase in the speed of productivity improvements or with enhancing the long run strength of the economy.

In order for CML to promote long-term growth, capital inflows need to go into investment and not be diverted into consumption. In the 1970s and, even more in 1990–97, capital did move to developing countries, but the basic conditions linking additional funds and growth were not met.[46] The capital inflows led mostly to increased consumption rather than investment. Moreover, much of the additional investment that did take place occurred in domestic non-tradable sectors that did not generate foreign exchange. With greater foreign debts unmatched by a greater ability to meet debt obligations, it is not surprising that balance of payment crises eventually developed.

The case for why capital market liberalization may be bad for growth is even broader. As we have seen, CML increases real macroeconomic instability, and instability is associated with a large average gap between potential GDP (full capacity) and actual GDP. Because the economy is more frequently operating below its full potential, productivity, profits, and incentives for investors are lower. Furthermore, higher risk increases the return investors require, limiting long-term investment. In turn, crises are characterized by an enormous destruction of organizational and informational capital, as firms and financial institutions are forced into bankruptcy. Policies that lead to more instability or lower income today are likely to inhibit growth and output in the future.

As a result, crises are often followed by an extended period of slow economic growth. A severe crisis always implies a significant loss of production and income that can last for several years, even if the recovery after the initial recession is strong. This is depicted in Figure 1.2 for the cases of Korea and Malaysia. But the crisis can also shift the growth trajectory, putting a country onto a lower GDP growth path even after recovery. Latin America after the debt crisis of the 1980s and Indonesia after the Asian crisis illustrate this.

The instability and periodic crises associated with capital market liberalization have other costs: they force governments intermittently to cut back

[46] Large inflows during boom periods often lead to an overvalued currency, making imported goods cheaper, and encouraging consumption. See Ffrench-Davis and Reisen (1998), particularly the 'Introduction' by the two editors and the chapter by A. Uthoff and D. Titelman, 'The Relationship Between Foreign and National Savings Under Financial Liberalization'.

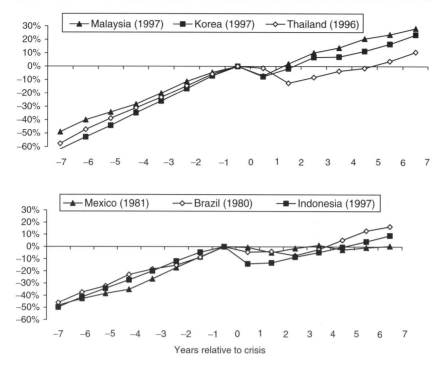

Figure 1.2. Growth trajectories before and after a major crisis (debt crisis of the 1980s, for Latin America, Asian crisis for Asian countries; log of GDP: percentage deviation from peak year before crisis)

on investments in infrastructure and human capital. This stop-and-go public sector investment pattern has long-term costs (Ocampo 2002a). The losses of foregone nutrition, education, or healthcare may never be undone for those who did not have access to the associated government programs and services during a crisis, and the services themselves may lose human and organizational capital, as spending may not be replenished for a long time. Public sector fixed capital investments (roads, energy projects) might be left unfinished, at least for several years, reducing the productivity of public sector investment.

1.3.4 *Recent Controversies*

The foregoing discussion indicates why CML has not brought the benefits of faster growth that were promised by its advocates and why it has often been associated with the increased volatility that its critics predicted. Even though the IMF and other economists have conceded this, they now contend that CML still has indirect benefits such as efficiency gains, faster development of the financial sector, and greater macroeconomic discipline. However, as we discuss, there is limited to no evidence that short-term capital inflows (as opposed to FDI) leads to efficiency gains or to sustained development of the financial system. In fact, CML leads to greater volatility, which has the opposite effect. And, as we discuss in greater detail below, the greater macroeconomic discipline imposed by CML is not appropriate for many developing countries.

Stiglitz, in his contribution to this volume, tries to explain what was wrong with the IMF 'model', why its predictions were so badly off the mark—and why the 'new' explanations are little better than the old. Indeed, our analysis suggests that the collateral consequences of CML are, in fact, negative, not positive. The 2006 IMF paper (Kose et al. 2006) simply ignores, for instance, the argument presented earlier that CML leads to more volatility, which has the consequence of slowing down the deepening of capital markets and contributing to capital market inefficiency. In addition, the paper misreads Stiglitz (2000), which, after considering the argument that CML helps bring discipline, argues that it is the *wrong* discipline, since short-term capital focuses on short-term returns—just the opposite of what is needed for long-term growth. The IMF paper argues that CML leads to better macroeconomic policies, ignoring the constraints that CML imposes on monetary policy, and it seems to measure success in macroeconomic policy in terms of inflation, not in terms of the more fundamental variables of *real* growth, *real* stability, and unemployment.

Most strikingly, their argument that while CML *appears* not to have had any growth effects, it really does because of hard-to-detect ancillary benefits that reveal the ideological basis of their stance: the regressions linking CML with growth are reduced form regressions. Hence if there were any significant effect, either through the direct channels they had originally argued for, or the new channels that form the basis of their current arguments, it would have shown up as a significant coefficient on the CML. Indeed, as Stiglitz points out, the failure to take adequate account of econometric problems like policy endogeneity may mean that the observed coefficient on the CML measure is biased upwards; that is, an observed small *positive* coefficient may mean that the effect of CML is actually negative. (In other words, countries that choose to liberalize may be those for whom liberalization has the most positive benefits—or least negative effects. If, given this 'selection' bias, there is still an insignificant effect on growth, it means that had a country that chose not to liberalize decided to do so, the likely effects would be negative.)[47]

[47] Some of the studies cited in the 2006 IMF paper (Kose et al. 2006) attempt to control for reverse causality, i.e., the biases that arise if higher growth leads to more liberalization. The issue just discussed is, however, quite different.

1.3.5 *Social Effects of Financial Volatility*

As the previous discussion indicates, capital market liberalization exacerbates real macroeconomic instability and the incidence of financial crises and is not clearly associated with faster economic growth. As Charlton argues in his contribution to this volume, these economic effects have social implications, because new opportunities accrue disproportionately to the rich, whereas adverse effects of volatility may disproportionately impact the poor. There is indeed, according to his review of the literature, an empirical relationship between capital account openness and income inequality, which is associated with the fact that inequality frequently increases following capital account liberalization.

He provides evidence of five channels through which capital account liberalization may affect the distribution of income and poverty. The first is that the poor are most vulnerable to macroeconomic volatility because they have the least ability to cope with risk. This is reflected in the greater volatility of consumption that has characterized countries with stronger integration into international financial markets. It is also reflected in the asymmetric behavior of poverty during the business cycle: crises generally increase poverty more than similarly sized recoveries reduce it. Second, orthodox management of crises is particularly harsh on the poor. Third, the increasing mobility of capital weakens the bargaining position of labor. Fourth, international financial integration may constrain governments' redistributive policies, affecting human capital investments in nutrition, schooling and health, and restricting the scope for progressive taxation, increasing the burden of taxation of labor. (The evidence presented by the author on this issue is somewhat mixed, however.) Finally, financial liberalization may increase the availability of credit for medium and large firms, but delivers few benefits in terms of increased credit availability and other financial services for the poor. This is evident in terms of direct access to international financial markets, which are only available for the largest firms, but it is also evident in the supply of financial services in most developing countries, which tend to be concentrated on a small sector of the population.

1.3.6 *Political Processes, Democracy, and Market Discipline*

Another debate about capital market liberalization concerns its impact on democracy and democratic political processes. Capital market liberalization can undermine the democratic process by giving a large 'vote' (influence) to capital market participants abroad and to the wealthiest strata at home. Indeed, it can put pressure on politicians so they are afraid to propose policies that might be interpreted as not 'market friendly'. During the Brazilian presidential campaign of 2002, for example, every time presidential candidate

Luiz Inácio Lula da Silva made a remark that the markets 'didn't like', market participants sold off Brazil's currency, causing the exchange rate to fall, risk margins and interest rates to rise, and voters to become increasingly nervous.

Supporters of capital market liberalization argue, on the contrary, that this intervention in the economy is beneficial: short-term foreign investors exert 'discipline', which, it is contended, is especially lacking in developing countries. Indeed, without the discipline provided by capital market liberalization, developing country democracies would be prone to listen to populists.

The critics of this market discipline theory worry, however, about the political consequences. While it is true that governments need to take into account how their actions affect the attractiveness of investment, they should balance this with a concern about how the structure of their economic system affects the democratic political process and true national sovereignty. The critics of CML reject the underlying premise of 'market discipline'—that democratic processes cannot provide an adequate check on economic policymakers and that countries should delegate economic policymaking to financial interests.

But the critics go further and argue that the discipline provided by the market is the wrong discipline. Even setting aside the increased volatility associated with CML, the policies demanded by capital markets are not those that maximize long-term growth. Who acts as economic 'disciplinarian' determines which policies get rewarded or punished, and this affects what a country does or does not do. Markets evaluate a country's performance against a benchmark reform agenda that, at the minimum, reflects the perspectives of particular interest groups and political players. Even worse, capital markets are myopic, and hence countries that are forced to listen to capital markets are forced to act more myopically. Capital market investors sometimes invest even when long-term fundamentals appear to be worsening, because the short term looks profitable. What matters from their point of view is that the crucial indicators (exchange rates and the prices of real estate, bonds, and stocks) continue to provide them with profits in the near term and that liquid markets allow them to reverse decisions rapidly.

Because CML forces countries to act myopically, economic performance over the long run might actually be worse—even ignoring the increased instability which is associated with CML. Market discipline can make it difficult for governments to engage in policies that are appropriate for long-term sustainable growth. For example, market analysts often do not differentiate clearly between increases in indebtedness that result from expenditures on productive investments and those due to increased consumption. Similarly, market sentiment generally approves of reductions in indebtedness, even if the country becomes poorer as a result—as, for example, happens when public assets are privatized cheaply. The markets focus on the reduced budget deficit and ignore the decline in government assets. This short-term focus also means that they often overlook or underestimate the consequences of factors such as deterioration in a country's infrastructure, inadequate investment in education and technology, and growing inequality.

There is one final objection to 'capital markets as disciplinarians': they are erratic. A good disciplinarian imposes discipline when one does the wrong thing but not when one does the right thing. But many countries learned that under CML they can be punished even if they do precisely what the disciplinarians—capital markets, international financial institutions, and risk-rating agencies—considered correct. With open capital markets, even these countries can face crises when international market sentiment changes.

1.4 Policy Options: Interventions in Capital Markets

Capital market interventions can serve multiple purposes. First, they can be used to stabilize short-term volatile capital flows, so that countries are exposed to less volatility. Second, they can give policymakers additional policy instruments that allow them more effective and less costly macroeconomic stabilization measures. Third, effective capital account regulations can promote growth and increase economic efficiency by reducing the volatility of financing and the volatility of real macroeconomic performance. Finally, they can also discourage long-term capital outflows. Of all the objectives of intervention listed, discouraging long-term capital outflows is perhaps the most difficult.

1.4.1 Capital Market Regulations in Practice

With the growing consensus that market interventions are desirable in theory, the critical question has become whether, in practice, policymakers can design interventions that work and for which the benefits to an economy outweigh any ancillary costs. There exist, of course, many alternative forms of intervention, each with its own strengths and limitations. While no regulatory system is perfect, they differ in their effectiveness and the extent that they can be circumvented. Still, it is important to realize that interventions, especially those designed to prevent crises, can be effective even if controls are partially circumvented. This idea is captured by two metaphors that were used during the critical debates in the late 1990s. Paul Volcker, former Chairman of the Federal Reserve Board, suggested that a leaky umbrella is better than no umbrella at all. Stiglitz pointed out that dams can prevent floods, even if they are leaky, and even if water finds alternative ways of going from the top of the mountain to the bottom. Given the importance that capital account interventions can play in macroeconomic policymaking, we devote several chapters in this book to analyzing alternative modes of regulations.

Capital controls include quantity and price-based regulations, both of which can be administered on either inflows or outflows. Some countries also use indirect regulations, such as prudential regulations on financial institutions or regulations on investments of pension funds, which have implications for capital flows. Thus, a broader concept of capital account restrictions is useful to understand the complementary use and even overlap among different forms of regulation. In their contribution to this volume, Esptein, Grabel and Jomo suggest the term *capital management techniques* to encompass financial policies that govern international private capital flows (capital account regulations) and that enforce prudential management of domestic financial institutions.

Traditional quantity-based capital restrictions (administrative restrictions and controls) continue to be widely used by developing countries, including key countries such as China and India, despite the gradual liberalization of their capital accounts. These regulations are used to target either inflows or outflows on either domestic or foreign residents. Regulations that affect domestic residents include restrictions on currency mismatches (only companies with foreign exchange revenues can borrow abroad), end-use limitations (borrowing abroad is allowed only for investment and foreign trade), minimum maturities for borrowing abroad, limitations on the type of agents that can raise funds abroad through ADRs and similar instruments, prohibition on borrowing in foreign currencies by non-corporate residents, and, in some countries, overall quantitative ceilings. Limitations on non-residents include restrictions or a prohibition on their capacity to borrow in the domestic markets, direct regulations of portfolio flows (including explicit approval and limitations on the assets in which they can invest), sectoral restrictions on FDI, and minimum stay periods.

Other countries, such as Chile and Colombia, have implemented price-based interventions on inflows (an unremunerated reserve requirement, which is equivalent to a tax on inflows). Argentina introduced a similar mechanism in 2005, and, under strong pressure from financial markets, Thailand limited restrictions on debt but not to portfolio flows in 2006. Malaysia introduced a tax on outflows during the Asian crisis after a short period in which it used quantitative controls. Such measures aim to discourage inflows or outflows by raising associated costs. Price-based interventions are usually mixed with some quantity based interventions. Thus, as Khor argues in his contribution to this volume, when Malaysia implemented its price-based restrictions, it still maintained quantity restrictions on currency mismatches by not allowing domestic agents without foreign exchange revenues to borrow abroad. Similarly, Chile maintained a one-year minimum maturity on most capital inflows, and Colombia directly regulated the inflows and investments of foreign investment funds throughout the 1990s.

Economists have a strong proclivity for price-based as opposed to quantity-based interventions. Price-based interventions are flexible, non-discretionary (thus less susceptible to bureaucratic manipulation), and are in line with market incentives. But the case for price-based interventions is far from clear. Theoretical work in economics has shown that sometimes quantity-based restrictions can reduce risk more effectively than price interventions.[48]

Most economists also prefer regulating inflows to outflows. There are several reasons for this. First, regulating inflows helps prevents crises, which is one of the principal goals of policymaking. Second, regulating inflows involves less uncertainty and more transparency: creditors know the regulations before they invest. But, again, the arguments against regulating outflows are not clear-cut, especially when market imperfections exist. For example, restrictions on outflows may be the only way to solve the collective action or coordination market failure discussed in the previous section. When markets exhibit herding behavior (and creditors and investors pull their funds out of a country during a crisis because they are afraid that others will pull their funds out first), restrictions on outflows may be the only instrument available to avoid a downward recessionary spiral. As we discussed earlier, markets generally overshoot in these circumstances, so the restrictions are welfare enhancing.

The empirical evidence shows that all types of instruments—i.e., both quantitative and price-based, on both inflows and outflows and, as we will see below, indirect interventions—can have positive effects, depending on the circumstances under which each mechanism is applied. In their contribution (Chapter 6), Epstein, Grabel, and Jomo argue that policymakers in China, India, and Malaysia were able to use quantitative capital account regulations to achieve critical macroeconomic objectives, including prevention of maturity mismatches, attraction of favored forms of foreign investment, reduction in overall financial fragility, and insulation from speculative pressures and contagion effects of financial crises—leading to greater economic policy autonomy.

Chapter 7 by Ocampo and Palma use the cases of Chile, Colombia, and Malaysia to analyze the effectiveness of price vs. quantity controls on inflows. They conclude that regulations on capital inflows in the three countries proved useful in inducing better debt profiles, restraining asset bubbles, and improving the macroeconomic trade-offs faced by authorities. The regulations succeeded in reducing overall inflows during boom periods, thus generating a higher domestic interest rate spread that allowed a more restrictive monetary policy to work. However, the macroeconomic effects depended on the

---

[48] See Weitzman (1974) for a general discussion. In the context of trade interventions, see Dasgupta and Stiglitz (1977).

strength of the regulations. In the case of the unremunerated reserve requirements used by Chile and Colombia, the macroeconomic effects tended to be
temporary; the regulations operated more as 'speed bumps'. In contrast, the
draconian quantity-based controls on inflows adopted by Malaysia in 1994
proved to be much stronger; they succeeded in stopping the massive capital
inflows that the country had experienced in the early 1990s. Therefore, when
immediate and drastic action is needed, quantitative controls may be more
effective.

The experience of Malaysia during the Asian crisis is further illustrated in
the contribution of Khor. In the face of contagion from Thailand in 1997,
the country first followed an orthodox macroeconomic package that led to a
strong domestic recession. A year later, though, it shifted its policy radically
towards an expansionary monetary and fiscal package supported by quantitative restrictions on capital outflows, some of which were soon replaced by an
exit tax. Two additional features of these capital account regulations were, as
already noted, the persistent policy of avoiding currency mismatches in the
balance sheets of residents and the decision to stop altogether the Singapore
trading of the domestic currency (the ringgit) and securities denominated in
that currency. The exchange rate was fixed after having depreciated strongly
during the period of orthodox policies. These measures were accompanied
by a set of policies aimed at restructuring the financial system and the corporate sector. The expansionary macro package soon led to recovery, and
because capital regulations were so effective, it was possible to ease them
when the storm passed, and they were dismantled after two and a half years
in place.

Malaysia illustrates the fallacy of another argument often put forward: that
controls on outflows 'deter future inflows of all kinds' (*Economist* 2003). This
argument was used to criticize Malaysia's controls when they were established in 1998. But even before the tax was lifted in 2001, Malaysia started
attracting additional flows. Investors are forward-looking, and Malaysia's positive fundamentals (its current account surplus, high savings ratio, moderate
external liabilities with a low share of short-term debts, and large international reserves—all of which capital controls had helped create or sustain) and strengthening stock market drew these additional funds into the
country.[49]

---

[49] After softening the controls in September 1999, Malaysia suffered immediate outflows
of 5.2 billion ringgit, with an additional 3.1 billion ringgit flowing out of the country during
the rest of the year. The net inflow of funds in the first quarter of 2000 was 8.5 billion
ringgit, roughly equal to the total amount of funds lost after the lifting of the controls (Bank
Negara Malaysia 2001b). Throughout 2000, private long-term capital inflows increased, and
foreign direct investments remained stable (Bank Negara Malaysia 2001a). Changes in levels
of inflows may be more attributable to changes in the overall magnitude of capital flows
from developed to developing countries than to changes in the relative attractiveness of
investments among developing countries.

1.4.2 *Market Segmentation: Regulations as Second-Best*

The history of interventions suggests that *capital market regulations are effective in large part because they segment the domestic capital market from international markets and capital flows*. Segmentation aims to protect the domestic economy from the volatility produced by capital market liberalization. In the best-case scenario, this would be done without affecting current account flows.[50]

Segmentation is most evident with traditional quantity-based controls, but also plays a role in price-based regulations. In addition, segmentation covers parallel regulations on the use of the domestic and foreign currencies in different markets, which are in fact more common than capital account regulations, such as forbidding the use of dollars for domestic transactions or for denominating (all or certain) domestic debts, and limiting or forbidding the 'internationalization' of the domestic currency (as Malaysia explicitly did in 1998).

In a previous section, we saw that a market failure prevalent in many developing countries is the lack of well developed capital markets. A first best solution might be to create long-term domestic markets for assets denominated in the domestic currency and develop good insurance markets as protection against exchange rate and interest rate fluctuations. Such a first best solution would also involve creating a stable external demand for assets denominated in the domestic currency. As these optimal solutions are not likely to be in place in the near term, a second best response is to segment the domestic market from international flows. This is, in fact, a special case of application of the theory of the second best.[51]

Since most developing countries do not have a stable source of foreign demand for the local currency and for local currency securities, their domestic capital markets are already in some sense segmented. Regulations can be used to help segment the markets more effectively, by restricting pro-cyclical—particularly short-term—inflows during boom periods and equally pro-cyclical outflows during crises. Reducing these fluctuations would ease the task of macroeconomic authorities in stabilizing the economy. On the other hand, it certainly does not make sense to design regulations as if segmentation does not exist.

Segmentation can have positive macroeconomic effects for at least four reasons: (1) it leads to a more stable demand for locally denominated assets; (2) it reduces risks associated with foreign borrowing; (3) it helps insulate the economy from pro-cyclical foreign borrowing; and (4) it enhances the ability of government to control the macroeconomy.

---

[50] Ironically, while many have worried that capital market restrictions might have adverse spillovers on the current account, the *absence* of capital market restrictions may lead to exchange rate volatility, which may have much stronger effects on the current account.

[51] Earlier, Newberry and Stiglitz (1984) showed how trade restrictions could reduce the risks faced by investors and, in the absence of insurance markets, make everyone better off!

It might make sense in the long run to develop an authentic stable international demand for these securities (among, for example, institutional investors). But until such demand exists, most domestic holdings by foreigners will tend to be short-term and speculative. The primary risk for these holdings is the exchange rate of the local currency, so foreign demand for domestic assets is largely determined by exchange rate expectations. Any shift in international sentiment can destabilize the foreign exchange market. It may thus make sense not to allow non-residents to hold domestic local currency denominated securities and to prevent the development of a premature offshore market for the domestic currency. One might develop anyway, but additional regulations could reduce its attractiveness.[52]

We should note that domestic residents also shift their investments between domestic and foreign assets based on currency expectations (and interest rate differentials). But unlike foreigners, domestic agents *do* have a clear long-term demand for the domestic currency and its associated assets. In any case, capital market interventions can be used to segment the market and reduce the capacity of domestic residents to substitute foreign assets for domestic assets. This will stabilize domestic demand for assets denominated in the local currency. The growth or 'thickening' of the market itself will contribute to stability.

The second reason why market segmentation can have a positive macroeconomic effect is based on the pro-cyclical nature of domestic demand for and the supply of foreign currency loans. The transactions, revenues, and assets of many domestic residents are denominated entirely in the domestic currency. But there is a temptation for domestic entities to borrow in foreign currency when external loans are available because these loans often carry a lower interest rate.[53] As we have noted, this currency mismatch between assets and liabilities creates considerable risk: any devaluation of the local currency will cause the value of foreign debt to rise. If the devaluation is large enough, local borrowers might be unable to repay their loans.[54]

Segmentation helps insulate the economy from pro-cyclical availability of external financing and foreign borrowing and their destabilizing dynamics. This point, too, depends on the pro-cyclical nature of domestic demand for foreign currency loans. External financing is most likely to be available during a boom, and lenders are likely to demand their money back in a downturn. Thus, the supply of funds intensifies economic fluctuations. The demand for loans in foreign currencies also appears to be pro-cyclical. But when domestic agents borrow abroad during booms, they often use much of those funds to buy local currency and assets. This increases the demand

[52] Malaysia, for example, was able to completely shut down the offshore market in ringgits.

[53] Newberry and Stiglitz (1984) showed how there is, admittedly, often a certain degree of irrationality.

[54] The problem is exacerbated when there are prospects of, say, a government bail-out of a bank: the public bears some of the downside risk of the foreign exchange exposure.

for the domestic currency and fuels the currency appreciation. In the opposite phase of the business cycle, domestic agents need to buy foreign currency to pay back their foreign debts. This means they will sell the local currency and assets, causing a large devaluation. So when domestic residents borrow in foreign currency, they can increase currency fluctuations, multiplying the destabilizing effects of cycles in the availability of external financing.

Forbidding domestic agents who do not have foreign currency revenues to borrow in those currencies would also have a major positive macroeconomic effect through another channel: it would reduce fluctuations in the *availability* of external financing. Since foreign lenders often demand repayment when borrowers are least able to comply, the overall adverse effects on individual borrowers over the course of an entire cycle would probably be limited; the systemic effects may even be positive—with less (uncovered) debt outstanding, lenders may be less inclined to demand repayment.

Segmentation can lead to reduced pro-cyclical exchange rate fluctuations (avoiding overvaluation in booms and undervaluation in downturns); in doing so, it reduces the magnitude of pro-cyclical wealth effects that characterize economies with large dollar- or euro-denominated debts. (As noted earlier, these wealth effects can offset the positive effects of these exchange rate adjustments on the trade balance.)

Finally, segmentation also enhances the ability of government to control the macroeconomy. The ability of policymakers to use restrictive monetary policies during times of euphoria and to avoid excessively contractionary policies during crises (in other words, the level of a government's monetary autonomy) depends on limited capital mobility which, in turn, depends on the extent of market segmentation. Similar arguments apply to the use of exchange rate policy. Segmentation increases the ability to use the exchange rate as a macroeconomic policy tool and improves the effectiveness of exchange rate management.

The problems of exchange rate adjustment become even clearer in economies with widespread use of a foreign currency in the domestic financial market. Given the significant effect that devaluation has on the ability to repay dollar- or euro-denominated debts and, consequently on the stability of the domestic financial system, there is a strong incentive for governments to avoid currency fluctuations. The experience of Argentina in 2001–2 serves as an example. The massive reduction in deposits throughout 2001, when the convertibility system was still in place, generated an illiquidity crisis that forced the government to restrict withdrawals of deposits from the financial system. This was in fact a first recognition that convertibility of the domestic deposits for dollars was not in place. After the devaluation, debtors with dollar-denominated debts were unable to pay their debts, while agents with net dollar assets were unwilling to give up their capital gains to subsidize the debtors. The domestic financial system became paralyzed while legal and legislative controversies undermined the economy.

This is why the most basic of all segmentations makes sense: avoiding dollar/euroization of the domestic financial system and, even more, of the domestic payments system. Of course, when dollar/euroization is in place, it is not easy to reverse, as it is generally the legacy of a period of high domestic price instability. But it can be induced by price incentives (e.g., taxing transactions denominated in the foreign currency but not in the domestic currency, higher reserve requirements for dollar- and euro-denominated deposits, higher prudential requirements for loans denominated in foreign currency), government debt strategies (not to issue debts in the domestic markets denominated in foreign currencies), and administrative or legal decisions (certain transactions cannot be denominated in foreign currencies and, if so, would not be legally protected). The history of dollarization in Latin America shows this: some countries avoided it altogether (Brazil and Colombia), others made a sharp change away from it after a crisis (Chile in the early 1980s, Argentina after 2002), and still others have been very gradually moving away from it (Bolivia, Peru, and Uruguay in the 2000s). Ecuador and El Salvador stand as opposite examples of countries that decided to entirely dollarize their economies (as Panama had done since independence a century ago).

1.4.3 *Soft Controls: Encouraging Market Segmentation*

The capital account interventions discussed above all serve the purpose of segmenting domestic markets from international markets. There is another category of restrictions called 'soft controls' that aim to segment the market directly. For example, soft controls can require domestic funds, such as social security or pension funds, to invest their assets in domestic markets and can prohibit them from investing abroad or limit the amount of funds that can be so invested. These restrictions limit the funds' potential to generate procyclical disturbances.

But soft controls have additional positive effects on the economy. They create a local demand for domestic securities, help to develop the local capital markets, and build a domestic capital base. In this way, soft controls can help remedy one of the market failures discussed earlier: that of under- and undeveloped capital markets.

This kind of control might become particularly relevant in the near future because of the growth of privately managed pension funds in many developing countries, especially in Latin America. In Chile (the pioneer in this area), such funds are equivalent to 70 percent of annual GDP. Most countries place limits on the extent to which domestic funds can invest abroad and have experienced new sustained growth in domestic markets in large part because of the increased demand for local securities from domestic pension funds. Once again, the Chilean experience demonstrates the stimulating role of pension funds on the development of domestic capital markets. But it also demonstrates how pension funds can generate macro-instability when the markets are not segmented and funds are allowed to invest abroad (Zahler 2003).

Some economists oppose these types of soft controls because they limit the ability of domestic funds to diversify their assets. This is true, but all economic policies involve trade-offs. Building a local capital market and domestic capital base is essential, and its benefits far outweigh the costs of controls—in fact, as we argued above, it is one of the 'first best' options to manage segmentation of domestic and external capital markets.[55] On the other hand, to the extent that domestic institutional investors add to the pro-cyclical nature of open capital markets, they impose an externality on the entire population. Soft controls can help turn this negative process into a positive one for long-term growth.[56]

1.4.4 *Indirect Interventions in Capital Account Transactions through Prudential Regulations*

In addition to direct quantity-based and priced-based regulations, governments can use a variety of indirect measures to control (or at least influence) capital account inflows and outflows. One of the most critical use of regulations is to avoid currency mismatches in the balance sheets of financial and non-financial agents.

Prudential regulations on the banking system are one such tool (Ocampo 2003). Numerous countries forbid, or strictly limit, banks from holding currency mismatches on their balance sheets. To avoid domestic financial dollar/euroization, many countries also forbid financial institutions from holding deposits from domestic residents in foreign currencies or limit the nature and use of such deposits. Bank regulators can also prohibit domestic banks from lending in foreign currencies to firms that do not have matching revenues in those currencies. For a more subtle approach, they can impose higher risk-adjusted capital adequacy requirements or additional liquidity and/or loan-loss provisioning (reserve) requirements on foreign currency loans made to domestic agents who lack matching revenues. In countries with deposit insurance, the government can impose higher insurance premiums on banks that have riskier practices. These softer regulations would discourage

---

[55] Moreover, one can 'balance' the risks, by allowing limited investment abroad.

[56] Government regulations allowing for swaps—an exchange of assets, say, between the pension funds of one country and that of another—could help diversify risk, without putting any pressure on the exchange rate, and without subjecting countries to pro-cyclical capital flows.

(although not eliminate) the indirect foreign exchange exposure of banks. To reduce the maturity mismatch of non-financial firms, regulators could similarly set higher capital, liquidity, or prudential requirements for short-term lending by domestic financial institutions.

One of the costs frequently associated with stronger prudential regulations is a higher domestic interest rate due to the higher cost of financial intermediation. But the costs of prudential regulations, higher reserve requirements, and higher deposit insurance premiums simply reflect the higher risks of certain kinds of borrowing. Since society otherwise will bear most of the costs of this borrowing (e.g., through the costs of crises), the regulations reduce the disparity between social costs and private benefits. By discouraging excessively risky borrowing, overall economic efficiency is enhanced.

Some policymakers worry that higher domestic interest rates may adversely affect small and medium-sized enterprises (SMEs).[57] However, if the government wants to promote lending to these firms, it should do so through explicit programs. Moreover, it is actually large firms that are most likely to have uncovered foreign exchange exposure. Competitive banks should pass on the costs of prudential regulations relating to foreign exposure to these large firms. This might discourage lending to these firms and, by leaving additional room for expanding domestic credit, even increase the supply of funds available to small and medium-sized enterprises.

There is obviously good reason for prudential regulations to take into account the foreign exchange exposure of firms that borrow from domestic banks. Otherwise, the risks assumed by corporations, particularly those operating in non-tradable sectors, can eventually translate into non-performing loans in domestic financial institutions. But a more systemic perspective also requires this same focus. Since banks traditionally mediate much of the capital flow in an economy, regulation of the financial sector has a significant impact on the overall economy. However, unless regulations focus adequate attention on the exposure of non-financial firms, the impact of the financial sector can be vitiated. For example, regulations that simply forbid banks from holding dollar-denominated liabilities might encourage firms to borrow directly from abroad. So banks must examine the entire asset and liability structure of the firms to which they lend (which they should do in any case). Since, for the most part, domestic firms borrow from domestic banks, if banks put restrictions on the foreign exposure of firms to whom they lend, this would act as an effective limit on foreign borrowing.

---

[57] We have argued, however, that there are social costs associated with these foreign exchange exposures. The increase in the risk-adjusted capital adequacy requirement (or other penalties imposed on banks with heavy exposure), if appropriately designed, would simply compensate for these external social costs.

Regulations can also be designed to target borrowing abroad by non-financial firms directly.[58] These might include rules on the types of firms that can borrow abroad (for example, only firms with revenues in foreign currencies) and the establishment of prudential ratios for such firms. Regulations might also include restrictions on the terms of corporate debt that can be contracted abroad (minimum maturities and maximum spreads, for example) and public disclosure of the short-term external liabilities of firms.

There can be problems administering these provisions because corporations will have an incentive to circumvent the rules by using derivatives. To address this, governments should require full disclosure of all derivative positions.[59] Foreign currency-denominated debt can also be subordinated to domestic currency-denominated debt in bankruptcy proceedings. An alternative (or complementary) approach is for governments to create adverse tax treatment for foreign currency-denominated borrowing, especially when it is short-term. For example, countries that have a corporate income tax with tax-deductible interest payments might exclude foreign-denominated debt from the tax deduction or make the interest payments only partially tax deductible.[60]

These alternative measures rely on a combination of banking regulations and complementary policies aimed at non-bank financial firms and non-financial firms. The direct capital-account regulations we discussed earlier might be simpler to administer than such a system. They may work better because they are aimed at the actual source of the disturbance—pro-cyclical capital flows.[61] For developing countries with strong administrative capabilities, a combination of direct and indirect measures can succeed in restricting flows and helping to limit circumvention through derivative products.

1.4.5 *The Broader Debate on Prudential Regulation, Norms, and Standards*

As we have noted, a broad consensus emerged after the Asian crisis on the need to strengthen financial and macroeconomic risk management in

---

[58] It is, of course, possible that some firms borrow exclusively from abroad. If only a few firms do so (with limited aggregate exposure), their default in the event, say, of a large change in the exchange rate would have much less of an effect than if those firms borrowed domestically. There would be no collateral damage to domestic financial institutions except through the impact of the bankruptcy on the firms' suppliers. But in the unlikely event that large numbers of firms borrow extensively from abroad (and not from domestic financial institutions), there can still be systemic effects. See Rajan and Zingales (2001); Forbes (2004).

[59] To do so, the government would need to add all the longs (investments) and shorts (borrowings) to get the net position and ascertain the actual extent of foreign-denominated borrowing.

[60] For an analysis of these issues, see World Bank (1999); and Bhattacharya and Stiglitz (2000).

[61] Still, these other interventions may be desirable to enhance economic efficiency, i.e., to reduce the disparity between private and social costs. One simple means of enforcement of disclosure requirements would be to make undisclosed derivative contracts not enforceable through legal action.

developing countries through prudential regulation and supervision of domestic financial systems, as well as through macroeconomic policy, good corporate governance, and data transparency. The papers in the third part of this book discuss some of the issues involved in the design of better risk management in developing countries and the spread of international 'standards and codes' in these areas.

One set of issues, analyzed in Rojas-Suarez' Chapter 9, relates to the usefulness of different regulatory tools in developing countries. She argues that reserve (or liquidity) requirements are most useful when bank deposits account for most of the liquid assets in the economy and reserves are invested in liquid foreign-denominated assets. These conditions are not generally met in developing countries, as reflected in the lack of a clear inverse relationship between reserve requirements and the ratio of liquid assets to international reserves. Reserve or liquidity requirements also have an additional draw-back: they are applied equally to weak and strong banks. Capital adequacy requirements discriminate better in this regard, but developing countries face problems associated with the 'quality' of bank capital due to inadequate accounting frameworks, the possibility of financing capital with loans from related parties, and the lack of a liquid market for bank shares that validates the value of bank capital, among other factors. For this reason, she argues that loan-loss provisions may be a better tool than capital requirements. Along the lines of the analysis presented in the previous section, one of the critical issues in designing both capital and loan-loss provisioning requirements in developing countries is the introduction of distinct charges for borrowers from tradable and non-tradable sectors. She also emphasizes the need to adequately assess the risks of banks holding government securities and lending short-term, so as to avoid creating incentives for banks to allocate excessive bank resources into government bonds or to reduce the maturity of the loans.

An additional issue that has been a focus of increasing attention in recent years is the pro-cyclical bias in the way traditional regulatory tools and risk management techniques operate. This issue is explored in Chapter 10 by Griffith-Jones and Persaud, who consider the implication of new Basel standards for lending by international banks to developing countries. The issue is also relevant to domestic regulation in all countries, but particularly in developing countries, where pro-cyclical biases in financial markets and macroeconomic policy are stronger.[62] Because traditional prudential regula-tions require higher loan-loss provisions (reserves) to offset riskier positions or cover actual loan losses during phases of slowdown, they tend to restrict lending during these periods. Losses associated with loan delinquencies that have not previously been adequately provisioned also reduce the capital of

---

[62] For recent analyses of these issues and policy options for managing them see BIS (2001); Borio et al. (2001); Clerc et al. (2001); Ocampo (2003); and Turner (2002).

financial institutions and thus their lending capacity during crises. This, in conjunction with a greater perceived level of risk, triggers the 'credit squeeze' that characterizes such periods and reinforces the downswing in economic activity. On the other hand, the apparently lower risks of lending may feed into the credit boom during periods of economic expansion. Thus, mandatory forward-looking provisioning systems may be an effective way to manage these pro-cyclical biases in regulation, as has been recognized in the design of bank regulation in a few countries. As Griffith-Jones and Persaud argue, the problem has been made worse by the spread of market price-sensitive risk analysis techniques, which tend to reflect the pro-cyclical swings in asset prices and may under- or over estimate the 'inherent risk' of lending during booms and crises, respectively, and increase contagion.

As we have noted, derivatives pose an additional set of risks, which has not been generally recognized in regulation, even in advanced countries. In Chapter 11, Dodd argues that although derivatives perform the useful functions of price discovery and facilitating hedging—and thus risk-shifting to those agents most able to bear it—they can also be potentially destabilizing. The reasons are associated with the potential abuse of these instruments through fraud, manipulation, tax evasion, and distortion of information, including information that regulatory and supervisory agencies use. Independent of such abuses, derivatives can also create new risks by facilitating leveraged transactions that generate greater levels of market risk for a given amount of capital in the financial system. Such risk taking can accelerate the spread of crises and contagion and can be particularly difficult to manage in the illiquid and one-sided markets that are likely to characterize developing countries during crises. Dodd argues in favor of regulating derivatives through three types of instruments: reporting and registration requirements; capital requirements for institutions operating in derivative markets and collateral requirements for derivative transactions; and orderly market provisions that would punish fraud and manipulation, establish position limits in derivatives markets, and require market dealers to act as market makers.

The chapters by Griffith-Jones and Persaud and Schneider (Chapters 10 and 12, respectively) explore some of the problems associated with international standards and codes. As mentioned earlier, the first two authors underscore three major problems in the reform of the new Basel standards for banking regulation (Basel II): whereas systemically important banks should be subject to additional regulatory costs and scrutiny, they receive favorable treatment under Basel II; the rules do not systematically treat risk diversification, as this criteria is taken into account for bank lending to SMEs but not to developing countries; and the rules favor market price-sensitive risk analysis that could spread pro-cyclicality and, more generally, underestimate the importance of the pro-cyclical bias in banking regulation.

Schneider explores the broader set of standards and codes that have spread since the Asian crisis and the new instrument created since the Asian crisis to spread them: the Reports on the Observance of Standards and Codes (ROSCs) based on the Financial Sector Assessment Programmes (FSAPs) prepared by the IMF and the World Bank. She identifies several major deficiencies in the current exercise. These include the fact that major industrial countries have lagged behind in the ROSC exercise and that many countries without capital account restrictions have no FSAPs, which implies that the degree of capital account liberalization has not figured prominently in prioritizing the codes. She also points out that there is no continuous stream of information, so that little information is effectively gained by markets and that, contrary to initial expectations, respect for standards of transparency in data dissemination standards does not seem to affect market responses. This reflects the muted response by the private sector to the standards and codes initiative. She forcefully argues for an alternative model: self-assessments combined with a peer review process, possibly coordinated by the Bretton Woods Institutions.

Both chapters underscore, finally, a major problem in current international institutions: the inadequate participation of developing countries in designing regulatory standards. This has also restricted the appropriateness of existing standards for developing countries. They argue that full participation and ownership of international standard setting by developing countries will not come without their adequate representation in standard-setting bodies.

1.5 Conclusion

This IPD project analyzing capital market liberalization is based on the premise that volatility is an inherent feature of financial markets. This financial instability implies that developing countries are likely to continue to be subject to strong pro-cyclical swings in external financing, with economic policy having at best a limited ability to manage such effects. We argue that, under these conditions, capital account liberalization has high economic and social costs, whereas its assumed benefits in terms of both economic stability and growth are unlikely to materialize.

We further argue that since financial and capital markets are not self-regulating and are highly segmented under the current globalization process, it makes sense to regulate them. This can be done directly through capital account regulations but also through more indirect norms that affect domestic financial intermediation and risk management by different economic agents. Finally, the experiences in developing countries reviewed in this book show that such regulations can work, both by reducing the sensitivity of developing countries to pro-cyclical swings of capital flows and by increasing the scope for counter-cyclical macroeconomic policy.

References

Aghion, P., Bacchetta, P., and Banerjee, A. (2001). 'A Corporate Balance Sheet Approach to Currency Crises'. CEPR Discussion Papers 3092.

Arnott, R. and Stiglitz, J. E. (1990). 'The Welfare Economics of Moral Hazard', in H. Louberge (ed.), *Risk, Information and Insurance: Essays in the Memory of Karl H. Borch.* Norwell: Kluwer Academic Publishers, 91–122.

——— ——— (1991). 'Price Equilibrium, Efficiency, and Decentralizability in Insurance Markets'. NBER Working Paper 3642.

Arrow, K. J. and Debreu, G. (1954). 'Existence of a Competitive Equilibrium for a Competitive Economy'. *Econometrica*, 22/3: 265–90.

Banerjee, A. (1992). 'A Simple Model of Herd Behavior'. *Quarterly Journal of Economics*, 107/3: 797–817.

Bank for International Settlements (BIS) (2001). *71st Annual Report.* Basel (June).

——— (2005). *75th Annual Report.* Basel (June).

Bank Negara Malaysia (2001a). *Annual Report 2000.* Available at: www.bnm.gov.my

——— (2001b). *Economic and Financial Developments in the Malaysian Economy in the First Quarter of 2000.* Available at: www.bnm.gov.my

Bhattacharya, A. and Stiglitz, J. E. (2000). 'The Underpinnings of a Stable and Equitable Global Financial System: From Old Debates to a New Paradigm'. *Annual World Bank Conference on Development Economics 1999*, B. Pleskovic and J. E. Stiglitz (eds.), Washington: World Bank, pp. 91–130. (Paper presented to the Annual World Bank Conference on Development Economics, April 28–30, 1999.)

Bikhchandani, S., Hirshleifer, D., and Welch, I. (1992). 'A Theory of Fads, Fashion, Custom, and Cultural Change as Informational Cascades'. *Journal of Political Economy*, 100/5: 992–1026.

Borio, C., Furfine, C., and Lowe, P. (2001). 'Procyclicality of the Financial System and Financial Stability: Issues and Policy Options', in *Marrying the Macro- and Micro-Prudential Dimensions of Financial Stability*, BIS Papers 1.

Calvo, G. and Mendoza, E. (2000). 'Rational Contagion and the Globalization of Securities Markets'. *Journal of International Economics*, 51/1: 79–113.

Caplin, A. S. and Lehay, J. (1994). 'Business as Usual, Market Crashes and Wisdom after the Fact'. *American Economic Review*, 84/3: 548–65.

Carlson, M. and Hernandez, L. (2002). 'Determinants and Repercussions of the Composition of Capital Inflows'. Board of Governors of the Federal Reserve System, International Finance Discussion Paper 717.

Chamley, C. P. (2004). *Rational Herds.* Cambridge: Cambridge University Press.

Clerc, L., Drumetz, F., and Jaudoin, O. (2001). 'To What Extent are Prudential and Accounting Arrangements Pro- or Countercyclical with Respect to Overall Financial Conditions?', in BIS, *Marrying the Macro- and Micro-Prudential Dimensions of Financial Stability*, BIS Papers 1.

Dasgupta, P. and Stiglitz, J. E. (1977). 'Tariffs versus Quotas as Revenue Raising Devices under Uncertainty'. *American Economic Review*, 67/5: 975–81.

Devlin, R., Ffrench-Davis, R., and Griffith-Jones, S. (1995). 'Surges in Capital Flows and Devlopment', in R. Ffrench-Davis and S. Griffith-Jones (eds.), *Coping with Capital Surges: The Return of Finance to Latin America.* Boulder, CO: Lynne Rienner Publishers.

Diamond, D. W. and Dybvig, P. (1983). 'Bank Runs, Deposit Insurance and Liquidity'. *Journal of Political Economy*, 91/3: 401–19.

Dodd, P. and Spiegel, S. (2005). 'Up From Sin: A Portfolio Approach to Salvation', in A. Buira (ed.), *The IMF and World Bank at Sixty*. London: Anthem Press.

Edison, H. J., Klein, M., Ricci, L., and Sloek, T. (2002). 'Capital Account Liberalization and Economic Performance: Survey and Synthesis'. NBER Working Paper 9100.

Edwards, F. R. (1999). 'Hedge Funds and the Collapse of the Long-Term Capital Term Management'. *Journal of Economic Perspectives*, 13/2: 189–219.

Eichengreen, B. (2001). 'Capital Account Liberalization: What Do Cross-Country Studies Tell Us?'. *The World Bank Economic Review*, 15/3: 341–65.

——, Hausmann, R. and Panizza, U. (2003). 'Currency Mismatches, Debt Intolerance and Original Sin: Why They are not the Same and Why it Matters'. NBER Working Paper 10036.

Economist (2003). 'A Place for Capital Controls'. May 3, p. 16.

Ferri, G., Liu, L.-G., and Stiglitz, J. E. (1999). 'The Procyclical Role of Rating Agencies: Evidence from the East Asian Crisis'. *Economic Notes* 28/3: 335–55.

Ffrench-Davis, R. (2004). 'Macroeconomics-for-Growth under Financial Globalization: Four Strategic Issues'. IPD Working Paper.

—— and Reisen, H. (eds.) (1998). *Capital Flows and Investment Performance in Latin America*. Paris: OECD Development Centre, and Santiago: ECLAC.

Forbes, K. (2004). 'Capital Controls: Mud in the Wheels of Market Discipline'. NBER Working Paper 10284.

Frenkel, R. (1998). 'Capital Market Liberalization and Economic Performance in Latin America'. Center for Economic Policy Analysis Working Paper No. 1.

—— (2005). 'External Debt, Growth, and Sustainability', in J. A. Ocampo (ed.), *Beyond Reforms: Structural Dynamics and Macroeconomic Vulnerability*. Palo Alto, CA: Stanford University Press, and Santiago: Economic Commission for Latin America and the Caribbean, 189–209.

Furman, J., and Stiglitz, J. E. (1998). 'Economic Crises: Evidence and Insights from East Asia'. *Brookings Papers on Economic Activity*, 2: 1–114 (presented at Brookings Panel on Economic Activity, Washington, DC, September 3, 1998).

Greenspan, A. (1996). 'The Challenge of the Central Banking System in a Democratic Society'. Remarks by Chairman Alan Greenspan at the Annual Dinner and Francis Boyer Lecture of The American Enterprise Institute for Public Policy Research, Washington, DC. Available at: www.federalreserve.gov/boarddocs/speeches/1996/19961205.htm

Greenwald, B. (1998). 'International Adjustments in the Face of Imperfect Financial Markets.' Paper presented to the Annual World Bank Conference on Development Economics, Washington DC, April 20–21, 1998.

—— (2003). *Towards a New Paradigm for Monetary Policy*. London: Cambridge University Press.

—— and Stiglitz, J. E. (1986). 'Externalities in Economies with Imperfect Information and Incomplete Markets'. *Quarterly Journal of Economics*, 101/2: 229–64.

Hahn, F. (1966). 'Equilibrium Dynamics with Heterogeneous Capital Goods'. *Quarterly Journal of Economics*, 80/4: 133–46.

Hernandez, L., Mellado, P., and Valdes, R. (2001). 'Determinants of Private Capital Flows in the 1970s and 1990s: Is There Evidence of Contagion?'. IMF Working Paper 01/64.

Jorion, P. (2000). 'Risk management lessons from Long-Term Capital Management'. *European Financial Management*, 6/3: 277–300.

Kaminsky, G. L., Schmukler, S., Reinhart, C., and Végh, C. (2004). 'When it Rains, it Pours: Procyclical Capital Flows and Macroeconomic Policies'. NBER Working Paper 10780.

Kindleberger, C. P. ([1978] 2000). *Manias, Panics, and Crashes: A History of Financial Crises*, 4th edn. New York: John Wiley and Sons, Inc.

Korinek, A. (2007). 'Excessive Dollar Borrowing in Emerging Markets: Balance Sheet Effects and Macroeconomic Externalities'. Columbia University. Mimeo.

Kose, M. A., Prasad, E., Rogoff, K., and Wei, S.-J. (2006). 'Financial Globalization: A Reappraisal'. IMF Working Paper 06/189. Washington, DC: International Monetary Fund.

Krugman, P. (2000). 'Balance Sheets, the Transfer Problem, and Financial Crises', in P. Isard, A. Razin, and A. Rosen (eds.), *International Finance and Financial Crises—Essays in Honor of Robert P. Flood, Jr.* Boston: Kluwer Academic Publishers.

Lucas, R. (1990). 'Why Doesn't Capital Flow from Rich to Poor Countries?'. AER Papers and Proc. 80: 92–6.

Maddison, A. (2001). *The World Economy: A Millenial Perspective*. Paris: OECD.

Majluf, N. S. and Myers, S. (1984). 'Corporate Financing and Investment Decisions When Firms Have Information that Investors Do Not Have'. *Journal of Financial Economics*, 13/2: 187–221.

Mishkin, F. (2006). 'Globalization: A Force for the Good?'. Weissman Center Distinguished Lecture Series, Baruch College, New York (October 12).

Mody, A. and Murshid, A. (2002). 'Growing Up with Capital Flow'. IMF Working Paper 02/75.

Montiel, P. and Reinhart, C. (1999). 'Do Capital Controls and Macroeconomic Policies Influence the Volume and Composition of Capital Flows? Evidence from the 1990s'. *Journal of International Money and Finance*, 18/4: 619–35.

Nalebuff, B. and Stiglitz, J. E. (1983). 'Information, Competition, and Markets'. *The American Economic Review*, 73/2: 278–83.

Newbery, D., and Stiglitz, J. E. (1984). 'Pareto Inferior Trade'. *Review of Economic Studies*, 51/1: 1–12.

Ocampo, J. A. (2002a). 'Developing Countries' Anti-Cyclical Policies in a Globalized World', in A. Dutt and J. Ros (eds.), *Development Economics and Structuralist Macroeconomics: Essays in Honour of Lance Taylor*. Aldershot: Edward Elgar, 374–405.

—— (2002b). 'Reforming the International Financial Architecture: Consensus and Divergence', in D. Nayyar (ed.), *Governing Globalization: Issues and Institutions*. UNU/WIDER, WIDER Studies in Development Economics. Oxford: Oxford University Press.

—— (2003). 'Capital Account and Counter-Cyclical Prudential Regulation in Developing Countries', in R. Ffrench-Davis and S. Griffith-Jones (eds.), *From Capital Surges to Drought: Seeking Stability for Emerging Markets*. London: Palgrave Macmillan, pp. 217–44.

—— (2005). 'A Broad View of Macroeconomic Stability'. DESA Working Paper No. 1 (October). Also in N. Serra and J. E. Stiglitz (eds.) (forthcoming). *From the Washington Consensus Towards a New Global Governance*. New York: Oxford University Press.

Ocampo, J. A., and Taylor, L. (1998). 'Trade Liberalisation in Developing Economies: Modest Benefits but Problems with Productivity Growth, Macro Prices, and Income Distribution'. *Economic Journal*, 108/450: 1523–46.

Persaud, A. (2000). *Sending the Herd off the Cliff Edge: The Disturbing Interaction between Herding and Market-Sensitive Risk Management Practices*. London: State Street Bank.

Prasad, E., Rogoff, K., Wei, S.-J., and Kose, M. A. (2003). 'Effects of Financial Globalization on Developing Countries: Some Empirical Evidence'. IMF Occasional Paper No. 220. Washington, DC: International Monetary Fund.

Rajan, R. G. and Zingales, L. (2001). 'The Great Reversals: The Politics of Financial Development in the 20th Centruy'. NBER Working Paper 8178.

Rey, P. and Stiglitz, J. E. (1993). 'Short-Term Contracts as a Monitoring Device'. NBER Working Paper 4514.

Rodrik, D. (1998). 'Who Needs Capital Account Convertibility?', in S. Fischer et al. (eds.), *Should the IMF Pursue Capital-Account Convertibility?*, Essays in International Finance no. 207. Princeton: Princeton University Press.

—— and Velasco, A. (2000). 'Short-Term Capital Flows', in B. Pleskovic and J. E. Stiglitz (eds.), *Annual World Bank Conference on Development Economics, World Bank 1999*. Washington, DC: The World Bank.

Shapiro, C. and Stiglitz, J. E. (1984). 'Equilibrium Unemployment as a Worker Discipline Device'. *American Economic Review*, 74/3: 433–44.

Shell, K. and Stiglitz, J. E. (1967). 'Allocation of Investment in a Dynamic Economy'. *Quarterly Journal of Economics*, 81: 592–609.

Shiller, R. J. (2000). *Irrational Exuberance*. Princeton: Princeton University Press.

Spiegel, S. (2007). 'Lessons from Moldova on How Not to Borrow', in *IPD Volume on Sovereign Debt*. Oxford: Oxford University Press.

Stiglitz, J. E. (1973). 'The Badly Behaved Economy with the Well Behaved Production Function', in J. Mirrlees (ed.), *Models of Economic Growth*. MacMillan Publishing Company, 118–37 (originally presented at the International Economic Association Conference on Growth Theory, Jerusalem, 1970).

—— (1982). 'The Inefficiency of the Stock Market Equilibrium.' *Review of Economic Studies*, 49/2: 241–61.

—— (1989). 'Economic Organization, Information, and Development', in H. Chenery and T. N. Srinivasan (eds.), *Handbook of Development Economics*. Amsterdam: North-Holland.

—— (1998). 'Knowledge for Development: Economic Science, Economic Policy, and Economic Advice', in B. Pleskovic and J. E. Stiglitz (eds.), *Annual World Bank Conference on Development Economics*. Washington, DC: The World Bank, 9–58.

—— (2000). 'Capital Market Liberalization, Economic Growth, and Instability'. *World Development*, 28/6: 1075–86.

—— (2002a). *Globalization and its Discontents*. New York: W. W. Norton & Company.

—— (2002b). 'Information and the Change in the Paradigm in Economics'. *American Economic Review*, 92/3: 460–501.

—— (2003). *The Roaring Nineties: A New History of the World's Most Prosperous Decade*. New York: W.W. Norton & Company.

—— (2004). 'Capital-Market Liberalization, Globalization, and the IMF'. *Oxford Review of Economic Policy*: 20/1: 57–71.

_____ , Ocampo, J. A., Spiegel, S., Ffrench-Davis, R., and Nayyar, D. (2006). *Stability with Growth: Macroeconomics, Liberalization, and Development*. New York: Oxford University Press.

Turner, P. (2002). 'Procyclicality of Regulatory Ratios', in J. Eatwell and L. Taylor (eds.), *International Capital Markets—Systems in Transition*. New York: Oxford University Press.

Weitzman, M. L. (1974). 'Prices vs. Quantities'. *Review of Economic Studies*, 41/4: 477–91.

White, W. R. (2005). 'Procyclicality in the Financial System: Do We Need a New Macro-financial Stabilization Framework?'. Kiel Economic Policy Papers. Kiel Institute for Economic Policy.

World Bank (1999). *Global Economic Prospects and the Developing Countries, 1998–99—Beyond Financial Crisis*. Washington, DC: The World Bank.

Zahler, R. (2003). 'Macroeconomic Stability under Pension Reform in Emerging Economies: The Case of Chile'. Proceedings of the Seminar on Management of Volatility, Financial Globalization, and Growth in Emerging Economies, ECLAC, Santiago.

2

The Benefits and Risks of Financial Globalization

Sergio L. Schmukler[1]

2.1 Introduction

The recent wave of globalization has generated an intense debate among economists, attracting both strong supporters and opponents. This chapter outlines the benefits and risks of financial globalization for developing countries. The chapter revisits the arguments and evidence that can be used in favor of and against globalization, as well as policy options.

In this chapter, financial globalization is understood as the integration of a country's local financial system with international financial markets and institutions. This integration typically requires that governments liberalize the domestic financial sector and the capital account. Integration takes place when liberalized economies experience an increase in cross-country capital movement, including an active participation of local borrowers and lenders in international markets and a widespread use of international financial intermediaries. Although developed countries are the most active participants in the financial globalization process, developing countries (primarily middle-income countries) have also started to participate. This chapter focuses on the integration of developing countries with the international financial system.[2]

[1] I thank David Dollar, Chang-Tai Hsieh, Rick Mishkin, and José Antonio Ocampo for several helpful comments on earlier versions of this work. I am grateful to Juan Carlos Gozzi Valdez, Marina Halac, and Pablo Zoido-Lobaton for excellent research assistance. The opinions expressed in this chapter represent those of the author(s) and not necessarily those of the Initiative for Policy Dialogue or the World Bank.
[2] In this paper, developing countries are all low- and middle-income countries as defined by the World Bank. Emerging markets are middle-income developing countries.

From a historical perspective, financial globalization is not a new phenom-enon, but today's depth and breadth are unprecedented.[3] Capital flows have existed for a long time. In fact, according to some measures, the extent of capital mobility and capital flows 100 years ago is comparable to that of today. At that time, however, only few countries and sectors participated in financial globalization. Capital flows tended to follow migration and were generally directed towards supporting trade flows. For the most part, capital flows took the form of bonds, and they were of a long-term nature. International investment was dominated by a small number of freestanding companies, and financial intermediation was concentrated on a few family groups. The international system was dominated by the gold standard, in which gold backed national currencies.

The advent of the First World War represented the first blow to this wave of financial globalization, which was followed by a period of insta-bility and crises ultimately leading to the Great Depression and the Second World War. After these events, governments reversed financial globaliza-tion, imposing capital controls to regain monetary policy autonomy. Capital flows reached an all-time low during the 1950s and 1960s. The interna-tional system was dominated by the Bretton Woods system of fixed but adjustable exchange rates, limited capital mobility, and autonomous mone-tary policies.

As Mundell (2000) argues, the 1970s witnessed the beginning of a new era in the international financial system. As a result of the oil shock and the breakup of the Bretton Woods system, a new wave of globalization began. The oil shock provided international banks with fresh funds to invest in developing countries. These funds were used mainly to finance public debt in the form of syndicated loans. With the disintegration of the Bretton Woods system of fixed exchange rates, countries were able to open up to greater capital mobility while keeping the autonomy of their monetary policies. The capital flows of the 1970s and early 1980s to developing countries preceded the debt crisis that started in Mexico in 1982. To solve the debt crisis of the 1980s, Brady Bonds were created, swapping bank debt in default with new bond debt. This led to the subsequent development of bond markets for emerging economies. Deregulation, privatization, and advances in technology made foreign direct investment (FDI) and equity investments in emerging markets more attractive to firms and households in developed countries. The 1990s witnessed an investment boom in FDI and portfolio flows to emerging markets.

---

[3] Several authors analyze different measures of financial globalization, arguing that there were periods of high financial globalization in the past. For a review of this literature see Baldwin and Martin (1999).

Today, despite the perception of increasing financial globalization, the international financial system is far from being completely integrated.[4] There is evidence of persistent capital market segmentation, home country bias, and correlation between domestic savings and investment. The recent deregulation of financial systems, the technological advances in financial services, and the increased diversity in the channels of financial globalization make a return to the past more costly and therefore more difficult.[5] Financial globalization is unlikely to be reversed, particularly for partially integrated economies, although the possibility of that happening does still exist.

The potential benefits of financial globalization likely will lead to a more financially interconnected world and a deeper degree of financial integration of developing countries with international financial markets. The main benefit of financial globalization for developing countries is most likely the development of their financial system, which involves more complete, deeper, more stable and better regulated financial markets. As discussed in Levine (2001), a better functioning financial system with more credit is important because it fosters economic growth.[6]

Financial globalization also carries some risks. These risks are more likely to appear in the short run, when countries first open up. One well-known risk is that globalization can be related to financial crises. The cases of the 1997–8 Asian and Russian crises, as well as those in Brazil in 1999, Ecuador in 2000, Turkey in 2001, Argentina in 2001, and Uruguay in 2002, are just some examples that captured worldwide interest. There are various links between globalization and crises. If the right financial infrastructure is not in place or is not put in place while integrating, liberalization followed by capital inflows can debilitate the health of the local financial system. If market fundamentals deteriorate, speculative attacks will occur with capital outflows generated by both domestic and foreign investors. For successful integration, economic fundamentals need to be strong and remain so. Strong fundamentals gain relevance because, other things equal, financial globalization tends to intensify a country's sensitivities to foreign shocks. Accordingly, local

[4] Frankel (2000) argues that 'though international financial markets, much like goods markets, have become far more integrated in recent decades, they have traversed less of the distance to perfect integration than is widely believed.'

[5] Mussa (2000) emphasizes the power of new technology and the powerlessness of public policy in the face of the current evolution of financial flows. He argues that public policy 'can spur or retard them, but it is unlikely to stop them.' He also claims that the last backlash against globalization was cemented on two world wars and a great depression and affirms that the likelihood of that happening again is low.

[6] For more than a century, the importance of capital markets for economic growth has been emphasized. Historically, the literature focused on the role of banks, beginning with the views of Bagehot (1873) and Schumpeter (1912). More recently, empirical work, such as Levine and Zervos (1998), documents the positive link between financial development (represented by different measures) and growth.

markets need to be regulated properly and supervised. Moreover, international market imperfections, such as herding, panics, and boom–bust cycles, and the fluctuating nature of capital flows can lead to crises and contagion, even in countries with good economic fundamentals. Another risk of globalization is the segmentation that it can create between those able to participate in the global financial system and those that need to rely on domestic financial sectors.

The net benefit of financial globalization for developing countries can be large, even despite the risks. But globalization also poses new challenges for policymakers. One main challenge is to manage financial globalization in a way that allows countries to take full advantage of the opportunities it generates, while minimizing the risks it implies. This is important because financial globalization is likely to deepen over time, led by its potential benefits. Another challenge of globalization is that, in a more integrated world, governments are left with fewer policy instruments. Thus, some type of international financial cooperation becomes more important.

The organization of this chapter is as follows. Section 2.2 discusses the recent developments and main agents of financial globalization. Section 2.3 studies the effects of financial globalization on the domestic financial sector. Section 2.4 analyzes the potential costs associated with globalization and discusses the net effects. Section 2.5 analyzes the policy options available to deal with financial globalization. Section 2.6 concludes and discusses the policy implications.

2.2 Financial Globalization: Latest Developments and Main Agents

The last 30 years witnessed many changes in financial globalization. New technological advances and the liberalization of the domestic financial sector and the capital account have led to new developments. The main agents driving financial globalization are governments, private investors and borrowers, and financial institutions.

2.2.1 Latest Developments in Financial Globalization

The new nature of capital flows and the increasing use of international financial intermediaries constitute two of the most important developments in financial globalization.

Figure 2.1 shows that net capital flows to emerging economies have increased sharply since the 1970s. The composition of capital flows to developing countries changed significantly during this period. The relative size of official flows more than halved, while private capital flows became the

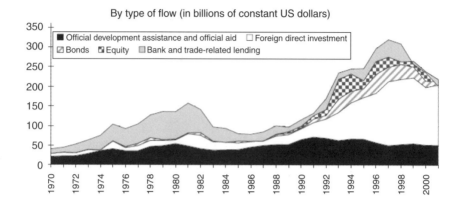

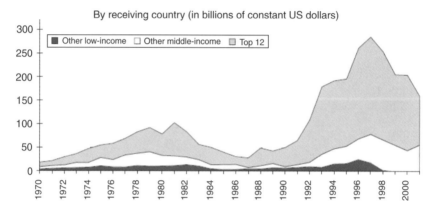

Figure 2.1. Net capital flows to developing countries 1970–2001

Notes: The figures display net capital flows to developing countries. The top panel plots the evolution of private capital flows and official capital flows. Private capital flows are dissagregated into foreign direct investment, portfolio bond flows, portfolio equity flows, and bank and trade related flows. The bottom panel depicts the distribution of private capital flows among developing countries. The top 12 receiving developing countries are: China, Brazil, Mexico, South Korea, Argentina, Malaysia, Chile, India, the Russian Federation, Thailand, Turkey, and South Africa.

The variables included are: total private capital flows, foreign direct investment (net inflows in reporting country), portolio investments-bonds and equity, bank and trade-related lending, and official development assistance and net official aid. All these variables are deflated using the US GDP deflator, the base year is 1995.

Source: World Bank, World Development Indicators 2003 (WDI).

major source of capital for a large number of emerging economies. The composition of private capital flows also changed markedly. FDI grew continuously throughout the 1990s. Figure 2.1 also shows the abrupt decline in capital flows to emerging markets following the Asian and Russian crises of 1997–8 and the Argentine crisis in 2001.

Even though net private capital flows to developing countries increased in recent years, private capital does not flow to all countries equally. Some countries tend to receive large amounts of inflows, while other countries receive little foreign capital. Figure 2.1 also shows that while capital flows to developing countries increased in general, the top 12 countries with the highest flows are receiving the overwhelming majority of the net inflows. Moreover, the top 12 countries are the ones that experienced the most rapid growth in private capital flows during the 1990s. As a consequence, the share of flows dedicated to low-income and middle-income countries (outside the top 12) has decreased over time.[7] This is important because if countries benefit from foreign capital, only a small group of countries are the ones benefiting the most. The unequal distribution of capital flows is consistent with the fact that income among developing countries is diverging, although the causality is difficult to determine.

The second development is the internationalization of financial services, which means the use of international financial intermediaries by local borrowers and investors. This internationalization is achieved through two main channels. The first channel is an increased presence of international financial intermediaries, mainly foreign banks, in local markets. The second channel involves the use of international financial intermediaries by local borrowers and investors; these international financial intermediaries are located outside the country. One example of the latter channel is the trading of local shares in major world stock exchanges, mostly in the form of depositary receipts.

Figure 2.2 presents evidence of the increased participation of companies from developing and developed countries in the US equity markets using depositary receipts. Companies from developing countries have been actively participating in the US equity markets since the early 1990s. The data show that the top six middle-income countries with the highest participation capture most of the activity among middle-income countries. As argued above in the case of capital flows, this might be creating a divergence among developing countries. If capital raised in international capital markets brings benefits to recipient countries, for example because the cost of capital is lower or because a longer maturity structure can be achieved, a group of middle-income countries has been benefiting more than other developing nations.

2.2.2 Main Agents

There are four main agents of financial globalization: governments, borrowers, investors, and financial institutions. Each of them is helping countries become more financially integrated.

---

[7] The share of private capital flows received by the 12 top countries decreased in 2001 as a consequence of the Argentine crisis and a reduction of international flows, mainly to Brazil and China.

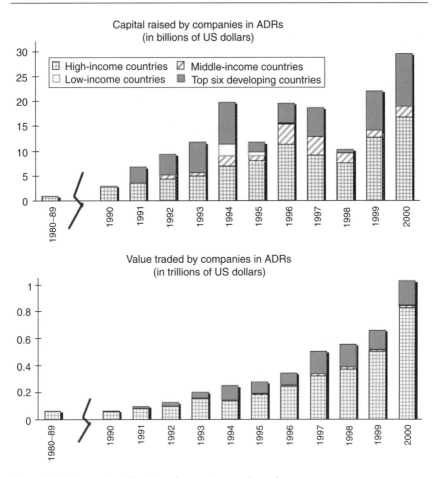

Figure 2.2. Internationalization of emerging stock markets

Notes: The figures illustrate the amount of equity capital raised by developing countries in international capital markets and the volume traded by developing countries ADRs during the 1990s. In these figures, the top six developing countries include Argentina, Brazil, China, India, South Korea, and Mexico; these countries were selected in accordance to their total capital raised during the period 1980–2000. High-income countries include Australia, Austria, Belgium, Denmark, Finland, France, Germany, Greece, Hong Kong, Ireland, Israel, Italy, Japan, Luxembourg, the Netherlands, New Zealand, Norway, Portugal, Singapore, Slovenia, Spain, Sweden, Switzerland, Taiwan, and the United Kingdom. Middle-income countries include Bahrain, Chile, Colombia, Croatia, the Czech Republic, the Dominican Republic, Egypt, Estonia, Hungary, Jordan, Kazakhstan, Latvia, Lebanon, Lithuania, Malta, Morocco, Papua New Guinea, Peru, the Philippines, Poland, Romania, Russia, the Slovak Republic, South Africa, Sri Lanka, Thailand, Tunisia, Turkey, Uruguay, and Venezuela. Low-income countries include Ghana, Indonesia, Malawi, and Pakistan.

Source: Bank of New York.

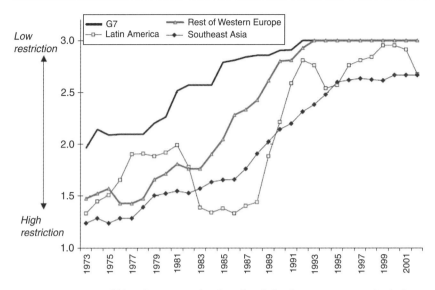

Figure 2.3. Financial liberalization in developed and developing countries (index)

Notes: The liberalization index is calculated as the simple average of three indexes (liberalization in the capital account, domestic financial system and stock market) that range between 1 and 3, where 1 means no liberalization and 3 means full liberalization. These data are then aggregated as the simple average between countries of each region. Figures correspond to annual averages calculated from monthly data.

Source: Kaminsky and Schmukler (2002).

Governments are one of the main agents of financial globalization. Governments allow globalization by liberalizing restrictions on the domestic financial sector and the capital account of the balance of payments. In the past, governments regulated the domestic financial sector by restricting the allocation of credit through controls on prices and quantities. Governments also imposed several constraints on cross-country capital movements. The list of instruments used to restrict the capital account is rather extensive, including restrictions on foreign exchange transactions, derivative transactions, lending and borrowing activities by banks and corporations, and the participation of foreign investors in the local financial system.

Even though the domestic financial sector and the capital account were heavily regulated for a long time, Kaminsky and Schmukler (2002) show how the restrictions have been lifted over time. Figure 2.3 presents the evolution of their index of financial liberalization that takes into account restrictions on the domestic financial system, the stock market, and the capital account. The figure illustrates the gradual lifting of restrictions in developed and emerging countries during the last 30 years. Although there has been a gradual lifting of restrictions over time, there were periods of reversals, in which restrictions were reimposed. The most substantial reversals took place in the aftermath of the 1982 debt crisis, in the mid-1990s, and after the Argentine crisis in Latin America.

Borrowers and investors, including households and firms, have also become main agents of financial globalization. By borrowing abroad, firms and individuals can relax their financial constraints to smooth consumption and investment, which allows them to invest when poor and repay when rich and to better withstand adverse shocks.[8] Firms can expand their financing alternatives by raising funds directly through bonds and equity issues in international markets and thereby reducing the cost of capital, expanding their investor base, and increasing liquidity. More financing alternatives help foreign investors overcome direct and indirect investment barriers. International investors, as argued in Obstfeld (1994) and Tesar and Werner (1998), have taken advantage of financial globalization to achieve cross-country risk diversification.

Financial institutions, through the internationalization of financial services, are also a major driving force of financial globalization. As discussed by the International Monetary Fund (IMF 2000), changes at the global level and changes in both developed and developing countries explain the role of financial institutions as a force of globalization. At a global level, the gains in information technology have diminished the importance of geography, allowing international corporations to service several markets from one location. In developed countries, increased competition has led banks and other non-bank financial firms to look at expanding their market shares into new businesses and markets and attracting customers from other countries, which allows them to diversify risk. Decreasing costs due to deregulation and technical improvements were accompanied by more competition. Moreover, the liberalization of the regulatory systems has opened the door for international firms to participate in local markets. Macroeconomic stabilization, better business environment and stronger fundamentals in emerging markets ensured a more attractive climate for foreign investment.

2.3 Financial Globalization and Financial Sector Development

Financial globalization can lead to the development of the financial system. A well-functioning financial sector provides funds to borrowers (households, firms, and governments) who have productive investment opportunities. As discussed in Mishkin (2003), financial systems do not usually operate as desired because lenders confront problems of asymmetric information, which can lead to adverse selection and moral hazard.

---

[8] To the extent that savings from developing countries are invested abroad, these nations can also achieve cross-country risk diversification.

Financial globalization can help improve the functioning of the financial system through two main channels. First, financial globalization can increase the availability of funds. Second, financial globalization can improve the financial infrastructure, which can reduce the problem of asymmetric information. As a consequence, financial globalization can decrease adverse selection and moral hazard, enhancing the availability of credit.

Regarding the first channel, in a financially integrated world, funds can flow freely from countries with excess funds to countries where the marginal product of capital is high. In this context, both foreign institutions and individuals might provide capital to developing countries if they expect these countries to grow faster than developed economies. As a consequence, countries can smooth consumption and make investments financed by foreign capital. This flow of capital from developed to developing countries is reflected in the large current account deficits typically observed in many developing nations.

The effects of capital flows on financial development take place because new sources of funds and more capital become available. New sources of funds mean that borrowers not only depend on domestic funds, they can also borrow from foreign countries willing to invest in domestic assets. The capital available from new sources means that market discipline is now stronger both at the macroeconomic level and at the financial sector level, as now local and foreign investors enforce market discipline on private and public borrowers. Foreign capital is particularly effective in imposing this kind of discipline given its footloose nature; foreign capital can more easily shift investment across countries. Domestic capital tends to have more restrictions to invest internationally.

Thanks in part to the availability of more capital, developing economies have developed their stock and bond markets as well as some of their local financial service industry. Capital markets have developed, in the sense that more domestic equity and bonds are issued and traded, but this does not imply that all domestic financial institutions have become more important. Borrowers and investors can just use international financial intermediaries, like stock exchanges and banks, to conduct their financial transactions. In fact, domestic financial institutions can actually shrink due to competition with international financial institutions. For example, local banks obtain a lower share of the domestic market. Moreover, as Claessens et al. (2002) argue, many stock markets are shrinking as trading moves from domestic markets to major global stock exchanges, as illustrated in Figure 2.4.

The second channel of financial globalization is an improved financial infrastructure. An improved financial sector infrastructure means that borrowers and lenders operate in a more transparent, competitive and efficient financial system. In this environment, problems of asymmetric information are minimized and credit is maximized.

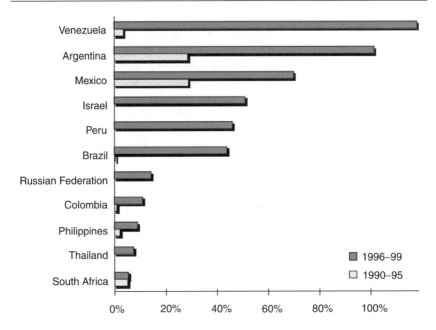

Figure 2.4. Share of trading in international markets to local markets in selected countries

Notes: The figure illustrates, for a group of selected countries, the equity trading in international markets relative to the domestic markets. The figure plots the average ratio of ADR trading in New York over the total value traded in the domestic markets for the years 1990–95 and 1996–99.

Source: Bank of New York (for ADRs) and International Financial Corporation Emerging Markets Fact Book.

In theory, there are different ways financial globalization can create improvements in the financial sector infrastructure. First, financial globalization can cause greater competition in the provision of funds, which can generate efficiency gains. Second, the adoption of international accounting standards can increase transparency. Third, the introduction of international financial intermediaries pushes the financial sector towards the international frontier. Fourth, Stulz (1999) argues that financial globalization improves corporate governance; new shareholders and potential bidders force a closer monitoring of management. Fifth, Crockett (2000) claims that the increase in the technical capabilities for engaging in precision financing results in a growing completeness of local and global markets.

Foreign bank entry is another way through which financial globalization can improve the financial infrastructure of developing countries. Mishkin (2003) argues that foreign banks enhance financial development for at least three main reasons. First, foreign banks have more diversified portfolios as they have access to sources of funds from all over the world, which means that they are exposed to less risk and are less affected by negative shocks to the home country economy. Second, foreign entry can lead to the adoption of best practices in the banking industry, particularly in risk management but also in management techniques, which leads to a more efficient banking sector. Third, if foreign banks dominate the banking sector, governments are less likely to bail out banks when they have solvency problems. A lower likelihood of bail-outs encourages more prudent behavior by banking institutions, increased discipline, and a reduction in moral hazard. The World Bank (2001) discusses this topic in greater depth.

2.4 Risks and Net Effects of Globalization

Although financial globalization has several potential benefits, financial globalization also carries risks. The recent stream of financial crises and contagion after countries liberalized their financial systems and became integrated with world financial markets might lead some to suggest that globalization generates financial volatility and crises.

Even though domestic factors tend to be key determinants of crises, there are different channels through which financial globalization can be related to crises. First, when a country liberalizes its financial system it becomes subject to market discipline exercised by both foreign and domestic investors. When an economy is closed, only domestic investors monitor the economy and react to unsound fundamentals. In open economies, the joint force of domestic and foreign investors might generate a crisis when fundamentals deteriorate. This might prompt countries to try to achieve sound fundamentals, though this might take a long time. Furthermore, investors might overreact, being overly optimistic in good times and overly pessimistic in bad ones. Therefore, small changes in fundamentals, or even news, can trigger sharp changes in investors' appetite for risk.

Second, globalization can also lead to crises if there are imperfections in international financial markets. The imperfections in financial markets can generate bubbles, herding behavior, speculative attacks, and crashes, among other things. Imperfections in international capital markets can lead to crises even in countries with sound fundamentals. For example, if investors believe that the exchange rate is unsustainable they might speculate against the currency, which can lead to a self-fulfilling balance of payments crisis regardless of market fundamentals. This is largely illustrated in the literature following Obstfeld (1986).[9] Imperfections can also deteriorate fundamentals. For example, moral hazard can lead to overborrowing syndromes when economies

---

[9] Note that self-fulfilling crises can also take place in a closed domestic banking sector as shown in the literature following Diamond and Dybvig (1983).

are liberalized and there are implicit government guarantees, increasing the likelihood of crises, as argued in McKinnon and Pill (1997).[10]

Third, globalization can lead to crises due to the importance of external factors, even in countries with sound fundamentals and even in the absence of imperfections in international capital markets. If a country becomes dependent on foreign capital, sudden shifts in foreign capital flows can create financing difficulties and economic downturns. These shifts do not necessarily depend on a country's fundamentals. Calvo et al. (1996) argue that external factors are important determinants of capital flows to developing countries. In particular, they find that world interest rates were a significant determinant of capital inflows into Asia and Latin America during the 1990s. Economic cyclical movements in developed countries, a global drive towards diversification of investments in major financial centers, and regional effects tend to be other important global factors.

Fourth, financial globalization can also lead to financial crises through contagion, namely by shocks that are transmitted across countries.[11] Three broad channels of contagion have been identified in the literature: real links, financial links, and herding behavior. Real links have usually been associated with trade links. When two countries trade among themselves or if they compete in the same external markets, a devaluation of the exchange rate in one country deteriorates the other country's competitive advantage. As a consequence, both countries will likely end up devaluing their currencies to balance their external sectors. Financial links exist when two economies are connected through the international financial system. One example of financial links is when leveraged institutions face margin calls. When the value of their collateral falls, due to a negative shock in one country, leveraged companies need to increase their reserves. Therefore, they sell part of their valuable holdings in the countries that are still unaffected by the initial shock. This mechanism propagates the shock to other economies.[12] Finally, financial markets might transmit shocks across countries due to herding behavior or panics. At the root of this herding behavior is asymmetric information. Information is costly so investors remain uniformed. Therefore, investors try to infer future price changes based on how other markets are reacting. In this context, a change in

---

[10] The arguments that claim that market imperfections are the cause of crises when countries integrate with financial markets imply that imperfections are more prevalent in international markets than in domestic markets. Imperfections in financial markets can exist even in closed countries. If imperfections are more important in domestic markets than in the foreign markets, as one can expect given their degree of development, financial globalization does not have to lead to crises.

[11] Dornbusch et al. (2000) survey the literature on contagion. Further references can be found at: www.worldbank.org/contagion.

[12] Another example of financial link is when open-end mutual funds foresee future redemptions after there is a shock in one country. Mutual funds need to raise cash and, consequently, they sell assets in third countries.

Thailand's asset prices might be considered useful information about future changes in Indonesia's or Brazil's asset prices with investors reacting accordingly, even when fundamentals do not warrant it. Additionally, in the context of asymmetric information, what the other market participants are doing might convey information that each uninformed investor does not have. This type of reaction leads to herding behavior or panics.

2.4.1 *Evidence on Crises and Contagion*

Though crises can be associated with financial liberalization, the evidence suggests that crises are complex. They are not just the consequence of globalization. The evidence indicates that crises have been a recurrent feature of financial markets for a long time, both in periods of economic integration and in periods of economic disintegration. Bordo et al. (2001*b*) study the frequency, duration, and impact of crises during the last 120 years and find the frequency of crises since 1973 has been double that of the Bretton Woods and classical gold standard periods and is rivaled only by the crisis-ridden 1920s and 1930s. However, they also find little evidence that crises have grown longer or output losses have become larger. Furthermore, evidence suggests several causes of financial crises, many of which are related to domestic factors. Frankel and Rose (1996) argue that domestic factors such as slow growth and a boom in domestic credit increase a country's likelihood of experiencing a financial crisis.[13]

The evidence also suggests that different channels of contagion have played important roles in the transmission of crises. Eichengreen et al. (1996), Glick and Rose (1999), and Forbes (2000) argue that trade links are important. Financial and non-fundamental links are also very important to understand contagion. Kaminsky and Reinhart (2000) argue that the contagion of Argentina and Brazil from Mexico in 1994, and that of Indonesia from Thailand in 1997–8, are best explained by financial sector linkages among these countries, in particular banks and international capital markets. Kaminsky et al. (2004) highlight the role of mutual funds and point out that in the aftermath of the Russian default in 1998 Malaysia suffered average mutual funds sales of 30 percent and the Czech Republic of 16 percent. The evidence is also consistent with contagion unrelated to fundamentals, either financial or trade related. Kaminsky and Schmukler (1999) and Favero and Giavazzi (2000) suggest that herding behavior can be a driving force of contagion.

---

[13] Kaminsky and Reinhart (1999) argue that crises occur mostly due to domestic factors, as the economy enters a recession following a period of prolonged boom in economic activity fueled by expanded credit, capital inflows, and an overvalued currency. Caprio and Klingebiel (1997) stress the importance of both macroeconomic and microeconomic factors in determining banking crises.

The evidence shows, furthermore, that financial crises are costly. For example, during the period 1973–97, there were 44 crises in developed countries and 95 in emerging markets, with average output losses of 6.25 and 9.21 percent of GDP respectively (see Bordo et al. 2001b; and Bordo and Eichengreen 2002). Moreover, the literature suggests that crises do not hit all groups of people equally, despite the overall negative impact on output. Crises affect disproportionately different ranges of the income distribution, hurting particularly the poor through adverse income and employment shocks, high inflation, relative price changes, and public spending cutbacks.[14]

2.4.2 Net Effects

The previous sections argued that globalization can bring benefits through the development of the domestic financial system. But globalization can also be associated with crises and contagion (and also with market segmentation). As discussed in Obstfeld (1998), this is inescapable in a world of asymmetric information and imperfect contract enforcement. Though many crises are triggered by domestic factors, and countries have had crises for a long time (even in periods of low financial integration), it is the case that globalization can increase the vulnerability of countries to crises. In open economies, countries are subject to the reaction of both domestic and international markets, which can trigger fundamental-based or self-fulfilling crises. Moreover, the cross-country transmission of crises is characteristic of open economies. Completely closed economies should be isolated from foreign shocks. But when a country integrates with the global economy, it becomes exposed to contagion effects of different types and, more generally, to foreign shocks.

Is the link between globalization, crises, and contagion important enough to outweigh the benefits of globalization? The evidence is still scarce, but it is far from clear that open countries are more volatile and suffer more from crises. The evidence suggests that, in the long run, volatility tends to decrease following liberalization and integration with world markets, probably because of the development of the financial sector. The evidence holds even when including crisis episodes, which might be considered particular events.

Any potential increase in volatility tends to occur in the short-run, immediately after liberalization begins. When countries first liberalize their financial sector, volatility and crises might arise, particularly in countries with vulnerable fundamentals. If the domestic financial sector is not prepared to cope with foreign flows and is not properly regulated and supervised, financial liberalization can lead to domestic crises. This is shown in Figure 2.5, which displays the typical boom–bust episode in stock markets. Kaminsky and Schmukler (2002) show that three years after liberalization the cycles in the stock market become

---

[14] See, for example, Ferreira et al. (1999).

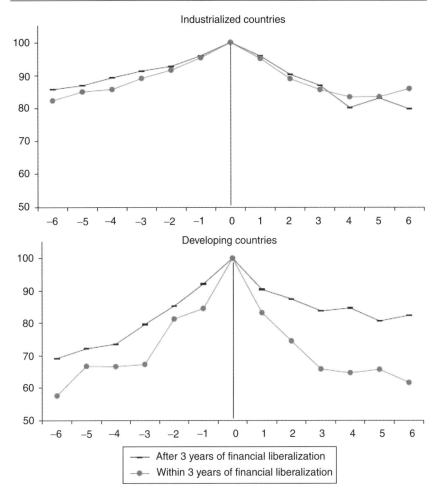

Figure 2.5. Average boom–bust cycles and financial liberalization

Notes: The figures show the average boom–bust cycle in financial markets for selected countries. Date 0 is the date of the peak in stock market prices. All stock market indices are normalized to 100 at the peak. Countries comprising industrialized countries are Canada, France, Germany, Italy, Japan, the United Kingdom, the United States, Denmark, Finland, Ireland, Norway, Portugal, Spain, and Sweden. Countries comprising developing countries are Argentina, Brazil, Chile, Colombia, Mexico, Peru, Venezuela, Hong Kong, Indonesia, Korea, Malaysia, the Philippines, Taiwan, and Thailand. Financial liberalization occurs when countries substantially lift the restrictions on cross-country capital movements.

Source: Kaminsky and Schmukler (2002).

less pronounced, while they become more pronounced in the aftermath of liberalization.

There is also some evidence on the positive impact of financial liberalization on output growth. Bekaert et al. (2001) estimate that output growth has increased about one percentage point following liberalization. Although financial liberalization spurs financial development, they show that measures of financial development fail to fully drive out the liberalization effect. Furthermore, Tornell et al. (2003) show that financial liberalization leads to higher average long-run growth even though it also leads to some crises and to boom–bust cycles.

2.5 Policy Options

There are different views on how governments can maximize the benefits of globalization and minimize its risks. As discussed above, one of the most important benefits of financial globalization is the development of the financial sector. This development tends to lead to deeper and less volatile financial markets. But, on the other hand, globalization can also be associated with some costs. The most important one involves a higher sensitivity to crises and contagion. The gains are likely to materialize in the long run, while the costs will tend to be more prevalent in the short run. In all the aspects of globalization, the action or inaction of governments can be important.

2.5.1 *Three Views on the Role of Government*

In the past, conventional wisdom favored unfettered capitalism, but the fact that globalization has been associated with crises and contagion has led many economists to believe that some degree of government intervention can be beneficial. Many economists would now agree that financial integration with the rest of the world is beneficial in the long run. However, the recent experience with crises and contagion has generated large disagreements about how to integrate and about what policies to recommend. These recent episodes have even led some economists to suggest isolating countries from the international financial system, or delaying integration for those countries that are closed. In sum, there are different views on what governments should do regarding financial integration.

A first view argues that government intervention is at the root of recent crises. This view believes that international capital markets are efficient and developed (or at least international financial markets are more efficient than financial markets in developing countries). Therefore, countries with underdeveloped financial markets would benefit from full financial liberalization, with minimal government intervention. Certain types of government intervention create distortions that can lead to moral hazard and crises. For example, Akerlof and Romer (1993) show that government guarantees can induce firms to go broke at society's expense (looting). They claim that once looting becomes established in one sector, it can distort production in other sectors.

A second view claims that cross-country capital flows should be restricted. According to this view, inefficient international financial markets debilitate the argument for unregulated financial integration. Anomalies such as asymmetric information, moral hazard, asset bubbles, speculative attacks, herding behavior, and contagion are present in international financial markets. So economies open to capital flows suffer the consequences of these imperfections. The recent crises showed that international financial markets punished similarly countries with different fundamentals and policies. Given this evidence, Krugman (1998), Tobin (2000), and Stiglitz (2000) argue that government intervention to restrict cross-country capital movements can be socially beneficial. Moreover, Stiglitz (1999) calls for developing countries to put some limits on capital inflows to moderate excessive boom-bust patterns in financial markets. Ocampo (2003) argues that two instruments can be used together to manage capital account volatility in developing countries—capital account regulation and counter-cyclical prudential regulation. Several economists, then, argue that governments can mitigate the cost of volatile capital flows—reducing excessive risk taking and making markets less vulnerable to external shocks—and still pursue integration with international financial markets.

A third view concentrates on risk management. This view focuses on strengthening the domestic financial sector and sequencing financial liberalization. This view argues that opening a weak domestic financial sector to large capital movements is potentially risky. If the domestic financial sector does not manage risk properly, does not have sufficient reserves and capital, or does not have the right incentives, large capital inflows and outflows can create severe problems in the domestic financial sector. Foreign competition can also debilitate local financial intermediaries. Since financial crises can be very costly, this view proposes an adequate regulation and supervision of the domestic financial system without distinguishing between capital that is foreign in origin and capital that is domestic. Additional proposals include the use of counter-cyclical fiscal policy, the stability of prices, the active management of reserve requirements, and the implementation of contingent liquidity arrangements. Also, improved prudential regulation and increased market discipline, through more transparency and information, have been recommended as a way to avoid excessive risk taking.

2.5.2 *Fewer Policy Instruments*

One of the main consequences of globalization for policymaking is that the number of instruments at a country's disposal diminishes when the economy is integrated. When the domestic financial system integrates with the rest of the world, it is more difficult for countries to monitor and regulate the transactions outside its borders. For example, local authorities are able to regulate the activities of the local subsidiary of an international bank, but it is more difficult to regulate the parent company and subsidiaries in other countries, which can be linked to the local bank. Also, the ability of capital to move freely in and out of the country makes government intervention more difficult to enforce. As countries become more integrated, the need for some kind of international financial cooperation grows.

The rest of the section illustrates, with two examples, how financial globalization influences the options available to policymakers. These policies have received significant attention in the discussions surrounding crises and financial globalization. The policies discussed below are the ones related to risk management and the choice of monetary and exchange rate regimes.

Before discussing examples of two policies, it is useful to mention the policies related to capital controls, which have received wide attention. The proposals on capital controls are designed to reduce the probability or mitigate the effects of sudden shifts in foreign capital. These proposals suggest that international capital flows should be restricted in particular and judicious ways. There is a large body of research on the effects of capital controls. This research is inconclusive about the effectiveness of capital controls. Some research suggests controls work as expected. Other research finds no impacts, or even negative impacts of such controls, or just temporary effects that dissipate over time. Since the evidence is inconclusive, we focus on two other policies about which there appears to be growing consensus.

RISK MANAGEMENT

As an alternative to capital controls, some economists have proposed focusing on managing risk by regulating and supervising the financial system, without distinguishing between domestic and foreign capital. When economies are partially integrated with the rest of the world, distinguishing between domestic and foreign capital becomes more difficult. That is why capital controls tend to be ineffective. In this case, governments can benefit by focusing on the stability of the overall financial sector to avoid financial crises or to make crises less costly. If there are imperfections in capital markets, it becomes even more important to avoid excessive risk taking, particularly maturity risk and currency risk, which have played central roles in recent crises. So the discussion shifts towards risk management.

Governments might want to regulate and supervise financial systems to ensure that the financial sector is managing risk well. Governments might want to avoid large asset-liability mismatches, like unhedged foreign exchange borrowings invested in non-tradable sectors and short-term assets for long-term investments, which can leave banks vulnerable to exchange rate depreciations and to interest rate surges. Also, regulation and supervision should ensure that banks are sufficiently capitalized with appropriate loan classification and adequate loan loss provisions. Transparency for investors and depositors through mandatory public disclosure of audited financial statements will help enforce market discipline. The removal of explicit or implicit government guarantees and sharing risk with investors will decrease the potential for moral hazard. The World Bank (2001) discusses in more detail the regulations of the financial sector in an integrated economy.

Financial sector policies also should be accompanied by the right incentives for sound corporate governance. Clear rules and adequate financial disclosure help regulators and market participants monitor corporations, which pushes corporations to achieve good practices. Clear governance rules help prevent insider and group lending not subject to loan evaluation and creditworthiness standards. Developed corporate bond and equity markets help companies obtain external financing, become more transparent, and be subject to market discipline.

Proper risk management helps to avoid and manage crises. First, as a preventive measure, countries with solid financial sectors will probably suffer fewer crises and less pronounced recessions. Second, countries with sound financial sectors will have more flexibility to cope with external shocks and to take corrective measures during a crisis. Countries with a solvent banking sector and low corporate leverage ratios will be able, to some extent, to raise interest rates to contain speculative attacks on the exchange rate. Countries with large foreign exchange reserves and access to contingent liquidity facilities will be able to inject liquidity in the system, avoiding credit squeeze and bank runs.

The recent experiences with crises and contagion stress the importance of adequate risk management. Kawai et al. (2005) argue that one of the more important lessons of the East Asian crisis was that highly leveraged and vulnerable corporate sectors were a key determinant of the depth of the crisis. Currency devaluations suddenly inflated the size of external debt (measured in terms of the domestic currency) and debt service obligations, thereby driving the domestic corporations into financial distress. High interest rates also sharply increased domestic debt service obligations of the corporations. These vulnerabilities affected the banks with exposures to the corporations. Krugman (1999) argues that company balance sheet problems may have a role in causing financial crises. Currency crises lead to an increase in foreign denominated debt, which combined with declining sales and higher interest rates weaken the corporate sector and, in turn, the financial system. Johnson et al. (2000) also show how weak corporate governance might hamper the economy and lead to currency depreciations and recessions.

MONETARY AND EXCHANGE RATE POLICY

The choice of exchange rate regime (floating, fixed, or somewhere in between) has been a recurrent question in international monetary economics. Obstfeld and Taylor (2003) argue that the different historical phases of financial glob-alization can be understood in terms of the so-called impossible trinity.[15] According to this proposition, a country can consistently pursue only two out of the three policy objectives: free capital mobility, a fixed (or highly stable) nominal exchange rate, and an autonomous monetary policy. Obstfeld and Taylor explain that international capital mobility has, thus, prevailed in peri-ods of political support either for subordinating monetary policy to exchange rate stability (as in the gold standard, 1880–1914), or for giving up exchange rate stability so as to enable monetary policy to pursue domestic objectives (as in the post-Bretton Woods era, 1971–2003). In contrast, when countries attempted simultaneously to target their exchange rates and use monetary policy in pursuit of domestic objectives (e.g., to combat the slowdown of economic activity in the interwar period), they had to impose controls to curtail capital movements (as in the interwar, 1914–45, and Bretton Woods, 1945–71 periods). After the crises of the 1990s, economists have become in favor of corner exchange rate regimes, according to which countries will either firmly fix their exchange rate or follow a flexible regime without pre-commitments, allowing for free capital movements.

By fixing the exchange rate, countries tend to then reduce transaction costs and exchange rate risk that can discourage trade and investment. At the same time, a fixed exchange rate has been used as a credible nominal anchor for monetary policy. On the other hand, a flexible exchange rate allows a country to pursue independent monetary policy. A flexible exchange rate allows countries to respond to shocks through changes in the exchange rate and interest rate to avoid going into recession. Under the combination of fixed exchange rates and complete integration of financial markets, monetary policy becomes completely powerless. Any fluctuations in the currency or cur-rencies to which the country fixes its exchange rate will impact the domestic currency. Under a fixed exchange rate regime, other variables need to do the adjustment.

Even though countries can choose a flexible exchange rate regime, some papers have argued that countries are not allowing their exchange rates to move in part because of the high degree of financial globalization. Among others, Calvo and Reinhart (2002) argue that there exists 'fear of floating' that prevents countries with *de jure* flexible regimes from allowing their exchange rates to move freely. According to this view, factors like lack of cred-ibility, exchange rate pass-through, and foreign currency liabilities prevent countries from pursuing an independent monetary policy, regardless of their announced regime. Therefore, many countries, even if formally floating, are *de facto* importing the monetary policy of major currency countries, much as

---

[15] The concept of an impossible trinity is not new. It dates back, at least, to the work of Mundell in the 1960s.

those with pegs. In fact, the empirical evidence seems to suggest that countries are not able or do not choose to pursue a completely independent monetary policy. Still, there are credible ways to adopt a flexible regime if the right monetary institutions are in place and if countries can commit to an inflation targeting policy, as discussed in Bernanke and Mishkin (1997) and Mishkin (2000).

After the fall of the Argentine peso peg, debate shifted again. Economists are now disregarding peg regimes that fall short of dollarization or euroization. Moreover, a one-dimensional emphasis on pure fix versus float dilemma now seems insufficient and can even be misleading. It would be more productive to focus on the weak currency problem that plagues most emerging economies and on the need to build healthy links between money and financial intermediation, while establishing adequate flexibility—including in financial contracting, to facilitate adjustment to shocks. De La Torre et al. (2002) and Calvo and Mishkin (2003) also highlight the importance of strengthening institutions. They argue that the choice of exchange rate regime is likely to be of second order importance to the development of good fiscal, financial, and monetary institutions in producing macroeconomic success in emerging market countries. A focus on institutional reforms rather than on the exchange rate regime may encourage emerging market countries to be healthier and less prone to crises.

2.6 Conclusions

In the last decades, countries around the world have become more financially integrated, driven by the potential benefits of financial globalization. One of the main benefits of financial globalization is the development of the financial sector. Financial markets become deeper and more sophisticated when they integrate with world markets, increasing the financial alternatives for borrowers and investors. Financial markets operating in a global environment enable international risk diversification and leveling of consumption. Although financial globalization has several potential benefits, financial globalization also poses new challenges. The crises of the 1990s, after many countries liberalized their financial system, have challenged the ideas stressing the gains of globalization. Countries become exposed to external shocks and crises, not only generated in their own country, but also from contagion effects. In the initial stages of liberalization, if the right infrastructure is not in or put in place, financial liberalization can lead to increased risks. Moreover, in a financially integrated economy, policymakers have fewer policy instruments to conduct economic policy.

The recent experiences with financial globalization yield some useful lessons for policymaking.

2.6.1 *Countries Can Benefit from Globalization*

Countries can benefit from financial globalization and should take advantage of it. Financial liberalization can have positive effects on the financial system. At the same time, the evidence does not suggest that financial volatility increases after financial liberalization. While it is true that crises have had a very large impact on growth in some countries like Indonesia, in other cases, the recovery has been rapid, as in South Korea and Mexico. Also, it would be hard to argue that economies would have grown as fast as they did if they had remained closed.

Though the potential benefits can be large, we are far from full financial globalization. Even in open countries there is still an important home bias. Given the potential benefits of globalization, the scope is for a much deeper financial globalization and for much larger gains. Many countries are already partially open and the prospect is for an increased globalization of financial markets. Paradoxically, increased globalization can reduce the scope for risk diversification, because integrated financial markets tend to be more correlated.

2.6.2 *Importance of Sound Fundamentals and Strong Institutions*

Sound macroeconomic and financial fundamentals are key to lowering the probability of crises and contagion and to be able to manage crises more effectively. Preventing currency and banking crises should be one of the primary objectives of any policymaker because of the high cost of crises. This is more important in a world of free capital mobility, because both foreign and domestic investors exercise market discipline and because foreign crises might have contagion effects at home. Attacks on currencies can occur whenever confidence is lost, even if a country has sound fundamentals. A crisis in a foreign country can rapidly trigger a crisis at home. Weak fundamentals tend to scare investors more easily and make crisis management more difficult. Countries with bad fundamentals, for example with large fiscal deficits and public debt, have fewer instruments to use in the midst of a crisis. Therefore, countries should focus on key policies that help them prevent and manage crises. These policies include avoiding large current account deficits financed through short term private capital inflows and large asset–liability currency mismatches.

Improving the contractual and regulatory environment is also important. Better institutions make an emerging country more fit to join in the financial globalization process. In particular, they increase the capacity of the domestic financial system to intermediate prudently large international capital flows. Also, improvements in the contractual and regulatory framework can enhance the access of resident corporations (at least in the case of larger countries and for the larger corporations) to financial services supplied abroad.

2.6.3 *Initial Conditions Matter*

Measures to isolate countries (like capital controls) are unlikely to work in the long run, particularly in countries that are partially integrated with the world economy. When there were attempts to isolate already open economies, investors have tended to find ways to avoid the restrictions over time. It is much easier to isolate countries with low levels of integration.

Initial conditions matter. The effectiveness of policies relies on the degree of integration with world markets. Countries with a relatively low degree of integration with world capital markets, like China and India, and with under-developed financial markets are more able to delay or revert the process of financial globalization than countries already partially integrated. Countries with a low level of integration should ensure that their financial sector is prepared to cope with open capital markets. If the domestic financial sector does not manage risk properly, does not have sufficient reserves and capital or does not have the right incentives, large capital inflows and outflows can create severe problems. However, it is not the case that all the conditions need to be met before governments liberalize the financial sector. As the discussion on sequencing shows, the process of integration itself can in some ways help improve the conditions of the domestic financial sector.

When countries develop, more comprehensive policies for risk manage-ment will be needed. These measures should try to avoid imperfections in cap-ital markets and the build up of vulnerabilities. In more developed economies, the distinction between foreign and domestic capital becomes increasingly difficult. As the economy becomes integrated with the rest of the world, constraints to capital movements are less effective since they can be easily circumvented. Therefore, a more comprehensive approach will be needed to build solid financial economies. This approach involves proper regulation and supervision of the financial system.

2.6.4 *Need for International Financial Cooperation*

As economies become more integrated, governments have fewer policy instru-ments and must rely more on international financial policies. For example, governments tend to have fewer options about their monetary policy and exchange rate policy. In open economies there is a higher transmission of international interest rates and prices to the domestic economy. Moreover, bank regulation and supervision by one government is more difficult when liabilities and prices are denominated in foreign currency and when the banking sector is part of an international banking system. Also, in the midst of contagious crises, governments tend to lack sufficient resources to stop a currency attack, and an individual government can do little to stop crises being originated in foreign countries. In these cases, international financial coordination can help individual governments achieve their goals.

There are different policies in which there is scope for cooperation. One policy is the timely mobilization of external liquidity of sufficient magnitude to reverse market expectations in a context of sound policies. That liquidity usually comes from the international financial institutions. Given the magnitude of capital flows and the clustering of crises, isolated actions of individual governments or institutions are not sufficient to gain the required confidence. A coordinated action among governments and the international financial institutions is necessary to overcome crises and contagion, at both regional and global levels. To minimize potential moral hazard, it would be necessary to involve the private sector so that private international investors share in the costs as penalty for excessive risk taking.

Another policy that requires international coordination is to build a strong international financial architecture to prevent and manage, in a systematic way, financial crises. Even though there are different meanings of this architecture, in general terms it refers to international arrangements for mutual consultation, monitoring and collaboration, covering a broad range of subjects of economic policy and possible financing in the event of crisis. The international financial architecture is still under construction. The initiatives under consideration focus on crisis prevention, crisis management and crisis resolution. The current initiatives include setting international standards for transparency and information dissemination, bank supervision and regulation, disclosure in securities markets, accounting and auditing rules, bankruptcy procedures, and corporate governance. The new initiatives also include private sector involvement in financing packages to complement IMF resources and to discourage the moral hazard that can be associated with bailouts.

2.6.5 Challenge: How to Integrate

One of the main challenges of financial globalization is integrating a country into the world financial system. Some economists would argue that the main challenge is to integrate all sectors and countries that do not participate in the globalization process. Though financial globalization can bring about many positive benefits, not all countries, sectors, or firms have access to global financial markets and services or can take advantage of the benefits induced by globalization. Among developing nations, only some countries receive foreign capital, particularly middle-income countries. Within each country, investment is concentrated in certain sectors. Selected companies can obtain foreign funds. The lack of participation in the financial globalization process might put countries, sectors, and companies in disadvantageous positions. There is no easy solution to integrate them.

Other economists would argue that the main challenge of globalization is to selectively integrate with the world economy and to adopt active capital account regulation. These measures would help to minimize the risks of crises and reduce the impact of fluctuations in the international financial markets. Future research might shed light on what strategies are optimal for different countries. Furthermore, future research might yield specific recommendations on how to broaden the extent of integration, or alternatively, which particular policies are best suited to regulate cross-border financial flows.

References

Akerlof, G. A. and Romer, P. M. (1993). 'Looting: the Economic Underworld of Bankruptcy for Profit'. *Brookings Papers on Economic Activity*, 2: 1–73.

Bagehot, W. ([1873]1962). *Lombard Street*. Homewood, IL: R. D. Irwin.

Baldwin, R. E. and Martin, P. (1999). 'Two Waves of Globalization: Superficial Similarities, Fundamental Differences', in H. Siebert (ed.), *Globalization and Labor*. Tübingen: Mohr Siebeck.

Bekaert, G., Harvey, C., and Lundblad, C. (2001). 'Does Financial Liberalization Spur Growth?' NBER Working Paper 8245.

Bernanke, B. and Mishkin, F. (1997). 'Inflation Targeting: A New Policy Framework for Monetary Policy?' *The Journal of Economic Perspectives*, 11/2: 97–116.

Bordo, M. and Eichengreen, B. (2002). 'Crises Now and Then: What Lessons from the Last Era of Financial Globalization?'. NBER Working Paper 8716.

—— —— Klingebiel, D., and Martinez Peria, M. S. (2001). 'Is the Crisis Problem Growing More Severe?' *Economic Policy*, 16/32: 51–82.

Calvo, G. and Mishkin, F. (2003). 'The Mirage of Exchange Rate Regimes for Emerging Market Countries'. NBER Working Paper 9808.

—— and Reinhart, C. (2002). 'Fear of Floating'. *Quarterly Journal of Economics*, 117/2: 379–408.

Calvo, S., Leiderman, L., and Reinhart, C. (1996). 'Inflows of Capital to Developing Countries in the 1990s'. *Journal of Economic Perspectives*, 10/2: 123–39.

Caprio, G. and Klingebiel, D. (1997). 'Bank Insolvency: Bad Luck, Bad Policy, or Bad Banking?' *World Bank Economic Review*.

Claessens, S., Klingebiel, D., and Schmukler, S. (2002). 'The Future of Stock Markets in Emerging Economies'. *Brookings-Wharton Papers on Financial Services 2002*, 167–202.

Crockett, A. (2000). 'How Should Financial Market Regulators Respond to the New Challenges of Global Economic Integration?' Paper presented at the Federal Reserve Bank of Kansas City conference Global Economic Integration: Opportunities and Challenges, Jackson Hole, WY, August.

De la Torre, A., Levy Yeyati, E., and Schmukler, S. (2002). 'Financial Globalization: Unequal Blessings'. *International Finance*, 5/3: 335–57.

Diamond, D. W. and Dybvig, P. H. (1983). 'Bank Runs, Deposit Insurance, and Liquidity'. *Journal of Political Economy*, 91: 401–19.

Dornbusch, R., Park, Y., and Claessens, S. (2000). 'Contagion: Understanding How it Spreads'. *World Bank Research Observer*, 15/2: 177–97.

Eichengreen, B., Rose, A., and Wyplosz C. (1996). 'Contagious Currency Crises'. *Scandinavian Journal of Economics*, 98/4: 463–84. (Also reprinted in T. M. Andersen and K. O. Moene (eds.) (1997). *Financial Liberalization and Macroeconomic Stability*. Oxford: Blackwell.)

Favero, C. A. and Giavazzi F. (2000). 'Looking for Contagion: Evidence From the ERM'. NBER Working Paper 7797.

Ferreira, F., Prennushi, G., and Ravallion, M. (1999). 'Protecting the Poor from Macroeconomic Shocks: An Agenda for Action in a Crisis and Beyond'. World Bank Working Paper 2160.

Forbes, K. (2000). 'The Asian Flu and Russian Virus: Firm-Level Evidence on How Crises Are Transmitted Internationally'. International Monetary Fund Seminar Series 2000–49 October, 1–57.

Frankel, J. (2000). 'Globalization of the Economy', in J. Nye and J. Donahue (eds.), *Governance in a Globalizing World*. Washington, DC: Brookings Institution Press.

—— and Rose, A. (1996). 'Currency Crashes in Emerging Markets: An Empirical Treatment'. *Journal of International Economics*, 41/3–4: 351–66.

Glick, R. and Rose, A. (1999). 'Contagion and Trade: Why are Currency Crises Regional?' *Journal of International Money and Finance*, 18/4: 603–17.

International Monetary Fund (IMF) (2000). 'International Capital Markets'. Washington, DC: IMF.

Johnson, S., Boone, P., Breach, A., and Friedman, E. (2000). 'Corporate Governance in the Asian Financial Crisis'. *Journal of Financial Economics*, 51/1–2: 141–86.

Kaminsky, G. and Reinhart, C. (1999). 'The Twin Crises: Causes of Banking and Balance of Payments Problems'. *American Economic Review*, 89: 473–500.

—— —— (2000). 'On Crises, Contagion, and Confusion'. *Journal of International Economics*, 51/1: 145–68.

—— and Schmukler, S. (1999). 'What Triggers Market Jitters? A Chronicle of the East Asian Crisis'. *Journal of International Money and Finance*, 18: 537–60.

—— —— (2002). 'Short-Run Pain, Long-Run Gain: The Effects of Financial Liberalization', World Bank Working Paper 2912.

——, Lyons, R., and Schmukler, S. (2004). 'Managers, Investors, and Crisis: Mutual Fund Strategies in Emerging Markets'. *Journal of International Economics*, 64/1: 113–34.

Kawai, M., Newfarmer, R., and Schmukler, S. (2005). 'Crisis and Contagion in East Asia: Nine Lessons'. *Eastern Economic Journal*, 31/2: 185–207.

Krugman, P. (1998). 'Saving Asia: It's Time to Get Radical'. *Fortune*, 138: 74–80.

—— (1999). 'Balance Sheets, the Transfer Problem, and Financial Crises'. Manuscript, Massachusetts Institute of Technology.

Levine, R. (2001). 'International Financial Liberalization and Economic Growth'. *Review of International Economics*, 9/4: 688–702.

—— and Zervos, S. (1998). 'Stock Markets, Banks, and Economic Growth'. *American Economic Review*, 88/3: 537–58.

McKinnon, R. and Pill, H. (1997). 'Credible Economic Liberalizations and Overborrowing'. *American Economic Review*, 87/2: 189–93.

Mishkin, F. (2000). 'Inflation Targeting in Emerging Market Countries'. *American Economic Review*, 90/2: 105–9.

_____ (2003). 'Financial Policies and the Prevention of Financial Crises in Emerging Market Countries', in M. Feldstein (ed.), *Economic and Financial Crises in Emerging Market Countries*. Chicago: University of Chicago Press.

Mundell, R. (2000). 'A Reconsideration of the 20th Century'. *American Economic Review*, 90/3: 327–40.

Mussa, M. (2000). 'Factors Driving Global Economic Integration'. Paper presented at the Federal Reserve Bank of Kansas City conference 'Global Economic Integration: Opportunities and Challenges'. Jackson Hole, WY, August.

Obstfeld, M. (1986). 'Rational and Self-fulfilling Balance of Payments Crises'. *The American Economic Review*, 76/1: 72–81.

_____ (1994). 'International Capital Mobility in the 1990s', in P. B. Kenen (ed.), *Understanding Interdependence: The Macroeconomics of the Open Economy*. Princeton: Princeton University Press.

_____ (1998). 'The Global Capital Market: Benefactor or Menace?' *Journal of Economic Perspectives*, 12: 9–30.

_____ and Taylor, A. M. (2003). 'Global Capital Markets', in M. D. Bordo, A. M. Taylor, and J. G. Williamson (eds.), *Globalization in Historical Perspective*. Chicago: University of Chicago Press.

Ocampo, J. A. (2003). 'Capital-Account and Counter-Cyclical Prudential Regulations in Developing Countries', in R. Ffrench-Davis and S. Griffith-Jones (eds.), *From Capital Surges to Drought: Seeking Stability for Emerging Economies*. London: Palgrave/MacMillan.

Schumpeter, J. A. (1912). *Theorie der Wirtschaftlichen Entwicklung*. Leipzig: Dunker & Humblot. (*The Theory of Economic Development*, trans. by R. Opie. Cambridge, MA: Harvard University Press, 1934.)

Stiglitz, J. E. (1999). 'Bleak Growth for the Developing World'. *International Herald Tribune* (10–11 April), 6.

_____ (2000). 'Capital Market Liberalization, Economic Growth, and Instability'. *World Development*, 28/6: 1075–86.

Stulz, R. (1999). 'Globalization, Corporate Finance and the Cost of Capital'. *Journal of Applied Corporate Finance*, 12/3: 8–25.

Tesar, L. and Werner, I. (1998). 'The Internationalization of Securities Markets Since the 1987 Crash', in R. E. Litan and A. Santomero (eds.), *Brookings-Wharton Papers on Financial Services*. Washington, DC: Brookings Institution Press.

Tobin, J. (2000). 'Financial Globalization'. *World Development*, 28/6: 1101–4.

Tornell, A., Westermann, F., and Martínez, L. (2003). 'Liberalization, Growth, and Financial Crises: Lessons from Mexico and the Developing World'.

World Bank (2001). *Finance for Growth: Policy Choices in a Volatile World*. Policy Research Report. Washington, DC: World Bank.

3

Capital Market Liberalization, Globalization, and the IMF

Joseph E. Stiglitz[1]

3.1 Introduction

One of the most controversial aspects of globalization is capital market liberalization (CML)—not so much the liberalization of rules governing foreign direct investment (FDI) but those affecting short-term capital flows, including speculative hot capital that can come into and out of a country. In the 1980s and 1990s, the IMF and the US Treasury tried to push capital market liberalization around the world, encountering enormous opposition not only from developing countries but from economists who were less enamored of the doctrines of free and unfettered markets, of market fundamentalism, that was at that time being preached by the international economic institutions. The economic crises of the late 1990s and early years of the new millennium, which were partly, or even largely, attributable to capital market liberalization, reinforced those reservations. This chapter takes as its point of departure a recent International Monetary Fund (IMF) paper and provides insights into how the IMF could have gone so wrong in its advocacy of capital market liberalization. It goes on to explain why it is that capital market liberalization has so often led to increased economic instability, not to economic growth.

A 2003 paper on the effects of financial globalization on developing countries by the IMF's former Chief Economist Ken Rogoff and his coauthors (Rogoff et al. 2003) and the *Financial Times* article summarizing some of their findings (Rogoff and Prasad 2003) are remarkable in many ways. The authors

[1] The author is a University Professor at Columbia University. He formerly served as Chief Economist of the World Bank (1997–2000) and in that period was actively engaged in policy debates concerning capital market liberalization. The author is indebted to Francesco Brindisi for research assistantship, and to the Ford, MacArthur, and Mott Foundations for financial support. This article is reprinted with permission from Oxford University Press. It originally appeared in the *Oxford Review of Economic Policy*, vol. 20 (1) 2004.

should be commended for the seriousness with which they addressed the task of assessing the consequences of financial market integration, and for their willingness openly to question the orthodoxy. They conclude that it becomes difficult to make a convincing connection between financial integration and economic growth once other factors, such as trade flows and political stability, are taken into account. And they find that 'those countries that made the effort to become financially integrated [...] faced more instability.' What makes this noteworthy is not *what is said*—much of the economics profession had long come to this view[2]—but who is saying it. Indeed, it would have been truly striking if they had come to any other conclusion.

The report should be read seriously by past and present policymakers— including those in the US Treasury who have in the past pushed and continue to push developing countries headlong into capital market liberalization (CML), who have attempted to impose demands for capital market liberalization as part of the Investment Agreement (one of the so-called Singapore issues) in trade negotiations, and who have insisted on CML as part of bilateral trade agreements with Chile and Singapore.[3]

3.2 Implicit Assumptions and Hidden Agenda

What is perhaps most striking about the report are not its conclusions but its starting point.

3.2.1 *What Does 'Theory' Say?*

The study begins repeatedly by asserting that 'theory' predicts that capital market liberalization should be good for economic growth and should reduce the volatility of consumption. It takes for granted that the reader will understand what is meant by 'theory': the neoclassical model, with perfect information, perfect capital markets, and perfect competition. But that is a model that provides a poor description of developed economies and an even poorer description of developing countries and international capital markets. Rogoff himself should have been well aware of the limitations of this 'theory.' He wrote a paper (Obstfeld and Rogoff 2000) in which he details several stylized facts that are hard to reconcile with this 'theory,' including the home bias

---

[2] See, for instance, Rodrik (2001); Rodrik and Velasco (2000); Stiglitz (2000, 2002); Furman and Stiglitz (1998); Bhagwati (1998); and a host of papers cited in those studies.

[3] For a critique of this provision in these treaties, see the testimonies given by Jagdish Bhagwati, Daniel Tarullo, Joseph E. Stiglitz, and Nancy Birdsall at the House Committee on Financial Services, Subcommittee on Domestic and International Monetary Policy, Trade and Technology 'Opening Trade in Financial Services—The Chile and Singapore Examples.' April 1, 2003 (http://financialservices.house.gov/). The testimony of Treasury Secretary John Taylor in those hearings shows either that he has not fully absorbed the lessons, and/or that ideology and interests still dominate at US Treasury.

in trade and portfolios, the dependence of investment on national savings,[4] the low international consumption correlations, the high volatility and high persistence of real exchange rate shocks and the weak relationship between the exchange rate and macroeconomic aggregates. Others have noted additional failings: the seeming failure of the interest arbitrage equation and the countercyclical nature of capital movements (see, e.g., Lewis 1995 and World Bank 2000).

'Theory'—theoretical developments in imperfect capital markets over the last quarter century, most of which are not cited in the extensive bibliography—provides an explanation for why capital market liberalization may lead to instability and not promote growth. The failure to take these theoretical developments on board, which contradict the market fundamentalism that underlies much of IMF policy, says as much about the institution as its earlier policy stances, in which it seemingly saw no need to look for evidence, when 'theory' (or more accurately, ideology and interests) provided such clear guidance.

3.2.2 Cognitive Dissonance

Beginning the analysis from the maintained hypothesis of a neoclassical economy with full employment, full information, and full rationality is even more striking, given the events occurring as, or shortly before, the paper was being written. An outflow of capital as a result of worries about the outcome of an election forced Brazil not only to turn to the IMF for help but also to raise interest rates to very high levels, helping precipitate a marked slowdown in the economy and leading to high unemployment. Note that Brazil had done nothing to justify these fears; the country's economic management after the election further showed how unjustified they were. On the other hand, the high interest rates that Brazil felt were necessary to stop the outflow of funds had the predictable adverse effect on output and employment.[5] Two of the standard criticisms of capital market liberalization, that it is systematically associated with a higher likelihood of a crisis and that it impairs the ability of the government to respond to negative macroeconomic shocks because it inhibits the ability to lower interest rates, can hardly be dealt with in a 'theory,' which assumes away problems of unemployment.

---

[4] The so-called Feldstein-Horioka puzzle. See Feldstein and Horioka (1980). For a survey of studies on the Feldstein-Horioka puzzle, see e.g., Coakley et al. (1998).

[5] In 1998 government interest rates reached 28.6%, or in real terms, 25.4%. Private sector borrowers, of course, had to pay considerably more. Growth slowed to 0.1% in 1998 and 0.8% in 1999 and unemployment increased to 9% in 1998 and to 10% in 1999. The average real interest rate between November 1998 and April 1999 was 33.7%. See IMF, International Financial Statistics; World Bank, World Development Indicators; Independent Evaluation Office of the IMF (2003).

In the East Asia crisis, the IMF and Treasury complained loudly about problems of lack of transparency—imperfections of information. The crisis itself was in part precipitated by lenders refusing to roll over loans, not just their demanding higher interest rates reflecting a changed risk perception, providing a dramatic illustration of the problems of credit rationing to which the theories of imperfect and asymmetric information had called attention much earlier. The IMF had complained, at the same time, about excessive leverage, yet in the neoclassical model, the 'theory' upon which the IMF paper rests, financial structure does not matter at all. Of course, the IMF was right about the problem of excessive leverage, but that is because financial structure does matter; there are real costs associated with bankruptcy. The neoclassical model, the 'theory' to which Rogoff and his colleagues repeatedly appeal, provides little insight into these issues.[6]

3.2.3 *Beyond Rationality*

Further, recent research in behavioral macroeconomics and finance (see, e.g., Akerlof 2002) has highlighted the importance of irrationalities. As Charles Kindleberger (1978) has noted, reviewing the long history of crises, these— together with market imperfections (including the exploitation of informa- tion asymmetries)—have been central in the economic fluctuations that have marked capitalism since its origins.[7] While these fluctuations may not fit neatly within the IMF 'theory,' they are nonetheless real. Even in the 1990s, Alan Greenspan, the Chairman of the Federal Reserve Bank, called attention to the role of 'irrational exuberance,' an irrationality that the subsequent events confirmed. On more than one occasion, even the IMF has referred to overshooting, the seemingly irrational pessimism that follows a crisis, to provide one of the main rationales for their interventions in exchange rates.

3.2.4 *FDI vs. CML*

There is another fundamental failing in the IMF paper. It talks about financial market integration, measured by gross capital flows, but does not sufficiently distinguish among types of capital flows. Most of the critics of capital mar- ket liberalization are not as concerned about foreign direct investment as

[6] The criticisms of neoclassical theory (Modigliani-Miller 1958), which plays such an important role in the IMF's theory and policy prescriptions, have long been noted. Stiglitz (1969) pointed out that with bankruptcy costs, financial structure does matter. But even more fundamental is the fact that when information is imperfect and asymmetric, decisions about financial structure convey information and affect incentives. See, e.g., Stiglitz (1982).

[7] In some cases, it is difficult to distinguish between behavior that is best explained by irrationality, and that which is best explained by information imperfections (e.g., herding). See Banerjee (1992); Bikhchandani et al. (1992); Howitt and McAfee (1992).

they are about short-term financial flows. It is the latter that many fear are particularly destabilizing—and not conducive to growth. The fact that total flows (which include both short-term and long-term flows) have failed to produce the desired effects is perhaps particularly condemning: it has long been presumed that foreign direct investment has a positive effect on growth. If total flows, long-term and short-term, have a negligible effect, it suggests that short-term flows may have a negative effect. This is, of course, consistent with 'theory'—not the naïve theory underlying the IMF paper's analysis but modern financial theory. But the analysis would have been greatly enriched if more effort had been put into parsing out the effects of different kinds of capital flows (including differentiating among different types of FDI, in particular among Greenfield investments and privatizations, and between natural resource investments and others). I shall return to this later in the chapter.

3.2.5 The Pre-conditions for Successful CML

Finally, given the seemingly mixed experience with capital market liberalization, the question to which countries contemplating capital market liberalization want an answer is, under what circumstances will capital market liberalization bring the promised benefits? The IMF paper provides only modest guidance to this critical question. It argues for the *flavor of the month* in policy circles: the critical role of 'good governance.' It neither defines precisely what good governance means, nor does it resolve the important issues of multicollinearity and reverse causation; the fact that countries that have good governance have a host of other attributes that make them both more attractive for investors and better able to absorb the shocks and instability associated with short-term capital flows. Nor does it provide a list of countries for which capital market liberalization, given their current governance, would be a mistake. But certainly theory—not the simplistic neoclassical theory underlying neoliberal doctrines, but the more realistic theories to which we have referred above—does not suggest that good governance by itself will eliminate the problems to which we have called attention. Good governance does not eliminate information imperfections, nor does it eliminate either irrational exuberance or pessimism. The Scandinavian countries are typically viewed as having good governance, but that did not prevent their having major crises a little more than a decade ago. The United States too is typically viewed as having good governance (though recent scandals have cast some pallor over such claims), and yet it too had a bubble that eventually burst.[8] The American economy is strong enough that it can withstand such events (though recent

---

[8] Even before that, the United States had had its mini-financial crisis, the S & L debacle that came to a head in 1989 and cost American taxpayers between $100 and $200 billion. The more recent sub-prime mortgage problems—the third major set of financial problems

reinterpretations of American data, including the increase in the rolls of those on disability, suggest that the downturn was not as mild as had previously been thought).[9] America could engage in stimulative deficit financing to help bring it out of the resulting recession, and short-term capital flows play a relatively modest role in America's macroeconomic fluctuations. By contrast, as we shall shortly see, developing countries are far weaker, and short-term capital flows that follow upon capital market liberalization have an important role in inducing economic fluctuations, on the one hand, and in inhibiting governments' ability to offset fluctuations that arise from other sources.

3.3 The Case Against Capital Market Liberalization

I have discussed at length the recent IMF paper, partly because it helps illustrate how simplistic models, combined with ideology and interests, have often dominated (at least at official levels) discussions of globalization. The presumption is that free markets must be welfare enhancing. In fact, we have known for a long time that when markets are imperfect, when information is limited or markets incomplete, competitive market equilibria are not, in general, constrained Pareto efficient. In the theory of the second best, the elimination of one imperfection ('liberalizing capital markets') may not lead to a welfare improvement in the presence of other market imperfections. In this part of the chapter, however, I want to go beyond these general considerations, to show more specifically how capital market liberalization may 'in theory' lead to more consumption and output variability and lower growth—in short, why it may be bad for developing countries.[10]

3.3.1 Why Capital Market Liberalization May Lead to More Consumption Volatility

The Rogoff et al. paper does make an important contribution in focusing on *consumption* volatility. Standard utility theory argues that individuals wish to smooth their consumption, and, according to 'theory,' well-functioning capital markets enable individuals to do this.

If short-term capital flows were smoothing consumption, then capital would flow into a country when the economy is weak and flow out (relative, at least, to steady state flows) when the economy is strong. Any casual observer

in the U.S. in twenty years—provides further confirmation that 'good governance' does not immunize a country against financial sector problems.

[9] There were not only massive misallocations of resources during the bubble, but the loss of output after the bubble broke—the disparity between the economy's potential and actual growth—was enormous (see Stiglitz 2003c).

[10] For more extensive and complementary discussions, see Stiglitz (2000, 2002); Ocampo and Martin (2003).

of capital flows recognizes, however, that capital flows (particularly short-term capital flows) in fact move pro-cyclically, not countercyclically (World Bank 1999: ch. 3). In Latin America, during the early years of the lost decade of the 1980s, oft cited statistics described the travails of most of the countries of the continent as they struggled to repay the loans.[11] *Given* the pro-cyclical movements of especially short-term capital flows, it is hard to see how they could perform the purported role of consumption smoothing. Had consumption volatility been reduced, Rogoff and his co-authors would have had to explain how, given the pro-cyclical nature of capital flows, this could have occurred.

The fact that, at least in certain critical cases, capital flows, especially short-term flows, appear to be pro-cyclical, suggests, of course, a failing in the standard 'theory.' But it is totally consistent with standard aphorisms about bankers—that they lend only to those who do not need their money—and with modern developments (that is, developments during the past quarter century) in finance, which emphasize credit rationing and other imperfections in credit markets.[12]

There is another reason that it should come as no surprise that (short-term) capital flows do not smooth consumption: 'theory' predicts that those more able to bear risks—the risks of exchange rate and interest rate fluctuations—should do so. But in fact, developing countries are forced to bear the brunt of such fluctuations, many of which have nothing to do with what is occurring in their own country. When the Fed raised interest rates to unheard of levels in the late 1970s and early 1980s, it precipitated the Latin American debt crisis; even if it had not lead to the crisis, it would have adversely affected the Latin American countries. Even if they had perfect access to capital markets, it would have led to a lowering of their 'life time income' and thus of their consumption, but with capital market imperfections, their consumption was lowered even more.

Matters are perhaps even worse when there is a perceived adverse shock (of unknown duration) to a country, e.g., an instance of political difficulties. Lenders immediately cut back, forcing an immediate reduction in consumption. Thus, adverse shocks are *amplified*. Consumption volatility is increased.

Of course, there may be some validity both to the view that consumption volatility is increased and decreased: financial integration may allow countries to smooth small disturbances but may lead to increased volatility in the event of a large adverse shock. Under normal assumptions of concavity, the gains

[11] In Latin American and Caribbean countries the annual GDP growth rate was nil in 1982–4. Net resource transfers (given by net capital inflows minus net payments of profits and interest) as a percentage of GDP were −3.8% in 1982–4 and −3.1% in 1985–90. Gross fixed capital formation declined by 2.4% in 1981–90 (see ECLAC 1996).

[12] See Appendices A and B for simple models that are consistent with these observations.

from consumption smoothing in the small shocks are, of course, of an order of magnitude smaller than the losses from induced volatility in the event of a large shock.

3.3.2 *Political Economy: Discipline and All That*

One of the standard arguments put forward for why capital market liberalization is good for growth is that it provides 'discipline.' Advocates of this position evidently have little faith in democracy. They do not believe that voters are capable of choosing economic leaders that will advance their economic interests (broadly defined, including within a broader social agenda). Instead, they believe that it is better to rely on the judgments of Wall Street financiers. This is called the 'discipline of the market place.' Later, I shall suggest that the capriciousness of such judgments—their volatility—and their extreme myopia actually may have adverse effects on long-term growth and stability. But to the extent that there is some validity in the concerns about lack of 'discipline,' financial market integration may actually have even more adverse effects. During the early 1990s, for instance, throughout Latin America, capital flows (spurred on by both capital market liberalization and privatizations) helped finance rapid increases in consumption (both public and private). Better measures of economic performance (which would have taken note of the increased indebtedness and the transfer of ownership of assets to foreigners) might have provided some warnings that things were not as rosy as GDP indicators suggested. To the extent that governments are short sighted, they have every incentive to take advantage of the further increases in consumption and the loosening of budget constraints that financial market liberalization provides in a boom—putting little weight on the consequences for the future. The tightening of the budget constraint when the bust that follows occurs is a problem that likely will be faced by another administration.

3.3.3 *Why Capital Market Liberalization Leads to More Overall Economic Volatility*

The previous two sections outlined why, given any level of output volatility, financial market integration might be expected not to reduce consumption volatility. But we should not take output volatility as given: the major criticism of capital market liberalization is that it has contributed to the volatility of output.

Anyone familiar with events in East Asia and Latin America in recent decades has seen the role that capital market liberalization has played in contributing to economic instability. Money rushed into the country, often financing a consumption binge, and then rushed out; as it left, financial institutions were weakened, often bankrupted, and exchange rates plummeted, leaving those with dollar denominated debts hard pressed to meet their obligations. During the inflow, the exchange rate appreciates, posing problems for the import competing and export sectors. Some governments, like that of Thailand, attempted to prevent this and at the same time avoid the economy overheating, which necessitates cutting back on high return public investments and raising interest rates. Investments other than in speculative real estate were accordingly dampened. During the outflow, financial institutions are devastated, and the lack of credit contributes to the economic downturn. One might have thought that the IMF paper would have begun from this oft-told tale, trying to identify the conditions that led to the outflows, including those that were generated by events inside or outside the country. (Indeed, for many developing countries that have liberalized their capital markets, a major source of shocks leading to economic volatility come through financial markets, e.g. with rapid changes in global risk premia and liquidity.)

There is another, important, reason that capital market liberalization leads to greater economic volatility: it inhibits the use of countercyclical monetary policy. In the East Asian crisis, Malaysia was able to avoid imposing the high interest rates that those with IMF programs had, which not only exacerbated the downturn but led also to more bankruptcies, thereby making the task of restructuring all the more difficult and costly.

3.3.4 Why Capital Market Liberalization Does Not Lead to Faster Growth or Higher Investment[13]

While the IMF paper attempts to identify some of the channels through which capital market liberalization leads to faster economic growth, it does not attempt to test the alternative hypotheses, if only to ascertain the relative importance of the possible explanations. The biased viewpoint from which the paper starts is evidenced by its failure to even consider the channels through which capital market liberalization might adversely affect growth. Since these are laid out at greater length elsewhere (Stiglitz 2003a, b; Stiglitz et al. 2006; and Chapter 1, this volume), I only sketch them here:

1. If CML leads to greater output or consumption instability[14] (as suggested by the previous section), then it increases the risk premium firms require for investment, thereby discouraging investment. Moreover, to the extent that investment depends on cash flow and balance sheet effects, downturns can have particularly adverse effects on investment.

---

[13] Even before the IMF report, the World Bank had come to the same conclusion (see World Bank 1999).

[14] Both are independently relevant: consumption instability may be especially linked to investments in non-traded consumption goods sectors; output instability may have an adverse effect on other sectors of the economy.

2. These problems are compounded by higher interest rate volatility, e.g., as noted above, required to stem outflows of capital.

3. Both output and interest rate volatility put severe limitations on the use of debt financing, which, in developing countries with underdeveloped equity markets,[15] can lead to less efficient resource allocations—lower output—and lower growth.

4. Short-term capital is highly myopic, and the often lauded discipline of the market accordingly forces countries to pursue more myopic policies than they otherwise would, again adversely affecting growth. Capital markets, for instance, often focus on budget deficits, without enquiring into how the money is spent. When the country is forced to cut back high return investments to balance the budget, long-term growth suffers.

5. Countries increasingly feel that prudence requires that they keep in reserves an amount equal to foreign denominated short-term debt, but there is a high cost to such reserves. Typically, they are held in the form of US (or other hard currency) T-bills, when the opportunity cost of such funds invested elsewhere in the economy is of an order of greater magnitude. If a firm in a developing country borrows $100 million abroad short term from an American bank, paying say 20 percent interest, then the country has to set aside a comparable amount of money, in reserves, paying but, say, 5 percent. There is as a result a net transfer *to* the United States: the country is almost surely worse off.[16]

Finally, the IMF paper seems, in many ways, unaware of one of the key issues: How do short-term capital flows translate into more *real* investment? Firms cannot (or should not) finance long-term investments with money that can quickly leave. (Consumption can, of course, be so financed, especially the purchase of durables.)

3.3.5 *Foreign Direct Investment*

The paper focuses on financial market integration—gross capital flows—which include foreign direct investment. While there was a broad consensus (outside of the IMF) that short-term flows did not lead to growth, but did enhance instability, there has been a broader sentiment in favor of foreign direct investment. Thus, the result that financial market integration, including foreign direct investment, does not have a strong positive effect on growth may come as a surprise.

---

[15] Even in developed countries, relatively little investment is financed by new equity issues, because of information asymmetries and imperfections.

[16] The only circumstance in which the country is better off would be if its ability to allocate its capital efficiently is much worse than that of the American bank.

Part of the reason may be that foreign direct investment statistics include a variety of forms of investment, and some of these may not lead to growth, or at least sustainable growth. If better measures of welfare were used, the results probably would be even less positive.[17] For instance, foreign direct investments include privatizations. If the privatization revenues are even partially spent on consumption, then the country's wealth (what the country as a whole owns) is decreased; the country is poorer. In some cases, privatizations do lead to increased efficiency—for instance, when there are public enterprises operating at a loss—but in other cases, it does not.[18] In many developing countries, much of the FDI is in the oil or other natural resource sectors; typical measures of GDP do not take account of the fact that the country is poorer as a result of the depletion of resources. Moreover, there is a large and growing literature (the paradox of the resource curse, see e.g., Sachs and Warner 2001) explaining why it is that natural resource development is often not associated with faster economic growth. There are typically few linkages with the rest of the economy; meanwhile 'Dutch disease' problems and (exchange rate appreciation), makes exports more difficult and weakens import competing sectors. Moreover, foreign firms may engage in bribery to obtain the natural resources at a 'discount' (or even in the case of manufactured goods, may use bribery to obtain protection or monopoly positions).

In the case of financial market integration associated with international banks acquiring domestic banks, there are other reasons for possible adverse effects: the international banks *may* be less willing or able to lend money to domestic small and medium sized enterprises.[19] Moreover, while in principle such integration holds out the possibility of greater stability in lending (since the risks are more diversified), in practice there have been important instances (such as in Bolivia in recent years) where shocks to the home country banking system or other events in the home country that have resulted in a change in willingness to bear risk in turn result in a market contraction in the credit supply, inducing a contraction in the economy of the developing country.[20]

---

[17] This is also true of other forms of capital flows. For instance, if, as the analysis above suggested, short-term borrowing in foreign denominated currencies is systematically associated with a higher probability of a crisis, a welfare oriented national income accounting framework ought to take into account some actuarial estimate of the resulting losses *at the time the borrowing occurs*.

[18] For a survey of studies on the effect of privatization see Megginson and Netter (2001). For a survey focused on economies in transition see Djankov and Murrell (2002).

[19] Similar concerns, of course, were at the center of restrictions on interstate banking in the United States, which was only finally repealed in 1995.

[20] The fact that the foreign lender is less informed about risks in the developing country may imply that there is a higher likelihood that certain categories of lending in the developing country will be 'red lined' i.e., rationed out of the market.

3.3.6 *Justifying Interventions*

The fact that short-term capital flows have potentially such large adverse effects on others—beyond those directly involved in the flows—implies that there is an *externality*, and as always, when there is an externality, there is a prima facie case for government intervention. The question is only whether there are interventions that can address the adverse consequences of the externality, without more than offsetting ancillary negative side effects and, if so, what is the best form of intervention. The experiences of Chile and Malaysia suggest that there are such interventions.[21]

Even the IMF recognizes the importance of externalities in this arena—witness their concern about contagion and their use of contagion as a justification for bail-outs. But if crises justify government actions, then it makes sense to address the underlying causes. (One should not just build a bigger hospital to address public health problems.) One of the causes of crises are destabilizing short-term capital flows. Accordingly, it makes sense to try to stabilize such flows. Even if interventions are *imperfect* (i.e., they are 'leaky'), there may be a large social benefit from the reduction in the overall magnitude of the volatility of short-term capital flows.

3.4 Concluding Comments

Economists, particularly in developing countries, had long expressed doubts about the virtues of capital market liberalization (see, e.g., the often cited paper by Diaz-Alejandro 1985). Even Summers, before he went to the US Treasury, expressed misgivings. As noted above, the seemingly pro-cyclical movements of capital flows and the structure of capital markets—which left developing countries bearing interest rate and exchange rate risks—has left little doubt of the risks imposed by capital market liberalization. Had the Rogoff et al. paper concluded that *on average* capital market liberalization reduced consumption volatility relative to output volatility, it would not have fully answered the critics of capital market liberalization, whose attention is focused not so much on *averages* but on the *extreme* events. But the fact that the paper, which begins with a clear bias towards capital market liberalization—and an analysis resting on theoretical presumptions so out of tune with many, if not most, developing countries—comes to such a skeptical conclusion about its virtues, should make a fundamental contribution to the debate on capital market liberalization. The IMF should change from pressuring countries to liberalize their capital markets to working with countries on how to design interventions in the capital markets that stabilize capital

---

[21] See Stiglitz et al. (2006); Chapter 1, this volume; and Chapter 6, this volume. China and India are two other examples. For the Indian case, see Vijayn (2003). See also Wypolsz (2002).

flows, or even better, ensure that they move counter cyclically. It should be working harder to address the underlying failures in capital markets, devising ways by which more of the risk of interest rate and exchange rate fluctuations can be shifted to developed countries and international financial institutions. And in the future, it should rely more on evidence and less on ideology in developing its policy agenda. The IMF's stance on capital market liberalization has, in many circles, undermined its credibility; in spite of its authors' claims that the paper represents 'an evolution, not a revolution' in IMF thinking, this paper confirms what many in the developing world have long known: IMF advice in this area confronted countries with risk without reward.

3.5 2007 Postscript: It's Hard to Change One's Mindset

An August 2006 IMF working paper, by the IMF's former Chief Economist and his colleagues, reinforces the conclusions that changing the mind set of the IMF about capital market liberalization—whatever the evidence—will not be easy (Kose et al. 2006). Again, they are to be commended for reporting honestly that 'there is still little robust evidence of the growth benefits of broad capital account liberalization . . . ' Yet they conclude 'our critical reading of the recent empirical literature is that it lends some qualified support to the view that developing countries can benefit from financial globalization.' The reason, they assert, is that there are 'potential collateral benefits,' such as financial market development, institutional development, better governance, and macroeconomic discipline, which themselves lead to higher growth and lower consumption volatility.

They never explain, however, why, if these collateral benefits exist, they do not show up in the reduced form regressions, regressions that should show growth benefits *regardless* of the channel through which they come. And, equally remarkably, they never test—indeed hardly mention—the potential ancillary channels through which capital market liberalization might adversely affect growth and volatility. Consider, for instance, one of the channels, 'market discipline.' In support of that, they mention my own earlier *World Development* paper (Stiglitz 2000). But as I point out, the problem with capital markets as disciplinarians is that they are myopic—they enforce a discipline that is not oriented towards long-term growth. Indeed, they typically focus more on a country's liabilities than on its assets, and therefore, CML may actually impede growth. (Even more so, they ignore other aspects of societal well-being, such as those reflected in health and the environment.) Moreover, capital markets are an *unreliable* disciplinarian, subjecting even well-behaved and well-performing countries to 'discipline' when the market appetite for developing country risk suddenly changes.

Indeed, what the IMF should have done was to look at the capital flow implications of their 'theory.' Their theory has it that CML is stabilizing because money flows into a country when it needs it, i.e., is counter cyclical, not pro-cyclical, and that it is growth enhancing, i.e., countries that liberalize have more investment, because of the greater availability of capital from the outside and/or increased domestic investment. Both theory and evidence cast doubt on both of these propositions, and the IMF study does little to dispel these doubts. It is largely because of the exposure to the risk of pro-cyclical capital movements that CML has been so roundly criticized.

The authors of the IMF study also remarkably fail to address directly most of the other criticisms of CML, either within their model or in more general models. They do not challenge the conclusion that capital market liberalization has exposed countries to a new set of shocks and that these external shocks are among the major sources of volatility in those countries that have become financially integrated. Moreover, they deal only partially with the claim that, while CML exposes countries to more shocks, it also makes it more difficult for countries to engage in countercyclical macroeconomic policy.[22] After noting the several ways in which liberalization has made the conduct of monetary policy more difficult, they note that 'the fact that so many emerging markets have successfully instituted more independent, inflation-focused central banks, is quite noteworthy.' They fail to observe that there is little evidence that independent, inflation-focused central banks lead to faster growth. (This is one of several instances where what should be treated as intermediate variables, of concern only to the extent that they promote growth or stability or a better distribution of income, are treated almost as ultimate objectives.) One of the main intentions of capital market restrictions (e.g., in the case of Chile) was to enhance the scope of monetary policy. They never even discuss this issue.

The underlying problem, of course, is that the authors continue to be wedded to the perfect capital markets view of the world (with infinitely lived individuals). Thus, they report, 'Lucas's (1987) claim that macroeconomic stabilization policies that reduce consumption volatility can have only minimal welfare benefits continues to be influential...' without noting that Lucas' result depends critically on individuals not facing borrowing constraints. Unfortunately, the empirical behavior of consumption can only be explained within models that assume that at least lower income individuals do face borrowing constraints. They conclude (notwithstanding the analysis of the models presented in this chapter, which they do not note): 'there is a strong presumption in theory that financial integration is good for growth and... it

---

[22] Of course, trade openness may have reduced inflationary pressures, and this may have allowed monetary authorities more scope to act. But we are concerned here with financial integration, not trade integration.

should unambiguously lead to reductions in the relative volatility of consumption.'

The IMF study does include a discussion of a number of recent papers on the relationship between crises and CML. On the basis of these studies, the authors conclude 'there is little formal empirical evidence to support the oft-cited claims that financial globalization in and of itself is responsible for the spate of financial crises that the world has seen over the past three decades' (Kose et al. 2006). But the study does not cite several World Bank studies that show that countries are more likely to have a crisis *after* liberalizing (financial and capital markets).[23] Moreover, the issue is not so much whether CML by itself leads to a crisis but whether it exposes a country to risks, which, together with one of the many other problems facing many developing countries, make a crisis more likely. Most students of the East Asian crises have come to the conclusion that capital market liberalization was a central factor in the crises in these countries, with capital rushing in during the early 1990s and rushing out in 1997. Without CML, these countries would not have faced the crises they faced. The same is true for the crises in Latin America at the end of the 1990s and early years of this decade.

A wealth of case studies—supported by economic theories that recognize market imperfections, including shortfalls in economic performance below potential—have provided the basis of much of the critique of CML. The IMF study, by contrast, reviews the cross-country econometric literature. This literature has been (rightly) criticized—its results often appear not to be robust, and the studies face numerous data and econometric problems. Unfortunately, the discussion of the IMF paper does not deal sufficiently with these problems to remove any skepticism that critics might have. For instance, while it notes the possible problem of 'reverse causality,' this is not the only source of endogeneity. There is, for instance, a problem of 'self-selection,' those countries that have chosen to liberalize their capital markets are those for which the benefits are the greatest (the costs are the lowest), even accounting for all the 'observed' variables. Assume, for instance, that (holding everything else constant), there are two kinds of countries: those for whom CML is good, and those for which it is not. Assume, moreover, each country knows whether CML is good for itself, but we (as outside observers) do not. Then, in a regression relating growth to CML the coefficient on the CML variable will provide an upwardly biased estimate of what will happen to a country that has not liberalized, should it decide to liberalize. Thus, if the regression coefficient comes out zero (as appears to be the case in many of the regressions), it means that the likely impact of liberalizing is negative.

While the IMF study does not take a look at most of the important ancillary costs of CML (e.g., the adverse effects on growth through the impact on debt

---

[23] See also Furman and Stiglitz (1998).

equity ratios resulting from the higher volatility of relevant variables), neither does it establish convincingly effective links through the alleged positive ancillary channels. This is illustrated by the discussion of governance. While no one would support the notion that it is a good thing for countries to have bad governance, the links between capital market liberalization and governance, on the one hand, and governance (as conventionally measured) and growth and stability on the other are tenuous at best. In some studies of corruption, for instance, China and Vietnam do not fare well; yet these countries have been among the best performing countries. Hoff and Stiglitz (2005) argue that capital market liberalization actually had an adverse effect on the development of the rule of law in the economies in transition. It enhanced incentives for asset stripping (relative to wealth creation) and thus undermined the constituency for the creation of a rule of law. With capital market liberalization, those in these countries could take their money outside the country, enjoying the protections of the rule of law in Western countries, and at the same time take advantage of the absence of the rule of law (e.g., the absence of good laws concerning corporate governance) to divert assets to their own benefit at home. Cross-country studies by Khan (2004), bolstered by theoretical analysis, suggest that there is, in fact, overall little relationship between growth and governance. He divides developing countries into two categories: fast growing countries (such as those in East Asia) and slow growing (which includes most of those in Africa). Within each category, differences in governance are unrelated to growth; by the same token, differences in governance have little to do with the category (fast or slow growing) into which the country falls.

The debate about capital market liberalization focuses on regulations affecting short-term capital flows. The IMF paper, by contrast, looks more broadly at financial globalization and, for the most part, does not separately address the issues of concern in this chapter. Even most critics of CML believe that Greenfield foreign direct investments can have a beneficial effect.[24]

By the same token, even had there been a finding that capital market liberalization *on average* was associated with lower growth, it would only prove that capital market liberalization can be—and in many countries has been—done poorly. It does not address the more relevant question, has it had these negative effects when it has been implemented well? Can countries with limited administrative capacity implement such controls well? Are there

---

[24] Much of what is classified as FDI is really a financial transaction, the purchase of an existing asset. The failure to distinguish among different categories of FDI undermines the usefulness of studies, such as the IMF study, that look simply at the relationship, e.g., between FDI and growth. Similarly, one should distinguish between FDI in natural resources (which typically creates few jobs and exposes countries to the risk of the Dutch disease) and in, say, manufacturing.

some controls that are more easily implemented by countries with limited administrative capacity?

The point of looking at historical lessons is to learn from them—it is not to imitate the mistakes of the past but to avoid them. Of course, this kind of reasoning has been at the center of the argument for capital market liberalization. Observing the many crises that have followed, they conclude that 'inadequate or mismanaged domestic financial sector liberalizations have been a major contributor to crises that may be associated with financial integration' (Kose et al. 2006).[25] The obvious lesson drawn—by the advocates of CML—is to strengthen one's financial institutions and manage financial sector liberalization well before liberalizing capital markets. But if countries have the capacity to do that, they may also have the capacity to administer an effective set of capital market regulations—regulations that can enhance growth and reduce volatility.

Appendix 3.1   A Simple Model of 'Regime Change' in which Financial Market Integration Leads to Increased Income and Consumption Volatility

Consider an economy in which there are two states of nature θ_1 and θ_2, and the economy stochastically shifts (in a Markovian way) from one to the other, with probability π. In both states there are two projects, one risky, one safe, and the lender cannot monitor which one the borrower will undertake. Projects take two periods to mature, and for simplicity, we assume that all loans are variable rate, with the interest rate set at the prevailing lending rate at the time. We focus on behavior along the equilibrium path. Both borrowers and lenders thus have (rational) expectations about what the lending interest rate *next* period will be, which will depend on the state.

Let $\beta_i^j(r, r')$, $j = S, R$, represent the expected return to an investor who must borrow to finance the project for an investment in the safe (S) or risky (R) project, when the economy is in state i, when it charges interest rate r, and it anticipates that if there is a regime change, the interest rate will be r'. (If the state is the same next period, then it is assumed, rationally, that the interest rate the next period will be the same as this period.) The borrower makes the decision about what type of project to undertake in period 1, but the outcome of the project is determined by the state of nature in the second period. Both the lender and the borrower know, of course, the likelihood that the state will change between today and tomorrow.

We can describe the set of interest rates over which the safe project will be undertaken in both states of nature: it is the state-dependent set $\{r_1, r_2\}_i$ such that

$$\{r_1, r_2\}_1 : \beta_1^S(r_1, r_2) \geq \beta_1^r(r_1, r_2)$$

$$\{r_1, r_2\}_2 : \beta_2^S(r_2, r_1) \geq \beta_2^r(r_2, r_1).$$

---

[25] See also Mishkin (2006).

We let $\rho_i(r_1, r_2)$ represent the expected return *to a lender* if the interest rate is $\{r_1, r_2\}$ for a loan made in state i. (Lenders can infer what kind of project the borrower will undertake.) Let ρ^* = the safe international rate of return. We assume that state 1 is the bad state, and that

$$\text{Max}\rho_1(r_1, r_2) < \rho^* < \text{Max}\rho_2(r_1, r_2)$$

so that, in state 1, no matter what interest rates are charged, the expected return to the lender is so small that no loans are made within the country *with financial market integration*; while, in state 2, loans will be made. The 'trick' in the analysis is that in a closed economy, the 'safe' rate of interest adjusts to the state of the economy, so that some loans will still be made even in state 1. Thus, the variability of output will be less.

We assume that there are M^* safe projects (each costing a dollar),[26] and that the lenders' expected returns are always maximized by the borrower undertaking the safe project, and indeed, that the lenders' expected return should the borrower undertake the risky project is so low that they would not make the loan. There is a weak enough credit culture that international lenders cannot lend to consumers directly. (Alternatively, they cannot tell the capitalists from the charlatans and their expected return to lending, given that they cannot distinguish and that there is a maximum interest rate above which the capitalists will not borrow, is negative. Accordingly, there are no consumption loans.)

We use a standard Keynesian aggregate demand macroeconomic framework, which we simplify by assuming that the fraction of income saved, s, is a function of the expected return, $\rho : s(\rho)$, with $s' > 0$, fixed exports, X, imports equal to a fraction m of income, fixed government expenditures, so that

$$Y_i = X + G + I/m + s(\rho_i).$$

Closed Financial Markets

With closed financial markets, ρ adjusts to equate savings with investment. In the 'good state,' all projects are undertaken, so $I = M^*$. This means that in the good state, the interest rate is such as to generate savings to finance all the investment projects;[27] while in the bad state, the interest rate is the maximum interest rate such that the borrower does not undertake the risky project.[28] We can then easily solve for (r_i, Y_i), through the simultaneous equations:

$$Y_2 = [X + G + M^*]/[m + s(\rho_2(r_1^0, r_2^0))],$$

the standard income–expenditure equation for state 2;

$$M^* = s(\rho_2(r_1^0, r_2^0))Y_2 = s(\rho_2(r_1^0, r_2^0))[X + G + M^*]/[m + s(\rho_2(r_1^0, r_2^0))]$$

[26] Moreover, all the investment entails non-traded (domestically produced) goods.

[27] Moreover, we assume the parameters are such that the interest rates lead borrowers to undertake the safe project in the good state.

[28] That is, if the interest rate increased to make the supply of funds equal to the potential demand for good projects, borrowers would in fact undertake the risky projects.

ensuring that in state 2 savings equals investments;

$$Y_1 = [X + G + I_1]/[m + s(\rho_1(r_1, r_2^0))],$$

the standard income–expenditure equation for state 1;

$$r_2^* : \beta_1^s(r_1^0, r_2^0) = \beta_1^r(r_1^0, r_2^0)$$

ensuring that the safe project is undertaken in state 1; and where

$$I_1 = s(\rho_1(r_1^0, r_2^0))Y_1 = s(\rho_1(r_1^0, r_2^0))[X + G + I_1]/[m + s(\rho_1(r_1^0, r_2^0))] = s_1^*[X + G]/m,$$

where r_i^0 denotes the equilibrium interest rate in state i.[29]
   It is easy to verify that for $i = 1, 2$

$$Y_i = [X + G]/m.$$

There is no output variability. There is some consumption variability, since savings must be higher in the good state (so consumption must actually be lower in the good state). The difference in consumption in the two states is equal to the difference in investment. Note that in more general versions of the model, there will be output as well as consumption variability, for instance, if m, X, or G are sensitive to the state of nature or the real interest rate.

Open Financial Markets

With fully open financial markets, the separation between investment and savings is almost complete—except through the effect of investment on income. There is an international interest rate that determines savings; we will denote that savings rate by s^{**}. In the good state, all the investment projects are undertaken; in the bad state, there is no interest rate at which it is profitable to invest. Hence

$$Y_2 = X + G + M^*/m + s^{**}$$

and

$$Y_1 = X + G/m + s^{**}.$$

Opening the capital market lowers income in the bad state and (assuming that in the good state, the country has a 'scarcity of capital', i.e. it borrows abroad), increases income in the good state (as the scarcity leads to higher savings and lower consumption). *Capital market liberalization thus increases output volatility*. It is ambiguous whether overall consumption variability is increased or reduced; the difference in consumption in the two states is now

$$(1 - s^{**})(Y_2 - Y_1) = [(1 - s^{**})/(m + s^{**})]M^*,$$

whereas in the closed economy model the difference in consumption in the two states is $I_1 - M^*$.
   The model also is consistent with observed patterns of capital mobility—capital flows into the country in good periods, and in bad periods, flows out (all of savings is invested abroad.)

[29] In the credit rationing equilibrium, r_1^0 is such that $\beta_1^s(r_1^0, r_1^0) = \beta_1^r(r_1^0, r_1^0)$.

Appendix 3.2   A Simple Model with Incomplete Risk Markets Where Financial Market Integration Leads to Increased Income and Consumption Volatility and Lower Welfare and Growth

Newbery and Stiglitz (1984) showed how, in the absence of risk markets, the opening of trade led to a Pareto inferior equilibrium. The idea was a simple one: with unitary demand elasticities, price and output vary inversely, so that the price system provides perfect revenue insurance. (With near unity demand elasticities, it provides good revenue insurance.) The opening of trade, however, weakens the inverse link between price and quantity, thus exposing producers to greater risk. This may discourage investment in the high return activity; tracing through the effects in a general equilibrium model, it is possible not only that the producers are worse off—because of their greater exposure to risk—but consumers are worse off as well.

A similar model can be used to show how capital market liberalization in the absence of good insurance markets can lead to lower welfare (and higher consumption and income volatility). Assume that the international lending rate to a country, r, is variable. Foreigners, however, only lend to enterprises (since they are unable to distinguish good from bad household borrowers). Individuals live for two periods, working in the first.

The budget constraints are given by[30]

$$C_1^t = w_t(1 - s_t)$$

$$C_2^t = [1 + r_{t+1}]s_t w_t$$

where the superscript t identifies the generation.

For simplicity, we assume that they have a logarithmic utility function

$$U^t = \ln C_1^t + \ln C_2^t$$

which means that $s = .5$, and

$$EU^t = 2\ln .5 + 2\ln w_t + E\ln(1 + r_{t+1}).$$

In the discussion below, we focus on two cases, the first where the only source of randomness is the interest rate, and the second where it is domestic productivity. In each, we focus on closed versus open capital markets. We begin with the case where the only source of uncertainty is the external interest rate.

For simplicity, we assume that the short-term capital actually is translated into investment goods. $F(K_t, L_t)$ is a constant returns production function, $f(k_t)$ is output per worker, with $k_t = K_t/L_t$. We assume that all capital depreciates each year. In a closed economy,

$$k_t = .5w_{t-1} = .5[f(k_{t-1}) - k_{t-1}f'(k_{t-1})] = .5g(k_{t-1}),$$

where $g \equiv f - kf'$.

The steady state is defined by

$$k^* = .5g(k^*).$$

---

[30] In the following, $E_t(X)$ denotes the conditional expectation of the random variable X given the information available at time t.

We assume that the economy is in steady state. There is no volatility in either wages, interest rate, or utility.

We now consider what happens when we open the economy. Now,

$$k_t = f'^{-1}(1 + r_t) \equiv h(r_t)$$

where r_t is a random variable. Hence $w_t = g(h(r_t))$ is a random variable, and expected utility, of an individual in period t

$$E_t U^t = 2 \ln .5 + 2 \ln w_t + E_t \ln(1 + r_{t+1})$$

and ex ante expected utility (of the *average generation*) is

$$E\{E_t U^t\} = 2 \ln .5 + 2E \ln w_t + E[E_t \ln(1 + r_{t+1})].$$

It follows that opening the capital market unambiguously leads to an increase in consumption variability.

The impact on social welfare is more difficult, for it depends in part on the relationship between the average interest rate in the international market and the interest rate in the closed economy, as well as the nature of the social welfare function. If, for instance, we denote by r_c the interest rate in the closed economy, and assume that the average interest rate in the international market is the interest rate in the domestic closed economy—$E[\ln(1 + r_t)] = \ln(1 + r_c)$—and that there is a utilitarian social welfare function, then social welfare is lowered or increased as the elasticity of substitution between labor and capital in the production function is less or greater than unity.[31] If the social welfare function is concave (i.e., is inequality or risk averse), then social welfare is reduced even when the elasticity of substitution is greater than unity, provided it is not too large. If the average interest rate in the open economy is equal to r_c, then it is even more likely that social welfare will be reduced.[32]

Variability in Productivity

A similar result holds even if there is variability in domestic production, e.g., domestic production function is of the form

$$Q_t = \theta_t f(k_t).$$

In a closed economy, now there is consumption and output variability. With our logarithmic utility function,

$$k_{t+1} = w_t/2 = \theta_t g(k_t)/2$$

and

$$E_t U^t = 2 \ln .5 + 2 \ln w_t + E \ln(1 + r_{t+1}) = 2 \ln .5 + 2 \ln w_t + E_t\{\ln \theta_{t+1} + \ln f'(w_t/2)\}$$

---

[31] Social welfare is lowered or increased as $\ln w$ is a concave or convex function of $\ln 1 + r$. It is straightforward to show that $d \ln w/d \ln(1 + r) = -a/1 - a$, where a is the share of capital in national income. The result is immediate.

[32] $\ln(1 + r)$ is a concave function of r.

and

$$E\{E_t U^t\} = -2\ln .5 + 3E[\ln \theta_t] + 2E[\ln g(k_t)] + E\ln f'[\theta_t g(k_t)/2].$$

In the case of an open capital market,

$$k_t^* = f'^{-1}((1 + r_t)/\theta_t) = h(r_t/\theta_t)$$

and

$$w_t = \theta_t[f(k_t^*) - k_t^* f'(k_t^*)] = \theta_t g(k_t^*) = \theta_t g(h(r_t/\theta_t))$$

so that

$$E_t U^t = 2\ln .5 + 2\ln w_t + E_t \ln(1 + r_{t+1}).$$

If we assume that there is no variability in the international interest rate, then

$$E\{E_t U^t\} = 2\ln .5 + 2E[\ln \theta_t] + 2E[\ln g(h(r/\theta_t))] + \ln(1 + r).$$

It should be clear that opening up capital markets allows for greater variability of wages (when θ is high, the country can borrow more, driving up the wage, and conversely, when θ is low, capital flows out of the country). And unlike the closed economy, a high level of wages today has no adverse effect on the interest rate next period. Hence, on average, consumption and expected utility will be more volatile than in a closed economy, and with a sufficient inequality/risk averse social welfare function, social welfare will be decreased. The only subtlety is presented by the fact that when the economy is more productive, it has access to more resources. We have to set this gain against the losses from greater variability. A full analysis is beyond the scope of this appendix. Here, we look only at the special case of a unitary elasticity production function, a utilitarian social welfare function, and a normalization where the expected logarithm of the interest rate in the closed economy is equal to the logarithm of the interest rate in the open economy, i.e.,

$$\ln a - (1 - a)E\ln k_c + E\ln \theta_t = \ln 1 + r_o.$$

So, in the obvious notation,

$$E\ln w_c = \ln(1 - a) + aE\ln k_c + E\ln \theta_t.$$

Meanwhile, for the open economy, for *each* θ

$$\ln a - (1 - a)\ln k_o + \ln \theta_t = \ln 1 + r_o$$

so that

$$\ln a - (1 - a)E\ln k_o + E\ln \theta = \ln 1 + r_o.$$

It immediately follows that

$$E\ln w_c = E\ln w_o.$$

And therefore the expected utility is the same. But with *individual* utility being

$$\ln w_t/2 + \ln w_t(1 + r_{t+1})/2,$$

and with w and r in a closed economy being negatively correlated, there is less variability in utility across generations in the closed economy; accordingly, with a concave social welfare function, social welfare is lower after capital market liberalization.

More generally, with capital market liberalization, variations in θ generate large variations in wages and therefore in lifetime utility, particularly if the share of labor is small.[33,34]

It is also clear that CML leads to an increase in the variance of output.

The intuition behind these results is simple. Before the opening of the capital market, utility will vary less than wages, since when there is a positive productivity shock, the wage is high, when the wage is high savings will be high, and so the interest rate will be low; life time consumption of the younger generation will not increase in tandem with productivity, i.e., with output and their wage. Moreover, the benefits of a productivity shock are shared with future generations, as the increased savings leads to increased wages in the next generation, which in turn benefits succeeding generations.

On the other hand, once the capital market has been liberalized, the first effect will no longer be present (since the interest rate does not depend on the country's own savings). Moreover, the impacts of a higher θ are felt only by the generation working at the time. (It thus affects consumption in only two periods, the two periods of life of the individual.)

References

Akerlof, G. (2002). 'Behavioral Macroeconomics and Macroeconomic Behavior'. *American Economic Review*, June, 92/3: 411–33.

Banerjee, A. V. (1992). 'A Simple Model of Herd Behavior'. *The Quarterly Journal of Economics*, August, 107/3: 797–817.

Bhagwati, J. (1998). 'The Capital Myth: The Difference Between Trade in Widgets and Dollars'. *Foreign Affairs*, May/June, 77/3: 7–12.

Bikhchandani, S., Hirshleifer, D., and Welch, I. (1992). 'A Theory of Fads, Fashion, Custom , and Cultural Change as Informational Cascades'. *Journal of Political Economy*, October, 100/5: 992–1026.

Coakley, J., Kulasi, F., and Smith, R. (1998). 'The Feldstein-Horioka Puzzle and Capital Mobility: A Review'. *International Journal of Finance and Economics*, April, 3/2: 169–88.

---

[33] In the open economy, $d\ln k/d\ln\theta = 1/\beta$ where $\beta = -(1/d\ln f'/d\ln k)$, so $d\ln w/d\ln\theta = 1 + \beta(a/1 - a)(d\ln k/d\ln\theta) = 1/1 - a$.

[34] The variations in wages and utility in a closed economy depend on the stochastic process for θ. Assume, for instance, that θ takes on two alternating values, θ_1 and θ_2. Then the steady state is defined by the pair of equations

$$k_2^* = \theta_1 g(k_1^*)/2$$

and

$$k_1^* = \theta_2 g(k_2^*)/2.$$

Demirgüç-Kunt, A., and Detragiache, E. (2001). 'Financial Liberalization and Financial Fragility', in G. Caprio, P. Honohan, and J. E. Stiglitz (eds.), *Financial Liberalization: How Far, How Fast?* Cambridge: Cambridge University Press, pp. 96–122.

Diaz-Alejandro, C. F. (1985). 'Goodbye Financial Repression, Hello Financial Crash'. *Journal of Development Economics*, 19/1–2: 1–25.

Djankov, S., and Murrell, P. (2002). 'Enterprise Restructuring: A Quantitative Survey'. *Journal of Economic Literature*, September, 40/3: 739–92.

Economic Commission for Latin America and the Caribbean (ECLAC) (1996). *The Economic Experience of the Last 15 Years. Latin America and the Caribbean, 1980–1995*. Santiago de Chile: United Nations/Economic Commission for Latin America and the Caribbean.

Feldstein, M. and Horioka, C. (1980). 'Domestic Savings and International Capital Flows'. *The Economic Journal*, June, 90/358: 314–29.

Furman, J. and Stiglitz, J. E. (1998). 'Economic Crises: Evidence and Insights from East Asia'. *Brookings Papers on Economic Activity*, 2: 1–135.

Hoff, K. and Stiglitz, J. E. (2005). 'The Creation of the Rule of Law and the Legitimacy of Property Rights: The Political and Economic Consequences of a Corrupt Privatization'. NBER Working Paper 11772 (November), forthcoming, Economic Journal.

Honohan, P. (2001). 'How Interest Rates Changed under Liberalization: A Statistical Review', in G. Caprio, P. Honohan, and J. E. Stiglitz (eds.), *Financial Liberalization: How Far, How Fast?* Cambridge: Cambridge University Press, pp. 63–95.

Howitt, P. and McAfee, P. R. (1992). 'Animal Spirits'. *The American Economic Review*, June, 82/3: 493–507.

Independent Evaluation Office of the IMF (2003). *The IMF and Recent Capital Account Crises—Indonesia, Korea, Brazil*. Washington, DC: IMF.

Khan, M. (2004). 'State Failure in Developing Countries and Strategies of Institutional Reform', in B. Tungodden, N. Stern, and I. Kolstad (eds.), *Towards Pro-Poor Policies: Aid Institutions and Globalization*. Proceedings of World Bank's Annual Bank Conference on Development Economics, 2002. Oxford: Oxford University Press and World Bank, pp. 165–96.

Kindleberger, C. P. ([1978]2000). *Manias, Panics and Crashes: A History of Financial Crises*, 4th edn. New York: John Wiley and Sons, Inc.

Kose, M. A., Prasad, E., Rogoff, K., and Wei, S-J. (2006). 'Financial Globalization: A Reappraisal'. IMF Working Paper WP/06/189. Washington, DC: International Monetary Fund.

Lewis, K. K. (1995). 'Puzzles in International Financial Markets', in G. Grossman and K. Rogoff (eds.), *Handbook of International Economics, Vol.3*. Oxford: Elsevier, pp. 1913–71.

Lucas, R. (1987). *Models of Business Cycles*. New York: Blackwell.

Megginson, W. L. and Netter, J. M. (2001). 'From State to Market: A Survey of Empirical Studies on Privatization'. *Journal of Economic Literature*, June, 39/2: 321–89.

Miller, M. H. and Modigliani, F. (1958). 'The Cost of Capital, Corporation Finance and the Theory of Investment.' *The American Economic Review*, 48/3: 261–97.

Mishkin, F. (2006). *The Next Great Globalization: How Disadvantaged Nations Can Harness Their Financial Systems to Get Rich*. Princeton: Princeton University Press.

Newbery, D., and Stiglitz, J. E. (1984). 'Pareto Inferior Trade'. *The Review of Economic Studies*, 51/1: 1–12.

Obstfeld, M. and Rogoff, K. (2000). 'The Six Major Puzzles in International Macroeconomics: Is There a Common Cause?', in B. S. Bernanke and K. Rogoff (eds.), *NBER Macroeconomics Annual 2000*. Cambridge, MA: MIT Press, pp. 339–90.

Ocampo, J. A. and Martin, J. (eds.) (2003). *Globalization and Development: A Latin American and Caribbean Perspective*. Stanford: Stanford University Press.

Rodrik, D. (2001). 'Development Strategies for the Next Century', in B. Pleskovic and N. Stern (eds.), *Annual World Bank Conference on Development Economics 2000*. Washington, DC: The World Bank.

—— and Velasco, A. (2000). 'Short-Term Capital Flows', in B. Pleskovic and J. E. Stiglitz (eds.), *Annual World Bank Conference on Development Economics, World Bank 1999*. Washington, DC: The World Bank.

Rogoff, K., Kose, A. M., Prasad, E., and Wei, S.-J. (2003). 'Effects of Financial Globalization on Developing Countries: Some Empirical Evidence'. IMF Occasional Paper No.220 (September).

—— and Prasad, E. (2003). 'The Emerging Truth of Going Global'. *Financial Times*, September 2, 21.

Sachs, J. and Warner, A. (2001). 'The Curse of Natural Resources'. *European Economic Review*, May, 45/4–6: 827–38.

Stiglitz, J. E. (1969). 'A Re-Examination of the Modigliani-Miller Theorem'. *American Economic Review*, December, 59/5: 784–93.

—— (1982). 'Information and Capital Markets,' in W. Sharpe and C. Cootner (eds.). New Jersey: Prentice Hall.

—— (1999). 'Knowledge for Development: Economic Science, Economic Policy, and Economic Advice', in B. Pleskovic and J. E. Stiglitz (eds.), *Annual World Bank Conference on Development Economics*. Washington, DC: The World Bank, pp. 9–58.

—— (2000). 'Capital Market Liberalization, Economic Growth and Instability'. *World Development*, 28/6: 1075–86.

—— (2002). 'Capital Market Liberalization and Exchange Rate Regimes: Risk Without Reward'. *The Annals of the American Academy of Political and Social Science*, January, 579: 219–48.

—— (2003a). 'Democratizing IMF and World Bank: Governance and Accountability'. *Governance*, January, 16/1: 111–39.

—— (2003b). 'Globalization and Growth in Emerging Markets and the New Economy'. *Journal of Policy Modeling*, July, 25/5: 505–24.

—— (2003c). *The Roaring Nineties*. New York: W. W. Norton.

—— Ocampo, J. A., Spiegel, S., Ffrench-Davis, R., and Nayyar, D. (2006). *Stability With Growth: Macroeconomics, Liberalization, and Development*. New York: Oxford University Press.

Vijayn, J. (2003). 'India and the Impossible Trinity'. *The World Economy*, April, 26/4: 555–83.

Wade, R. H. (2002). 'US Hegemony and the World Bank: The Fight over People and Ideas'. *Review of International Political Economy*, (Summer), 9/2: 215–43.

World Bank (1999). *Global Economic Prospects 1998/1999*. Washington, DC: The World Bank.

—— (2000). *Global Development Finance 2000*. Washington, DC: The World Bank.

Wyplosz, C. (2002). 'How Risky is Financial Liberalization in the Developing Countries?' *Comparative Economic Studies*, (Summer), 44/2–3: 1–26.

4

From the Boom in Capital Inflows to Financial Traps

Roberto Frenkel[1]

4.1 Introduction

This chapter examines the performance of highly indebted countries that are linked with the international financial markets. The paths followed by some countries in the globalization process led to segmented integration. Persistently high country risk premiums place these countries in a financial trap, with high interest rates and low growth, vulnerability to contagion and other sources of volatility and the imposition of narrow limits to the degrees of freedom of economic policy.

Domestic policies implemented during the process of financial integration account for most of the variation in the present situations of the different emergent markets.

Although the analytical parts of this chapter do not refer specifically to Latin America, the experiences of these regional emergent markets provide useful examples and historical background. Two reasons explain this focus. First, Latin American countries participated in the earliest stages of the financial globalization process in the late 1960s and early 1970s. Second, the most important cases of high indebtedness took place in this region. The chapter is divided into three sections. The first presents the historical background and briefly discusses domestic policies of the 1990s. The second section analyzes the links between individual countries and the international financial market and characterizes financial traps. Conclusions are presented in the third section.

---

[1] This chapter was prepared for the Capital Market Liberalization Task Force of the Initiative for Policy Dialogue (IPD), Columbia University. The author extends his thanks for the collaboration of Daniel Kampel and the comments of Ricardo Ffrench-Davis and other participants in the meeting organized by IPD in Barcelona, Spain, June 2–3, 2003.

4.2 Latin America in the Process of Financial Globalization

Latin American countries took part in the financial globalization process from the beginning, in the late 1960s and early 1970s. Financial globalization itself combines two complementary processes. One is the adoption of institutional and legal measures allowing capital to freely flow across borders, namely capital market liberalization. The other is the increase in the amount of capital actually flowing between countries.

Those trends were neither smooth nor continuous in the region. The first boom in capital flows into the developing economies came to an abrupt halt with the financial and external crises in 1981 and 1982. The transfer of a large proportion of the private external debt to the public sector—through different mechanisms—followed. Then an institutional arrangement was established in which each country's external financing would involve simultaneous negotiation with both creditor banks and the IMF. During the rest of the 1980s, the region evolved under a regime characterized by two salient features: (1) rationed external financing; and (2) negotiations with creditors and multilateral lending agencies. These features generally imposed significant net transfers abroad. In this period, some of the capital market liberalization measures previously adopted were overturned. This temporary reversal of financial liberalization and openness was mainly motivated by the need to restrain the explosive trends set by the crises.

Another feature of the early globalization period must also be stressed. The first policy experiments involving complete trade opening and financial liberalization were implemented in the region. Argentina, Chile, and Uruguay implemented similar policy packages—the so-called Southern Cone experiments—in the last quarter of the 1970s (Frenkel 2002). They all ended in financial and currency crises, debt default, and deep recessions. Second, Latin American debt crises showed the first episodes of regional contagion. For instance, voluntary financing shrunk in Colombia, forcing a country with relatively small debt ratios and no sustainability problems to renegotiate its debt.

The region was not untied from the process of globalization in the 1980s. Although it was virtually impossible to obtain fresh voluntary financing, Latin American countries and the international system still maintained closed links through the negotiated service of the debts they had contracted in the previous period. When, in the 1990s, several of the region's economies, particularly the largest ones, entered a new period of financial boom, they carried the legacy of large external debt that resulted from their early involvement in financial globalization and the economic disaster it created.

The region was reinserted into the process in the early 1990s and experienced a new boom in capital flows that came to a sudden stop (Calvo 1998) with the Mexican crisis in 1994–5. This time the shrinkage period was abbreviated and capital flows resumed with the greater weight of foreign direct investment. This cyclical behavior did not reappear after the new shrinkage period triggered by the Asian crisis.

Many participants saw the first boom of the 1990s as an early stage of a long period of growth in capital flows to emerging markets, as a result of continual financial deepening on a global scale. This was the basic analytical view that predominated in multilateral lending agencies and some governments. Many international investors and financial intermediaries also shared it. It was thought that the process would lead, without interruption, to the complete integration of the emerging markets into a global market. The possibility of a crisis was simply ruled out in this scheme. Possible herd behavior of international investors was not considered. The phenomenon was familiar to financial market analysts, but concepts such as sudden stops and contagion effects were born and applied to the international market only after the Mexican crisis (Krugman 1997).

The scope and magnitude of the first boom in the 1990s was linked to this underestimation of risks by investors, which encouraged the intensity of capital flows. There was a bubble led by Mexican assets. The Mexican crisis and its repercussions exposed both the risks involved and the volatility of capital flows. But it also showed the possibility and effectiveness of an international intervention in an unprecedented scale. The rescue packages allowed Mexico and other affected countries—mainly Argentina—to fulfill all their financial commitments. This set up the environment for a new boom that endured until the Asian crisis.

The idea that the international financial integration was a cyclical process had been accepted as conventional wisdom after the Asian, Russian, and Brazilian crises, and hence, a boom was expected. Such was, for example, the belief of the economic authorities of the Argentine administration that took office at the end of 1999. The optimistic outlook was encouraged by the effectiveness of most interventions by the international lending agencies in order to avoid default, and also by the relatively benign nature of the Brazilian crisis.

However, other events indicated that the process had taken a new direction. First, the volume of net capital inflows did not recover from the low levels registered in 1998. Second, the risk premium remained systematically high for some countries with heavy weight in emerging markets average, above a floor that doubles the values of the premiums observed during previous periods of boom.

New aspects in price dynamics were also revealed as events unfolded. Risk premium and private capital movements oscillated at the pace of new forms of contagion. Oil price increases and the NASDAQ collapse in 2000–1 can be cited as examples—for example, Mexico's country risk grew together with the rest of emergent market risk indexes even though it is an oil exporting country.

Reductions in capital flows and innovations in their dynamics were associated with other significant changes that substantially modified the context that had prevailed in the 1990s. Simultaneously, the United States ended a long period of growth as the bubble in technology stocks burst, triggering an important negative wealth effect. That bubble had grown parallel to the boom in the emerging markets, and both types of assets represented a new set of opportunities for investors looking for high returns. The restraint in demand for emerging market assets that resulted from revised income expectations and the losses caused by the fall in the prices of shares were further augmented by the impact of greater uncertainty.

On the supply side, assets issued by regional emerging markets had lost the attractiveness they showed in the early 1990s. The external sector of these countries along with their ability to pay their external obligations changed over the decade, largely as an effect of the globalization process itself. The international positioning of the involved economies changed. The counterpart of the net capital flows is a growing trend in foreign capital and international public and private debts. That was reflected in the current account of the balance of payments as a continuous growth in external factor income. In some relevant cases, growth in the capital income account has not been counterbalanced by growth in net exports and it led to structural deficits in the current account. A large part of the problems facing these countries was precisely the result of this mismatch between their financial and trade positions in the global economy.

At the end of the 1990s, in the face of an exhausted external supply of funds, heavily indebted countries needed desperately to roll over their debt and acquire additional financing to cover the current account deficit, chiefly determined by capital service (interest and profits). In 2001, this situation affected countries like Argentina and Brazil, which account for a large percentage of the debt of emerging markets and of the Latin American debt. At the end of 2002, Argentina was in default on its debt and the market for fresh borrowing was closed to Brazil.[2] Before continuing with the main issue of this chapter, it is worth taking a look at the origins of the differences in the present situations of Latin America's emergent markets.

4.2.1 The Importance of Domestic Policies During the Capital Inflows Boom Periods

In contrast with Argentina and Brazil, other Latin American emerging markets show more robust situations. Differences in present positions have mainly resulted from the different paths of international integration followed

---

[2] In April 2003 the market for Brazilian bonds was reopened. The government issued $1 billion of new debt at an annual cost of 10.7%.

throughout the 1990s. Important in determining such differences was the role played by domestic policies applied during that decade.

A closer look finds significant differences in both the pace and nature of the capital market liberalization measures adopted by each emerging market, on the one hand, and in the volume and composition of capital inflows, on the other. Although participating in the same globalization process, these countries have followed different paths towards trade and financial international integration.

The full deregulation of the capital account, fixed or quasi-fixed exchange rate, real exchange rate appreciation, and a passive role of monetary policy characterized the path that led to high debt and greater vulnerability. Argentina throughout the 1990s, Brazil in the 1994–8 period and Mexico until 1995 are all examples of this path. On the other hand, some sort of capital account regulation, in coordination with more active monetary and exchange rate policies, developed into more robust situations. Chile and Colombia in the first half of the 1990s are examples of this path.[3]

Decisions regarding capital market regulations were not isolated measures but complementary features of different policy strategies. In the cases where such regulations were implemented, they were intended to allow or reinforce monetary and exchange rate policies focused on growth and price stability without losing sight of the real exchange rate. Chile and Colombia initially adopted crawling bands exchange regimes, regulated capital flows by imposing tax rates differentiated by type of flow—which meant that some control had to be maintained over the foreign exchange market—and implemented sterilization policies. On the other hand, in the cases where the capital account was completely deregulated, the economic policy was oriented towards full integration with the international financial system and the capital inflows were an essential component of those policies.

Chile and Colombia, on the one hand, and Argentina and Brazil, on the other hand, are examples of different integration paths closely correlated with different policy strategies. The Mexican experiences in the 1990s encompass both kinds. Its experience in the first half of the decade undoubtedly belongs to the second group, both regarding policy and performance. In contrast, in the second half of the decade the country followed a different path, with higher rates of growth and an impressive increase in manufactured goods exports that led the economy to a comparatively more robust situation at the end of the period. Mexico, then, as it developed in the first half of the 1990s, can be included with the same group as Argentina and Brazil, while its

---

[3] The differences in policy strategies vis-à-vis financial globalization are related to the different priorities posed by the macroeconomic situation at the end of the 80s. Mexico, Argentina, and Brazil had to control inflation and recover growth after a long period of very high inflation and stagnation. In contrast, in Chile and Colombia inflation was under control and the economies were growing at relatively high rates (Damill et al. 1993; Frenkel 1995).

experience in the second half of the decade puts it in the same group as Chile and Colombia.

That classification of experiences and policies stresses the role of the real exchange rate as a crucial determinant of the difference between the two groups.[4] This is so because the only remarkable policy change in the strategy implemented by Mexico after its crisis was the adoption of a floating exchange rate regime that led to significant exchange rate depreciation in the following three years (but not in the entire second half of the decade). This does not mean that the improvement of Mexico's performance in the second half of the 1990s was caused solely by a more depreciated exchange rate. Obviously, the creation of NAFTA and the long period of high growth of the US economy contributed. Could Mexico have taken advantage of NAFTA and the US growth if the country had persisted in its previous policy regime? Actually, the crisis made persistence impossible, but one can imagine that it would have been very difficult for Mexico to reverse the low growth rates and the high trade deficit trends in those circumstances.

4.3 The Financial Traps

4.3.1 *The International Positioning of Emergent Market Countries*

The evolution of trade flows and financial commitments describes the different paths of international integration. The evolution of trade and financial links are important aspects of the development trajectories of the countries. Those are historical processes characterized by path dependence, in which the conditions found at any moment depend on the earlier course of events. For instance, the external financial commitments resulting from the previous path can impose heavy constraints on the present performance and future evolution of the economy. Certain paths can drive the economy to a dead end, such as a financial trap of low growth and high vulnerability.

The stock of the external debt and the proportion of local capital owned by foreigners are the basic indicators of the evolution of financial commitments. Both are the result of foreign capital inflows that take the form of debt contracts or direct investment (portfolio investment is included in this category to simplify the discussion). Trade payments and international financial commitments are generally made and contracted in international currency. In contrast, no emerging market country issues any international currency and thus their financial commitments are almost always denominated in foreign currency. This point deserves to be stressed. The point is not related to what

---

[4] In comparison with the average real exchange rate of the second half of the 1980s, in the period 1991–4, Chile and Colombia appreciated significantly less than Argentina and Mexico (Frenkel 1995).

currency is domestically used to make transactions or endorse local contracts. The observation is valid even in the case of a dollarized economy, like Panama.

The path of international integration is reflected in the changing structure of the balance of payments. In the process of financial globalization, the accumulation of debt commitments and foreign direct investment implies a growing deficit in the capital services payments item (interests and profits) of the current account. On the other hand, the evolution of the trade account balance is a consequence of the path of trade integration, which evolves more or less independently—without coordination—of the financial integration process.[5] Moreover, as mentioned above, a badly managed boom in capital inflows can significantly deteriorate the trade performance of the country through its effect on relative prices and incentives. Besides, the volume and structure of the external debt determine the committed amounts of capital amortization payments.

The sum of the capital amortization payments plus the current account balance amounts to the so-called 'financing needs', i.e., the amount of international currency liquidity needed to meet international payments in a certain period—a year, for example.

Aside from its own reserves, a country can obtain the international currency needed to meet its financial commitments from four sources: (1) trade surplus; (2) the transfer of the ownership of existing domestic assets; (3) new investment financed by foreigners; and (4) new foreign debt. The last three categories entail new capital inflows. On the one hand, financing needs measure the amount of new capital inflows needed to endorse international payments, under the current trade trends and policy setting and maintaining stable reserves. On the other hand, the concept also measures the necessary adjustment that the reserves and/or the trade balance have to experience in case there are no new capital inflows.

In the real world there is no mechanism able to coordinate in every circumstance the myriad of individual decisions involved in the above-mentioned transactions, in order to assure the ability of the country to endorse its international payments commitments.

A priori, the interest rate and the exchange rate would be the main candidates to perform the coordinating role, as flexible prices capable of equilibrating the demand and supply of foreign currency. The role of the first variable is limited, because we know both from experience and theory (Stiglitz and Weiss 1981; Jaffe and Stiglitz 1990) that the international financial market may at times ration the supply of new funds, precisely when the interest rate of the country's assets reaches some (high) level. On the other hand, given the constraint on new foreign funds, an adjustment exclusively

---

[5] In the mainstream literature of the 80s this was seen as a problem related to the sequencing of the structural reforms (McKinnon 1991; Fanelli and Frenkel 1993).

based on the exchange rate depreciation could be at times impossible or intolerable.

In other terms, the capital inflows may at times experience sudden stops. In this case, the endorsement of international commitments would require an adjustment in the trade balance and/or the level of reserves. Reserves could be insufficient, or a significant decline could trigger a speculative attack. The increase in the trade surplus throughout the depreciation of the exchange rate may have an upper limit, because exports cannot expand sufficiently or imports could not be reduced beyond some limit without affecting exports-production capacity. Besides, the contraction in consumption and/or investment could also affect the production of exportable goods or be socially intolerable. Even if there are non-binding real constraints, the necessary adjustment of the trade surplus may not be feasible for other reasons. A very high nominal depreciation has a negative effect on indebted firms and the balance sheets of the banks and, consequently, a destabilizing impact on the financial system. The financial crisis would be in that case a self-defeating effect of the devaluation on the ability to endorse international payments. If there is not enough availability of international currency to meet the country's obligations, some of the contracts have to be defaulted. This may happen independently of the particular financial situation of the domestic agent engaged in the international contract. For example, a firm can be forced to meet an international interest payment commitment at the current exchange rate, but the government can suspend convertibility to make financial transactions. The government could appeal to convertibility suspension in order to avoid the depletion of reserves— in the case of a fixed exchange rate. Or to avoid a financial crisis and slow down the acceleration of inflation (in the case of a floating exchange rate).

So, international contracts involving developing countries almost always carry a specific country-risk of default. It is imposed by the potential inability of the country to meet its obligations in international currency. It reflects the potential lack of international currency liquidity at the country-aggregate level. Solvency considerations are not entirely useful for the purpose of assessing the country risk of default. Sustainability is a more relevant concept. In this context it means the ability of the country to fulfill its financial commitments as they are written in the involved contracts. External debt sustainability means that no serious difficulties should be expected for the attainment of the contracts in due time. Obviously, sustainability is not a guarantee that the contracts will actually be fulfilled. As with other financial concepts, sustainability is an assessment about future uncertain events, based on present information and probable conjectures.

An international investor has to evaluate both the prospects of the capital inflows and the ability of the country to make necessary adjustments in trade account and reserves while assessing the risk of default of a particular country. Obviously, possibilities are related to the quantities involved. For instance, usual indicators compare financing needs (or some components of financing needs, such as current account deficit or interest plus amortization) with the amount of foreign debt, reserves, exports, and output. The first indicator focuses on the international market capacity to absorbing new country debt. The second points to immediate liquidity availability and to how long the country could endorse international payments without new capital inflows. The third and fourth indicators point to the relative size of the trade adjustment as an essential ingredient of feasibility considerations. Other usual inputs of the assessment are the situation of the financial system and the specific situation of particularly important agents or debtors, for instance, the public sector.

Domestic information cannot provide a complete assessment of the risk, whatever the amount and detail of the collected information and the sophistication of the models used to evaluate it. Even the quantitative components of the sustainability assessment depend on the behavior of the international market. Present and expected interest rates and country risk premium are necessary information to forecast the evolution of the debt burden and the future financing needs of a specific country. The amount of new debt that has to be issued in order to meet its financing needs depends on the country risk premium. A higher country risk premium implies that a greater amount of debt has to be issued to get a certain net amount of international currency. This is one of the ways in which the sustainability assessment depends on the behavior of the market. Because of that, an increase in the country risk premium caused, for example by a contagion effect, can substantially change the assessments of external debt sustainability.

Because the prospects of capital inflows and country risk premium are essential components of a sustainability assessment, each of the investors has to conjecture the behavior of the rest of the market. Consequently, there is room for multiple equilibria and self-fulfilling prophecies, as in most financial markets. But beyond this general observation, different situations can be identified in this regard.

4.3.2 *The More Robust Situations*

If the above-mentioned quantitative indicators are relatively low and there is real exchange rate flexibility to perform any needed non-disruptive adjustments, the fundamental component of the assessment will point to a low risk of default. At the same time, the evaluation by an individual investor does not greatly depend on the behavior of the rest of the market. Fundamentals are, in this case, the main component of the risk evaluation process. Each investor can presume that the market will easily back the financing needs. And, in case they are not, the necessary adjustment will take place. Thus, the risk of default is low.

Under the mentioned conditions, low-risk fundamentals coordinate a good equilibrium. This equilibrium seems robust, but this is not always the case. Experience shows that a contagion effect, even with unaffected fundamentals, can trigger a significant reduction in capital inflows and push the country into important adjustments. However, the country could carry out the adjustment and avoid default. This does not mean that there are not negative impacts on growth and employment. Capital flows volatility imposes high economic and social costs in this case as in other cases (Stiglitz 2000). But here we want to stress its financial aspects. Even though there is no guarantee of the stability of this 'good equilibrium', the situation is more robust than in the highly indebted cases. In the set of Latin American countries considered above, the description applies to the international positioning of Chile, Mexico, and Colombia.

4.3.3 The More Fragile Situations

A country whose fundamentals show a relatively high risk presents a different scenario. Financing needs are relatively high and there is less room for non-disruptive adjustment. In this case, the individual investor assessment of the risk of default heavily depends on the behavior of the rest of the market. To clarify this point it is useful to consider the managing possibilities of the main components of the financing needs: trade deficit, foreign capital profit remittances, and the aggregate of interests and amortization payments. The classification differentiates the components according to how manageable they are by the country's authorities or to what extent they are responsive to domestic variables.

The trade account balance is the most manageable and responsive component. A country can devalue—with the above-mentioned caveats—or implement other measures intended to reduce the trade deficit or generate trade surpluses.

The remittances of foreign capital profits rank second on this scale. Exchange rate devaluation reduces the international currency value of foreign capital profits in non-tradable activities. Besides, the country's authorities could provide incentives to locally reinvest foreign firms' profits, negotiate a suspension of remittances with foreign firms, or directly impose restrictions. In any of these alternatives, this component of the financing needs would be backed by foreign direct investment without affecting the country's foreign currency liquidity. Lastly, the debt services and amortization components are mostly beyond the reach of government policies. Currently, this is particularly true, since most of the external debt has been placed through bonds and commercial papers that are traded in a secondary market and held by numerous bondholders. (In this respect, bank debt is more manageable because banks are more prone to individually renegotiate their credit contracts when difficulties in debt servicing are foreseen.)[6] The debt services and amortization commitments have to be fulfilled or defaulted.[7] In this regard, the debt burden is an inertial component of the financing needs because its amount is a consequence of contracts subscribed in the past.

The composition of the present and forecasted financing needs informs about the proportion that should inescapably be backed by new lending in the international market, even after correcting policy measures and feasible adjustments have been taken. When debt burden accounts for the bulk of present and projected financing needs, the effects of domestic policies and the adjustment on the financing needs are relatively small. Consequently, the individual sustainability assessment depends in this case mostly on conjectures about the behavior of the rest of the financial market (including, to be more realistic, the behavior of the IMF and other multilateral lenders).

Sustainability is then a self-fulfilling prophecy of the average opinion of the market. The average opinion can suddenly change from sustainable to unsustainable. The changes can be triggered by relatively small variations in the country risk premium, trade prospects, or other news affecting the fundamentals. Alternatively, the change can be caused by domestic or international news less connected to the fundamentals. The sufficient condition for that to happen is a conventional opinion shared by most of the market participants. Consequently, sustainability is more vulnerable to contagion effects or other sources of volatility, international or domestic.

4.3.4 *The Constraints to Domestic Policy*

The valuation of the assets issued by a country in the above situation is a neat example of the Keynesian beauty contest. What can this country do to make their financial assets look more beautiful? The government's domestic policies have relatively little room for improving the fundamentals in which the sustainability assessments are based in the short run. But this does not mean that domestic policies are irrelevant. They are relevant, not because of their effect on the fundamentals, but as signals to the international market (Rodrik 2000). The signals should make the country look more attractive, according to market criteria. Signals are intended to convince individual investors that the average opinion will be favorably influenced. So, they have to harmonize with

[6] For example, the standstill on short-term debt negotiated in the crisis by the Korean government would have been practically impossible if short-term obligations were bond services instead of bank debt.

[7] There is another alternative: bondholders could agree to voluntary swaps intended to reduce liquidity needs and avoid formal default. Let us consider this alternative as default, for the purpose of this discussion.

the more generalized conventions of the market participants. For instance, if most of the players think that an agreement with the IMF will favorably influence average market opinion, then the agreement will actually have a powerful coordinating role. Fiscal austerity measures are valuable signals if, as it is actually the case, generalized conventions see them always positively, even if an independent analysis could easily show that they worsen the sustainability fundamentals. The fiscal issue will be discussed in more detail below.

The country loses most of its policy degrees of freedom. The external financing becomes the center of the relations of the country with the rest of the world. It also becomes the main focus of domestic policies because it is the most important and urgent government target. The default would be followed by financial and currency crises (or a burst of inflation in a floating exchange regime). Moreover, the anticipation of default would trigger the financial and currency crisis. In any case the crisis would impose a high political cost and consequently, the government perceives the loss of international funding as the most important threat it faces.

Policy signals to the market may be, and usually are, socially or politically problematic and may actually have negative impacts on economic performance. Experience shows that governments choose to confront domestic, social, and political conflicts and risk worsening the economic performance to give priority to the issuing of signals to the market. Governments always prefer to play for time. The default and crisis threat is tangible and easily foreseeable, while the local effects of the signals are more uncertain, take more time to appear or simply are comparatively less costly for the government in the short run.

4.3.5 *The Real Interest Rate and the Country Risk Premium*

The loss of policy degrees of freedom is one of the elements of the financing trap. The other element results from the high real interest that the highly indebted country has to bear. High real interest rate is a consequence of the domestic open financial market functioning in a situation of high country risk premium. The sum of the international interest rate plus the country risk premium sets up a floor for the local interest rate. As an example, we consider the determination of the lending interest rate. A bit of simple algebra is useful to present the issue.

The market quotation of the bonds issued by the country determines their yield i. Let's suppose they are sovereign bonds, to simplify the presentation. Conventionally, this yield can be decomposed in two terms:

$$i = r^* + k. \tag{1}$$

In expression (1), r^* is the yield of the US Treasury bond of the same maturity and k is the country risk premium.

In the first place, it has to be stressed that i is the opportunity cost of any foreign investment in the country, to the extent that the asset under consideration, real or financial, is subject to country risk. So, the cost of international credit to local banks or to other private agents should generally be equal to or greater than i. In order to ease the discussion of the real interest rate determination, we suppose that the domestic financial system is partially dollarized. This means that assets and liabilities denominated in dollars are issued by the financial system together with assets and liabilities in local currency (pesos, for example). Because local banks can buy sovereign bonds yielding i, this rate is the opportunity cost of local bank lending in dollars. Consequently, this rate sets the floor for local lending in dollars, even if the credit has not been funded in the international market. The local lending interest rate in dollars should be equal to or higher than i. Let us assume that it equals i.

To determine the rate in pesos, the banks have to take into account the expected trend of the exchange rate:

$$j = i + E(e) + \pi$$
$$\pi > 0. \tag{2}$$

In expression (2), j is the nominal interest rate in pesos, $E(e)$ is the expected rate of nominal devaluation and π represents the exchange risk premium. Let p and p^* represent the local and international inflation rates respectively. We can subtract p from both members of (2) and add and subtract p^* in the second member:

$$j - p = (i - p^*) + [E(e) - p + p^*] + \pi. \tag{3}$$

In (3), $j - p$ is the real interest rate in pesos and $E(e) - p + p^*$ is the expected real devaluation rate.

With expression (3) it is easy to see that the real interest rate in pesos should be equal or higher than $i - p^*$, except in the case of an expected real appreciation trend strong enough to compensate for the exchange risk premium π. We can disregard this case because an expected appreciation trend is not consistent with a situation in which there is a high country risk. Consequently,

$$j - p \geq i - p^* = r^* - p^* + k. \tag{4}$$

Expression (4) indicates that the real international lending rate plus the country risk premium normally set a floor for the real lending interest rate.

Already mentioned were the negative cumulative effects of high country-risk premium on external debt dynamics, the evolution of the country's financing needs and sustainability. Persistently high real interest rates, on the other hand, impair the growth capacity of the country and tend to increase the fragility of the financial system. Low rates of growth or recession trends plus increasing financial fragility further contribute to the worsening of sustainability. Once the country is caught in the financial trap, market forces themselves lead the economy to contraction or low growth and increasing financial fragility. Together with external financial fragility, these trends contribute to increase the likelihood of a crisis.[8]

In fact, most high-risk situations did lead to financial and external crises. The experience also shows that situations of high country risk premium can last for years. Argentina in 1998–2001 is a clear example in this regard. Argentina was a case of a very rigid fixed exchange commitment—a currency board regime enacted by law. Are fixed exchange rate regimes a necessary condition for the configuration of financing traps? The Brazilian situation suggests a negative answer. Brazil experienced low growth and high country risk since 1998. This case shows that countries can fall and remain caught in financing traps even if they have already experienced and overcome currency crises and adopted a floating exchange rate regime. It is a neat example of path-dependence. In 1999, Brazil corrected many of the features that characterized its previous policy approach. But it wasn't enough, because the country could not rid itself of the heavy financial commitments inherited from its previous path. Country-risk premium and interest rate remained high and the country did not find a way out of the financing trap.

4.3.6 *The Fiscal Signals*

We have already mentioned that fiscal austerity measures are highly valued by the consensus opinion of the financial markets. On the other hand, the generation of fiscal primary surpluses is also important in the policy packages promoted by the IMF, both in the programs intended to prevent crisis as well as in the post-crisis stabilization programs.

In the beauty contest in which the country is involved, the IMF plays the game side-by-side with the rest of the market players. But it is also true that the institution has a significant coordination role, not only because of the amount of resources it manages—vis-à-vis the rest of individual players—but because of the importance given by the market to its seal of approval. So clever IMF officials could blame the incorrect average opinion of the market

[8] We have formulated a model of the macroeconomic dynamics generated by capital inflow booms in fixed exchange rate contexts. There is a cycle with a first expansionary phase, followed by domestic financial distress and a second phase of contraction that leads to a final financial and currency crisis. The rise in the real interest rate is an endogenous consequence of increasing external fragility. The model was inspired by the Argentina and Chile experiences of the late 1970s to early 1980s (Frenkel 1983; Williamson 1991). It was applied to explain similar crises in the 1990s (Taylor 1998; Eatwell and Taylor 2000; Frenkel 2002; Frenkel 2003).

for promoting inappropriate policies while, at the same time, smart market participants say that they do well following the IMF assessments.

The reduction of fiscal deficit or the generation of a surplus was a crucial component of the IMF stabilization programs before financial globalization. Balance of payments crises were caused primarily by difficulties in the financing of trade deficit. Excessive trade deficit was always attributed to excessive domestic absorption, which simultaneously caused exchange rate appreciation. Sometimes the problem originated with fiscal and monetary policies that were too expansionary, and the diagnosis was right. Sometimes the external deficit originated in exogenous negative shocks—for instance, on the terms of trade—and the same diagnosis was wrong. In any case, the stabilization program combined exchange rate devaluation with domestic absorption contraction induced by contracting fiscal and monetary policies. With the implicit assumptions of full employment and expansionary effects of devaluation, the main effect of the policy package was supposed to be the change in the composition of aggregate demand. In practice, there was an output contraction and an increase in unemployment in the majority of cases. However, the policy packages reached their most important objective anyway, i.e., the rise in net exports, although mostly through a fall in imports and at the cost of a loss of output (the program was said to 'overkill' the target).

Balance of payments crises are now different. The external financial difficulties of highly indebted economies originate in different sources. It is not a rather simple problem of flows adjustment, but rather a problem rooted in the stocks of debt and foreign capital. Next, the role of fiscal policy is discussed in cases where public debt sustainability is a significant component of the country's external sustainability uncertainties. This situation creates different scenarios.

The first scenario is one in which the public debt burden represents a significant proportion of the external financing needs. The country can arrive at this situation in different ways. For instance, the external public debt could have been borrowed to finance public sector primary deficits. It has to be mentioned that in Latin America, none of the emergent market countries have followed this pattern, although there is a controversy about the causes of Argentina's public external indebtedness in the second half of the 1990s.

The other possible way to arrive at the above situation is through the cumulative effect of high country risk premiums. The rise in the country-risk premium can originate either in a deterioration of the external sustainability not related to the fiscal performance, or caused by a contagion effect. Given some initial stock of external public debt, high country risk premiums generate a faster accumulation of external public debt and growing interests payments, even if there are primary surpluses in the fiscal accounts. In this case, fiscal deficits originate exclusively in the interest component of current public expenses.

In the second scenario, public debt is not an important component of external debt. Even so, the dubious public domestic debt sustainability negatively affects the assessments of external sustainability. The same distinction of origins of the situation holds in this scenario. Public debt growth can originate either in the financing of primary deficits or it can be a consequence of high domestic interest rates caused by high country risk premiums.

When public debt is a significant proportion of external debt, fiscal sustainability overlaps with external sustainability, however the country arrived at that situation. If there are doubts about fiscal sustainability, measures intended to reinforce it are directly connected with the fundamentals of external sustainability. The same holds in the second scenario. Measures intended to improve the sustainability of the domestic debt would have a beneficial effect on the external sustainability assessments.

But the measures intended to reinforce fiscal sustainability could not be the same in every case. When the growth of public debt originated in public sector accounts for primary deficits, measures focused on generating or raising the primary surplus point to the fundamentals of sustainability assessments. However, this is not always the correct treatment. The recessive effects of the measures could deteriorate the sustainability of private external debt while recession and financial fragility could impair the whole sustainability assessment. Besides, the measures could actually have no significant effect on the fiscal accounts, because the effects of recession or lower growth on collected taxes neutralize the impact of the policy measures.

An alternative case is when there is a primary surplus in the public sector accounts and doubts about the sustainability of public debt originate in the high country risk premium itself. In this situation, the variable that is out of line is the interest rate that the country has to face to back its financing needs. A lower interest rate would reduce the fiscal deficits and the growth of public debt, improving public debt sustainability prospects. From a strict macroeconomic point of view, the only variable that is 'wrong' and should be adjusted is the country risk premium itself. Obviously, there is no way to do that in the present setting of international financial markets.

What could be the rationale for raising primary surplus through expense cuts or higher taxes in this situation? First of all, if primary surplus actually rises, public debt sustainability fundamentals may improve. However, governments mainly adopt fiscal austerity measures not because of their effects on the public debt sustainability fundamentals, but as signals to the market. Fiscal signals point to a target that has to be reached well before any quantitative evaluation of the measures' effects is possible. Their main purpose is to gain credibility; namely, preserving or re-opening the country's access to the markets to back the external financing needs. The issuing of signals bets on a quick reduction in the country risk premium. Sometimes the signals do their short-run job (as in Argentina in 2000 and Brazil in early 2003); sometimes they do not (as in Argentina in 2001).

In any case, fiscal austerity measures are not only inappropriate from a macroeconomic and development point of view, but also risky in relation to their own credibility target. The negative impacts on the economic performance, the financial distress and the social conflicts may actually end up worsening the sustainability assessments.

Why do governments take the risks? Often, because the situation is worrisome and the administration in charge is responsible for its management. Governments must show action. So, they implement fiscal austerity measures as one of the few ways they have to show policy initiatives 'in the right direction'. Maybe the same argument is applicable to the IMF policy proposals. IMF lending has necessarily to be submitted to conditionality. When there is not much room for correcting policies and the IMF has decided on new lending—Argentina in 2000 is probably the best example—the institution appeals to fiscal contracting measures as a solution to the problem of establishing some conditions for their disbursements. Ultimately, fiscal austerity always looks respectable and the policy is deeply rooted in the institution's traditional orthodoxy.

The suggested explanation can shed some light on the more intriguing case of the IMF fiscal austerity measures' recommendation: the situation in which there are not fiscal sustainability problems nor even significant public debt. In this case the norm followed by IMF officials seems to be the following: if you don't know what to do and you have to do something, raise taxes and reduce public expenses. The justification of this orientation is archaeological residue from the pre-globalization period.

4.3.7 Segmented Integration

The paths of international integration followed by the highly indebted countries led them into situations of segmented financial integration in which the domestic rate of interest is significantly higher than the international rate.

Persistently high country risk premiums are an unforeseen effect of financial globalization. Since the process began, its advocates have presented full integration between the domestic and international financial markets as its ideal final stage. Full integration is tantamount of global financial intermediation whereby the yield on the assets, on the one hand, and the cost of capital for borrowers, on the other, are the same for economically equivalent transactions, regardless of the location of savers and borrowers.

Ideally, full integration would minimize intermediation costs and reduce the cost of capital to developed country levels. Assuming that developing countries offer greater opportunities for investment, full integration would also result in investment and financing flows tending to narrow the development gap.

Convergence towards full integration would have meant a continuous reduction in country risk premiums. This has not happened. The evolution of country risk premiums provides no evidence to suggest that the international system that has developed along with globalization is moving towards full financial integration. Quite the contrary, the experience of the period that began with the Asian crisis suggests that the system has evolved into segmented integration. The cost of capital is systematically much higher for some emerging market economies than for the developed countries. Segmented integration is not a marginal phenomenon; it has developed precisely in emerging market countries that concentrated an important proportion of capital flows.

4.4 Conclusions

The volatility of capital flows imposes high economic and social costs to every country participating in the system created by the financial globalization process, regardless of each particular situation. However, some countries have managed their insertion in such ways that they show more robust situations vis-à-vis international financial markets. In contrast, other important emergent market countries found themselves caught in financial traps.

The comparative analysis of Latin American experiences, together with the negative and positive lessons learned from other cases, makes it possible to extract a series of policy recommendations to avoid the riskier paths of international integration.

First, there is a consensus regarding the importance of prudential regulations. However, the conventional criteria for regulation are largely pro-cyclical. Besides microeconomic risks, prudential regulation should also consider the macroeconomic and systemic risks, such as mismatches in currencies and the stockpiling of debt in foreign currency (Ocampo 2003). Moreover, the burden from prudential regulation should be distributed beyond recipient countries and shared by developed countries.

Second, experience leaves no doubts as to the incompatibility between fixed exchange rates and the volatility of capital flows. Nevertheless, although there is consensus regarding the need for exchange rate flexibility, there is an open debate on the possibilities and benefits of intervening in the exchange market. The IMF advocates pure flotation and assigns all responsibility for price and exchange rate stability to monetary policy. A flexible exchange rate discourages certain types of short-term capital flows, but free floating in contexts of volatile capital flows can result in intolerable volatility in the nominal and real exchange rates. Besides, policies should never lose sight of the real exchange rate. Application of direct controls—or application of reserve requirements to the entry of capital as Chile and Colombia used—(Ffrench-Davis and Villar 2003) can contribute to the stability of the exchange market and the capital flows. It can also influence the duration of inflows by discouraging short-term investments. Aside from its role as short term stabilizer, the objective of regulatory policy is to harness capital inflows to turn their behavior into a stable and predictable flow.

The Economic Commission for Latin America and the Caribbean (ECLAC) has been a leader in promoting the mentioned policy outlook and approach (ECLAC 2000, 2002). The so-called crisis prevention measures incorporate the lessons that can be learned from the region's experience, but their implementation is most suitable for periods of capital inflow booms. Besides, even optimal domestic policies cannot guarantee robustness. Moreover, even countries in relatively robust situations cannot avoid significant real effects from capital flows volatility. Under the current international financial architecture, once a country has fallen into a financial trap, there is no mechanism able to take it out (Eatwell and Taylor 2000; Stiglitz 2002). Massive rescue packages coordinated by the IMF are the only policy initiative at the international level in this area. In fact, these packages did contribute to avoiding default in most cases. But the existence of this policy instrument did not impede the outbreak of crises and, particularly in the Russian crisis, did not prevent persistently high country risks and the development of financial traps.

To make things worse, rescue packages are no longer allowed while the new IMF initiative points toward an international reform with the exclusive purpose of facilitating post-default negotiations. Even this very limited initiative has not prospered.

The prospects of high-risk countries are not encouraging.

References

Calvo, G. (1998). 'Capital Flows and Capital Market Crises: The Simple Economics of Sudden Stops'. *Journal of Applied Economics*, 1.

Damill, M., Fanelli, J. M., and Frenkel, R. (1996). 'De México a México: el desempeño de América Latina en los noventa'. *Desarrollo Económico*, Special Issue, 36.

——————Rozenwurcel, G. (1993). 'Crecimiento económico en América Latina: Experiencia reciente y perspectivas'. *Desarrollo Económico*, July–September, 130.

Eatwell, J. and Taylor, L. (2000). *Global Finance at Risk: The Case for International Regulation*. New York: The New Press.

Economic Commission for Latin America and the Caribbean (ECLAC) (2000). *Equidad, Desarrollo y Ciudadanía*. Santiago de Chile: ECLAC.

——(2002). *Growth with Stability. Financing for Development in the New International Context*. Santiago de Chile: ECLAC.

Fanelli, J. M. and Frenkel, R. (1993). 'On Gradualism, Shock Treatment and Sequencing', *International Monetary and Financial Issues for the 1990s*, Vol. II. New York: United Nations.

Ffrench-Davis, R. and Villar, L. (2003). 'The Capital Account and Real Macroeconomic Stabilization: Chile and Colombia'. ECLAC. Mimeo.

Frenkel, R. (1983). 'Mercado Financiero, Expectativas Cambiarias y Movimientos de Capital'. *El Trimestre Económico*, 4/200.

——(1995). 'Macroeconomic Sustainability and Development Prospects: Latin American Performance in the 1990s'. UNCTAD Discussion Papers No. 100, Geneva, August.

——(2002). 'Capital Market Liberalization and Economic Performance in Latin America', in J. Eatwell and L. Taylor (eds.), *International Capital Markets. Systems in Transition*. Oxford: Oxford University Press.

——(2003). 'Globalización y Crisis Financieras en América Latina', *Revista de la CEPAL* (forthcoming).

Jaffe, D. and Stiglitz, J. E. (1990). 'Credit Rationing', in B. M. Friedman and F. H. Hahn (eds.), *Handbook of Monetary Economics*. Amsterdam: North-Holland.

Krugman, P. (1997). 'Currency Crises'. Mimeo.

——(1999). 'Balance Sheets, the Transfer Problem, and Financial Crises', in Isard, P., Razin, A., and Rose, A. (eds.), *International Finance and Financial Crises: Essays in Honor of Robert P. Flood, Jr.* Amsterdam: Kluwer Academic Publishers.

McKinnon, R. I. (1991). *The Order of Economic Liberalization: Financial Control in the Transition to a Market Economy*. London: John Hopkins University Press.

Ocampo, J. A. (2003). 'Capital-Account and Counter-Cyclical Prudential Regulations in Developing Countries'. *Series Informes y Estudios Especiales*, No. 6. Santiago de Chile: ECLAC.

Rodrik, D. (2000). 'How Far will International Economic Integration Go?'. *Journal of Economic Perspectives*, 14/1.

Stiglitz, J. E. (2000). 'Capital Market Liberalization, Economic Growth and Instability'. *World Development*, 28/6.

——(2002). *Globalization and its Discontents*. New York: W. W. Norton & Company.

——Weiss, A. (1981). 'Credit Rationing in Markets with Imperfect Information'. *American Economic Review*, 71.

Taylor, L. (1998). 'Lax Public Sector and Destabilizing Private Sector: Origins of Capital Market Crises', in United Nations Conference on Trade and Development, *International Monetary and Financial Issues for 1990s*, Vol. 10. New York: United Nations.

Williamson, J. (1983). *The Open Economy and the World Economy*. New York: Basic Books.

5

Capital Market Liberalization and Poverty

Andrew Charlton[1]

5.1 Introduction

In developing countries, the poverty effects of macroeconomic reforms are determined by the impact of those policies on income growth and the extent to which any new prosperity is distributed progressively to the lowest income groups. A number of studies have investigated the effects of capital market liberalization on the growth of average incomes. In general, this literature establishes a compelling case for caution: capital market liberalization is not robustly associated with economic growth in developing countries, but it does appear to exacerbate macroeconomic volatility and increase the incidence of financial crises (Rodrik 1998; Singh 2002; Prasad et al. 2003).

To the extent that liberalization offers compensatory advantages, these lie in improved access to advanced credit markets and new opportunities to diversify risk and insure against volatility. However, not all sectors of the economy are equally equipped to take advantage of these benefits, and not all sectors are equally affected by increased volatility. In general, empirical evidence suggests that new opportunities accrue disproportionately to the rich, while the adverse effects of volatility impact disproportionately on the poor. For these reasons, it is not surprising that cross-country empirical studies link capital market liberalization with deterioration in various measures of inequality (Quinn 1997; Calderon and Chong 2001; Harrison 2002; Das and Mohapatra 2003; Jayadev 2004).

In this chapter, we review analytical studies and cross-country empirical evidence on the effects of capital market liberalization on the lives of the poor. We should be clear that this chapter focuses on the effects of liberalization

[1] Centre for Economic Performance, London School of Economics. The author would like to thank Andrew Glyn and Sujit Kapadia.

polices which facilitate short term capital flows. Other types of capital flows, such as foreign direct investment, may have different effects on economic growth and poverty.[2]

Orthodox capital market liberalization policies have been derived from the neoclassical theoretical framework. This paradigm does not take into account the idiosyncrasies of financial markets which distinguish capital market liberalization from other reforms that have been shown to be generally pro-poor, such as (carefully implemented) trade liberalization. The weaknesses of the orthodox paradigm are reflected in cross-country empirical studies which, contrary to neoclassical predictions, generally establish a negative relationship between the extent of capital market liberalization and various measures of inequality.

After reviewing this evidence, the remainder of the chapter is devoted to explaining this relationship by considering five channels through which liberalization may affect the distribution of income and poverty levels in developing countries. In each channel, we find that the overwhelming share of risks fall on the poor. One channel is the effect of capital market liberalization on macroeconomic volatility. The poor are particularly vulnerable to macroeconomic volatility because they have the least ability to cope with risk and the weakest access to insurance markets. Second, to the extent that capital market liberalization increases the incidence of crises (an extreme case of volatility), it has a substantial effect on poverty. The poor are the hardest hit by financial crises: their welfare losses are severe and persist long after the crisis abates. Third, there is considerable evidence that the increasing mobility of capital has weakened the bargaining position of poor laborers and may lead to a reduction in their share of total output. Fourth, international financial integration may reduce governments' autonomy over fiscal policy and can restrict the scope for progressive transfers, social protection, and anti-poverty programs. Finally, financial liberalization increases competition from foreign banks, potentially increasing financial efficiency, but also reducing credit availability to rural and poor sections of the economy.

5.2 The Empirical Relationship between Capital Market Liberalization, Inequality, and Poverty

While there is no conclusive evidence demonstrating that CML will benefit the poor through increased economic growth, there is evidence that CML worsens the income distribution and increases poverty.

Early research suggested that capital account openness is related to inequitable distributional outcomes. For a sample of 66 countries over the

---

[2] There is fairly strong evidence of the positive effects of FDI on economic growth. See Borensztein et al. (1998); De Mello (1999).

period 1960–89, Quinn (1997) reports a positive correlation between the change in his capital account openness indicator[3] and the GINI index. Quinn's results are statistically significant and robust across various specifications including controls for government expenditures and controls for international convergence of the GINI index over time. This relationship has been subsequently supported by further research. Das and Mohapatra (2003) analyze whether capital market reforms are associated with changes in inequality for 11 developing countries that undertook extensive economic reforms between 1986 and 1995. Rather than focusing on the GINI index, they attempt to investigate the dynamics of the income distribution, by observing the trend in the share of income owned by the jth quintile. Importantly, they control for global shocks and contemporaneously introduced stabilization policies.[4] Their results show that inequality increased following financial reform in almost all countries. The mean share of income held by the top quintile increased on average by 1.3 percent. They also found that the income share of the middle class is strongly negatively correlated with liberalization, and there is a mixed reaction for the lowest income group, whose income share rose in some countries and fell in others but generally fell relative to their control group of eight countries which did not experience liberalization. These results are consistent with Bekaert and Harvey (2000).

Calderon and Chong (2001) estimate a dynamic panel model to analyze the effects of various measures of international interdependence on income inequality using data for 97 countries over the period 1960–95. They find contrasting results for the effects of trade and financial openness. Whereas an increase in trade volumes reduces inequality, measured by the GINI index, they find a negative and significant relationship between the intensity of balance of payments controls, as expressed by distortions in the foreign exchange market, and income inequality.

Considerable research has documented a relationship between financial openness and the size of the labor share of output (Harrison 2002; Jayadev 2004). Diwan (2001) analyzes 67 financial crises and finds that the labor share of output falls sharply during the crisis and only partially recovers.[5]

Instead of examining the effect of financial liberalization on the poverty rate or through income variables, several researchers have turned to poverty proxies derived from other aspects of the life of the poor, including life expectancy, infant mortality, and the status of women. Not only are these

[3] Quinn's (1997) measure of capital account liberalization is the change in a constructed index of openness over the period. The openness index is based on the intensity of capital restrictions in seven areas.

[4] Henry (2000) shows that financial liberalization almost always occurs as part of broader macroeconomic regime change including reforms to exchange rate policies, trade liberalization, and privatization.

[5] We review the link between financial openness and the incidence of financial crises in a later section.

questions interesting in their own right, but they offer a number of advantages as an approach to poverty analysis. Arguably these variables provide a more direct link to welfare, and additionally their use avoids the multitude of problems associated with comparing income data across countries.[6]

Singh and Zammit (2000) examine the implications of capital flows for wages, employment, and the unpaid labor of women in developing countries. They argue that there are good reasons to believe that women are more disadvantaged by cyclical instability and economic depressions than are men. In developed countries, downturns usually throw more men out of work, but the opposite is true in developing countries where the gender structure of employment is different (Howes and Singh 1995). In addition women suffer from the knock-on effects of downturns including the effect of any reduction in social expenditure on the well-being of their family, and the introduction of charges for previously free public services. As a consequence, the volume of unpaid work done by women may increase (Ozler 1999). There have been a number of studies of the effects of the Asian financial crisis on women. Nathan and Kelkar (1999) identified a drastic drop in women's incomes in the informal sector; for example, in Indonesia, income in weaving declined by more than 75 percent during the crisis. Women also made up a majority of the migrant worker populations who were expelled from their host countries during the crisis.

Wei and Wu (2002) analyze the differential effects of financial and trade integration[7] on improvements in health, as measured by life expectancy and infant mortality. In a sample of 79 countries over the period 1962–97, they find that more trade openness is associated with longer life expectancy and lower infant mortality, after controlling for fixed effects, other macro and policy variables, and possible endogeneity of the openness variable. But they find that financial integration (measured as the ratio of total gross private inflows and outflows to GDP) is different. In their results, financial integration is associated with lower life expectancy and higher infant mortality, although both relationships are weak.

5.3 Channels of Causation

What explains this positive relationship between capital market liberalization and inequality and poverty? And why are the empirical results above so different to the predictions of the simplest theoretical models? From the Heckscher-Ohlin model we expect real openness to lead to an increase in the

---

[6] Avoiding potentially important problems associated with variation in data across countries and, in the case of income measures, purchasing power parity adjustments which may not be reliable.

[7] Wei and Wu's (2002) study analyzes trade integration rather than trade openness.

labor share of income in labor-abundant countries, and since the movement of commodities is a substitute for the movement of factors, we expect a similar result from financial openness. This implies that capital account openness should improve equity and *reduce* poverty. In this section we describe five channels through which capital market liberalization could affect income distribution and poverty in the context of these features.

5.3.1 Volatility and Poverty

Macroeconomic volatility is one channel through which financial liberalization increases both inequality and poverty. Theory suggests that international financial liberalization should facilitate international risk sharing (Obstfeld and Rogoff 1998), and thereby increase the scope for consumption smoothing, a key determinant of economic welfare. However the evidence leads strongly towards the conclusion that financial liberalization increases the volatility of consumption.[8] Kose, Prasad, and Terrones (2003) examine the macro volatility experienced by a large group of industrial and developing economies over the period 1960–99. They find that, on average, the volatility of consumption growth relative to that of income growth has increased for more financially integrated developing economies in the 1990s. Their results are robust using financial openness measures based on actual capital flows or indices measuring the extent of capital controls. They also report a threshold effect, where the adverse effects of increasing financial openness diminish for more developed countries. Prasad et al. (2003) report similar results from a comparison of the volatility experiences of a sample of 22 more financially integrated developing countries and 33 less financially integrated developing countries. They find that the most financially integrated have experienced an increase in consumption volatility over the 1990s while the less financially integrated group of developing countries and the industrialized countries both experienced average declines in consumption volatility relative to the previous decade. Prasad et al. conclude 'financial integration has not provided better consumption smoothing opportunities for these economies'.

How should this empirical relationship be interpreted? Stiglitz (2000) identifies three links between financial openness and volatility: the pro-cyclical nature of capital flows, the sensitivity of international markets to changes in information, and the systemic risk through contagion from one economy

---

[8] Evidence on the effect of financial liberalization on the volatility of output is more mixed, but fluctuations in output are less important for poverty than consumption. Razin and Rose (1994) find that financial openness has no effect on the volatility of output in their sample of 138 countries. Similarly Easterly et al. (2001) found neither the volatility of capital flows nor measures of financial openness had a significant impact on output volatility. O'Donnell (2001) finds that financial integration reduces output volatility in rich countries but increases it in poor countries.

to another. On the first link, there is considerable evidence that capital inflows are positively correlated with domestic business cycle conditions (see Kaminsky and Reinhart 2002; Reinhart 2002), i.e., flows are pro-cyclical, supporting the popular cynicism that bankers only lend money to people who don't need it. On the second link, international financial liberalization increases the liquidity to which domestic borrowers have access and thereby amplify the effects of changes in international market sentiment. When market sentiment is high, capital market liberalization permits inflows of speculative capital which, in the East Asian case, were often associated with booms in real estate and construction. When market sentiment changes, inflows may be subject to 'sudden stops' as bankers pull their money out of the economy (see Calvo and Reinhart 1999).[9] East Asia experienced a dramatic $109 billion reversal in net capital flows (more than 10 percent of GDP in the region) between 1996 and 1997. As capital flows out, banks are deprived of lending resources, forcing a credit contraction; exchange rates also fall, leading to increases in the value of dollar denominated debt.

Increased volatility induced by openness is almost certainly part of the reason why financial market liberalization does not appear to be correlated with growth in cross-country studies,[10] and it is also a smoking gun for investigations into the poverty effects of financial openness. Volatility has profound and persistent effects on the poor. Crises hurt both the poor and the rich, but the poor have the fewest resources and insurance mechanisms to respond. Empirical evidence shows that economic cycles have an asymmetric effect on poverty in the sense that contractions increase poverty more than similarly sized expansions (Morely 1994; Londono and Szekely 1997). In an analysis of inequality in Latin America between 1970 and 1994, De Janvry and Sadoulet (1998) found that, on average, one year of recession had six times the (negative) impact on inequality that one year of growth was able to achieve. This may be because the poorest and least skilled workers also have the least secure employment, leading economic fluctuations to disproportionately harm the poor (Agenor 1998). Thus volatility may have an effect on poverty, independent of its effect on growth. In Mexico from 1984 to 1994 the poverty headcount rose from 28 to 34 percent of the population, much of this increase (86 percent) was due to the increase in inequality rather than falling GDP per capita (World Bank 2001). Hausmann and Gavin (1995) highlight the

---

[9] The causes of changes in market sentiment are difficult to identify ex ante. In Thailand the speculative inflows led to a real estate bubble, and when that bubble broke so did expectations of high returns. What seemed to be a change in market feeling about the risks of emerging markets hit Latin America in 1998.

[10] One plausible explanation is that irreversibilities or asymmetric costs associated with investment increase uncertainty (see Pindyck 1991). For further theoretical discussion of the relationship between growth and volatility in developing countries see Turnovsky and Chattopadhyay (1998). For an analysis of the effect of volatility on Africa, see Guillaumont et al. (1999) and for Latin America, see Hausmann and Gavin (1995).

importance of macroeconomic volatility in explaining the weak economic performance of Latin America relative to East Asia. In particular, they find that a higher standard deviation of real GDP is associated with higher poverty, after controlling for other factors.

The asymmetric response of poverty to GDP levels is partly due to the effects of crises and recessions on the investment choices of the poor. Shocks may have long term effects on poverty through their impact on health, schooling, physical investment, and nutrition. For example, evidence from Indonesia suggest that the East Asian crisis led to a 5 percent decline in secondary enrollment rates and a sharp drop in household expenditure on health services (Frankenberg et al. 1999). Through these mechanisms, negative shocks may have a chronic impact on poverty long after average incomes recover.

The effect of volatility on the poor has another dimension beyond income levels. Traditional poverty measures neglect several important dimensions of household welfare, perhaps most importantly the effects of risk on household welfare. Ligon and Schechter (2003) decompose the welfare of the poor into a contribution from poverty and a contribution from various sources of uncertainty. Using household data from Bulgaria, they find that risk plays a large role in reducing the welfare of the poor.

5.3.2 *Financial Crises, Poverty, and Liberalization*

In 1998, the number of people living in poverty in the four countries hardest hit by the Asian crisis increased by more than 60 percent. In that year approximately 20 million people in those countries fell into poverty.[11] Smaller but nonetheless significant increases in poverty were experienced in Latin America (World Bank 1998; Lustig 1999). If capital market liberalization significantly increases the risk of crises, these experiences provide a powerful rationale for maintaining controls in some form.

The link between capital account liberalization and the incidence of crises has not been uncontroversial. Crises have occurred in countries with both closed and open capital accounts, but, although it is too strong to claim a direct causal link, there is evidence (and good reasons) to believe that liberalization increases the incidence of crises.[12] Eichengreen and Wyplosz (1993) argue that the relaxation of capital controls in Europe exposed governments to speculative pressures and reduced their ability to deal with the 1992 crisis.

---

[11] World Bank (1998) estimates of the increase in poverty in Indonesia (17 million), Thailand (2.3 million), the Philippines (665,000), and Malaysia (500,000). The estimates use the US$1 a day poverty line for Indonesia and the Philippines and US$2 a day for Malaysia and Thailand. Total poverty in these countries almost doubled from approximately 30 million to 50 million.

[12] See Williamson and Mahar (1998) for a survey.

Furman and Stiglitz (1998) find that capital account liberalization in East Asia exacerbated moral hazard problems associated with government guarantees and led to structural instability in the banking system. By contrast, China's stunning resilience during the East Asian crisis may be partly explained by its controls on outflows of yuan and the absence of an onshore futures market, both of which limited the impact of speculation on the currency (Fernald and Babson 1999; Eichengreen 2001).

There are a small number of cross-country studies on this issue. They face the twin problems of nailing down a definition of currency crisis and dealing with reverse causality. In particular, if crisis risk causes governments to change their capital account policies, it will be difficult to identify a direction of causality in cross-country data. Using data for 90 countries over the period 1975–97, Glick and Huchinson (2000) find that the presence of capital controls in one year is *positively* correlated with the occurrence of a crisis in the next. Their interpretation is that controls send a bad signal to the market, inciting investors to become suspicious of the government's macroeconomic policies. An alternative but related interpretation is that the results haven't identified the direction of causality. For example Malaysia's efforts to tighten controls during the crisis were a consequence of instability rather than a cause of it. Other cross-country studies have found evidence that financial liberalization increases the vulnerability of countries to crises. Kaminsky and Reinhart (1998) find that 'in 18 out of 26 banking crises studied ... the financial sector had been liberalized during the preceding five years'. In a panel of 53 countries Demirgüç-Kunt and Detragiache (1998) find that banking crises are more likely to occur in liberalized financial systems. However, they also note that the effect of financial liberalization on the fragility of the banking sector is weaker when the institutional environment is strong. Case study evidence from several countries, beginning with the careful analysis of Chile's 1982 crisis by Diaz Alejandro (1985) presents more detailed analysis which has generally supported the role of financial liberalization in increasing exposure to risk of crises.[13]

Where does this evidence leave us in relation to the impact of financial market liberalization on poverty through the incidence of crises? It is perhaps not clear which of financial contagion (facilitated by international financial liberalization) or weak macroeconomic fundamentals should bear the primary blame for causing crises. Most of the detailed evidence suggests that exposure to large foreign capital flows plays an important role. But for the analysis of poverty there is perhaps a more important issue. Whatever the role played by financial market liberalization in causing crises, there is clear evidence that it exacerbates their effect on the poor. Financial openness increases the

---

[13] For other national and regional studies see, for example, Steigum (1992); Kiander and Vartia (1996); Furman and Stiglitz (1998).

incidence of crises on the lives of the poor and simultaneously reduces the scope for government safety nets to protect them.

Independent of the issue of whether financial openness causes crises, there has been considerable debate about whether countries in crisis suffer more with open financial regimes. Certainly, the orthodox prescription for dealing with crises are particularly harsh for the poor. In response to the East Asian crisis Thailand, South Korea, and Indonesia embarked on IMF-supported programs to cope. They committed to floating their exchange rates, opening financial markets to foreigners, tightening fiscal policy (at least initially), dramatically lifting interest rates, closing insolvent banks, as well as other structural reforms. These policies had disproportionately adverse effects on the poor. High interest rates (proscribed to protect the currency) had a debilitating effect on net borrowers and many small businesses (in Thailand small businesses were going bankrupt at the rate of almost 1000 per month, see Chomthongdi 2000) leading to lower wages and increased unemployment. In addition, falling exchange rates increased the price of imported food and other products, lifting costs for poor households that are net consumers of food.

5.3.3 *Capital Mobility and Bargaining Power*

Financial openness might affect inequality and poverty by altering the relative bargaining power of labor and capital and thereby changing the labor share of GDP (Glyn 1995; Rodrik 1997). Rodrik (1997) argues that the increasing mobility of capital might be increasing its bargaining power over labor.[14] Supporting this thesis, Slaughter (2001) documents a rise in the elasticity of labor demand in many countries, which seems to be correlated with, among other things, measures of openness.

In an imperfectly competitive theoretical framework, Harrison (2002) determines the division of excess profits between capital and labor as the outcome of bargaining process between them. In her model, bargaining strength is a function of the fixed costs of relocating and the alternative return available elsewhere. Applying the model to data for more than 100 countries over 40 years, Harrison finds that rising trade openness and exchange rate crises reduce labor's share of output, while capital controls and government spending increase labor's share. Jayadev (2004) estimates the effect of financial liberalization on the labor share of output using a constructed index of capital account restrictions for up to 140 countries over the period 1972–96. This enables panel estimation of the effect of liberalization controlling for macroeconomic trends and changes in endowments. Jayadev finds that capital account openness exerts a robust and significant negative effect on the labor

---

[14] Similar arguments have been made by Freeman (1995), Slaughter (1998), and Budd and Slaughter (2000).

share of income. The effect is robust across subsets of developing and developed countries, contrary to the predictions of the Heckscher-Ohlin theory. Jayadev finds that labor's losses are not temporary, but persist through the medium term.

5.3.4 Anti-poverty Policies and Market Disciplines

Capital account liberalization may constrain domestic policies to alleviate poverty. In particular, the government may lose some autonomy over fiscal policy and to the extent that this leads to a reduction in transfers, social programs, or public investment, the poor may be adversely affected. The openness constraint on fiscal policy is an application of the 'impossible trinity'; where a country cannot simultaneously maintain autonomous macro policy with an open capital account and a fixed exchange rate. Increased exposure to short-term capital flows may affect the fiscal balance in several ways. The primary effect works through the government bond market: in particular the ability to maintain or increase the planned public sector borrowing requirement at reasonable rates of interest (FitzGerald 2001). Second, the budget balance will be affected by fluctuations in the costs of servicing external debt caused by changes in the exchange rate. Capital inflows causing appreciation improve the budget balance; capital outflows reduce it. As well as suffering a potential loss due to reduced government expenditure, Rodrik (1997) argues that the increasing mobility of capital may shift a greater share of the tax burden onto labor.

This implies that one way that capital market liberalization may lead to lower government expenditure is through a reduction in the scope for debt-financed deficits. There is some empirical evidence of the effect of openness on the size of government expenditure. Garrett and Mitchell (2001) find that international financial openness is negatively correlated with total government spending in 18 OECD countries. However, importantly for poverty, they did not find that capital mobility had a deleterious effect on the welfare state: openness was not significantly related to social security transfers. Jayadev (2004) reports some evidence that capital account openness reduces budget deficits, but this was only true for developing countries. Garrett (1995) provides a potential explanation. He finds some evidence that countries with fewer capital controls have proportionately smaller government expenditure and smaller budget deficits, but determines that the relationship is conditional on the bargaining power of labor. This might explain the absence of a relationship between openness and reduced expenditure in OECD countries. Quinn (1997), in a sample of 64 countries finds no evidence that capital account liberalization reduces government expenditures. All these studies should be interpreted with caution since the effects of openness are difficult to separate from the effects of other reforms which may have been implemented at the same time. Case study evidence indicates that changes to capital account regimes are often introduced contemporaneously with other macroeconomic polices from which it is difficult to isolate the effects. In any case, even if financial openness results in only a small reduction in social spending, this may have a large effect on the poor, for whom transfers represent an important part of their incomes.

Externally imposed fiscal discipline may have long-term effects on the poor if it leads developing countries to reduce their investment in infrastructure. Biggs (1998) finds that fiscal contractions in developing countries usually comprise larger reductions in investment spending than in social spending. FitzGerald (2001) argues that developing countries will find it politically easier to postpone promised investment programs rather than cut recurrent spending by, for example, laying off teachers and nurses. However the consequences of fluctuations in public investment may have large negative effects on the poor who rely on public services such as transport, education, health, and development programs.

As well as experiencing a decline in social spending and public investment, financial openness may increase the share of the tax burden borne by labor. International financial liberalization may enable firms to shift taxable income between jurisdictions, leading to a reduction in tax revenue for many countries. As the elasticity of capital supply increases, countries may respond by reducing the rate of capital taxation. However, the evidence for a link between financial openness and corporate taxation rates is quite weak (see Garrett 1995; Quinn 1997; Garrett and Mitchell 2000). Eichengreen (2001) points out that part of the empirical confusion may be explained by the fact that most countries with open capital accounts are relatively high income, with large public sectors and large tax rates.

Management of volatile capital flows through sterilized intervention in foreign exchange markets may impose additional constraints on government expenditure. In response to large capital inflows, governments often simultaneously sell domestic currency and government bonds. The first softens any exchange rate appreciation caused by capital inflows, while the second neutralizes its inflationary effect. These prudential management policies are associated with potentially significant costs if the government faces an interest rate premium on the foreign currency it borrows and holds as an asset. In addition, there is an opportunity cost of foregone expenditure. An increase in reserves is a government investment that could otherwise have been made in infrastructure, education, or health.

The disciplining effect of market forces on national policies is often advanced by proponents of capital market liberalization as a positive force, since countries that fail to pursue 'good' policies are quickly punished. As Stanley Fischer, former First Deputy Managing Director of the International Monetary Fund, said in 1997, capital markets serve as an important discipline on government macroeconomic policies 'which improves overall economic performance by rewarding good policies and penalising bad'. But underlying this belief is a fundamentally undemocratic ethic which would transfer authority from national democratic processes toward foreign financial interests. Market discipline may also be inefficient if capital market behavior is subject to certain biases: for example, fund managers may take a myopic view of government expenditures and fail to sufficiently differentiate between deficits which fund long-term investments and those which fund consumption. In addition, international financial interests can be an erratic and arbitrary source of discipline. Eichengreen (2001) points out that international investors are prone to overlook domestic policy weaknesses until they are abruptly brought to their attention, at which point markets overreact. As Calvo and Mendoza (1996) suggest, the punishment may be greater than the crime if creditors' reactions cause a financial crisis.

5.3.5 Access to Credit

Capital market liberalization facilitates the entry of foreign banks into the domestic market, as well as increasing the scope for domestic banks to engage in international transactions. Such reforms may alter the allocation of credit to different sectors in the economy and impact on poverty. Theory predicts that when allowed to freely compete, banks will become more efficient and support more profitable projects, leading to greater economy-wide efficiency (Fry 1988). There is considerable evidence to suggest that increasing financial depth leads to income growth (King and Levine 1993), and there is also evidence that improving access of the poor to financial services, particularly to credit and insurance against risk, strengthens the capacity of the poor to accumulate productive assets and maintain sustainable livelihoods (World Bank 2001). But this evidence coexists with doubts about whether capital market liberalization actually promotes financial depth for the poor as well as for the rich, i.e., whether it increases the distribution of credit or mainly increases access for the rich. Greenwood and Jovanovic (1990) argue that financial sector reform tends to exclude the poor from its benefits because they are unable to pay upfront set-up and access charges. Consequently financial liberalization leads to further inequality.

Information problems are also an important limitation on credit distribution. The cost of obtaining information about the profitability of potential projects is often a key determinant of lending decisions (Rothschild and Stiglitz 1976). Stiglitz and Weiss (1981) show that where these information costs are high, credit may be withheld from potentially viable projects. While foreign banks may bring increased competition and efficiency to the domestic banking system of developing countries, they may have less local knowledge (and hence higher information costs in the domestic sector), which could cause them to shift the allocation of credit away from the poor.

The empirical evidence generally supports this conclusion. In a cross-country study, Klein and Olivei (1999) find that financial openness increases the ratio of liquid liabilities to GDP, suggesting that controls limit financial depth. However, this result is limited to advanced industrial countries and breaks down when poor countries are considered, and, as we will see below, there is reason to believe that the relationship is even weaker when considering credit availability to the poor within developing countries.[15]

The empirical evidence from more detailed country-level studies suggests that following capital market liberalization there is an expansion of credit to medium and large businesses, the foreign sector, and urban areas, but no effect (or even a contraction) to small enterprises and rural areas.[16] Brownbridge and Gayi (1999) found evidence of credit expansion and financial innovation in the financial sector reform experiences of eight low income countries. In each country, there was a growth in the number of foreign banks and increased competition precipitated several identifiable improvements in service. Some of the new entrants introduced longer banking hours, expanded credit and debit card services, increased the speed of check clearing and introduced automated teller machines. Financial depth—measured as the ratio of bank deposits and M2 to GDP—increased in three LDCs but declined in four after reform. The authors attribute the difference to the complementary effects of macroeconomic stability in the three countries experiencing financial deepening (all of which were in Asia) and the higher and more volatile inflation experiences of the other five countries (all of which were in Sub-Saharan Africa).

Brownbridge and Gayi (1999) found that rural areas were likely to suffer a deterioration in the availability of financial services in the period following financial liberalization. The new foreign banks typically avoided rural areas and serviced mainly large and/or foreign corporate customers. The elimination of special lending and financing schemes and the closure of rural branches led to a reduction in credit to agriculture and small farmers. In particular, the share of agriculture in bank lending fell sharply in Malawi and Bangladesh in the wake of financial sector reforms.

Mosely (1999) analyzes the availability of credit during the period of financial reform in four African countries: Uganda, Kenya, Malawi, and Lesotho. The study concludes that credit availability to the poor increased only in

[15] Levine and Zervos (1998) find that capital account openness leads to growth and increased liquidity in stock markets in developing countries. However stock market liquidity is not likely to directly benefit the poor in these countries.

[16] These results have been confirmed in a number of analyzes of the financial sectors reforms of developing and transition countries. Several studies find that levels of savings and investment have not increased (Gibson and Tsakolotos 1992) and access to bank credit has not improved (Nissanke 1990 and Kariuki 1995, for Africa; Mosley 1996, for eastern Europe; Cho and Khatkhate 1989, for Asia).

Kenya and Uganda and that this was mainly accounted for by large increases in NGO lending in these countries. Where NGO lending did not increase, credit access to the poorest 10 percent of the population actually declined over the period. Financial liberalization had similarly mixed consequences in Cambodia where liberalization proceeded rapidly after 1992. UNDP (2004) reports that reduced government intervention and increased competition among new commercial banks have brought benefits to the dollarized urban economy but have delivered little to the 90 percent of the population living in rural areas. Bank branches are concentrated in large population centers and 48 percent of the population live in provinces with no bank branches at all.

5.4 Conclusion

The determination of the net effects of macroeconomic liberalization programs usually involves weighing the gains to average incomes against the costs to vulnerable groups who will be disadvantaged. The challenge for policymakers is to select a program of reform that appropriately balances risks and returns. For capital market liberalization in developing countries, the returns have been difficult to identify: there is no convincing empirical evidence linking open capital markets to economic growth. There is, however, considerable evidence of increased risk. Capital market liberalization increases consumption volatility and heightens countries' vulnerability to crises.

Our analysis of five channels of causation suggests that the poor receive a small share of the gains from capital market liberalization and a large share of the risks. The poor are least equipped to cope with increased volatility, and they are most affected by financial crises. Capital mobility reduces workers' bargaining power relative to capital and leads to a decline in the labor share of output. Financial openness delivers the poor few benefits in terms of increased access to credit and other financial services, and it constrains governments' redistributive efforts and anti-poverty fiscal policies. While it is difficult to establish a conclusive direct link between capital market liberalization and increased rates of poverty, the evidence presented above suggests a compelling case that capital market liberalization is bad for the poor in developing countries.

References

Agénor, P.-R. (1998). 'Stabilization Policies, Poverty and the Labor Market: Analytical Issues and Empirical Evidence'. Washington, DC: EDI, World Bank (December).

Ariyoshi, A., Habermeier, K., Laurens, B., Ötker-Robe, I., Canales-Kriljenko, J. I., and Kirilenko, A. (2000). 'Capital Controls: Country Experiences with Their Use and Liberalization'. IMF Occasional Paper No. 190 (May 17).

Bekaert, G. and Harvey, C. R. (2000). 'Capital Flows and the Behavior of Emerging Market Equity Returns', in S. Edwards (ed.), *Capital Flows and the Emerging Economies: Theory, Evidence and Controversies*. Washington, DC: National Bureau of Economic Research, pp. 159–94.

Biggs, M. (1998). 'Deficits and Economic Growth: Lessons from Developing Countries,' in I. Abedian and M. Biggs (eds.), *Economic Globalization and Fiscal Policy*. Oxford: Oxford University Press.

Borensztein, E. and Gaston Gelos, R. (2002). 'A Panic-Prone Pack? The Behavior of Emerging Market Funds'. IMF Working Paper 00/198. Washington, DC: International Monetary Fund.

—— and De Gregorio, J., and Lee, J.-W. (1998), 'How Does Foreign Direct Investment Affect Growth?'. *Journal of International Economics*, 45: 115–35.

Brownbridge, M. and Gayi, S. (1999). 'Progress, Constraints and Limitations of Financial Sector Reforms in the Least Developed Countries'. Finance and Development Research Programme Working Paper Series, Paper No. 7, University of Manchester, IDPM.

Budd, J. W. and Slaughter, M. J. (2000). 'Are Profits Shared Across Borders? Evidence on International Rent Sharing.' National Bureau of Economic Research Working Paper, No. 8014.

Calvo, G. and Mendoza, E. (1996). 'Petty Crime and Cruel Punishment: Lessons from the Mexican Debacle'. American Economic Review Papers and Proceedings, 96: 170–5.

—— and Reinhart, C. M. (1999). 'Capital Flow Reversals, the Exchange Rate Debate, and Dollarization'. *Finance and Development*, September, 36: 13–15.

Cho, Y.-J. and Khatkhate, D. (1989). 'Lessons of Financial Liberalization in Asia: a Comparative Study'. World Bank Discussion Papers, No. 50.

Chomthongdi, J. (2000). 'The IMF's Asian Legacy'. Focus on the Global South. Mimeo.

De Janvry, A. and Sadoulet, E. (1998). 'Growth, Poverty and Inequality in Latin America: a Causal Analysis, 1970–94'. Univeristy of California at Berkeley (September). (Presented at the Inter-American Development Bank Conference on Social Protection and Poverty, February 1999.)

De Mello, L. (1999). 'Foreign Direct Investment-Led Growth: Evidence from Time Series and Panel Date'. *Oxford Economic Papers*, January, 51/1: 133–51.

Demirguç-Kunt, A. and Detragiache, E. (1998). 'Financial Liberalization and Financial Fragility'. Working Paper WP/98/83. Washington, DC: International Monetary Fund.

Diaz-Alejandro, C. F. (1985). 'Good-Bye Financial Repression, Hello Financial Crash.' *Journal of Development Economics*, 19.

Diwan, I. (2001). 'Debt As Sweat: Labor Financial Crisis and The Globalization of Capital'. World Bank. Mimeo.

Easterly, W., Islam, R., and Stiglitz, J. E. (2001). 'Shaken and Stirred: Explaining Growth Volatility', in B. Pleskovic and N. Stern. (eds), *Annual World Bank Conference Volume on Development Economics*. Washington, DC: The World Bank.

Eichengreen, B. (2001). 'Capital Account Liberalization: What Do the Cross-Country Studies Tell Us?' *The World Bank Economic Review*. 15/3: 341–65.

—— and Wyplosz, C. (1993). 'The Unstable EMS'. Brookings Papers on Economic Activity, 1, The Brookings Institution, Washington, DC.

Fernald, J. G. and Babson, O. D. (1999). 'Why has China Survived the Asian Crisis so Well? What Risks Remain?' International Finance Discussion Papers, No. 633 (February), Board of Governors of the Federal Reserve System.

Fischer, S. (1997). 'Capital Account Liberalization and the Role of the IMF'. Paper presented at the seminar 'Asia and the IMF', held in Hong Kong, China, on September 19, 1997.

FitzGerald, E. V. K. (2001). 'Short-Term Capital Flows, The Real Economy And Income Distribution In Developing Countries'. QEH Working Paper Series, No. 8, QEHWPS08.

Frankenberg, E., Thomas, D., and Beegle, K. (1999). 'The Real Costs of Indonesia's Economic Crisis: Preliminary Findings from the Indonesia Family Life Surveys'. Labor and Population Program Working Paper Series 99–04, March, Rand, Santa Monica, CA.

Freeman, R. B. (1995). 'Are Your Wages Set in Beijing?' Journal of Economic Perspectives, 9/3: 15–32.

Fry, M. (1988). Money, Interest and Banking in Economic Development. Baltimore, MD: Johns Hopkins University Press.

Garrett, G. (1995). 'Capital Mobility, Trade, and the Domestic Politics of Economic Policy'. International Organization, 49/4: 657–87.

_____ and Mitchell, D. (2001). 'Globalization, Government Spending, and Taxation in the OECD'. European Journal of Political Research, 39: 145–77.

Gibson, H. and Tsokolotos, E. (1994). 'The Scope and Limits of Financial Liberalization in Developing Countries: A Critical Survey'. Journal of Development Studies, 30: 562–78.

Glick, R. and Hutchinson, M. (2000). 'Stopping "Hot Money" or Signaling Bad Policy? Capital Controls and the Onset of Currency Crises'. Unpublished Manuscript. Federal Reserve Bank of San Francisco and UC Santa Cruz.

Glyn, A. (1995). 'Social Democracy and Full Employment'. New Left Review, 211: 33–55.

Greenwald, B. and Stiglitz, J. E. (1986). 'Externalities in Economies with Imperfect Information and Incomplete Markets'. Quarterly Journal of Economics, May, 229–64.

Greenwood, J. and Jovanovic, B. (1990). 'Financial Development, Growth, and the Distribution of Income'. The Journal of Political Economy, 98/5: 1076–107.

Guillaumont, P., Guillaumont Jeanneney, S., and Brun, J.-F. (1999). 'How Instability Lowers African Growth'. Journal of African Economies, 8/1: 87–107.

Hausmann, R. and Gavin, M. (1995). 'Overcoming Volatility in Latin America'. International Monetary Fund Seminar Series (International), No. 1995-34: 1–86 (August).

Jayadev, A. and Lee, K. K. (2004). 'The Effects of Capital Account Liberalization on Growth and Labor Share of Income: Reviewing and Extending the Cross-Country Evidence,' in G. Epstein (ed.), Capital Flight and Capital Controls in Developing Contries. Northhampton, MA: Edward Elgar.

Jomo, K. S. (2001). 'Capital Controls', in K. S. Jomo (ed.), Malaysian Eclipse: Economic Crisis and Recovery. London and New York: Zed Books.

Kaminsky, G. and Reinhart, C. M. (1998). 'The Twin Crises: The Causes of Banking and Balance of Payments Problems'. Board of Governors, Federal Reserve System. Mimeo.

____ ____ and (2002). 'The Center and Periphery: The Globalization of Financial Turmoil'. *NBER Working* Paper W9479.

Kariuki, P. W. (1995). 'The Effects of Liberalization on Access to Bank Credit in Kenya'. *Small Enterprise Development*, March, 6/1: 15–23.

Kiander, J. and Vartia, P. (1996). 'The Great Depression of the 1990s in Finland'. Finnish Economic Papers, 9: 72–88.

King, R. G. and Levine, R. (1993). 'Finance, Entrepreneurship, and Growth: Theory and Evidence'. *Journal of Monetary Economics*, 32: 513–42.

Klein, M. and Olivei, G. (1999). 'Capital Account Liberalization, Financial Depth and Economic Growth'. NBER working paper 7384.

Kose, M. A., Prasad, E. S., and Terrones, M. E. (2003). 'Financial Integration and Macroeconomic Volatility'. Staff Papers, International Monetary Fund.

Levine, R. and Zervos, S. (1998). 'Capital Control Liberalization and Stock Market Development'. *World Development*, 26/7: 1169–83.

Ligon, E. and Schechter, L. (2003). 'Measuring Vulnerability'. *The Economic Journal*, 113(486).

Londoño, J. L. and Székely, M. (1997). 'Distributional Surprises After a Decade of Reforms: Latin America in the Nineties'. Working Paper 352. (August) Office of the Chief Economist. Washington, DC: Inter-American Development Bank.

Lustig, N. (1999). 'Crises and the Poor: Socially Responsible Macroeconomics'. Inter-American Development Bank, Washington, DC. Mimeo.

Morley, S. (1994). *Poverty and Inequality in Latin America: Past Evidence, Future Prospects.* Washington, DC: Overseas Development Committee.

Mosley, P. (1996). 'Financial Reform in Transitional Economies: A Preliminary Assessment of Impact.' Paper presented to conference on Economic Reform in the Post Soviet World (November).

____ (1999). 'Micro–Macro Linkages in Financial Markets: The Impact of Financial Liberalization on Access to Rural Credit in Four African Countries'. Finance and Development Research Programme Working Paper Series, Paper No. 4 (March), Institute for Development Policy and Management (IDPM), Manchester.

O'Donnell, B. (2001). 'Financial Openness and Economic Performance'. Trinity College Dublin. Mimeo.

Pindyck, R. S. (1991). 'Irreversibility, Uncertainty and Investment.' *Journal of Economic Literature*, September 29(3): 1110–48.

Prasad, E., Rogoff, K., Wei, S.-J., and Kose, M. A. (2003). 'Effects of Financial Globalization on Developing Countries: Some Empirical Evidence'. International Monetary Fund.

Razin, A. and Rose, A. K. (1994). 'Business-Cycle Volatility and Openness: An Exploratory Cross-Sectional Analysis', in L. Leiderman and A. Razin (eds.), *Capital Mobility: The Impact on Consumption, Investment, and Growth*. Cambridge: Cambridge University Press, pp. 48–76.

Reinhart, C. M. (2002). 'Credit Ratings, Default and Financial Crises: Evidence from Emerging Markets'. *World Bank Economic Review*, 16/2: 151–70.

Rodrik, D. (1997). 'Has Globalization Gone Too Far?', Washington, DC: Institute for International Economics.

____ (1998). 'Who Needs Capital Account Convertibility?', *Princeton Essays in International Finance*, 207: 55–65.

Rothschild, M. and Stiglitz, J. E. (1976). 'Equilibrium in Competitive Insurance Markets: An Essay in the Economics of Imperfect Information'. *Quarterly Journal of Economics*, 86: 629–49.

Singh, A. (2002). 'Capital Account Liberalization, Free Long-term Capital Flows, Financial Crises and Economic Development'. ESRC Centre for Business Research—Working Papers, No. 245.

Slaughter, M. (1999). 'Globalisation and Wages'. *The World Economy*, 22: 609–30.

―― (2001). 'International Trade and Labor-Demand Elasticities'. *Journal of International Economics*, June 54/1: 27–56.

Steigum, E. (1992). 'Financial Deregulation, Credit Boom and Banking Crisis: The Case of Norway'. Norwegian School of Economics and Business Administration Discussion Paper 15/92.

Stiglitz, J. E. (1994). 'The Role of the State in Financial Markets', in *Proceedings of the World Bank Annual Conference on Development Economics 1993*, Washington, DC: The World Bank, 19–52.

―― (2000). 'Capital Market Liberalization, Economic Growth, and Instability'. *World Development*, 28/6: 1075–86.

―― and Weiss, A. (1981). 'Credit Rationing in Markets with Imperfect Information'. *American Economic Review*, 71: 393–410.

Turnovsky, S. and Chattopadhyay, P. (1998). 'Volatility and Growth in Developing Economies: Some Numerical Results and Empirical Evidence'. Discussion Paper in Economics, Department of Economics, University of Washington.

UNDP (2004). 'The Macroeconomics of Poverty Reduction in Cambodia'. *Asia-Pacific Regional Programme on the Macroeconomics of Poverty Reduction*. New York: UNDP.

Williamson, J. and Mahar, M. (1998). 'A Survey of Financial Liberalization'. *Princeton Essays in International Finance*, November 211.

World Bank, (1998). *Global Economic Prospects*. New York: Oxford University Press.

―― (2001). *World Development Report*. New York: Oxford University Press.

6

Capital Management Techniques in Developing Countries: Managing Capital Flows in Malaysia, India, and China

Gerald Epstein, Ilene Grabel, and K. S. Jomo[1]

6.1 Introduction

The external macroeconomic and normative environment facing developing countries in the last several decades has been decidedly neoliberal as well as challenging. Aspects include:

- norms of domestic and international financial liberalization;
- increasingly unstable international capital mobility;
- a focus on export-led growth in an increasingly competitive environment;
- intense competition to attract foreign direct investment (FDI);
- privatization and a focus on private (as opposed to public) investment; and

[1] This chapter is a revised version of a paper that was presented at the XVIth Technical Group Meeting (TGM) of the G-24 in Port of Spain, Trinidad, and Tobago, February 13–14 2003. Gerald Epstein is Professor of Economics and Co-Director of the Political Economy Research Institute (PERI) at the University of Massachusetts, Amherst. Ilene Grabel is Professor of International Finance at the Graduate School of International Studies, University of Denver. K. S. Jomo was then Professor of Economics, University of Malaya. Epstein acknowledges the financial support of the Ford and Rockefeller Foundations. In addition, we thank Arjun Jayadev and Peter Zawadzki for excellent research assistance, and Jayadev for his contributions to the India case study. We are grateful to Robert McCauley and Dani Rodrik for their help at the early stages of this project, and to José Antonio Ocampo for advice. We are also grateful to the participants at the TGM for helpful comments, especially Ariel Buira, Aziz Ali Mohammed, Esteban Pérez, and Benu Schneider.

- monetary policy oriented toward achieving low inflation (inflation targeting) (Taylor and Pieper 1998).

Policymaking dilemmas abound in such an environment. Economists are fond of discussing the so-called impossible trinity of independent monetary policy, fixed exchange rates, and free capital mobility. Yet the experiences of developing countries over the last several decades suggest some trade-offs that are much more troublesome both for the neoliberal policy prescription and for policymakers. In particular, it is increasingly evident that inflation targeting, free capital mobility, financial liberalization, and export-led growth are inherently contradictory policy options. To state the issue starkly: the problems created by free capital mobility are at the very heart of these contradictions.

A few examples illustrate the problem. Inflation targeting with free capital mobility has led to excessive capital inflows, over-valued exchange rates and a shifting of resources from traded to non-traded sectors, harming the prospects for export-led growth, while encouraging financial fragility. At other times or in other places, capital mobility, inflation targeting and a hands-off attitude toward the exchange rate have led to speculative attacks and a depreciating exchange rate. Those impacts, in turn, lead to inflationary pressures and confusion about the proper role for monetary policy. Free capital mobility has led to currency mismatches on balance sheets of banks and non-financial corporations and unsustainable asset bubbles, leading, in turn, to bankruptcies and the need for bail-outs of liberalized financial institutions (Taylor 2002; Chapter 7, this volume).

In short, open capital markets in combination with other neoliberal prescriptions have undermined some key policy tenets of the Washington consensus, and more importantly, led to serious economic problems for a number of developing countries.

The financial crises of the 1990s—including those in Mexico, Turkey, Asia, and Russia—brought many of these problems center stage. In response there has been a renewed interest in the role of capital controls in developing countries within both policy and academic circles. Even strong proponents of capital account liberalization have acknowledged that many countries that avoided the worst effects of financial crises were also those that used capital controls, including the three countries we study here: Malaysia, India, and China. Consequently, prominent mainstream economists and even the IMF have relaxed their insistence that immediate capital account liberalization is the best policy for all countries in all circumstances (IMF 2000; Fischer 2002; Eichengreen 2002a).[2] Adding momentum to the discussion over the last several years, a number of highly respected economists have actively argued

---

[2] Of course, doctrinaire hold-outs on capital account liberalization still exist. For instance, some members of the US Treasury took this stance in recent negotiations with Chile and Singapore over free trade agreements.

in favor of capital controls (e.g., Bhagwati 1998; Krugman 1998; Rodrik 1998; Stiglitz 2002).

Despite this apparent increase in the tolerance for capital controls, most mainstream academic and policy economists remain skeptical about the viability and desirability of controls, at least in two specific senses. Increased tolerance for capital controls applies, if at all, only to controls on inflows, not to controls on outflows. Moreover, controls on inflows are generally seen as a temporary evil, useful only until all of the institutional prerequisites for full financial and capital account liberalization are in place.

In this chapter we present case studies of three countries—China, India, and Malaysia—that counter both of these claims. China, India, and Malaysia successfully have utilized controls on outflows as well as inflows (see Chapter 7, this volume, for a discussion of controls on inflows). Furthermore, in the case of two of these (China and India), controls have been in place for a significant period of time. Moreover, though both China and India are currently engaged in liberalizing their controls, both countries still retain effective controls while insisting on retaining the right to reimpose stronger controls when necessary. In the words of our taxonomy described below, these countries have implemented and presumably will retain for a considerable period of time both static and dynamic controls. Moreover, all three countries can be cited as success stories in terms of having avoided the worst of the Asian financial crisis, as well as having achieved highly respectable and in some cases (especially China and India) spectacular rates of economic growth.

In discussing these three cases, we emphasize that a thorough understanding of their policies as well as the policy options facing developing countries necessitates that we expand the discussion of capital controls to include what we term capital management techniques (Epstein et al. 2003). Capital management techniques include the traditional menu of capital controls but add a set of policies that we term prudential financial regulations. We argue that certain types of prudential financial regulations actually function as a type of capital control in the sense that they alter the opportunities or affect the incentives facing resident and non-resident investors to exchange domestic and foreign financial assets or liabilities. Moreover, we argue that capital controls themselves can function as prudential financial regulations or complement other regulations already in place. Our research demonstrates that there is often a great deal of synergy between prudential financial regulations and traditional capital controls (see Ocampo 2002).

Moreover, it can be difficult (and sometimes impossible) to draw a firm line between prudential domestic financial regulation and capital controls. For example, domestic financial regulations that curtail the extent of maturity or locational mismatches may influence the composition of international capital flows, even though these types of regulations are commonly classified as prudential domestic financial regulations and not as capital controls.

We believe these three case studies show that properly construed and in the right context, capital management techniques—even ones that manage outflows—can ameliorate some of the dilemmas and problems described above. More importantly, they can contribute to development and growth. Controls on outflows can help countries manage exchange rates, avoid external debt problems and help promote the quantity and quality of investment. They can do this in several ways. Controls can support industrial policies designed to channel credit and savings to productive uses. They can reduce the availability of domestic currency offshore that can be used by non-residents to speculate against the domestic currency, thereby helping to maintain exchange rates within targeted ranges (i.e., policies to prevent the *internationalization* of the domestic currency; see Ishi et al. 2001; Watanabe et al. 2002; Ma et al. 2004; and Section 6.3 below). Controls also can reduce the need for foreign borrowing to finance capital outflows and thereby lower domestic vulnerability. They can create degrees of freedom for monetary and credit policy to lower interest rates to foster investment. They can reduce the vulnerability to sudden capital outflows that threaten the exchange rate and add to inflationary pressures.

Controls on inflow also can help. They help countries manage accumulation of external debts and help maintain healthy balance sheets of financial and non-financial firms. They can help avoid asset bubbles and over-valuation of exchange rates in inflation targeting contexts. They also can maintain export competitiveness and employment. They can help avoid costly sterilization measures that can erode government balance sheets, and finally, they can reduce the economy's vulnerability to asset bubbles and financial crashes.

Experience in several countries has shown, moreover, that capital management techniques comprise a multifaceted tool box of fine instruments—not just one blunt, one-size-fits-all tool as some critics imply (Epstein et al. 2003; Tables 6.1–6.4, below). Individual countries have developed a rich array of instruments that affect different assets, different liabilities, and various actors in varying combinations to address local needs in different contexts. With such a large variety of tools, governments can tailor their approaches to reach the governments' goals while trying to avoid high costs.

Of course, no set of tools is perfect or cost-free, and capital management techniques are no exception. Furthermore, tools often need to be changed to fit changing circumstances. For example, all three countries discussed here have chosen to foster integration between their domestic financial markets and global financial markets. Given the decision to do that, the questions facing their governments include these: What is the best way to integrate? What markets? What agents? How far? How fast? These are all questions that do not have *prima facie* answers as some advocates of financial liberalization imply. The useful question is not, as many analysts suggest, what are the prerequisites to full capital account liberalization? Rather, the important question is: How much and what type of capital management techniques do countries want and what is the right path to find them? These are the issues we hope this chapter can help illuminate.

The rest of this chapter is organized as follows. In Section 6.2 we discuss capital management techniques in more depth, focusing on types of techniques, goals, achievements, and costs. In Section 6.3 we present the three case studies of the capital management techniques employed during the 1990s and describe their effects, including benefits and costs. There we focus on controls on outflows. In Section 6.4 we summarize our chief findings and discuss some issues of broader policy relevance.

6.2 Capital Management Techniques: Tools, Objectives, and Costs

6.2.1 What are Capital Management Techniques?

We use the term capital management techniques to refer to two complementary and often overlapping types of financial policies: policies that govern international private capital flows, called capital controls, and those that enforce prudential management of domestic financial institutions. Regimes of capital management take diverse forms and are multifaceted. Capital management techniques, as actually implemented by governments around the world, make a number of fine distinctions (Rajaraman 2001; Nayyar 2000; Epstein et al. 2003; Reddy 2004). Governments make the following distinctions:

- between residents and non-residents (and sometimes between nationally affiliated and not, for example, between non-resident Indian nationals and other non-residents);
- among non-financial corporations, financial institutions, and individuals;
- among foreign exchange (i.e., exchange controls), equity and debt instruments (and derivatives);
- between portfolio investment (PI) and foreign direct investment (FDI);
- between short-term and long-term debt regulations;
- between on-shore and offshore markets;
- between quantitative and administrative regulations; and
- between administrative techniques that involve strict penalties (civil or criminal) or those that involve only monitoring and reporting.

These many distinctions are not incidental, but highlight the rich array of capital management techniques that governments implement.

COMPLEMENTARY POLICIES: CAPITAL CONTROLS
AND PRUDENTIAL FINANCIAL REGULATION

Capital controls refer to measures that manage the volume, composition, or allocation of international private capital flows (see Neely 1999). Capital controls can target inflows or outflows. Inflow or outflow controls generally target particular flows, such as portfolio investment, based on their perceived risks and opportunities. Capital controls can be tax-based or quantitative. Reserve requirement taxes against certain types of investments are an example of a tax-based control. Quantitative capital controls involve outright bans on certain investments (e.g., the purchase of equities by foreign investors), restrictions or quotas, or license requirements.

Prudential domestic financial regulations are another type of capital management technique. These refer to policies, such as capital adequacy standards, reporting requirements, or restrictions on the ability and terms under which domestic financial institutions can provide capital to certain types of projects. They also refer to prudential rules on currency mismatching on balance sheets and to restrictions on issuing certain types of derivatives or forward contracts.

As the last examples suggest, a strict bifurcation between capital controls and prudential regulations often cannot be maintained in practice (as Ocampo 2002 and Schneider 2001 observe). Policymakers frequently implement multifaceted regimes of capital management as no single measure can achieve diverse objectives (as we will see in section 6.3). Moreover, the effectiveness of any single management technique magnifies the effectiveness of other techniques, and enhances the efficacy of the entire regime of capital management. For example, certain prudential financial regulations magnify the effectiveness of capital controls (and vice versa). In this case, the stabilizing aspect of prudential regulation reduces the need for the most stringent form of capital control. Thus, a program of complementary capital management techniques reduces the necessary severity of any one technique, and magnifies the effectiveness of the regime of financial control.

STATIC VERSUS DYNAMIC CAPITAL MANAGEMENT TECHNIQUES

Capital management techniques can be static or dynamic (though here, too, the strict distinction is not always maintained in practice). Static management techniques are those that authorities do not modify in response to changes in circumstances. Examples of static management techniques include restrictions on the convertibility of the currency, restrictions on certain types of activities (such as short selling the currency), and maintenance of minimum stay requirements on foreign investment.

Capital management techniques also can be dynamic, meaning that they can be activated or adjusted as circumstances warrant. Three types of circumstances trigger implementation of management techniques or lead authorities to strengthen or adjust existing regulations.

First, capital management techniques are activated in response to changes in the economic environment (e.g., changes in the volume of international capital flows or the emergence of an asset bubble).[3] For example, the Malaysian government implemented stringent temporary inflow controls in 1994 to dampen pressures associated with large capital inflows (see Chapter 7, this volume). Second, capital management techniques are activated to reduce the severity of a crisis.[4] For example, the Malaysian government implemented stringent capital controls in 1998 to stabilize the economy and to protect it from the contagion effects of the regional crisis. Both China and Taiwan POC strengthened existing capital management techniques and added new measures to insulate themselves from the emerging regional crisis. Third, capital management techniques are strengthened or modified as authorities attempt to close loopholes in existing measures. For example, authorities in Taiwan POC, Chile, and China adjusted their capital management techniques several times during the 1990s as loopholes in existing measures were identified.

INFLOWS, OUTFLOWS, AND NON-INTERNATIONALIZATION POLICIES

As mentioned earlier, management policies can focus on managing inflows or outflows. Watanabe et al. (2002) present a useful discussion of channels through which outflows can affect exchange rates and reserves:

- short positions in the local currency taken by non-residents;
- withdrawal of short-term funds and portfolio investments by non-residents; and
- capital flight by residents.

Capital management techniques for outflows have been designed to manage these three channels.

Increasingly common in Asia, policies manage outflows, prevent the internationalization of domestic currencies, and more specifically, reduce offshore access to domestic currency by non-residents (see Table 6.3 below). The aims of these regulations are to reduce exchange rate volatility, reduce the likelihood of financial crises, and restore some autonomy to monetary policy through the suppression or elimination of offshore markets in the home

---

[3] Ocampo (2002) proposes dynamic, counter-cyclical domestic financial regulation as a complement to permanent, adjustable capital controls. Palley (2004) proposes counter-cyclical, variable asset-based reserve requirements.

[4] Grabel (1999, 2003a) proposes 'trip wires and speed bumps' as a framework for dynamic capital management. This approach aims to identify the risks to which individual countries are most vulnerable, and to prevent these risks from culminating in crisis.

currency (McCauley 2001; Watanabe et al. 2002). In response to these policies, markets in non-deliverable forwards have sprung up in some offshore
financial centers in currencies restricted by non-internationalization policies
(Ma et al. 2004; Table 6.3, below), raising questions about the viability of these
practices. However, as discussed later, most evidence suggests that the non-
internationalization policies are effective despite the non-deliverable forward
markets.

6.2.2 Objectives of Capital Management Techniques

Policymakers use capital management techniques to achieve some or all of
the following five objectives.[5]

CAPITAL MANAGEMENT TECHNIQUES CAN PROMOTE FINANCIAL
STABILITY

Capital management techniques can promote financial stability through their
ability to reduce currency, flight, fragility, and contagion risks. Capital management can thereby reduce the potential for financial crisis and related
economic and social devastation.

Currency risk refers to the risk that a currency will appreciate or depreciate
significantly over a short period of time. Currency risk can be curtailed if
capital management techniques reduce the opportunities for sudden, large
purchases or sales of domestic assets by investors (via controls on inflows
and outflows, respectively). Capital management can protect the domestic currency from dramatic fluctuation via restrictions on its convertibility.
Finally, capital management can provide authorities with the ability to engage
in macroeconomic policies that sterilize the effects of sudden large capital
inflows or outflows on the currency.

Investor flight risk refers to the likelihood that holders of liquid financial
assets will sell their holdings *en masse* in the face of perceived difficulty.
Lender flight risk refers to the likelihood that lenders will terminate lending
programs or will only extend loans on prohibitive terms. Capital management
can reduce investor and lender flight risk by discouraging the types of inflows
that are subject to rapid reversal (namely, PI, short-term foreign loans, and
liquid forms of FDI). Capital management can also reduce investor and lender
flight risk by reducing or discouraging the opportunities for exit via outflow
controls.

Fragility risk refers to the vulnerability of an economy's private and public
borrowers to internal or external shocks that jeopardize their ability to meet

---

[5] Discussion of objectives and costs draws on Chang and Grabel (2004: ch. 10) and Grabel
(2003b), whereas discussion of the means by which capital management techniques attain
their objectives draws on Grabel (2003a).

current obligations. Fragility risk arises in a number of ways. Borrowers might employ financing strategies that involve maturity or locational mismatch. Agents might finance private investment with capital that is prone to flight risk. Investors (domestic and foreign) may over-invest in certain sectors, thereby creating overcapacity and fueling unsustainable speculative bubbles. Capital management techniques can reduce fragility risk through inflow controls that influence the volume, allocation, and prudence of lending and investing decisions.

Contagion risk refers to the threat that a country will fall victim to financial and macroeconomic instability that originates elsewhere. Capital management techniques can reduce contagion risk by managing the degree of financial integration and by reducing the vulnerability of individual countries to currency, flight, and fragility risks.

CAPITAL MANAGEMENT TECHNIQUES CAN PROMOTE DESIRABLE TYPES OF INVESTMENT AND FINANCING ARRANGEMENTS AND DISCOURAGE LESS DESIRABLE TYPES OF INVESTMENT/FINANCING STRATEGIES

Capital management techniques can influence the composition of the economy's aggregate investment portfolio, and can influence the financing arrangements that underpin these investments. Capital management techniques (particularly those that involve inflow controls) can promote desirable types of investment and financing strategies by rewarding investors and borrowers for engaging in them. Desirable types of investment are those that create employment, improve living standards, promote greater income equality, foster technology transfer, learning by doing, and/or long-term growth. Desirable types of financing are those that are long-term, stable, and sustainable. Capital management can discourage less desirable types of investment and financing strategies by increasing their cost or precluding them altogether.

CAPITAL MANAGEMENT CAN ENHANCE THE AUTONOMY OF ECONOMIC AND SOCIAL POLICY

Capital management techniques can enhance policy autonomy in a number of ways. Capital management techniques can reduce the severity of currency risk and can thereby allow authorities to protect a currency peg. Capital management can create space for the government or the central bank to use macroeconomic policies that promote growth or spur inflation by neutralizing the threat of capital flight (via restrictions on capital inflows or outflows). They can also help countries fight inflation without inducing over-valued exchange rates (Ho and McCauley 2003). Moreover, by reducing the risk of financial crisis in the first place, capital management can reduce the likelihood that governments may be compelled to use contractionary macro and micro economic and social policy as a signal to attract foreign investment back to the country or as a precondition for financial assistance from the International Monetary Fund (IMF).

CAPITAL MANAGEMENT CAN HELP MANAGE THE EXCHANGE RATE FOR TRADE PURPOSES

Capital management techniques give policymakers extra degrees of freedom to manage their exchange rates. Despite the mainstream advice to either freely float or adopt a hard peg through a currency board or dollarization, many developing countries, including emerging market economies, use capital management techniques to help them manage their exchange rates (McCauley 2001; Klau and Mohanty 2004). Use of capital management techniques is widespread among those countries that adopt inflation targeting as well. Despite the mainstream advice, few countries completely ignore exchange rates when attempting to lower inflation. This helps them avoid over-valued exchange rates, which harm trade competitiveness and can lead to financial crises, and on the other hand can help avoid under-valuations that can worsen inflation. In the latter case, inflation targeting central banks would be forced to raise interest rates and restrict credit which could harm employment and growth.

CAPITAL MANAGEMENT TECHNIQUES CAN ENHANCE DEMOCRACY

It follows from point three that capital management can enhance democracy by reducing the potential for speculators and external actors to exercise undue influence over domestic decision making directly or indirectly (via the threat of capital flight). Capital management techniques can reduce the veto power of the financial community and the IMF and create space for the interests of other groups (such as advocates for the poor) to play a role in the design of economic and social policy. Capital management techniques, then, can enhance democracy because they create the opportunity for pluralism in policy design.

6.2.3 Costs of Capital Management Techniques

Critics of capital management techniques argue that they impose four types of costs:

- reduce growth;
- reduce efficiency and policy discipline;
- promote corruption and waste; and
- aggravate credit scarcity, policy abuse, uncertainty, and error.

Critics argue that the benefits that derive from capital management (such as financial stability) come at an unacceptably high price. However, the evidence for these costs is quite limited (Epstein et al. 2003). As suggested above, the strongest criticism is reserved for controls on outflows and permanent controls. But as we argue in the case studies below, controls on outflows have been applied successfully in three dynamic economies, and the *prima facie* evidence is that, even assuming there have been costs, the success is even more apparent.

6.3 Case Studies: Capital Management Techniques in China, India, and Malaysia Since the 1990s

6.3.1 Objectives and Case Selection

In this section we present case studies that analyze the capital management techniques employed during the 1990s in Malaysia, India, and China. As mentioned above, we have chosen these three because they represent important counter examples to the mainstream claim that controls on outflows and long term controls do not work.

6.3.2 The General Context

Table 6.1 presents a summary of the major capital management techniques and their objectives in each of our cases. We will describe in detail the types of management techniques used by Malaysia, India, and China, what their costs and benefits have been, and what the countries' likely prospects are. The focus will be on controls on outflows, though we will also discuss, when relevant, prudential controls on inflows. Of course, managing inflows can be important in reducing the vulnerability to outflows. So inflows and outflows are not easily separated in the policy context.

MALAYSIA[6]

Context: In the first two-thirds of the 1990s, Malaysia experienced rapid economic growth due to increased government spending, FDI, and exports. During this period, the Malaysian capital account was so liberalized that there was an offshore market in ringgit, perhaps the only case of an offshore market in an emerging-market currency (Rajaraman 2001). Indeed, by most conventional measures, Malaysia had had one of the longest running open capital accounts in the developing world (Rajaraman 2001).

---

[6] This section draws mainly on BNM (various years), Jomo (2001), Mahathir (2001), Rajamaran (2001), Kaplan and Rodrik (2002). We focus here on the 1998 controls on outflows. For a discussion of the earlier controls on inflows see Chapter 7 (this volume) and Epstein et al. (2003).

Table 6.1. Summary: Types and Objectives of Capital Management Techniques Employed During the 1990s

Country	Types of Capital Management Techniques	Objectives of Capital Management Techniques
Malaysia (1998)	**Inflows** restrictions on foreign borrowing **Outflows** *non-residents* 12-month repatriation waiting period graduated exit levies inversely proportional to length of stay *residents* exchange controls **Domestic financial regulations** *non-residents* restrict access to ringgit *residents* encourage to borrow domestically and invest	maintain political and economic sovereignty kill the offshore ringgit market shut down offshore share market help reflate the economy help create financial stability and insulate the economy from contagion
India	**Inflows** *non-residents* strict regulation of FDI and PI **Outflows** *non-residents* none *residents* exchange controls **Domestic Financial Regulations** strict limitations on development of domestic financial markets	support industrial policy pursue capital account liberalization in an incremental and controlled fashion insulate domestic economy from financial contagion preserve domestic savings and forex reserves help stabilize exchange rate
China	**Inflows** *non-residents* strict regulation on sectoral FDI investment regulation of equity investments: segmented stock market **Outflows** *non-residents* no restrictions on repatriation of funds strict limitations on borrowing Chinese Renminbi for speculative purposes *residents* exchange controls **Domestic Financial Regulations** strict limitations on *residents* and *non-residents*	support industrial policy pursue capital account liberalization in incremental and controlled fashion insulate domestic economy from financial contagion increase political sovereignty preserve domestic savings and foreign exchange reserves help keep exchange rates at competitive levels

Sources: See Section 6.4.

Rapid economic growth in Malaysia came to a halt with the Asian financial crisis of 1997. The Malaysian government bucked trends in the region and, rather than implement an IMF stabilization program, implemented capital controls, and adopted an expansionary monetary policy 14 months after

September 1998. Malaysia's introduction of capital controls widely was seen as a major departure from its long reputation for a liberal capital account. The Malaysian government, of course, had implemented capital controls in 1994, but these were eliminated within a few months.

Objectives: The 1998 controls had somewhat different goals. These were designed to accelerate expansionary macroeconomic policy while defending the exchange rate, reduce capital flight, preserve foreign exchange reserves, and avoid an IMF stabilization program (Kaplan and Rodrik 2002).

Capital Management Techniques in Malaysia, September 1998: The policy package generally is recognized as comprehensive and well designed to limit foreign exchange outflows and ringgit speculation by non-residents as well as residents, while not adversely affecting foreign direct investors. The offshore ringgit market had facilitated exchange rate turbulence in 1997–8. Thus, the measures were designed to eliminate this source of disturbance. Table 6.2 describes some of these policies according to the channels of outflows mentioned above (Watanabe et al. 2002).

The measures introduced on September 1, 1998 were designed to achieve the following objectives (BNM various years; Jomo 2001; Mahathir 2001; Rajaraman 2001):

- Eliminate the offshore ringgit market. The measures prohibited the transfer of funds into the country from externally held ringgit accounts except for investment in Malaysia (excluding credit to residents) or for purchase of goods in Malaysia. The offshore ringgit market could only function with externally held ringgit accounts in correspondent banks in Malaysia because offshore banks required freely usable access to onshore ringgit bank accounts to match their ringgit liabilities, which the new ruling prohibited. Holders of offshore deposits were given the month of September 1998 to repatriate their deposits to Malaysia. This eliminated the major source of ringgit for speculative buying of US dollars in anticipation of a ringgit crash. Large denomination ringgit notes were later demonetized to make the circulation of the ringgit currency outside Malaysia more difficult.

- Eliminate access by non-residents to domestic ringgit sources by prohibiting ringgit credit facilities to them. All trade transactions now had to be settled in foreign currencies, and only authorized depository institutions were allowed to handle transactions in ringgit financial assets.

- Shut down the offshore market in Malaysian shares conducted through the Central Limit Order Book (CLOB) in Singapore.

- Obstruct speculative outward capital flows by requiring prior approval for Malaysian residents to invest abroad in any form and limiting exports

Table 6.2. Controls on Outflows Pre- and Post-Crisis Malaysia

Channel for outflows	Transactions	Malaysia	
		Pre-Crisis	*Post-Crisis*
Short selling of local currency by non-residents	Lending to non-residents in local currency	Subject to a maximum outstanding limit	Not permitted Not permitted after Sept. 1998
	Swap transactions with non-residents	Free, subject to a maximum outstanding limit of $2 million	
	Accounts in domestic currency held abroad	Not permitted	Not permitted
Withdrawal of capital by non-residents	External borrowing	Free for approved borrowing	Unchanged
	Purchase of stocks by non-residents	Purchase share limited to maximum of 30% of total shares issued by individual company	
Capital flight by residents	Convertibility from domestic currency to foreign exchange without underlying trade & investment activities	Not permitted	Not permitted
	Foreign exchange accounts held domestically (surrender requirement)	Exporters allowed to hold up to RM10 million with designated banks	Unchanged
	Foreign exchange accounts held abroad (repatriation requirement)	Export proceeds must be repatriated when contractually due, and in any case no more than 180 days from the date of exports. Proceeds must be retained in local ringgit accounts.	Unchanged
Memo: Existence of non-deliverable forward market?	No	No	

Source: Watanabe et al. (2002).

of foreign currency by residents for anything other than valid current account purposes.

- Protect the ringgit's value and raise foreign exchange reserves by requiring repatriation of export proceeds within six months from the time of export.

- Further insulate monetary policy from the foreign exchange market by imposing a 12-month ban on the outflow of external portfolio capital (only on the principal; interest and dividend payments could be freely repatriated).

The September 1998 measures imposed a 12 month waiting period for repatriation of investment proceeds from the liquidation of external portfolio investments. To pre-empt a large scale outflow at the end of the 12 month period in September 1999 and to try to attract new portfolio investments from abroad, a system of graduated exit levies was introduced on February 15, 1999, with different rules for capital already in the country and for capital brought in after that date. For capital already in the country, there was an exit tax inversely proportional to the duration of stay within the earlier stipulated period of 12 months. Capital that had entered the country before February 15, 1998 was free to leave without paying any exit tax. For new capital yet to come in, the levy would only be imposed on profits, defined to exclude dividends and interest, also graduated by length of stay. In effect, profits were being defined by the new rules as realized capital gains.

Credit facilities for share as well as property purchases actually were increased as part of the package. The government has even encouraged its employees to take second mortgages for additional property purchases at its heavily discounted interest rate.

The exchange controls, still in place, limit access to ringgit for non-residents, preventing the re-emergence of an offshore ringgit market. Free movement from ringgit to dollars for residents is possible, but dollars must be held in foreign exchange accounts in Malaysia, e.g., at the officially approved foreign currency offshore banking center on Labuan.

Assessment: Did Malaysia's September 1998 selective capital control measures succeed? They clearly succeeded in meeting some of the government's objectives. The offshore ringgit market was eliminated by the September 1998 measures. By late 1999, international rating agencies had begun restoring Malaysia's credit rating. For example, the Malaysian market was listed again on the Morgan Stanley Capital International Indices in May 2000.

But, did these controls succeed in the sense of allowing more rapid recovery of the Malaysian economy? The merits and demerits of the Malaysian government's regime of capital controls to deal with the regional currency and financial crises will be debated for a long time to come. Proponents claim that the economic and stock market decline came to a stop soon after the controls were implemented (Palma 2000; Jomo 2001; Dornbusch 2002; Kaplan and Rodrik 2002). On the other hand, opponents argue that such reversals have been more pronounced in the rest of the region. Kaplan and Rodrik present strong evidence that the controls did have a significant positive effect on the ability of Malaysia to weather the 1997 crisis and reflate its economy. While this debate is likely to go on for some time, our reading of the evidence suggests that Kaplan and Rodrik are correct. Controls segmented financial markets and provided breathing room for domestic monetary and financial policies, and they promoted a speedier recovery than would have been possible via the orthodox IMF route.

Supporting Factors: It is often argued that prior experience with capital management techniques has been important to the success of capital management in the 1990s. However, the case of Malaysia seems quite different. The country had a highly liberalized capital account prior to the 1990s. Nonetheless, the government was able to implement numerous capital management techniques, all under rather difficult circumstances. This suggests that a history of capital management is not a necessary condition for policy success.

Costs: It is difficult to identify any significant costs associated with the short-lived 1994 controls. The most important cost of the 1998 controls was the political favoritism associated with their implementation. It is difficult, however, to estimate the economic costs of political favoritism (Jomo 2001; Johnson and Mitton 2003; Kaplan and Rodrik 2002). Moreover, these costs (if quantified) must be weighed against the significant evidence of the macroeconomic benefits of the 1998 controls.

INDIA[7]

Following Independence from Britain, India had for many decades a highly controlled economy, with exchange and capital controls an integral part of the developmental state apparatus. Over time, and partly in response to economic crisis in 1991, India gradually liberalized and with respect to the capital account, this process of liberalization greatly accelerated in the 1990s. Most mainstream observers have suggested that the pace of liberalization is far too slow. However, supporters of gradual liberalization point to the relative success India has had in insulating itself from the excesses of the international financial markets which led to the crises of some of its neighbors in 1997. Moreover, key officials in India insist that despite its commitment to liberalization, India must retain the right to re-impose controls when necessary.

Context: The Indian financial system and Indian approach to capital management are best understood in the context of its history of colonization, and the subsequent development plan that it pursued following independence in 1947. Given the history of British colonialism, policymakers were understandably reluctant to open their economy to foreign capital. In terms of the external account, in the first few years following independence, an intricate set of controls evolved for all external transactions. Equity investments were further restricted in 1977 when many multinational companies left India, rejecting the government's effort to enforce a law that required them to dilute their equity in their Indian operations to 40 percent. Although India ushered in industrial reforms in the 1980s, the general consensus was that export orientation and openness could not provide a reasonable basis for growth.

Like many other developing countries, India's decision to dramatically liberalize its intricately planned economy in 1991 was necessitated by a balance

---

[7] This section draws mainly on Rajaraman (2001) and Nayyar (2000).

of payments crisis. By March 1991, the crisis had reached severe proportions. India turned to the IMF for an emergency loan, and the conditions imposed led to the adoption of extensive liberalization measures.

Objectives: The goals of India's capital management techniques are to foster financial development (through gradual capital account liberalization) and attract foreign investment. Prudential financial regulations aim to reduce the likelihood of speculative crises driven by excessive foreign borrowing and to help authorities manage the exchange rate. To further this goal, capital management has attempted to shift the composition of capital inflows from debt to equity. In addition, capital management techniques have been oriented towards maintenance of domestic financial stability by limiting foreign equity and foreign currency deposit investments in the financial sector. In addition, the government tried to retain domestic savings, stabilize the domestic financial sector by limiting the deposits of foreign currencies, and allocate foreign equity investment to strategic sectors, such as information technology.

Capital Management Techniques in India: India has had significant controls on both inflows and outflows. These controls have applied to a broad spectrum of assets and liabilities, applying to debt, equity and currency. These capital management techniques have involved strict regulation of financial institutions, as well as controls of external transactions. Although the Indian economy has moved towards a progressively freer capital market, this has been an extremely gradual process.[8] In particular, the management of integration into the world financial market has been based, until very recently, on fundamental asymmetries between residents and non-residents, and between corporations and individuals. While non-resident corporations enjoy substantial freedom to repatriate funds, until recently this has been severely limited in the case of individual residents. Resident corporations have had to obtain approval before exporting capital, and resident individuals have been, for all practical purposes, subject to strict and low limits with respect to these. Moreover, there have been restrictions on debt accumulation as well as foreign currency deposits and loans by domestic financial institutions. (See Table 6.1.)

Controls on Outflows: As mentioned above, the liberalization process has maintained a clear distinction between residents and non-residents. It has maintained strict controls on outflows by residents, while giving significant latitude to non-residents to repatriate funds. Table 6.3 presents information on Indian policies with respect to the non-internationalization of the currency. As Table 6.3 shows, a market in non-deliverable forwards has developed. In principle, this market (and other moves toward financial liberalization) could impair India's central bank's ability to affect to domestic interest rates relative to foreign rates. But a study by the Bank for International Settlements suggests that India has been able to maintain a differential between onshore

---

[8] Rajaraman (2001) calls this the 'incremental dribble' of Indian policymaking.

Table 6.3. Limits on International Capital Flows in East Asia and India and the Existence of Non-Deliverable Offshore Forward Markets

	Non-deliverable offshore forward market for domestic currency	Limits on non-resident access to domestic currency liabilities	Limits on foreign currency deposits in domestic banks	Limits on corporate borrowing in foreign currency	Limits on non-resident equity purchases
China	Y	Y	N	Y	Y[a]
Hong Kong	N	N	N	N	N
India	Y	Y	Y	Y	Y
Indonesia	Y	Y	N	N	N
Korea	Y	Y	N	N	N
Malaysia	N	Y	N[b]	Y	N
Philippines	Y	Y	N	Y[c]	N
Singapore	N[d]	Y	N	N	N
Thailand	N	Y	Y	N	N
Taiwan	Y	Y	N	Y[e]	Y

Notes: [a] Non-residents not allowed to buy A-shares listed in Shanghai and Shenzhen but are allowed to buy B-shares; [b] Only corporate accounts permitted; [c] Registration of foreign loans with the Bangko Sentral ng Pilipinas is necessary only in order to obtain foreign exchange from the central bank; [d] Borrowing of Singapore dollars to buy Singaporean equities, bonds, and real estate now permitted; offshore issuers of Singapore dollar bonds without local need for the funds are required to swap the proceeds into foreign currency; [e] Taiwanese corporations are allowed to borrow foreign currency freely but not to exchange the proceeds for New Taiwan dollars.

Sources: McCauley (2001); Ma et al. (2004); Economist Intelligence Unit (EIU).

and offshore rates, an indication that their controls are still working despite substantial financial liberalization (Ma et al. 2004).

Borrowing and Short-Term Debt Accumulation and Prudential Regulation: Prudential regulations having capital account implications are widespread in India. Responding to the lessons of the 1997 Asian crisis, commercial borrowing in foreign currencies has remained significantly curtailed. Commercial banks, unlike in some East Asian countries, have not been and are still not allowed to accept deposits or to extend loans which are denominated in foreign currencies. As Nayyar (2000) describes the crisis context of India's initial reform:

> It prompted strict regulation of external commercial borrowing especially short-term debt. It led to a systematic effort to discourage volatile capital flows associated with repatriable non-resident deposits. Most important, perhaps, it was responsible for the change in emphasis and the shift in preference from debt creating capital flows to non-debt creating capital flows. (Nayyar 2000)

Foreign Direct Investment: Before liberalization, FDI and equity investments were strictly controlled in virtually all sectors. By the early 2000s, however, these restrictions have been lifted. The first steps in liberalization involved lifting restrictions on FDI. By 1993 the government enacted far-reaching changes in the Foreign Exchange Regulation Act (FERA) of 1973. Some of these reforms may have been used as a tool of industrial policy, guiding FDI into certain industries, including computer hardware and software, engineering industries, services, electronics and electrical equipment, infrastructure projects, chemical and allied products, and food and dairy products. Recent changes have meant that by 2001–2, most sectors are open to FDI. Still, important restrictions remain. In particular, FDI is severely restricted in banking, finance, real estate, and infrastructure.

Portfolio Investment: The attitude towards portfolio investment liberalization has been gradual, as well. India's first attempt to capture part of the growing funds being channeled into emerging markets came during the second half of the 1980s, as India opened five closed-end mutual funds for sale on offshore markets. They also reformed the structure of equity regulations on the stock exchanges. By the late 1990s, the limits on foreign institutional investor ownership of share capital had been eased.

Assessment: India has had some success and a few question marks in this decade of capital account management. On the credit side, India has had consistent net inflows (a legacy of its discrimination between residents and non-residents) and has not had any major financial meltdowns in a decade that saw three serious crises around the world (and one next door). Some of this has certainly been due to the prudential discrimination between various types of capital flows.

Another major element on the credit side has been India's success in increasing the share of non-debt creating inflows. There has been a particularly impressive reduction in short-term loans. However, India has had only limited success in attracting foreign direct investment instead of portfolio investment. In fact, the decade has seen a marginally greater percentage of foreign inflows being accounted for by FPI than by FDI (52 percent to 48 percent).

India's exchange rate policy seems to have worked. Although there has been a steady decline in the external value of the rupee, there have been relatively few periods of volatility, and the only really difficult period (in 1997) saw the external value fall by 16 percent.

Supporting Factors: Among the contributing factors to the success of India's partial liberalization process and continuing use of capital management techniques, three are most important. First is the widespread institutional experience of the Indian authorities in managing controls, including long-standing experience with regulating Indian financial institutions. Second, the controls themselves were well-designed, clearly demarcating the distinction between resident and non-resident transactions. Finally, liberalization of FDI and the very success of the controls themselves contributed to the ability of India to accumulate foreign exchange reserves and limit the accumulation of foreign debt, both of which reduced the vulnerability of the Indian economy.

Costs: In India's case, this is a complex question because the Indian economy has been undergoing a dramatic liberalization process, which is only ten years old. It is hard to untangle the costs of the controls from the costs of previous controls, or indeed, from the costs of the liberalization process itself and other factors, both internal and external. For example, many observers still point to the relatively underdeveloped financial markets in India compared to other semi-industrialized economies. But these are certainly due to many factors, including previous controls, and cannot be necessarily attributed to the current controls, which fall mostly on residents. In any case, controls have been in place for a relatively short time. In short, assessing the costs of the current system will undoubtedly have to wait for more information.

Other Achievements: As suggested above, India's capital management techniques clearly helped to insulate India's economy from the ravages of the 1997 Asian financial crisis (Rajaraman 2001). By limiting capital flight by residents, they also have helped to retain domestic savings that are critical for domestic investment.

The Future: Recently, Indian policies on outflows have changed substantially, at least on an experimental basis. Restrictions on individuals and domestic corporates have been eased to allow substantial investments abroad. Most significantly, mutual funds in India are now permitted to invest up to $1 billion abroad. Moreover, individuals are now permitted to invest abroad without limit. In addition, companies can now invest in foreign companies too, but there is a quantitative restriction on the amount (less than 25 percent of the company's worth). If this recent liberalization is retained on a permanent basis, it will represent a fundamental change in India's capital management techniques.

Still, the Governor of India's central bank, Dr Y. V. Reddy, insists that India places enormous importance on capital management techniques, not only for the short run but also in the long run, thereby bucking the common view among economists that controls are simply a temporary evil (Reddy 2004). At the same time, some critics are concerned that capital account liberalization has gone too far and it will be difficult for the authorities to respond to future crises, an issue we address further below (Nayyar 2000; Ghosh 2004).

CHINA[9]

Among the cases we study in this paper, the People's Republic of China (PRC) has the most comprehensive foreign exchange and capital controls. At the same time, China's record of economic growth and development in the last several decades, as well as its ability to attract high levels of FDI has been admired by many countries both in the developed and developing world. Finally, like its neighbor India, China avoided significant negative repercussions from the Asian financial crisis of the late 1990s. The relatively

[9] This section is based on Naughton (1996), Lardy (1998), Fernald and Babson (1999), Gao (2000), Icard (2002), and Jingu (2002).

strict capital controls alongside enviable economic growth and the ability to attract large quantities of foreign capital starkly calls into question the common view among economists that capital controls on outflows necessarily hinder economic growth and deter capital inflows. Indeed, China's policies suggest that, under the right conditions, strong capital management techniques might be useful in protecting macroeconomic stability, and enhancing economic growth and development.

Context: The People's Republic of China has achieved an admirable record of success in terms of economic growth and development in the last decade or more, averaging an annual growth rate of GDP of 8 percent or more, depending on one's view of the accuracy of the PRC's government statistics. This record has been associated with high savings rates (40 percent of GDP or more), a long record of current account surpluses, a large inflow of FDI (even discounting for the fact that half or more of it may really be domestic investment that is round-tripped through Hong Kong or elsewhere in order to take advantage of preferential treatment afforded to foreign investors), a huge stock of foreign exchange reserves, and, even in light of a substantial foreign debt, a likely net creditor status (see, for example, Icard 2002).[10] After a short period of high inflation and interest rates in the mid-1990s, China has experienced low domestic interest rates and, until recently, deflation.[11] In terms of exchange rate management, China has maintained a fairly consistent US dollar peg. Whether this is a hard or soft peg is a matter of some controversy.

Objectives: Capital management techniques in China are an integral part of China's development strategy. The objectives of the controls evolved over time, but generally have included the following: to retain savings; to help channel savings to desired uses; to help insulate China's pegged exchange rate in order to maintain export competitiveness; to reduce the circumvention of other controls such as tariffs; to protect domestic sectors from foreign investment; to strengthen China's macroeconomic policy autonomy; and to insulate the economy from foreign financial crises.

Capital Management Techniques in China: China has followed a fascinating pattern of economic liberalization since the early 1980s, one that does not conform to any simplistic view of sequencing commonly found in the economics literature. The typical, currently prescribed liberalization sequence starts with liberalizing the trade account, then relaxing foreign exchange restrictions, then the long-term capital account, then the short-term capital account. Instead, China has liberalized quite selectively within each of these categories, often on an experimental basis, and sometimes moving a step or

---

[10] A recent estimate of round-tripping finds a large amount, equal to 25–40 percent of FDI (Xiao 2004).

[11] Of course, the Chinese economy and society also face significant problems and challenges, including high unemployment and underemployment, significant environmental destruction, and the perceptions, if not reality, of widespread government corruption.

two backwards before moving once again forward. This complex pattern of experimentation and liberalization thus defies easy description, and makes over-simplification in a short summary such as this almost inevitable.

When China, under the leadership of Deng Xiao Ping embarked on its experimentation with liberalization and integration into the world economy, it had comprehensive controls over foreign exchange, current account and capital account transactions. In its experimentation with Special Economic Zones it began to allow foreign investment in foreign minority owned joint ventures, and liberalized to some extent controls over necessary imports for these 'foreign invested enterprises' (see Braunstein and Epstein 2004 for a brief summary and references).

Many of these restrictions were loosened over time and a major change in capital management techniques occurred in 1996 with China's acceptance of IMF Article VIII and the consequent liberalization of foreign exchange controls with respect to current account transactions. Moreover, since that time, controls over inflows and outflows by non-residents have been significantly loosened. Still, strict foreign exchange controls have been retained. In addition controls over foreign ownership of domestic assets have been retained to allow industrial policy tools with respect to foreign investment to be effective. In addition, strict controls over outflows and inflows of capital by domestic residents have been retained. Still, significant exceptions have been made, partly by choice and partly by necessity, to allow a somewhat porous capital account, thereby facilitating some capital outflows (capital flight) and round tripping of foreign direct investment.

China's current capital management techniques have the following characteristics (IMF 2000; Gao 2000; Icard 2002):[12]

- strict exchange controls on the capital account but few restrictions on the current account;
- some liberalized sectors for equity inflows and outflows by non-residents accompanied by some sectors of quite strict controls on non-resident equity inflows, e.g., banking, insurance, and the stock market;
- strict controls on foreign borrowing by residents, including on currency denomination and maturity structure of debt inflows;
- strict but porous controls on inflows and outflows by residents; and
- tight regulations over domestic interest rates.

Dynamic Controls: China's experience during the Asian financial crisis illustrates not only how successful management of the capital account can be in

---

[12] This list is a very short summary of a very long and complex set of controls. See the references cited above for much more detail.

terms of insulating an economy from crisis, but also how active management of the techniques can be required to deal with a dynamic, unfolding crisis.

The State Administration of Foreign Exchange (SAFE) managed the 1997 crisis by re-enforcing regulations and instituting new ones (SAFE 2002). First, given China's relatively high foreign debt, in 1998 SAFE moved to control risk and improve the management of foreign debt by tightening control over the scale and structure of foreign borrowing. For example, borrowing for real estate speculation was sharply curtailed. SAFE's ability to limit short-term debt borrowing is recognized as a key factor in helping China to avoid the worst of the crisis.

SAFE also had to confront capital fight stemming from the expectation that China would devalue the renminbi. Speculators found loopholes to the exchange controls, including borrowing renminbi from domestic banks. For example, SAFE noticed a sharp increase in stand-by letters of credit unaccompanied by increases in trade figures, so it swiftly moved to ban early redemption of foreign currency loans. Also, firms were falsifying documents to get hard currency for imports. SAFE tightened monitoring of such behavior. SAFE also tightened penalties for the holdings of foreign exchange offshore. For example, SAFE supported legislation to make holding such foreign exchange offshore a more serious crime. Foreign exchange swap centers had become transit points for the outflow of foreign currency, so SAFE closed most of the centers, and closely supervised the ones that remained open.

SAFE also took measures to build up China's foreign exchange reserves as a treasure chest to deter speculation and defend the currency. They raised the interest rates paid to residents on foreign exchange accounts to get them to turn foreign exchange into banks. They also took measures to prevent exporters from holding earnings overseas. For those with low repatriation rates, banks were supposed to examine their books before issuing loans, and the firms could lose their export licenses.

These are just some of the examples of dynamic techniques the SAFE implemented to strengthen the management of capital outflows during the Asian financial crisis. After the crisis eased, many of these restrictions were eased.

Assessment: The system of capital and exchange controls has been an integral part of China's development strategy for the last 20 years. The Chinese government could not have pursued its policy of incremental liberalization based on exports, extensive infrastructure spending, labor-intensive FDI, expansionary monetary and fiscal policy, and competitiveness-oriented exchange rate policy without its system of exchange and capital controls. Given that China's growth record in the past 20 years is the envy of much of the world, and the important role played by the capital management techniques in that economic expansion, one must deem them a success in terms of reaching the Chinese government's objectives.

Most recent commentary has focused on the role that the controls may have played in insulating the Chinese economy from speculative excesses. More specifically, this system of controls is widely credited with helping China avoid the boom-and-bust cycle associated with the Asian financial crisis (e.g., Fernald and Babson 1999; Gao 2000; and Eichengreen 2002a). Controls on foreign debt accumulation prevented the excessive accumulation of unsustainable amounts and maturities of foreign debt by resident institutions. Controls on equity inflows prevented a speculative bubble in the stock market from spilling over into other sectors of the economy, and limited, to some extent, the fall out from bubbles in real estate and other assets. Controls on outflows prevented devastating surges of capital flight. Exchange controls and the control over derivative and futures markets limited the desirability and feasibility of domestic and foreign residents speculating on the renminbi.

As liberalization in China and elsewhere proceeds, China's controls still have bite. China has been able to reach its exchange rate targets. Offshore markets in non-deliverable forwards have developed, but differentials between onshore and offshore interest rates remain (Ma et al. 2004). (See Table 6.3.)

At the same time, we note the paradox of tight controls with large amounts of capital flight and round-tripped investment (Xiao 2004; Zhu et al. 2004). The Chinese authorities clearly have tolerated a degree of flexibility in the controls. Some of this is undoubtedly related to possible corruption and unwanted evasion. But some of it reflects a safety valve, allowing some evasion at the margins in order to protect the average effectiveness of the controls. Some of the evasion is allowed in order to facilitate other objectives. This ebb and flow of capital flight to some extent reflects the dynamic nature of the controls, with the Chinese authorities tightening enforcement during periods of perceived need, including during crisis periods and loosening them when a crisis subsides.

Supporting Factors: The most important factors supporting the success of capital management techniques in China are the government's extensive experience with implementing economic controls, the comprehensive nature of the controls, the success in building foreign exchange reserves through exports and FDI, and the flexibility of policy.

Costs: Capital management in China is not without cost. China's financial system does not have the breadth and depth of financial systems in more advanced economies, such as the United States. Capital management, while facilitating China's industrial policies, has also facilitated the accumulation of bad debts at China's state banks (Lardy 1998). Capital management (as with other aspects of China's state-guided policies) has facilitated credit allocation and industrial policies. But it has also created opportunities for corruption by government officials. These costs are likely to have been outweighed by the significant contributions that capital management has played in China's highly successful economic development over the past several decades.

Other Achievements: Even though there has been significant capital flight from China, most observers have suggested that capital flight would have been significantly greater in the absence of the capital management techniques employed. Further, capital management policies have allowed the Chinese government to follow an expansionary monetary policy to try to counter the strong deflationary forces pressures facing the Chinese economy. Finally, China is the largest recipient of FDI among developing countries. While some argue that capital management discourages FDI inflows (Wei 2000), the econometric evidence on this point lacks robustness. Moreover, interviews on this subject do not suggest that capital management has been an obstacle to FDI. Indeed, sound capital management appears to encourage FDI inflows (Rosen 1999).

6.4 Lessons and Opportunities for Capital Management in Developing Countries

6.4.1 *Lessons*

What lessons can we learn from these case studies about capital management techniques and their possible use to developing countries that are trying to navigate the often treacherous waters of the world economy? To clear the field for the positive lessons that we draw from our cases, we first consider five commonly held erroneous claims about capital management techniques.

One common view of capital management is that it can only work in the short run but not the long run. However, with the exception of Malaysia, two of our three cases show that management can achieve important objectives over a significant number of years. Taking China and Singapore as two cases at different ends of the spectrum in terms of types of controls, one can see that both countries effectively employed capital management techniques for more than a decade in the service of important policy objectives.

A second common view is that for capital management to work for a long period of time, measures have to be strengthened consistently. In fact, reality is much more complex. As the cases of Malaysia and China show, at times of stress, it may be necessary to strengthen controls to address leakages that are exploited by the private sector. However, as these same cases demonstrate, controls can be loosened when a crisis subsides or when the international environment changes, and then reinstated or strengthened as necessary. More generally, looking at a broad cross-section of country experiences, one finds that the use of dynamic capital management means that management evolves endogenously according to the situation and the evolution of government goals (Cardoso and Goldfajn 1999).

A third common but misleading view is that for capital management to work, there must be an experienced bureaucracy in place. It is certainly true that experience helps. China and India have many years of experience. Malaysia, however, is an important counter-example. It successfully implemented capital management even without having had a great deal of experience. In the case of Chile, to take another example, the central bank had had no obvious previous experience implementing the reserve requirement scheme, though it had had some negative experiences in trying to implement capital controls in the 1970s. In short, experience is no doubt helpful, but it does not seem to be a pre-requisite for implementing successful capital management techniques. What is more important is state capacity and administrative capacity as discussed in Sections 6.3 and 6.4.

Fourth, a recent view that has gained currency is that controls on capital inflows work, but those on outflows do not. However, our examples show policy success in both dimensions.

Fifth, a common view is that capital management techniques impose significant costs by leading to higher costs of capital, especially for small firms. As we have seen, in some cases there may be some merit to these arguments. But much more evidence needs to be presented before this is established as a widespread cost. [13]

6.4.2 The Bottom Line

Table 6.4 summarizes the main achievements and costs of the capital management techniques in Malaysia, India, and China in the 1990s. As we have suggested, there is strong evidence these policies have had many positive impacts on these three countries, including helping to insulate them from the worst effects of the Asian financial crisis. However, as Table 6.4 suggests, the positive impacts have been greater.

In recent years, all three countries have continued to liberalize their capital account and exchange controls. Indeed, as this process of liberalization is ongoing, any snap shot of controls is bound to soon be out of date. Many economists and policymakers maintain the full capital account liberalization must be the obvious and ultimate goal, and that these countries must continue to travel down the path to full liberalization as soon as is feasible.

We have argued, on the contrary, the capital management techniques, not only with respect to inflows but also outflows, must be available to developing

---

[13] In any case, this observation is just the beginning of the analysis since it says nothing about the balance of costs and benefits. As economists are fond of pointing out, there are always trade-offs. Our cases demonstrate that capital management techniques can have important macroeconomic or prudential benefits. Of course, these benefits must be weighed against the micro costs. But as James Tobin was fond of remarking, 'It takes a lot of Harberger Triangles to fill an Okun Gap'.

Table 6.4. Summary: Assessment of the Capital Management Techniques Employed During the 1990s

Country	Achievements	Supporting Factors	Costs
Malaysia 1998	facilitated macroeconomic reflation helped to maintain domestic economic sovereignty	public support for policies strong state and administrative capacity dynamic capital management	possibly contributed to cronyism and corruption
India	facilitated incremental liberalization insulated from financial contagion helped preserve domestic saving helped maintain economic sovereignty	strong state and administrative capacity strong public support for policies experience with state governance of the economy success of broader economic policy regime gradual economic liberalization	possibly hindered development of financial sector possibly facilitated corruption
China	facilitated industrial policy-insulated economy from financial contagion helped preserve savings helped manage exchange rate and facilitate export-led growth helped maintain expansionary macro policy helped maintain economic sovereignty	strong state and administrative capacity strong economic fundamentals experience with state governance of the economy gradual economic liberalization dynamic capital management	possibly constrained the development of the financial sector possibly encouraged non-performing loans possibly facilitated corruption

Sources: See Section 6.3.

country governments over the long term as they try to stay afloat in the treacherous waters of international finance. Dr Y. V. Reddy, Governor of India's Central Bank, perhaps summarizes our argument best. In a recent speech to the Central Bank Governors' Symposium at the Bank of England in London, Reddy (2004) made the following points:

First, capital account liberalization 'has to be managed.' Second, 'caution' must be exercised in implementing liberalization. Third, the capital account itself needs to be managed during the process of 'capital account liberalization.' Fourth, the management of capital account requires 'safeguards against misuse of liberalized current account regime to effect capital transfers.' Fifth, prudential regulations over financial intermediaries, and especially banks, with regard to their forex transactions and exposures are crucial. 'Such prudential regulations should not be treated as capital controls.' Moreover, capital controls should be treated as one component of the management of the capital account. Sixth, 'the freedom to change the mix of controls and to reimpose controls should always be demonstrably available.' Finally, 'in respect of emerging economies, the conduct of market participants show the automatic self-correcting mechanisms do not operate in the forex markets. Hence, the need to manage capital account—which may or may not include special prudential regulations and capital controls.'

A recent symposium on capital account liberalization sponsored by the Bank for International Settlements and China's SAFE reached similar conclusions. Among them is the following:

... in the course of capital account liberalisation, it is important to maintain a proper balance between the treatment of transactions by residents and non-residents, capital inflows and outflows, and different types of financial institutions. The authorities may pay more attention to issues related to capital outflows when inflows are excessive. How to effectively manage capital outflows could present a major challenge to the process of capital account liberalisation. (Wang and Xie 2002)

Indeed, critics are not mistaken to worry that liberalization may be proceeding too far and too fast in some cases. The main point, though, as we have tried to argue, is that retaining the prerogative and the capacity to manage capital inflows and outflows over the long term, should be a permanent part of most developing countries' economic toolkits.

References

Akyuz, Y. (2000). 'The Debate on the International Financial Architecture: Reforming the Reformers'. UNCTAD Discussion Paper No. 143, UNCTAD, Geneva.

Ariyoshi, A., Habermeier, K., Laurens, B., Ötker-Robe, I., Ivan Canales-Kriljenko, J., and Kirilenko, A. (2000). 'Capital Controls: Country Experiences with their Use and Liberalization'. IMF Occasional Paper No. 190, International Monetary Fund, Washington, DC.

Bank of International Settlements/State Administration of Foreign Exchange (BIS/SAFE) (2003). *Symposium on China's Capital Account Liberalization in International Perspective.* BIS Papers, No. 15. Available at: www.bis.org/publ/.

Bank Negara Malaysia (BNM) (various years). *Annual Report.* Kuala Lumpur: Bank Negara Malaysia.

Bhagwati, J. (1998). 'The Capital Myth: The Difference Between Trade in Widgets and Dollars'. *Foreign Affairs,* 77/3: 7–12.

Braunstein, E. and Epstein, G. (2005). 'Bargaining Power and Foreign Direct Investment in China: Can 1.3 Billion Consumers Tame the Multinationals?' in W. Milberg (ed.), *Labor and the Globalization of Production; Causes and Consequences of Industrial Upgrading.* London: Palgrave Macmillan.

Cardoso, E. and Goldfajn, I. (1998). 'Capital Flows to Brazil: The Endogeneity of Capital Controls'. International Monitary Fund Staff Papers, vol. 45.

Chang, H.-J. and Grabel, I. (2004). *Reclaiming Development: An Alternative Economic Policy Manual.* London: Zed Press.

Dornbusch, R. (2002). 'Malaysia's Crisis: Was it Different?', in S. Edwards and J. A. Frankel (eds.), *Preventing Currency Crises in Emerging Markets*. Chicago: The University of Chicago Press, pp. 441–60.

Eichengreen, B. (2002). *Financial Crises and What to Do About them?* New York: Oxford University Press.

Epstein, G. and Schor, J. (1992). 'Structural Determinants and Economic Effects of Capital Controls in OECD Countries', in T. Banuri and J. Schor (eds.), *Financial Openness and National Autonomy*. Oxford: Clarendon Press, pp. 136–62.

—— and Grabel, I., and Jomo, K. S. (2003). 'Capital Management Techniques In Developing Countries', in A. Buira (ed.), *Challenges to the World Bank and IMF*. London: Anthem Press, pp. 141–75.

Fernald, J. G. and O. D. Babson (1999). 'Why Has China Survived the Asian Crisis So Well? What Risks Remain?' International Finance Discussion Papers, Board of Governors of the Federal Reserve System, Washington, DC.

Fischer, S. (1998). 'Capital Account Liberalization and the Role of the IMF', in 'Should the IMF Pursue Capital-Account Convertibility'. *Princeton Essays in International Finance*, 207: 1–10.

—— (2001). 'Exchange Rate Regimes: Is the Bipolar View Correct?' *Journal of Economic Perspectives*, 15/2: 3–24.

—— (2002). 'Financial Crises and Reform of the International Financial System'. NBER Working Paper No. 9297.

Gao, H. (2000). 'Liberalising China's Capital Account: Lessons Drawn from Thailand's Experience'. Visiting Researchers Series No. 6. Institute of Southeast Asian Studies, Singapore.

Ghosh, J. (2004). 'Regulating Capital Flows'. International Development Economics Associates (IDEAs). Available at: www.networkideas.org/alt/jul2004/alt05_Capital_Flows.htm.

Grabel, I. (1999). 'Rejecting Exceptionalism: Reinterpreting the Asian Financial Crises', in J. Michie and J. G. Smith (eds.), *Global Instability: The Political Economy of World Economic Governance*. London: Routledge, pp. 37–67.

—— (2003a). 'Averting Crisis: Assessing Measures to Manage Financial Integration in Emerging Economies'. *Cambridge Journal of Economics*, 27: 317–36.

—— (2003b). 'International Private Capital Flows and Developing Countries', in H.-J. Chang (ed.), *Rethinking Development Economics*. London: Anthem Press.

Ho, C. and R. N. McCauley (2003). 'Living With Flexible Exchange Rates: Issues and Recent Experience in Inflation Targeting Emerging Market Economies'. BIS Working Papers No. 130.

Icard, A. (2002). 'China's Capital Account Liberalization in Perspective'. Paper presented to BIS/SAFE Seminar on Capital Account Liberalization in China: International Perspectives, Beijing, September 12–13.

International Monetary Fund (IMF) (2000). *Annual Report on Exchange Arrangements and Exchange Restrictions*. Washington, DC: International Monetary Fund.

Ishi, S., Ötker-Robe, I., and Cui, L. (2001). 'Measures to Limit the Offshore Use of Currencies: Pros and Cons'. IMF Working Paper, WP/01/43. International Monetary Fund, Washington, DC.

Jayadev, A. and Lee, K.-K. (2004). 'The Effects of Capital Account Liberalization on Growth and the Labor Share of Income: Reviewing and Extending the Cross-Country

Evidence', in G. Epstein (ed.), *Capital Flight and Capital Controls in Developing Countries*. Northampton, MA: Edward Elgar.

Jianping, D. (2001). 'Liberalization of Capital Account With China's Characteristics'. Mimeo.

Jingu, T. (2002). 'Moving Forward in Reforming China's Capital Market'. NRI Paper No. 40. Nomura Research Institute, Tokyo.

Johnson, S. and Mitton, T. (2003). 'Cronyism and Capital Controls: Evidence from Malaysia'. *Journal of Financial Economics*, 67: 351–82.

Johnston, R. B. with M. Swinburne, A. Kyei, B. Laurens, D. Mitchem, I. Ötker-Robe, S. Sosa, and N. Tamirisa (1999). *Exchange Rate Arrangements and Currency Convertibility: Developments and Issues*. Washington, DC: International Monetary Fund.

Jomo, K.S. (ed.) (2001). *Malaysian Eclipse*. London: Zed Press.

Kaplan, E. and Rodrik, D. (2002). 'Did the Malaysian Capital Controls Work?', in S. Edwards and J. A. Frankel (eds.), *Preventing Currency Crises in Emerging Markets*. Chicago: The University of Chicago Press, pp. 393–441.

Klau, M. and Mohanty, M. S. (2004). 'Monetary Policy Rules in Emerging Market Economics: Issues and Evidence'. BIS Working Paper No. 149. Available at SSRN: http://ssrn.com/abstract=901388.

Krugman, P. (1998). 'Open Letter to Mr. Mahathir'. *Fortune*, 28 September.

Lardy, N. R. (1998). *China's Unfinished Economic Revolution*. Washington, DC: Brookings Institution Press.

Ma, G., Ho, C., and McCauley, R. N. (2004). 'The Markets for Non-Deliverable Forwards in Asian Currencies'. *BIS Quarterly Review*, June, 81–94.

McCauley, R. N. (2001). 'Setting Monetary Policy in East Asia: Goals, Developments and Polices'. *Future Directions for Monetary Policies in East Asia*. Sydney: Reserve Bank of Australia.

Mahathir, M. (2001). *The Malaysian Currency Crisis: How and Why it Happened*. Petaling Jaya: Pelanduk.

Miller, M. (1999). 'Malaysian Capital Controls a Failure, Says Nobel Prize Winner Merton Miller'. *Asian Wall Street Journal*, 9 July, A18.

Naughton, B. (1996). 'China's Emergence and Future as a Trading Nation'. Brookings Papers on Economic Activity, 1992: 2, pp. 273–344.

Nayyar, D. (2000). 'Capital Controls and the World Financial Authority: What Can We Learn from the Indian Experience'. CEPA Working Paper Series III No. 14.

Neely, C. (1999). *An Introduction to Capital Controls*. St Louis: Federal Reserve Bank of St Louis, Nov–Dec. 81: 13–30.

Nembhard, J. G. (1996). *Capital Control, Financial Policy and Industrial Policy In South Korea and Brazil*. New York: Praeger Press.

Ocampo, J. A. (2002). 'Capital-Account and Counter-Cyclical Prudential Regulations in Developing Countries'. UNU/WIDER Discussion Paper, August.

Padmanabhan, G. (2002). 'Operationalising Capital Account Liberalisation: The Indian Experience'. Paper presented to the BIS/SAFE Seminar on Capital Account Liberalisation in China: International Perspectives, Beijing, September 12–13.

Palley, T. I. (2004). 'Asset-based Reserve Requirements: Reasserting Domestic Monetary Control in an Era of Financial Innovation and Instability'. *Review of Political Economy*, vol. 16, no. 1, pp. 43–58.

Palma, G. (2000). 'The Three Routes to Financial Crises: The Need for Capital Controls', CEPA Working Paper Series III, no. 18.

Prasad, E., Rogoff, K., Wei, S.-J., and Ayhan Kose, M. (2003). 'Effects of Financial Globalization on Developing Countries: Some Empirical Evidence'. Available at: www.imf.org/external/np/res/docs/2003/031703.htm.

Rajaraman, I. (2001). 'Capital Account Regimes in India and Malaysia'. National Institute of Public Finance and Policy, New Delhi. Mimeo.

Reddy, Y. V. (2004). 'Remarks on Capital Account Liberalisation and Capital Controls'. Central Bank Governors' Symposium, 25 June.

Rodrik, D. (1998). 'Who Needs Capital-Account Convertibility?' *Princeton Essays in International Finance*, 207: 55–65.

Rosen, D. H. (1999). *Behind the Open Door: Foreign Enterprises in the Chinese Marketplace*. Washington, DC: Institute for International Economics.

Schneider, B. (2000). *Conference Report: Conference on Capital Account Liberalization—A Developing Country Perspective*. London: Overseas Development Institute.

____ (2001). 'Issues in Capital Account Convertibility in Developing Countries'. *Development Policy Review*, 19/1: 31–84.

State Administration of Foreign Exchange (SAFE) (2002). 'Recent History of Capital Controls'. Available at: www.chinaonline.com/refer/ministry_profiles/C00041154.asp.

Stiglitz, J. E. (2002). *Globalization and Its Discontents*. New York: W. W. Norton & Co.

Taylor, L. (2002). 'External Liberalization In Asia, Post-Socialist Europe and Brazil'. Available at: www.networkideas.org.

____ and Pieper, U. (1998). 'The Revival of the Liberal Creed: the IMF, the World Bank, and Inequality in a Globalized Economy' in D. Baker, G. Epstein, and R. Pollin (eds.), *Globalization and Progressive Economic Policy*. Cambridge: Cambridge University Press.

Wang, Y. and Xie, Y. (2002). 'Summary'. BIS/SAFE Seminar on Capital Account Liberalisation in China: International Perspectives. Available at: www.bis.org.

Watanabe, K., Akama, H., and Mifune, J. (2002). 'The Effectiveness of Capital Controls and Monitoring: The Case of Non-Internationalization of Emerging Market Currencies'. EMEAP (Executives' Meeting of East Asia-Pacific Central Banks) Discussion Paper.

Wei, S.-I. (2000). 'Local Corruption and Global Capital Flows'. Brookings Papers on Economic Activity, 2: 303–54.

Xiao, G. (2004). 'Round-Tripping Foreign Direct Investment in the People's Republic of China: Scale, Causes and Implications'. Asian Development Bank Institute Discussion Paper No. 7, Tokyo.

Zhu, A., Li, C., and Epstein, G. (2004). 'Capital Flight From China', in G. Epstein (ed.), *Capital Flight and Capital Controls in Developing Countries*. Northampton, MA: Edward Elgar.

7

The Role of Preventative Capital Account Regulations

José Antonio Ocampo and José Gabriel Palma

7.1 Introduction

Since the 1970s, developing countries have faced significant problems with their capital accounts in the face of rapidly expanding but highly volatile and unregulated international financial liquidity. In the case of Latin America, which has some of the most open capital accounts in the Third World, few practical economic problems have been as complex as the question of how to handle sharp externally-generated financial cycles. These financial cycles have been characterized by phases of large inflows (such as those created by bank lending in the 1970s and portfolio inflows during the 1990s), followed by sharp reversals and large negative transfers (1980s and 1999–2003).[1] Asian economies experienced a similar process in the 1990s, leading to a crash in 1997 that brought the world financial system to the brink of a global crisis.

For developing countries, the crucial issue is whether domestic markets can deal with these sharp financial cycles on their own and, in particular, whether domestic financial and asset markets can absorb positive and negative external shocks of this magnitude without manias and crashes. At the same time, there is the issue of whether the real economy has the capacity to adjust effectively to the rapidly changing economic environment that results from

[1] According to the database of the United Nations Economic Commission for Latin America and the Caribbean (ECLAC), between 1973 and 1981, net private inflows into Latin America reached US$(2000) 440 billion; in the 1990s, this figure jumped to US$(2000) 580 billion (see Figure 7.2 below). In turn, between 1982 and 1990, net transfer of resources (net inflows minus net factor payments; for this calculation net inflows includes 'errors and omissions', but excludes the use of IMF credit, IMF loans, and exceptional financing) became *negative* to the tune of US$(2000) 650 billion; again, between 1999 and 2003, Latin America had to deal with negative transfers of more than US$(2000) 100 billion (see Figure 7.4).

these cycles. In terms of policy in a capital-importing developing country, the optimal policy mix for dealing with these cycles is not obvious. This paper underscores the role of preventive capital account regulations on capital flows in this policy mix.

Unfortunately, recent experiences of developing countries with open capital accounts have shown that these sharp financial cycles are highly likely to lead to financial crises. There are three reasons for this. First, during periods of surges in inflows, the incentive mechanisms and resource allocation dynamics of financial markets have failed under the pressures generated by the increased liquidity brought about by these surges.[2] As a result, borrowers and lenders ended up accumulating more risk than was privately, let alone socially, efficient; this risk has become evident in the alternate phase of the cycle (that of the 'sudden stop' in external financing).[3] Second, the real economy has found it extremely difficult to deal with financial cycles of the magnitude experienced by countries with open capital accounts. Indeed, in developing economies characterized by significant currency mismatches in their financial portfolios, some typical adjustment mechanisms—such as the relative price (real exchange) adjustment—have failed when faced with sharp changes in external liquidity; instead of helping to bring these economies back to equilibrium, these adjustment mechanisms have tended to exacerbate cyclical swings through their pro-cyclical wealth effects. Third, in financially liberalized economies, governments and central banks have found their degrees of freedom for counter-cyclical macroeconomic policies to offset the effects of these externally generated cycles seriously limited; indeed, market forces have often pushed them into opposite, pro-cyclical, macroeconomic policies.

These recurrent financial crises in developing countries have opened up political and academic debates at least on two fronts: first, on whether these crises have been the result of market interferences (mostly in the form of unhelpful government interventions that distorted the working of otherwise efficient financial and other markets), or the result of actual market failures; second, on the policy responses most likely to help developing countries to absorb the sharp swings in capital inflows characteristic of the last two decades.

Regarding the first issue, those who argue that primarily exogenous destabilizing mechanisms led developing countries into financial crises have

---

[2] The remarkable size of net inflows into East Asia before the 1997 crisis—according to the WEO database, 'Developing Asia' received more than US$(2000) 500 billion between 1989 and 1996—makes Alan Greenspan's oft quoted post-East Asian crisis remarks something of an understatement: 'In retrospect, it is clear that more investment monies flowed into these economies than could be profitably employed at modest risks'.

[3] According to Kindleberger, international financial markets can do one thing that is more damaging for developing countries than over-lending: to halt that lending abruptly.

emphasized the moral hazards created by government deposit insurance and bailouts by international institutions, as well as the 'crony-mechanisms' that have often distorted the access to finance. In turn, those who emphasize the existence of endogenous market failures are primarily concerned with the study of how the combination of a particular type of international financial market and a particular form of financial liberalization in developing countries may have led to the creation of an economic environment in which the maximization-cum-equilibrium process failed. One of the issues at the centre of the resulting debate regarding the policy options most appropriate to reduce the likelihood of financial crises is the relative effectiveness of price-based and quantity-based controls of capital *inflows*.

This chapter reviews the experiences of three developing countries—Chile, Colombia, and Malaysia. After having opened up their capital accounts, these countries fine-tuned their integration into international financial markets through the reintroduction of capital controls, in order to deal with the 1990s surge in private capital inflows, particularly short-term portfolio inflows. The following section of the chapter examines the dynamics of capital flows into developing countries, and presents some contrasting experiences of Latin America and East Asia. The chapter then analyses the nature and effects of regulations on capital inflows in these three countries during the 1990s—in particular, their effects on the magnitude and composition of capital flows, on the macroeconomic policy space that the authorities enjoyed under these circumstances, and on asset prices. Finally, the chapter presents some conclusions.

7.2 The Dynamics of Capital Flows: The Contrast Between Latin America and East Asia

One of the most clear stylized facts of developing countries' access to international finance is that when international financial markets have opened up their doors to these countries they have done so in the form of sharp cycles (e.g., the 1820s, 1860s, 1890s, 1920s, 1970s, and 1990s). Figure 7.1 shows this phenomenon during the last three decades.

A remarkable feature of the 1990s cycles is that while the 1970s surge in inflows had to wait for a half century after the previous boom (1920s), the one in 1990s took place less than a decade after the 1982 debt crisis (see Figure 7.2). In the case of Latin America, one well-known reason for this rapid return of inflows is that the US government had to act in the late 1980s to sort out the problems left by the 1970s cycle and the subsequent problems of the highly exposed US banks. This eventually led to the 'Brady Plan', which effectively created a secondary market for Latin American securities. This new market not only helped US banks to unload their Latin American debt, but also facilitated

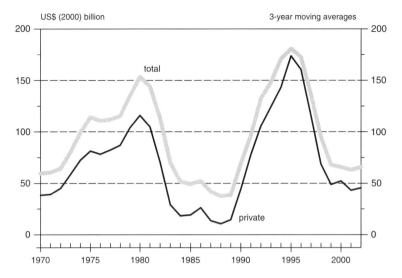

Figure 7.1. Africa, Asia, and Latin America: total and private net capital inflows, 1970–2002

Note: total = total net capital inflows; private = net private inflows. In this and other graphs below that show values in terms of 3-year moving averages, the value shown for the last year is the actual value of the year.

Source: IMF (2004a). With respect to Africa, as the IMF data-set only includes information for Sub-Saharan Africa, in order to have an estimate for the whole continent (and despite the problems of mixing data from IMF and World Bank sources), data for North Africa (Algeria, Morocco, Tunisia, and Egypt) was added to that of Sub-Saharan Africa using information from World Bank (2004).

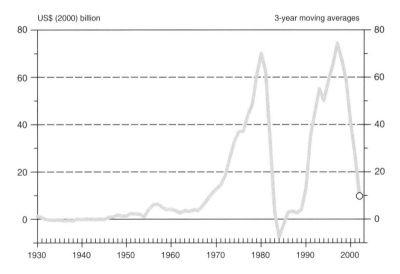

Figure 7.2. Latin America: net private capital inflows, 1930–2002

Source: 1930–49, B. Stallings (1990; this source only including inflows from the USA); 1950–69, ECLAC Statistical Division (during this period, portfolio inflows include a very small amount of government bonds because Latin American countries report their balance of payments according to the IMF methodology, revision 5; in this methodology, under 'net portfolio inflows' public and private sector bonds are reported together); and 1970–2002, IMF (2004a).

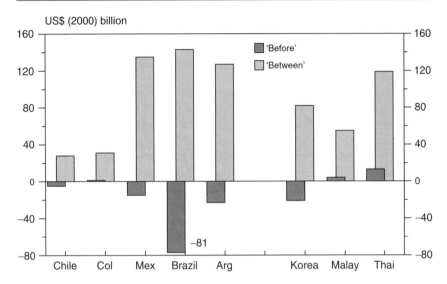

Figure 7.3. Latin America and East Asia: aggregate Net capital flows before financial liberalization and between financial liberalization and financial crisis

Note: **Col** = Colombia; **Mex** = Mexico; **Arg** = Argentina; **Malay** = Malaysia; **Thai** = Thailand. In each case the period '**between**' covers the years between financial liberalisation and financial crisis—Chile, 1975–82; Colombia, 1993–98; Mexico, 1988–94; Brazil, 1992–98; Argentina, 1991–01; and Korea, Malaysia, and Thailand, 1988–96. The period '**before**' covers a similar number of years before financial liberalization (in the case of East Asia and Argentina, however, as the period 'before' would have included years preceding the previous 1982 debt crisis, only years since 1982 have been included).

Source: World Bank (2004).

the inclusion of Latin America—and emerging markets in general—into the booming security markets that had been developing in the industrial world in the 1980s.

Although these capital flow cycles were *external* from the point of view of the developing world, domestic policies did play a role in the specific timing of the capital account booms, both in their composition and in their effect on the recipient countries. Figure 7.3 shows the remarkable turnaround in the capital account of some Latin American and East Asian countries after their respective processes of domestic financial and capital account liberalizations; this striking turnaround generated the dynamics that eventually led to financial crises in these countries. It is also widely recognized that the macroeconomic policy followed by different countries during periods of booming inflows also influenced the vulnerability of countries once a sharp turnaround in the capital account had taken place. This chapter deals with precisely that positive role that preventive regulations on capital inflows had on a group of developing countries willing to apply them (see also Chapters 4 and 6, this volume).

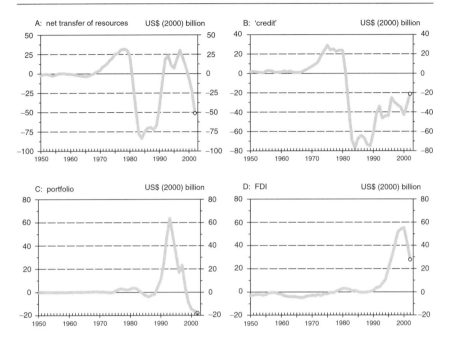

Figure 7.4. Latin America: net transfer of resources and its composition, 1950–02

Note: Net transfer of resources = net inflows minus net factor payments; as mentioned above, net inflows includes 'errors and omissions' but excludes the use of IMF credit, IMF loans and exceptional financing. 3-year moving averages.

Source: ECLAC's Statistical Division.

The cyclical movement of the aggregate net inflows hides the sharply different dynamics of the three main components of private capital inflows and, in particular, their sequential booms: first came credit inflows (particularly bank lending), then portfolio inflows and finally FDI inflows. This is illustrated in Figure 7.4 for Latin America through the evolution of the net transfer of resources (net capital inflows minus interest and dividend payments). In the case of bank lending, the boom of the 1970s was followed by an extended period of net resource outflows that lasted more than two decades. Indeed, strikingly, bank lending continued to generate strong negative resource flows to Latin America at the same time as the Asian economies were experiencing a surge in bank lending between 1990 and 1996. Also, the net transfer of resources accumulated during the boom periods are moderate— US$(2000) 243 billion from 1972 to 1981 and US$(2000) 203 billion from 1991 to 1998—and, even then, these two periods are among only a very few years out of the last two centuries when the net transfer of resources has actually been positive for Latin America. Put in other terms, interest and dividend payments have most of the time exceeded net capital inflows into

175

the region or have reinforced the negative effect of capital outflows during crises.

A comparison of the relationship between changes in current and capital accounts in Latin America and East Asia also reveals two crucial differences between these two regions, differences that are critical for the analysis of the appropriate macroeconomic and regulatory policies. One is the asymmetric nature of the cycle in Latin America—i.e., the inability of Latin America up to 2002 to generate current account surpluses even at times of capital outflows and domestic recession—which contrasts with a very different pattern in East Asia (see Figure 7.5). This is mainly the result of both the problems generated by the composition of Latin American exports (particularly the high sensitivity to commodity price fluctuations and the low share of manufacturers that are dynamic in world trade due to Latin America's endemic underinvestment in export diversification. A major implication of this incapacity to generate current account surpluses up to 2002 was that it inevitably affects its capacity to repay principal, thus increasing the likelihood of running into Ponzi-type finance.

The other is the different time sequence that characterizes the joint dynamics of the current and capital accounts in the two regions. This difference between Latin America and East Asia can be tested with the help of the Granger time-precedence test (often misleadingly called the Granger-causality test). The results of this test show a major difference between Latin America and East Asia in the time sequencing between the changes in the current and the capital accounts. In Latin America, changes in the capital account tend to precede changes in the current account, while in East Asia the time precedence is the opposite (see the Appendix). This is an important finding because if the primary source of the Latin American financial cycle is an externally induced change in the capital account, capital controls are more likely to be an obvious counter-cyclical policy option to deal with the cycle at its source.

In East Asia, the results of the test indicate a more macroeconomic textbook time-sequence: changes in the current account—the result of developments in the domestic real economy—precede changes in the capital account. It therefore seems less clear that in this region capital controls should be the dominant component of a policy to deal with the inflow problems at source. This does not mean that capital control cannot help—as discussed below, inflow controls in Malaysia in 1994 were remarkably effective in the short run; it means that the best policy in this case would be to deal with the domestic problems leading to the changes in the current account: in this case, mainly the huge levels of deficit finances of corporate investment. For example, in the case of the Republic of Korea (mainly due to declining profitability—a decline that had little to do with productivity trends and much with collapsing micro

A: Latin America, 1950–2002

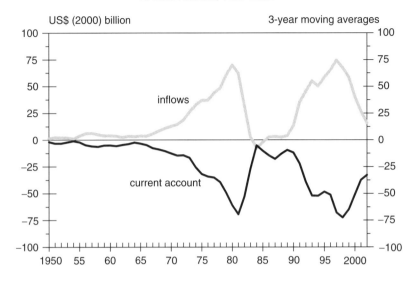

B: East Asia (3), 1975–2002

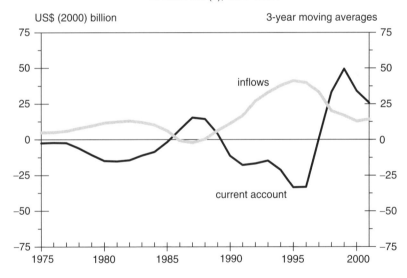

Figure 7.5. Latin America and East Asia: net private inflows and current account

Note: East Asia (3): Korea, Malaysia, and Thailand.

Source: Latin America, 1950–69, ECLAC's Statistical Division; 1970–02, World Bank (2004). East Asia, (2004; data available only from 1975).

electronic prices)[4]—the corporate sector had to finance its high, but relatively stable, levels of investment (of just under 30 percent of GDP) switching from own profits to external finance. This change led to a rapid increase in the deficit of the corporate sector, from about 5 percent of GNP (1987) to nearly 20 percent of GNP (1996), which absorbed not only all the increase in the surplus of the capital account but also that of the household and government sectors as well (Palma 2002, 2003).

Not surprisingly, Latin America and East Asia followed different routes to their respective financial crises. Even though there was a similarity in terms of the surges in capital inflows and in the speed of credit expansion between these two regions, there also was a crucial difference in the use made of this additional credit. While in Latin America additional credit to the private sector was mainly directed towards increased consumption and asset speculation, in East Asia it helped to sustain high levels of corporate investment (in the face of falling profitability). As mentioned above, the difference was related to the macroeconomic dynamics that had led to booming capital inflows in the first place. In East Asia, it was mainly an endogenous pull: additional finance was actually needed to sustain high levels of investment at a time of rapidly falling profit levels. In Latin America, meanwhile, it was a mixed response. First, though there was an endogenous pull, it was of a very different nature from that of East Asia, based on the need to attract foreign finance to help service the huge foreign debt in the face of the then region's inability to generate current account surpluses. Second, there was a crucial exogenous push of foreign capital—particularly portfolio flows—searching for new market outlets (see Figure 7.6). Among the many macroeconomic challenges that emerged, of course, was how to absorb the surge of liquidity resulting from non-sterilized inflows; an age-old mechanism was followed: additional inflows eased the access and reduced the price and the transaction costs of liquidity. In turn, easy access to cheap credit fuelled expectations regarding the performance of the economy, a performance that was enhanced by the additional expenditure brought about by extra borrowing and availability of foreign exchange. Thus, for a while, improved expectations fed a self-fulfilling prophecy. As a result, from the point of view of this exogenous push of foreign capital, in Latin America the propensity to 'over-lend' led to the propensity to 'over-borrow'.

---

[4] The D-Ram price per megabyte, for example, fell from US$26 in 1995 to US$10 in 1996, US$4 in 1997 and less than US$1 in 1998. Memory chips were one of the Republic of Korea's main export items. The collapse of the price of the D-Ram memory in 1995 was triggered by massive Taiwanese new investment in memory chips of more advanced technology, which came on-stream at a time when markets were already saturated. As is well known, in micro electronic markets competitiveness only exists at the cutting edge of technology; so Korean corporations had little choice but to invest in the new technology even though collapsing prices had drastically cut short-term returns (Palma 2003).

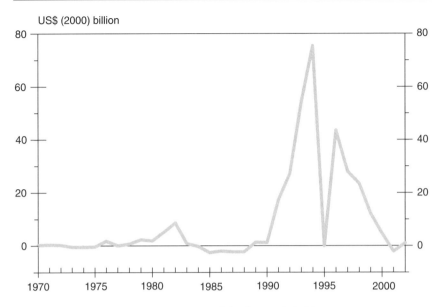

US$ (2000) billion

Figure 7.6. Latin America: net private portfolio flows, 1970–02
Source: IMF (2004a).

From this perspective, therefore, the path to financial crises in Latin America started with a surge in inflows, an explosion of credit to the private sector, and low levels of interest rates (after stabilization); all these produced rapid real-exchange appreciation, consumption booms, asset bubbles in stock and real estate markets, a reduction in savings, and a deterioration of current accounts (massive in several cases). In the meantime, not only did foreign debt levels increase but also their term structure deteriorated. It did not take much for this Latin route of inflow absorption to lead to a state of such financial fragility that a sudden collapse of confidence and withdrawal of finance were almost inevitable.

In East Asia, there were also massive inflow surges and an increase in private credit and low interest rates, but there were no consumption booms and only more limited asset bubbles. In fact, there were none at all in the Republic of Korea, whereas in Malaysia and Thailand asset bubbles were not anywhere near as huge as in Latin America. Rather, in the context of declining profitability and rapid technological change, there were high levels of investment that ended up producing remarkably high corporate debt/equity ratios. Despite stunning growth records, a high degree of competitiveness and fundamentals that although not perfect were the envy of most developing countries, this East Asian route to financial fragility also led to financial crisis.

7.3 Capital Account Regulations in Chile, Colombia, and Malaysia

7.3.1 *The Nature of the Regulations*

In a world of highly volatile and unregulated international liquidity, the basic task of capital controls is both to help avoid the pro-cyclical dynamics created by surges in inflows and to counteract the strong market incentives to adopt pro-cyclical macroeconomic policies that tend to develop in economies that have chosen to integrate into international capital markets with open capital accounts.[5] From this perspective, there are two basic issues for developing countries; the first is how to deal with the remarkable volatility of capital flows, particularly in some of its components—see Figure 7.6. The second, the fact that the liberalization of capital accounts, instead of creating automatic stabilizers vis-à-vis these volatile flows, tends effectively to create, in the words of Stiglitz (2003), 'automatic destabilizers'. In this context, preventive capital account regulations attempt to deal both with the first problem at source, and to give monetary authorities more room for manoeuvre in order to deal with the second.

In the 1990s, most countries in Latin America and some in East Asia opted for rapid liberalization of their capital accounts. However, the experiences of China, India, and Taiwan show that a more selective path of participation in international capital markets was also possible, and proved a more effective way of avoiding the pro-cyclical swings associated to the volatility generated by unrestricted capital flows (see Chapter 6, this volume). In turn, what the experiences of Chile, Colombia, and Malaysia have in common is the fact that although they initially opted for a process that was eventually to lead to practically unrestricted integration into international capital markets, they later decided to 'fine-tune' this integration using different forms of preventive regulations to control unwanted capital *inflows*.

The central instrument used by Chile and Colombia was price-based regulation, namely unremunerated reserve requirements (URR) for specific foreign currency liabilities. The advantage of this system was that it created a simple, non-discretionary and preventive price-based incentive to regulate capital inflows; in particular, these measures penalized short-term foreign currency liabilities. In the case of Chile, these price-based capital account regulations were established in June 1991 and strengthened in May 1992. Some other modifications were also made in that time period, particularly the closing of a major loophole: foreign currency term deposits in domestic institutions.

---

[5] Among the pro-cyclical macroeconomic policies that developing countries tend to follow in the face of large inflows, the tendency to let interest rates fall and/or exchange rate appreciate stands out (see Ocampo 2003b).

Capital inflows were subject to a flat rate foreign currency deposit in the Central Bank, originally 20 percent but raised to 30 percent in May 1992; these unremunerated deposits continued until June 1998. These deposits were originally meant to be kept for a three month period, but they were soon extended to 12 months. In 1995 these regulations were strengthened, particularly by extending them to some portfolio flows that until then had been exempted from reserve requirements (another major loophole in the system). There were also other less important changes throughout the period, particularly those aiming at closing ambiguities and adjusting other secondary provisions.

In 1993, Colombia adopted the unremunerated reserve requirement system. Initially, these reserve requirements only applied to credits with maturities below a specified term (initially 18 months), with the amount of the deposit originally being inversely proportional to the term of the credit. It is interesting to emphasize that the introduction of this system was initially conceived to help *liberalize* the capital account, as it replaced a more traditional system of capital controls in which regulations were based on the final use of the loans.[6] Reserve requirements were modified in Colombia more frequently than in Chile, including not only changes to the minimum maturity of loans subject to regulations but also to the rates and maturities of the reserve requirements (Ocampo and Tovar 2003). In 1994, the regulatory system was strengthened on two occasions; initially the minimum maturity subject to the deposit was increased to three years and later again to five years. However, in early 1996, the regulatory system was put in reverse, the minimum maturity was decreased to three years, and a unique deposit rate was established; regulations were strengthened again in 1997, when the minimum maturity was restored to five years;[7] soon afterwards, the whole system was replaced by a scheme more clearly resembling that of Chile, a system which applied to all loans and thus eliminated the principle of a minimum maturity-period. The main difference from the Chilean system was that the deposit (originally

[6] The previous regulations, dating from 1991 (which, in turn, were reformed versions of the 1967 foreign exchange regulations) had established a minimum maturity of one year for foreign loans and maintained the traditional regulations on the final use of funds from such loans; i.e., these could only be used for trade or investment financing. In February 1992 for the first time, firms were allowed to contract foreign credits abroad for short-term working capital. In September 1993, when the URR were introduced, the traditional system of regulations based on final use was replaced by a system based on maturity. Additionally, domestic financial intermediaries were authorized to lend in foreign currency to domestic firms and residents regardless of the final use of the credit, to lend to foreigners in international currencies and to invest liquid assets abroad. The fact that the 1993 regulations were an effective liberalization of the capital account is emphasized by Ocampo and Tovar (1998, 2003), who show that they actually increased the sensitivity of capital flows to interest rate differentials (arbitrage incentives).

[7] This occurred after a short experiment with an explicit (Tobin) tax on all capital inflows, which was declared unconstitutional by the Constitutional Court two months after it was decreed.

30 percent of the inflows, which had to be kept in the central bank for 18 months) was made in the local currency and was therefore not protected from devaluation.

In both Chile and Colombia, economic agents could opt to substitute the unremunerated deposit with a one-off payment to the Central Bank of a sum equivalent to the opportunity cost of the deposit. This made the regulation into a *de facto* 'Tobin-type' tax—i.e., a fixed cost for external borrowing. However, by Tobin tax standards, the tax was very high; in Chile it was about 3 percent for one year loans during most of the period, and tended to fluctuate in response to changes in certain macroeconomic factors, such as international interest rates. The level for Colombia was higher, being on average equivalent to 13.6 percent for one year loans and 6.4 percent for three year loans during the 1994–98 period. In the case of Colombia, the domestic interest rate and devaluation expectations also determined the magnitude of the implicit tax. These taxes were meant to have a counter-cyclical role, which is why they were raised (particularly in Colombia) during periods of surges in capital inflows and lowered—eventually to a zero rate in both countries—when external conditions deteriorated following the 1997 East Asian crisis and the 1998 Russian default.

Although the central feature of the system was price-based, other administrative regulations on capital flows complemented reserve requirements. To contrast them with price-based regulations, we will refer to them as 'quantitative' in nature. In Chile, all inflows (including FDI) were subject to one year minimum stay requirements (a requirement that was lifted in May 2000), and the issuing of ADRs and similar instruments were subject to minimum amounts of issues and adequate risk classification; they also were subject to direct approval by the central bank. In Colombia, the Superintendence of Securities regulated the amount of the funds that portfolio investors could bring into the country and their domestic use, as well as bond and ADR issues made by Colombian firms on foreign markets. And although, unlike in Chile, trade loans were exempt from reserve requirements, other types of regulation were used to control this type of borrowing (minimum repayment periods for imports, except capital goods). Finally, in both cases, the reserve requirement implied an obligation to register all loans at the central bank. In Colombia, this included short-term commercial credits, which prior to the regulation had not been subject to this requirement.

Malaysia also offered major innovations in the area of capital account regulations in the 1990s, but relied more on provisions of a quantitative nature. After a surge of net private capital inflows that in relative terms climbed to extraordinary heights, net private inflows (including errors and omissions) increased as a share of GDP from minus 3 percent in 1988 to 25 percent in 1993 (see Palma 2000)—the Malaysian authorities decided to take radical action. To stop this surge, in January 1994 this country adopted a series of drastic measures that were mostly quantitative in character. It prohibited non-residents from buying a wide range of short-term securities, placed limits on non-trade-related liabilities of commercial banks, and prohibited commercial banks from making swaps and forward transactions with foreigners (see Negara Bank 1994; Park and Song 1997; Ötker-Robe 2000; and Palma 2000). Also, deposit interest rates were drastically reduced: real deposit rates fell from an annual average of 4.2 percent in 1993 to one of minus 0.9 percent in 1994, and real lending rates from 6.2 percent to 1.8 percent, respectively (Palma 2000). This was done in order to reverse arbitrage flows.

As these measures were so drastic, and as they included such a strong quantitative component, the effect was not only immediate but also remarkable, so much so that as early as August of the same year, some of the controls were already beginning to be lifted, and by the end of the year most had disappeared. The Malaysian authorities seemed to have developed some anxiety about the degree of effectiveness of these controls.[8] In fact, net private inflows fell in one year by no less than 18 percentage points of GDP; the main component of this fall was short-term flows, which fell by an amount equivalent to more than 13 percentage points of GDP.[9] These measures seem to have been particularly effective vis-à-vis short-term flows, which fell by more than 13 percentage points of GDP in just one year. Although these restrictions were lifted relatively soon, some in August 1994 and others in January 1995, the shock effect they generated seems to have affected the expectations of economic agents in a more permanent way than the Latin American-style price-based mechanisms (see below).

The other Malaysian innovation came in 1998 with the East Asian financial crisis but applied to capital outflows. These regulations were aimed at limiting ringgit speculation by both residents and non-residents, particularly by eliminating offshore trading of the domestic currency. As in the case of the 1994 regulations, they effectively segmented access to domestic financial transactions between residents and non-residents. In February 1999, a price-based instrument, an exit tax, which would be phased out in the following years, replaced this regulation. As these regulations affected outflows rather than inflows, they will not be considered in this chapter.[10]

---

[8] There is also evidence of a strong lobby from the domestic financial sector for the government to lift the most drastic controls.

[9] Non-FDI inflows, which had reached more than US$(2000) 11 billion in 1993, turned sharply negative in 1994; FDI was the only component of capital inflows that remained unaffected by these controls.

[10] On the effect of these regulations, see particularly, Kaplan and Rodrik (2002); Rajaraman (2002); and Epstein et al. (2003).

7.3.2 Policy Objectives of Regulations

As extensive literature on the subject has emphasized, the accumulation of risks during periods of surges of capital inflows depends not only on the flow imbalances that can eventually lead to unsustainable private and public sector debts, but also on their effects on corporate balance sheets and asset prices (especially stocks and real estate). Regulations on capital inflows, therefore, have three potential roles. The first is as a macroeconomic policy tool; the key aims are to provide some room for counter-cyclical macroeconomic policies, to help to cool aggregate demand, and try to avoid the accumulation of unsustainable debt burdens. The second role is as a 'liability policy' which helps to avoid both risky corporate balance sheet structures (especially due to excessive reliance on short-term external debts, and the maturity and currency mismatches typical of private sector financial structures in developing countries), and thus the worst effects of the volatility of capital inflows. Finally, capital controls help to avoid asset bubbles, given the sharp cyclical pattern that characterizes asset prices in developing countries.

Viewed as a macroeconomic policy tool, regulations on capital inflows can provide some room to 'lean against the wind' during periods of financial euphoria, through the adoption of a contractionary monetary policy and/or reduced appreciation pressures. Furthermore, if they are effective in reducing the magnitude of inflows, they can reduce or eliminate the quasi-fiscal costs of sterilized foreign exchange accumulation. Their role depends on the dynamics of capital inflows and their relation to current account deficits and their domestic counterparts (savings and investment behavior). If capital flows generate an exogenous push on current account and domestic imbalances, as they seemed to have done in Latin America, they can help to control the direct source of the financial disturbance. If they respond to an endogenous pull, as in East Asia, they can work in an indirect way to limit the finance available for domestic investment. In either case, the effect of regulations may be limited by the fact that integration into capital markets tends to generate strong pressure to adopt pro-cyclical macroeconomic policies (in particular, as discussed above, to allow domestic interest rates to fall to unreasonable levels, or to allow the exchange rate to appreciate excessively).

Viewed as a liability policy, capital account regulations take on board the fact that markets usually reward sound external debt profiles (Rodrik and Velasco 2000). This phenomenon reflects the fact that, during times of uncertainty, markets tend to respond to gross (and not merely to net) financing requirements; this means that the rollover of short-term liabilities is not financially neutral. Under these circumstances, a loan and bond maturity profile that leans towards longer term external obligations will reduce the risk of a balance of payments crisis. At the same time, on the equity side, foreign direct investment (FDI)—properly defined—also should be preferred to other portfolio flows, as it has proved in practice to be least volatile. Equity flows have the additional advantage that they allow all risks associated with the business cycle to be shared with foreign investors, and FDI may bring parallel benefits (access to technology and external markets). These benefits should be balanced against the generally higher costs of equity financing.

From the point of view of domestic balance sheets, the lack of depth in developing countries' financial markets can lead agents in the private and public sectors to hold variable mixes of maturity and currency mismatches in their portfolios. These mismatches tend to be interrelated. Indeed, due to the limited availability of domestic financing—and long-term domestic financing in particular—agents may be inclined to borrow abroad if external financing is easily available, but will then accumulate currency mismatches if their revenues are generated in domestic currencies (e.g., if they operate in the non-tradable sector). Capital account regulations thus can help avoid currency mismatches, particularly if they establish different rules on access to external capital markets by firms in the non-tradable sector (or, to the extent that this can serve as an imperfect proxy, by residents). Domestic prudential regulations that take into account the particular currency mismatch that characterizes non-tradable sectors can serve as a partial substitute in this regard (see Ocampo 2003a; Chapter 9, this volume). To the extent that maturity and currency mismatches are interrelated, obvious but long-term solutions are policies aimed at deepening domestic financial markets.

Recent literature has also emphasized the crucial role that asset prices play in the business cycle. In developing countries, a surge in capital inflows often generates over-optimism (or 'irrational exuberance', to use Robert Shiller and Alan Greenspan's terminology) and, as such, may well end up producing excessively high market valuation of stocks and real estate. Portfolio inflows may directly fuel stock price booms and may lead to speculative financing to profit from stock market revaluation. In turn, rising real estate prices may generate excessive investment in residential construction as well as help fuel the boom in domestic financing, based on overpriced loan collaterals. These booms can produce increased financial fragility; and when there is a (in the case of developing countries, practically inevitable) sudden stop in external financing, this would lead to large price corrections; also, after a collapse of asset prices, banks may find that their loan portfolios lack adequate collateral and this may even fuel further downward corrections in prices if they decide (or need) to sell at large discounts the collateral they had received in lieu of debts.

A look at the rationale behind the imposition of regulations of capital inflows in Chile, Colombia, and Malaysia indicates that authorities were

explicitly aiming to increase their room for macroeconomic policy manoeu-
vres and to change the composition of external finance towards less volatile
flows. Averting asset bubbles seems to have figured less prominently in their
explicit policy objectives. In the following sections, the extent to which there
is evidence that they were successful in their task will be explored.

7.3.3 Effects on the Magnitude of Capital Inflows

Figure 7.7a shows the level and composition by source of net private capital
inflows in Chile before, during and after capital controls. As is fairly evident
from the graph, capital controls in Chile seem to have had a significant but
rather short-term effect, at least in terms of levels. By 1994, the 1991 reduction
seems to have evaporated, even in the face of the strengthened regulations
adopted in May 1992. The reduction brought about by the 1995 strengthening
of controls seems to have lasted for only one year. Of course, what levels
these inflows would have reached had it not been for these controls may
never be known, but the evidence seems to indicate that private inflows did
bounce back after having been affected briefly by the imposition of controls.
In terms of volume, then, these controls seem to have had the effect of 'speed
bumps' rather than permanent restrictions (Palma 2000). There also were
changes in the composition of capital flows towards foreign direct investment,
but this was a broader regional (and global) trend which also occurred in
countries that did not open their capital accounts in any significant way
and those that did open them but did not rely on preventive capital account
regulations.

The speed bump character of inflow regulations in Chile is even clearer in
Figure 7.7b. In terms of volume, net equity securities and 'other' investments,
went from generating large negative flows in 1988 to large positive flows in
1990. The 1991 regulations did interrupt this process, but only by a year,
and their strengthening in 1992 does not seem to have prevented a renewed
capital account boom. The 1995 regulations generated a new lull that, as
had happened in 1991, only lasted for a year. The fact that the effects of
regulations on capital inflows were only temporary may, of course, not be
independent from the level of the implicit tax, which was much lower in
Chile than in Colombia (see below). Also, loopholes in the regulations were
a constant source of concern and led to a series of measures aimed at closing
them.

In Colombia, frequent changes in the regulations make annual data an
unreliable clue to their effect on capital flows. So Figure 7.8 concentrates
on the most widely used series in Colombia to analyze capital flows: private
capital flows involving cash transactions (thus eliminating those flows that are
tied to trade transactions or involve investment in kind, both of which were
not subject to the URR. As the figure makes clear, the major turning points

a. Composition of net private capital inflows, 1988–97

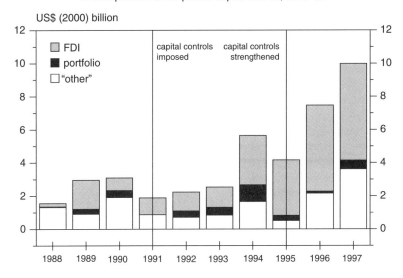

b. Net equity securities and 'other' inflows, 1988–97

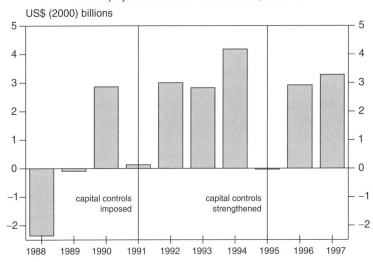

Figure 7.7. Chile: composition of net private capital inflows, net equity securities, and 'other' inflows, 1988–97

Source: Panel A, World Bank (2004); and Panel B, IMF (2004b). See respective sources for different definition of components of private capital flows.

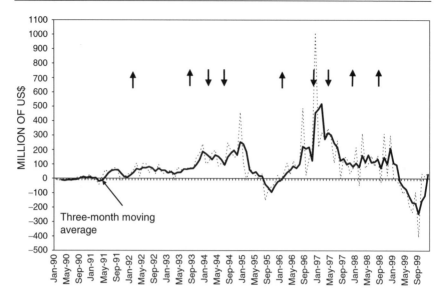

Figure 7.8. Colombia: Private cash capital flows

Note: Imposition or relaxation of restrictions on capital inflows, respectively (the direction of the arrows indicates expected effect on the index).

Source: Calculations based on data from the Central Bank of Colombia (Banco de la República).

in the dynamics of private capital flows in Colombia during the 1990s closely followed the timing of policy decisions.

Indeed, capital account liberalization, which came in two steps (February 1992 and September 1993),[11] led to a boom in external financing. The strengthening of controls in March 1994 had only moderate effects, but the stronger decisions adopted in August 1994 generated, with a lag, a sharp reversal of the trend. The lag was due to the fact that there were broad-based expectations, based on policy announcements by the new Administration (which took power in that month) that controls would be strengthened; this led to a speculative wave of registrations of new loans in anticipation of such policy change. The less restrictive regulations introduced in early 1996 prompted, in turn, a rapid increase in capital inflows. By late 1996, speculative attacks threatened to break the floor of the currency exchange band (as reflected by the peak observed in the data for December 1996). The series of regulations imposed early in 1997 reversed that trend again, bringing capital inflows to more moderate levels; these levels were maintained until early 1999, when the Brazilian crisis triggered rapid capital outflows.

Figure 7.9 shows the very strong surge in private capital inflows experienced by Malaysia between 1988 and 1993. This was the background for the

[11] See footnote 6.

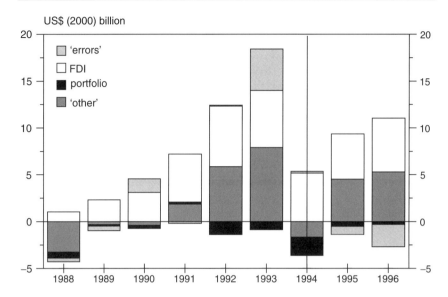

Figure 7.9. Malaysia: composition of net private capital inflows, 1988–96

Source: IMF (2004a; includes 'errors and omissions'). See source for definition of components of private capital flows.

decision adopted by the Malaysian authorities to impose strict controls on capital inflows at the beginning of 1994. As we have seen, and unlike the Chilean and Colombian experiments with capital account regulation, the key characteristic of these controls was their quantitative administrative character. Also, domestic interest rates were reduced to reverse arbitrage flows.

As mentioned above, these measures were so drastic that the effect was immediate. In part due to the very success of these controls, and in part due to strong political pressure from the domestic and foreign financial systems, some of the controls began to be lifted as early as August of the same year; by January most had disappeared.

Although capital flows recovered with the lifting of controls, the recovery was relatively mild compared, for example, with the recovery of net private inflows in Chile after 1995. Moreover, the recovery took place only in 'other' inflows, leaving net portfolio inflows still negative; in turn, 'errors and omissions' changed from a large positive figure in 1993 to a large negative one in both 1995 and 1996. Thus, quantitative controls generated a short but sharp shock, which had both stronger short-term and longer lasting effects than the continuing (and strengthening) Chilean or Colombian price-based controls.

One of the main peculiarities of the Malaysian case is the large size of the balance of payments 'errors and omissions' item. This is relevant not only because it reveals pre-1994 deficiencies in Malaysia's Central Bank accounting practices, but also because, with controls in place, they first disappeared and then became negative. The relevance of this is that one of the most repeated criticisms of controls is that they tend to be ineffective because capital will always find ways of bypassing them. In Malaysia it seems to have been the other way around: with controls came a successful tightening of procedures for recording inflows and a massive reduction, rather than an increase, in this item.[12]

In any case, not all elements of the macroeconomic policy package were dismantled at the end of 1994: low interest rates were maintained to discourage a possible rapid return of private capital inflows after the end of quantitative restrictions. This certainly helped to maintain the volume of arbitrage inflows at a relatively stable level, but may have helped to fuel the real estate bubble of 1996, which made the 1997 crisis much worse than it would have been otherwise (see below).

7.3.4 The Broader Macroeconomic Effects

While there is little room to doubt the capacity of the 1994 Malaysian controls to affect capital flows, the price-based capital account regulations of Chile and Colombia have generated a great deal of debate. In particular, contrary to the broad agreement on the positive impact they had on external debt profiles (see below), their effectiveness as a macroeconomic policy tool has been subject to a great deal of controversy.[13]

Nonetheless, judging from the solid evidence with respect to the sensitivity of capital flows to interest rate spreads in both Chile and Colombia, it can be asserted that URR do influence the volume of capital flows at given interest rate spreads.[14] This may reflect the fact that available mechanisms for evading or eluding regulations are costly,[15] and that national firms' access to longer

---

[12] The negative figures for this item in 1995 and 1996 probably reflect capital flight by Malaysian citizens. If this was the case, like their counterparts in Mexico before the December 1994 crisis, these domestic agents may have predicted trouble with better foresight than international funds and bank managers did.

[13] For documents that support the effectiveness of these regulations in Chile, see Agosin (1998); Larraín et al. (2000); Le Fort and Lehman (2000, 2003); Palma (2000) and Agosin and Ffrench-Davis (2001). For a more mixed view, see Valdés-Prieto and Soto (1998); Ariyoshi et al. (2000); De Gregorio et al. (2000); Laurens (2000). Similarly, for strong views on their positive effects in Colombia, see Ocampo and Tovar (1998, 2003) and Villar and Rincón (2002), and for a more mixed view, Cárdenas and Barrera (1997) and Cárdenas and Steiner (2000).

[14] Indeed, evidence on the insensitivity of the volume of capital flows to capital account regulations comes from econometric analysis in which URR is not included as a determinant of interest rate spreads but rather as an additional factor affecting capital flows; this may therefore be interpreted as an inadequate econometric specification.

[15] Some of these mechanisms, such as the use of hedging, enable investors to cover some of the effects of these regulations, but in large part this is done by transferring risks (more specifically, the risk associated with longer term financing) to other agents who would only

term external funds is more limited than access to shorter term funds. In Colombia, where these regulations were modified more extensively over the 1990s, there is strong evidence that increases in URR reduced overall flows; this evidence is consistent with the more qualitative evidence of the links between the timing of major turnarounds in the capital flows and policy decisions regarding the capital account (Ocampo and Tovar 1998, 2003). In any case, as mentioned above, a significant part of the history of these regulations, particularly in Chile, was associated with the closing of regulatory loopholes.

However, the macroeconomic effect of price-based regulations cannot be judged only on the basis of their effect on the magnitude of capital flows. Indeed, one of the explicit policy objectives of their introduction in Chile was allowing interest rates to remain at levels that were higher than parities; at the same time, at least according to some analysts, URR were meant to avoid further exchange rate appreciation. In turn, in Colombia, the strengthening of such regulations in 1994 was aimed at both opening up the space for a contractionary monetary policy (as the central bank judged that the credit and demand boom of 1992–4 was generating undesirable effects), and reversing the exchange rate appreciation that the country had been experiencing.

In terms of interest rates, the available econometric evidence regarding the effects of capital account regulations is less controversial. It indicates that URR were able to increase domestic interest rates in both Chile and Colombia.[16] The evidence of the effects of URR on exchange rates is more mixed, but this may well reflect more the difficulties inherent in exchange rate modelling (see Williamson 2000: ch. 4), or the inability of URR to affect exchange rates at the levels they were actually applied (rather than any intrinsic ineffectiveness of URRs vis-à-vis exchange rates).

The links between the different macroeconomic effects of regulations is also clear in the evolution of the regulatory instruments themselves. Thus, in Chile a basic problem of regulations was the variability of the rules pertaining to the exchange rate, since the lower limits of the exchange rate bands were changed several times during the period of controls (1991 to 1999). During capital account booms, this gave rise to a safe bet for agents bringing in capital, because when the exchange rate neared the floor of the band (in pesos per dollar) it was highly likely that the floor would be adjusted downwards. In Colombia, the main problem was the frequency of the changes made in reserve requirements. Changes that were foreseen by the market (particularly

be willing to assume them for an adequate reward. More generally, if there is no stable external demand for the domestic currency, hedging may be available only in limited quantities, a fact that affects the maturities and costs involved.

[16] For the case of Chile see De Gregorio et al. (2000); Larraín et al. (2000); and Le Fort and Lehman (2000, 2003); for Colombia, Villar and Rincón (2002).

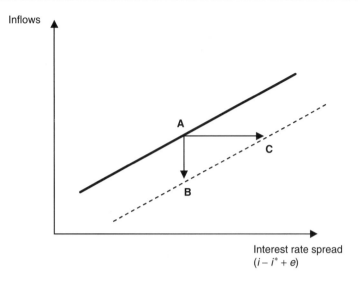

Figure 7.10. Macroeconomic effects of capital regulations

Note: *i*: Domestic real interest rate; *i**: External real interest rate; *e*: Annual variation of of the real exchange rate.

those of August 1994) led to speculatory movements that reduced the effectiveness of such measures for some time.

Thus, in broader terms, the usefulness of capital controls as a macroeconomic policy tool must be evaluated first on their ability to give monetary authorities improved policy choice—particularly between reducing capital flows (and thus the money supply or the magnitude of sterilization) and increasing domestic interest rate spreads; and between higher domestic interest rates and exchange rate devaluation.[17] The fact that policy choice and other macroeconomic factors play a role brings into focus the fact that URR are a complement to, rather than a substitute for, other macroeconomic policies; this fact was explicitly recognized in both Latin American experiments with price-based controls. In Chile, these other macroeconomic policies were applied more effectively, particularly in relation to fiscal policy.

The macroeconomic effect of capital regulations is shown in Figure 7.10 in a simple diagram that relates capital inflows to the interest rate spread under imperfect capital mobility. Regulations shift the relationship between both variables downwards, allowing either lower levels of inflows (and sterilization) for a given level of interest rate spread (i.e., a movement from A to B), or higher interest rates/exchange rate devaluation for a given level of inflows

[17] This is the very apt interpretation provided by Williamson (2000: ch. 4). Indeed, under this interpretation, the apparently conflicting evidence on the Chilean case largely disappears.

(a movement from A to C). The final equilibrium (including, of course, an intermediate outcome between B and C) will depend on other policy variables and macroeconomic conditions.

Given the multiple channels through which the URR can affect the economy, the effectiveness of these regulations can be best measured by a broad index of monetary pressures that includes the three possible channels through which capital inflows can affect the economy: the accumulation of international reserves, exchange rate appreciation, and a reduction in interest rates. Figure 7.11 provides an index similar to others used in the relevant literature, in which the weights for the three indicators are their standard deviation during the period analyzed.

An inspection of the graph indicates that the 1994 Malaysian controls were extremely effective in reversing the strong expansionary effect of capital surges in previous years, particularly in 1993. The price-based capital account regulations of Chile and Colombia had weaker effects, particularly in the first case. Indeed, the introduction of such regulations in Chile in June 1991 and their strengthening in May 1992 was not accompanied by a reversal of the expansionary trend (though the index remained stagnant for a few months);[18] those instituted in July 1995 had a more discernible effect. In Colombia, which used price-based regulations more aggressively, the effects were stronger. In particular, the movement in the index of expansionary pressures is more closely tied to the changes in capital account regulations in 1993–7. In both Chile and Colombia, the capital account turned contractionary in 1998, with the reduction in the URR having only a negligible effect on this trend.

As Table 7.1 indicates, the mix in the evolution of the three components of the index varied significantly from one episode to another, even within the same country. Thus, taking Malaysia as a standard, controls had major effects on international reserves accumulation with an additional moderate impact on the exchange rate, whereas the policy decision to reduce interest rates supported the reduction of capital inflows. The effects of the June 1991 Chilean decisions are unclear, but those of May 1992 allowed a higher interest-rate-cum-devaluation mix but were incapable of affecting reserve accumulation. In turn, those of July 1995 did have a broadly desirable outcome: they stopped reserve accumulation as well as exchange rate appreciation while allowing authorities to maintain fairly high interest rates. In Colombia, the August 1994 regulations allowed the authorities to undertake a contractionary monetary policy while avoiding exchange rate appreciation. In the context of

---

[18] The low level of the URR may account for this result. Valdés-Prieto and Soto (1998) find evidence of a 'threshold effect', which would explain why these regulations were only effective in reducing capital flows in 1995–6. Despite this, Agosin and Ffrench-Davis (2001) have argued that on broader grounds the macroeconomic management undertaken in the earlier part of the 1990s was more appropriate than in 1995–6.

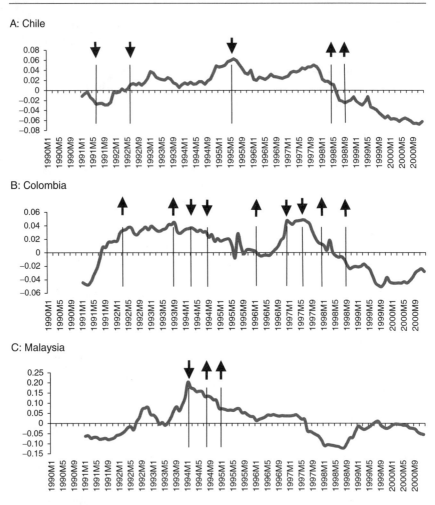

Figure 7.11. Chile, Colombia, and Malaysia: index of expansionary monetary pressure

Note: Imposition or relaxation of restrictions on capital inflows, respectively (the direction of the arrows indicates expected effect on the index). Index $= aR + be - ci$. R = International reserves corrected by log trend. e = Twelve-month variation of the real exchange rate. i = Real deposit interest rate. a, b, c = Standard deviation of R, e and i respectively.

Source: Authors' estimates based on IMF data.

the continuation (or, more precisely, only a gradual weakening) of such contractionary monetary policy, the decision to loosen regulations in February 1996 generated an avalanche of reserve accumulation and exchange rate appreciation, which in turn was stopped by the return to controls in January 1997 (or, to be more accurate, by a series of decisions between that month and May 1997).

Table 7.1. Change in Key Variables Preceding and Following Major Capital Control Episodes

		Reserves accumulation	Real effective exchange rate percent variation*	Average real interest rate
Chile				
June 1991	Year before	1775.0	3.6%	3.9
	Year after	2160.6	1.4%	1.5
May 1992	Year before	1540.6	7.0%	1.5
	Year after	2263.6	−4.8%	3.7
	Second year after	175.2	6.8%	6.0
July 1995	Year before	4115.2	9.5%	3.8
	Year after	−189.9	1.3%	6.0
	Second year after	2267.4	9.3%	5.3
Colombia				
August 1994	Year before	−287.4	14.6%	2.0
	Year after	217.1	−1.3%	9.5
February 1996	Year before	−87.5	−2.9%	9.4
	Year after	1725.0	18.0%	8.7
January 1997	Year before	1570.6	19.4%	9.1
	Year after	−105.4	−4.5%	4.4
	Second year after	−1020.8	−5.4%	10.2
Malaysia				
January 1994	Year before	19881.5	−3.5%	3.4
	Year after	−12060.2	−0.2%	1.2
January 1995	Year before	−12060.2	−0.2%	1.2
	Year after	−2813.7	2.9%	2.4
	Second year after	4586.3	6.7%	3.5

Note: *Any increase means an appreciation of the domestic currency.

Source: Authors' estimates based on IMF, International Financial Statistics (2003).

Both Figure 7.11 and Table 7.1 indicate, however, that much of these macroeconomic effects were temporary in nature. In Table 7.1, in particular, their effect is hardly visible in the second year after regulations were imposed or strengthened. In the terminology used above, they operated more as speed bumps rather than as permanent restrictions. Of course, this may be associated with the fact that in several cases the regulations were designed to be temporary, or that their strong initial effect prompted authorities to take immediate steps in the opposite direction. This was particularly the case of the January 1994 Malaysian controls, and the August 1994 Colombian ones. In yet another episode (the January 1997 Colombian regulations), the effects were overwhelmed by new events (the Asian and Russian crises). Thus, the temporary character of the effects is more clearly perceived in the history of Chilean regulations.

However, more broadly, this is reflected in the fact that none of the three countries was able to avoid the cycle that developing countries experienced in the 1990s: rapid expansion up to the Asian crisis followed by a contraction when faced with the events that began with the 1997 Asian crisis. In this respect, there is a sharp contrast between the experience of these countries and those of China, India, and Taiwan, which followed a strategy of keeping quantitative controls and only liberalizing them very gradually. Combined with the stronger effects of Malaysian vs. Chilean/Colombian regulations, these are clear indications of the stronger macroeconomic effects of quantitative vs. price-based regulations.

7.3.5 Effects on the Composition of Capital Inflows

Figure 7.12a demonstrates a fact that is less controversial about the effects of inflow regulations in the three countries: the regulations were effective in helping the countries to maintain a debt profile with a low share of short-term debt, a fact that proved to be very beneficial during the turbulent events of 1997–8. Indeed, in some cases, some regulations led to changes in trends that proved permanent. This is particularly true of the decisions adopted by Chile and Colombia in the mid-1990s. The 1994 Malaysian regulations also interrupted a rising trend of short-term borrowing that was only partially reversed in the following years. As demonstrated above, in all three countries there is also clear evidence that regulations did not have any adverse effects on FDI.

Figure 7.12b, however, highlights a major problem in studying the effects of controls on debt profiles. The crucial question is: what is the counterfactual— i.e., were controls effective because they reduced the share of short-term debt vis-à-vis the historical trend, or were they effective because they helped the countries that adopted capital account regulation (Chile, in this case) to avoid the trend of rising shares of short-term debt experienced by other developing countries that did not impose controls?

As it happened, until 1995 capital controls seem to have had little lasting effect in Chile, vis-à-vis its own trend of capital flows, but a significant effect after the strengthening of controls in that year.[19] However, if the comparison is made with the trend of capital flows in countries that did *not* impose similar controls, such as Thailand and Brazil, then controls in Chile seem to have had quite a remarkable effect from the very beginning. In fact, in Chile the share of short-term debt was at a similar level to Thailand's before the imposition of controls (about one-quarter of the total), but by 1995 Thailand had a share twice as large as Chile's. Furthermore, at the beginning of the *Plano Real* and full financial liberalization in Brazil in 1994, Chile actually had a share of short-term debt five percentage points higher than that of

[19] In fact, according to Chile's Central Bank balance of payments statistics, after 1995 this share fell even further than is indicated by the IMF source used in this graph—from more than 18 percent in 1994, to 16 percent in 1995, 12 percent in 1996, and less than 5 percent in 1997.

a. Chile, Colombia, and Malaysia: short-term external debt, 1988–98

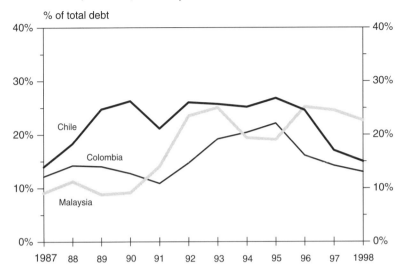

b. Chile, Brazil, and Thailand: short-term external debt, 1989–98

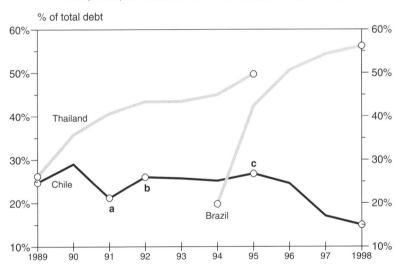

Figure 7.12. Chile, Colombia, Malaysia, Brazil, and Thailand: short term external debt, 1988–98

Note: **a** = capital controls imposed; **b** and **c** = capital control strengthened.

Source: IMF (2004a).

197

Brazil; however, by 1998 Brazil's share was nearly four times higher than Chile's (Palma 2006).

In the case of Malaysia following its 1994 controls, a new wave of debt accumulation developed in that country, but the debt profile was kept at more prudential levels than in other Asian countries that were hit by the 1997 crisis (Palma 2000; Kaplan and Rodrik 2002).

7.3.6 Effects on Asset Price Dynamics

Finally, Figures 7.13 and 7.14 show that, in the three countries, capital account regulations had sufficient capacity to slow down and, in some cases, to pierce asset bubbles. As is clear from Figure 7.13a, Chile was experiencing an asset bubble in its stock market in early 1991. In the four quarters preceding the first imposition of controls, the index had jumped more than three-fold; the 1991 and 1992 regulations stopped this trend for about seven quarters. However, as with the levels of net private inflows and the broader macroeconomic effects studied above, this effect soon ran its course and together with the huge new increase in inflows in 1994 the index jumped again, this time more than two-fold. The strengthening of controls in 1995 had an immediate impact on this new bubble, bringing the index down considerably. When it began to recover again in early 1997, with the new increases in inflows, its progress was halted by the mid-1997 East Asian crisis.

Something similar, but even more pronounced, took place in real estate after 1995 (see Figure 7.14). In this market, Chile was facing another bubble when capital controls were imposed in 1991. In this case, the (short-term) reduction in net private inflows that came with inflow controls did not have such an immediate effect as on the stock market. However, the strengthening of regulations in May 1992 coincided with the interruption of the real estate boom. By then, the index of real estate prices (in US dollar terms) had already increased close to five-fold in just six quarters. Nevertheless, as in the stock market, the respite was only temporary, and the real estate price index doubled again between the end of 1993 and the strengthening of capital controls in the third quarter of 1995 (following the renewed increase in inflows). The subsequent fall is remarkable (more so than in the stock market), even though the economy continued to grow rapidly until 1998.[20]

In Colombia, booming capital inflows since 1992, partly fuelled by growing capital account liberalization, led to a seven-fold increase in stock prices. This

---

[20] Chile's GDP grew at 7.4 percent in 1996 and 6.6 percent in 1997.

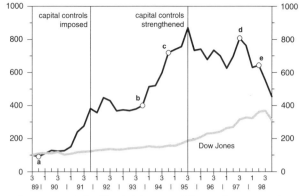

Notes: **a** = first democratic government after Pinochet; **b** = second democratic government; **c** = Mexican crisis; **d** = East Asian crisis; and **e** = Russian default.

b. Colombia

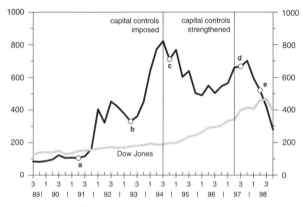

Notes: **a** and **b** = progressive opening of the capital account; **c** = Mexican crisis; **d** = East Asian crisis; and **e** = Russian default.

c. Malaysia

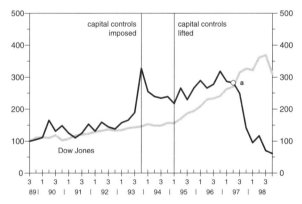

Notes: **a** = East Asian crisis.

Figure 7.13. Chile, Colombia, and Malaysia: quarterly stock market index (US), 1989–98

Source: DataStream.

a. Chile

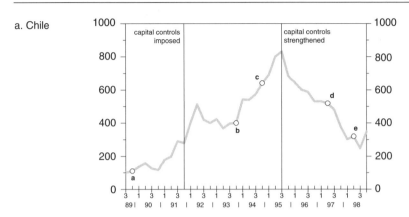

Notes: **a** = first democratic government after Pinochet; **b** = second democratic government; **c** = Mexican crisis; **d** = East Asian crisis; and **e** = Russian default.

b. Malaysia

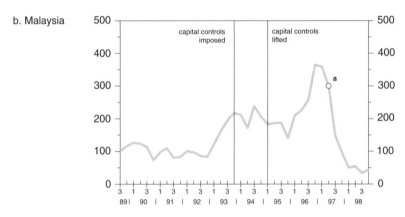

Notes: **a** = East Asian crisis.

Figure 7.14. Chile, and Malaysia: quarterly real estate index, 1989–98
Source: DataStream.

process was sharply reversed by the August 1994 controls and the accompanying monetary policy. A similar reversal took place after the controls adopted in early 1997, but here the preceding boom had not reached its peak. Although no similar indices exist for real estate prices, partial evidence in this regard (the evolution of housing rents) indicates that a similar reversal took place, coinciding with the 1994 regulations.

Figure 7.13 also shows the remarkable jump in stock prices at the time of the surge in inflows into Malaysia in 1993. Before the imposition of controls, this index jumped more than two-fold in just four quarters. During the three quarters that these controls lasted in full, this index fell by 30 percent; it then began to recover somewhat erratically, almost reaching its previous peak again in the last quarter of 1996.[21]

A rapid bubble in real estate prices in Malaysia also took off in the four quarters before the imposition of controls in 1994. As in Chile, the piercing of this bubble was not as immediate as the one in the stock exchange. However, in contrast to Chile, the return of inflows in 1995 pushed this index back up with a vengeance. One major difference between the two countries was the level of interest rates. As Table 7.1 indicates, interest rates remained relatively high in Chile two years after the July 1995 controls. The return of inflows, low deposit rates, and calm in the stock market (by pre-crisis standards), together with low mortgage rates, set in motion another real estate bubble. In just four quarters the real estate index jumped again more than two-fold.

7.4 Conclusions

Overall, the experiences of Chilean, Colombian, and Malaysian regulations on capital inflows indicate that they served as useful instruments for improving both debt profiles and the macroeconomic trade-offs faced by the authorities, and for restraining asset bubbles. However, the macroeconomic effects, including on asset prices, depended on the strength of the regulations and tended to be temporary—operating more as 'speed bumps' than as permanent speed restrictions. The basic advantage of the price-based instrument used by Chile and Colombia is its non-discretionary character, whereas quantity-based controls in Malaysia proved to be stronger in terms of short-term macroeconomic effects. Thus, when immediate and drastic action is needed, quantitative controls are more effective.

The dynamics of capital flows must be taken into account when analysing the overall and relative virtues of the different types of regulations. Interestingly, given the links between the dynamics of capital flows and current account deficits in Latin America vis-à-vis East Asia, the policy prescription should perhaps have been the opposite of what actually happened: quantitative controls for Latin America (where exogenous inflow surges dominate) and price controls for East Asia (a region in which inflow surges have tended to be mostly endogenous).

In any case, it must be emphasized that these systems were designed for countries that initially had chosen to be fully integrated into international

[21] The crash after the mid-1997 crisis was equally remarkable; by the third quarter of 1998 the local currency denominated index had fallen to just 38 percent of its early 1997 level.

capital markets, but later decided to fine-tune this integration—at least temporarily. Traditional exchange controls and capital account regulations—when applied effectively and transparently—may thus be superior if the policy objective is to reduce significantly domestic macroeconomic sensitivity to volatile and unregulated international capital flows, as the experiences of China, India, and Taiwan have indicated.

Appendix: Results of the 'Granger-Predictability' Test Between Net Private Capital Inflows and Current Account

In all Latin American countries the test spans the period from 1950 to 2002, and the source of the data is ECLAC's Statistical Division. Due to lack of data, for the East Asian countries it was only possible to study the period 1975–2002; the source of these data was IMF (2004a). Following the 'Perron-sequential procedure', unit root tests indicate that all series of net private capital inflows and current account in both regions have a unit root; furthermore, with the (significant) exceptions of Chile and Malaysia, all series cointegrate. Therefore, the Granger-test for Argentina, Brazil, Colombia, Mexico, Korea, and Thailand was done in levels, while for Chile and Malaysia it was done in first differences. The specification of the regressions (i.e., the number of lags) within which the null hypothesis (of no 'predictability') was tested both ways was determined by the rule of choosing the minimum number of lags that would produce a residual that was not serially correlated (see Table 7A.1).

The results of the Granger tests (in levels) indicate that in Argentina, Brazil, Colombia, and Mexico net private capital inflows are a good predictor of the current account, while in Korea and Thailand there is evidence of predictability the other way around. In Chile (tested in first differences), there seems to be a two-way predictability phenomenon; in Malaysia, meanwhile, (also in first differences and up to a 10 percent level of significance) the null hypothesis of no predictability cannot be rejected either

Table 7A.1. Results of the 'Granger-Predictability' Test Between Net Private Capital Inflows and Current Account

	'p' of T1	'p' of T2	Lags T1	lags T2	'p' of Q T1	'p' of Q T2
Argentina	1.9E-08	0.50630	2	2	0.138	0.361
Brazil	0.00610	0.32485	2	2	0.375	0.784
Colombia	3.1E-07	0.16296	2	2	0.505	0.862
Mexico	0.07166	0.15202	2	2	0.503	0.871
Korea	0.32344	0.06342	2	2	0.291	0.640
Thailand	0.12219	0.01066	2	2	0.307	0.099
Chile	0.08340	3.6E-05	2	2	0.844	0.995
Malaysia	0.73646	0.10611	1	1	0.978	0.869

Notes: T1 = test of the null hypothesis that net private capital inflows do not 'Granger-predict' the current account. T2 = test of the null hypothesis that the current account does not 'Granger-predict' net private capital inflows. 'p' of Q = is the level of significance at which the null hypothesis of no autocorrelation up to order 3 is rejected using the 'Ljung-Box Q-statistics'.

way; however, if the level of significance is increased to 10.7 percent, the test indicates that Malaysia seems to follow the same pattern as Korea and Thailand.

References

Agosin, M. (1998). 'Capital Inflow and Investment Performance: Chile in the 1990s', in R. Ffrench-Davis and H. Reisen (eds.), *Capital Inflows and Investment Performance: Lessons from Latin America.* Paris and Santiago: OECD Development Centre/ECLAC.

_____ and Ffrench-Davis, R. (2001). 'Managing Capital Inflows in Chile', in S. Griffith–Jones, M. F. Montes and A. Nasution (eds.), *Short term Capital Flows and Economic Crises.* New York: Oxford University Press/United Nations University (UNU)/World Institute for Development Economics Research (WIDER).

Ariyoshi, A., Habermeier, K., Laurens, B., Ötker-Robe, I., Canales-Kriljenko, J. I., and Kirilenko, A. (2000). 'Capital Controls: Country Experiences with Their Use and Liberalization'. Occasional Paper 190, International Monetary Fund, Washington, DC.

Cárdenas, M. and Barrera, F. (1997). 'On the Effectiveness of Capital Controls: The Experience of Colombia During the 1990s'. *Journal of Development Economics*, October, 54/1.

_____ and Steiner, R. (2000). 'Private Capital Flows in Colombia', in F. Larraín (ed.), *Capital Flows, Capital Controls, and Currency Crises: Latin America in the 1990s.* Ann Arbor, MI: The University of Michigan Press.

De Gregorio, J., Edwards, S., and Valdés, R. (2000). 'Controls on Capital Inflows: Do They Work?' *Journal of Development Economics*, October, 63/1.

Epstein, G., Grabel, I., and Jomo, K. S. (2003). 'Capital Management Techniques in Developing Countries', in A. Buira (ed.), *Challenges to the World Bank and the IMF: Developing Country Perspectives.* London: Anthem Press, ch. 6.

Kaplan, E. and Rodrik, D. (2002). 'Did the Malaysian Capital Controls Work?'. NBER Working Paper Series, No. 8142 (February), Cambridge, MA.

Larraín, F., Labán, R., and Chumacero, R. (2000). 'What Determines Capital Inflows? An Empirical Analysis for Chile', in F. Larraín (ed.), *Capital Flows, Capital Controls, and Currency Crises: Latin America in the 1990s.* Ann Arbor, MI: University of Michigan Press.

Laurens, B. (2000). 'Chile's Experience with Controls on Capital Inflows in the 1990s', in A. Ariyoshi, K. Habermeier, B. Laurens, I. Ötker-Robe, J. I. Canales-Kriljenko, and A. Kirilenko, *Capital Controls: Country Experiences with Their Use and Liberalization.* Occasional Paper 190, International Monetary Fund, Washington, DC.

Le Fort, G. and Lehmann, S. (2000). 'El encaje, los flujos de capitales y el gasto: una evaluación empírica'. Documento de Trabajo No. 64 (February), Central Bank of Chile.

Negara Bank (2004). *Annual Report.* Kuala Lumpur: Negara Bank.

Ocampo, J. A. (2003a). 'Capital Account and Counter-Cyclical Prudential Regulations in Developing Countries', in R. Ffrench-Davis and S. Griffith-Jones (eds.), *From Capital Surges to Drought: Seeking Stability for Emerging Markets.* London: WIDER/ECLAC/Palgrave.

Ocampo, J. A. (2003b). 'Developing Countries' Anti-Cyclical Policies in a Globalized World', in A. Dutt and J. Ros (eds.), *Development Economics and Structuralist Macroeconomics: Essays in Honor of Lance Taylor*. Aldershot: Edward Elgar.

—— and Tovar, C. (1998). 'Capital Flows, Savings and Investment in Colombia, 1990–96', in R. Ffrench-Davis and H. Reisen (eds.), *Capital Flows and Investment Performance: Lessons from Latin America*. Paris and Santiago: OECD Development Centre/ECLAC.

—— —— (2003). 'Managing the Capital Account: Colombia's Experience with Price-based Controls on Capital Inflows'. *CEPAL Review*, December, 81.

Ötker-Robe, I. (2000). 'Malaysia's Experience with the Use of Capital Controls', in A. Ariyoshi, K. Habermeier, B. Laurens, I. Ötker-Robe, J. I. Canales-Kriljenko, and A. Kirilenko, *Capital Controls: Country Experiences with Their Use and Liberalization*. Occasional Paper 190, International Monetary Fund, Washington, DC.

Palma, G. (2000). 'The Three Routes to Financial Crises: The Need for Capital Controls'. CEPA Working papers No. 17. Also published in J. Eatwell and L. Taylor (eds.), *International Capital Markets—Systems in Transition*. New York: Oxford University Press, 2002.

—— (2003). 'The Three Routes to Financial Crises: Chile, Mexico, and Argentina [1]; Brazil [2]; and Korea, Malaysia, and Thailand [3]', in H.-J. Chang, *Rethinking Development Economics*. London: Anthem Press. Reprinted in R. E. Allen (ed.) (2004). *The International Library of Writings on the New Global Economy: The Political Economy of Financial Crises*. Northampton, NH: Edward Elgar.

—— (2006). 'The 1999 Financial Crises in Brazil: "Macho-Monetarism" in Action'. *Economic and Political Weekly*, vol. 41, no. 9, March 4.

Park, Y. C. and Song, C.-Y. (1997). 'Managing Foreign Capital Flows: The Experience of the Republic of Korea, Thailand, Malaysia and Indonesia'. *International Monetary and Financial Issues for the 1990s*, Vol. VIII. New York: UNCTAD.

Rodrik, D. and Velasco, A. (2000). *Short Term Capital Flows*. (Paper presented at the Annual World Bank Conference on Development Economics 1999.) Washington, DC: The World Bank.

Stiglitz, J. E. (2003). 'Whither reform? Toward a new agenda for Latin America'. *CEPAL Review*, August, 80.

Valdés-Prieto, S. and Soto, M. (1998). 'The Effectiveness of Capital Controls: Theory and Evidence from Chile'. *Empirica*, No. 25. Amsterdam: Kluwer Academic Publishers.

Villar, L. and Rincón, H. (2002). 'The Colombian Economy in the Nineties: Capital Flows and Foreign Exchange Regimes', in Albert Berry (ed.), *Critical Issues in Financial Reform: A View from the South*. New Brunswick, NJ: Transaction Publishers.

Williamson, J. (2000). 'Exchange Rate Regimes for Emerging Markets: Reviving the Intermediate Option'. Policy Analyses in International Economics 60 (September), Institute for International Economics, Washington, DC.

8

The Malaysian Experience in Financial-Economic Crisis Management: An Alternative to the IMF-Style Approach

Martin Khor

8.1 General Background to the Issue

8.1.1 *The Onset of Financial Crisis: Some Elements*

In the 1980s and 1990s, many developing countries fell into an external debt-led financial crisis. In the first generation of these crises, the inability to service debt was due to a combination of factors, including depression in commodity export prices, an increase in the price of oil imports, a rapid increase in foreign loans, and the inability to utilize these loans productively or appropriately.

In the 1990s, several more countries (including the more economically advanced of the developing countries) experienced financial crises. A major cause of many of these second generation crises was the inappropriate design and implementation of capital account liberalization. Some countries that had hitherto succeeded in attaining high economic growth rates and in using export expansion for this growth faced difficulties in managing rapid liberalization in financial flows.

In 1997 several East Asian countries began to experience serious financial problems. Because of financial deregulation, they had received large inflows of capital, including bank loans (denominated in foreign currencies) and portfolio capital (especially foreign purchase of equity in the local stock exchanges). A significant part of the foreign loans was not channelled to activities that yielded revenue in foreign exchange, and thus a mismatch occurred, at least in the short term, that resulted in pressures building up on foreign reserves.

In some of the countries that experienced this financial fragility, currency speculators took advantage of the deregulated environment (which allowed them to function), borrowed in local currency and sold the currency short against the US dollar.

In Thailand, the Thai central bank sold dollars against the baht in an attempt to maintain the baht's exchange rate level. When its foreign reserves dried up, and it could no longer defend the baht, the local currency depreciated sharply. This made it even more difficult for the country to service its high foreign debt. The Thai crisis spread by means of the contagion effect to other East Asian countries.

In Indonesia, there had also been a rapid buildup of foreign loans, especially to the private sector. There was a very sharp depreciation of the rupiah (at one stage its value against the US dollar had fallen by more than 80 percent), rendering the country unable to meet its foreign loan obligations.

In South Korea, following the financial deregulation and liberalization that occurred as the country prepared to join the Organization for Economic Cooperation and Development (OECD), private banks and companies had also accumulated large quantities of foreign loans. As a result of a sharp depreciation of the won, the country also experienced debt servicing difficulties.

In Malaysia, the ringgit came under speculative attack and also declined significantly. However, the country had not liberalized its capital account to the same extent as the other three countries, at least in one important respect: local companies were allowed to obtain foreign loans only with central bank permission, which would be given only if the borrower could show that the loan would be used for activities that would yield revenue in foreign exchange that could be used for loan servicing. Partly as a result of this restriction, Malaysia's debt situation remained manageable, but fragile, since there was also a possibility of debt servicing difficulty if the ringgit depreciated even more sharply, or if there was a rapid enough outflow of capital.

8.1.2 Orthodox IMF-Style Policy Response

On the verge of external debt default, Thailand, Indonesia, and South Korea sought the assistance of the International Monetary Fund (IMF) and World Bank for loan assistance. Credit was forthcoming on the condition that the recipient countries agreed to adopt a package of policies embodied in successive letters of intent. The main elements of the loan conditionalities were common to the countries. They included the following:

- floating of the currency;
- the capital account should remain open, deepening financial liberalization, disallowing capital controls, and allowing foreigners and locals to take out and bring in funds with little or no restriction;

- a sharp increase in the interest rate (to counter inflation and to maintain investor confidence in the local currency);

- contractionary monetary policies;

- austere fiscal policies;

- minimal or no government financial assistance to local banks and companies facing difficulties;[1]

- liberalization of foreign ownership in local assets and companies;[2]

- privatization of state enterprises and agencies and state economic activities; and

- reduction or elimination of state subsidies.

Some of these policies contributed to transforming the financial crisis into an economic recession and crisis. The contractionary interest rate, monetary, and fiscal policies depressed domestic demand and adversely affected GDP growth. The closure of some banks, without guarantee that the government would protect deposits in other banks, led to a general decline in depositor confidence in the banking system. The high interest rates strained the ability of companies to service their loans and this in turn increased the banks' incidence of non-performing loans. Thus the macroeconomic policies had significant influence on the viability of the microeconomy, and the crisis in the financial economy was transformed into a crisis in the real economy.

Many local enterprises closed down, and many thousands of jobs were lost. The rates of unemployment and poverty rose significantly. The deteriorating condition of the real economy in turn adversely affected the confidence of investors (both foreign and local). The value of shares in the stock market fell significantly. There was a flight of foreign and local capital abroad, facilitated by the liberal capital account regime. Despite the rise in interest rates, the local currency's exchange rate continued to be low or declined further (especially in Indonesia). The open door policy to foreign ownership as a result of the IMF-World Bank loan conditionality enabled foreign companies to more easily purchase local assets, often at bargain prices. The government in Indonesia reduced or eliminated some subsidies, resulting in price increases in fuel and in transport fees, and giving rise to social instability.

---

[1] In Indonesia and Thailand the governments were asked to take measures to close down several financial institutions.

[2] Thailand raised its limit on foreign ownership of local banks from 10% to 100%; South Korea raised the foreign ownership limit in local companies listed on the stock exchange from 10% to 100%, and Indonesia's letter of intent specified allowing foreign ownership of plantations and wholesale trade.

8.1.3 *Needs and Goals of a Country Facing Crisis*

A country undergoing a financial crisis caused by capital account liberalization would like to be able to adopt policies that meet the following goals:

- stabilization of the exchange rate, or at least the prevention of so sharp a currency depreciation that it faces a crisis in debt servicing, or the prevention of currency exchange volatility which makes it difficult or impossible for businesses that rely on trade to predict costs or revenues;

- maintenance of capital funds in the country and creation of conditions that prevent outflow of foreign or local capital;

- lowering of interest rates, or maintaining relatively low interest rates so that businesses can continue servicing their loans and consumer demand can be kept up or increased in order to maintain or raise effective demand;

- an increase in government expenditure to give a boost to effective demand;

- expansionary credit and monetary policy to encourage viable businesses to maintain or increase their investment and to encourage maintenance or growth of consumer demand;

- relative stability of consumer prices;

- increase in the financial and economic viability of enterprises, and of the banks and banking system;

- maintenance of employment and of the meeting of social needs (health, education, welfare, etc.); and

- maintenance of policy space and flexibility to decide on issues such as privatization, subsidies, trade and trade liberalization, and the degree of opening up to foreign ownership.

It is difficult to formulate and implement policies that can meet all or many of the above goals. Often, there are policy trade-offs. For example, lowering the interest rate may have a positive effect on the financial position of enterprises and on effective demand, but may reduce the incentive to save in the local currency and lead to capital outflow and currency depreciation (under conditions of an open capital regime and a floating exchange rate). However, the deliberate increase in interest rates (an important plank of the IMF package) is intended to maintain or increase investor confidence in the currency and in the economy generally but would have an adverse effect on the microeconomy as firms and banks suffer a deterioration in their financial situation, and this in turn undermines investor confidence.

When there are policy trade-offs—in other words, when one policy tool can lead to both positive and negative effects—it is important to seek more policy tools so that more of the goals can be met. The IMF package has been unable to meet many of the policy challenges and goals since the policies failed not only to fulfill the needs of the real economy but also to resolve the problems in the financial economy. They also had damaging effects on economic institutions, including local enterprises and banks. This raises the question of whether an alternative approach can be found that works better than the IMF policies and avoids their damaging effects.

8.2 Background to the Malaysian Crisis and Response

8.2.1 *The Malaysian Crisis: The Start*

Shortly after the Thai currency was floated and devalued sharply, there was a 'contagion effect' on the Malaysian economy. The first effect occurred through the exchange rate. The Malaysian ringgit (RM) had for several years been relatively stable at around RM2.40–2.50 to the US dollar. It steadily depreciated to 2.80, and in several steps to a low point of 4.88 on January 7, 1998. For a while, it appeared that the 5.00 level would be breached.

The drastic decline was caused in large part by speculation, because speculators sold the ringgit 'short'.[3] There were at least two mechanisms for this short selling: in one such mechanism, the speculator sold the ringgit in the forward market at the current exchange rate with a view to delivering the ringgit at a future date; in the other mechanism, the speculator borrowed the ringgit in order to sell it immediately and hold dollars. These actions contributed to the weakening of the ringgit as the demand for the US dollar increased.

When the ringgit depreciated, the speculators could reap the profit. In the first mechanism, the speculator delivers the agreed ringgit amount at the previous rate and obtains the agreed dollar amount, which in turn can now be exchanged for greater amounts of ringgit (since the ringgit has since depreciated). In the second mechanism, when the time comes for the speculator to repay his or her ringgit denominated loan at the previous exchange rate, the speculator needs to use only a part of the dollars that have been accumulated (since the ringgit has now depreciated); thus the balance of the dollars is his profit.

Speculation on the ringgit was carried out not only in the local markets but also abroad, since the ringgit was being traded in overseas markets, such as Singapore.

The currency depreciation had several negative effects. First, it increased the burden of external debt servicing. At the start of the crisis, the country's

---

[3] See Mahani (2002: 283–6) for a summary of examples of three main ways in which speculation on the Malaysian currency took place. The examples are taken from Lin (1998).

external debt servicing position was rather comfortable. However, the depreciation increased the debt burden in that the debtors had to pay more in local currency amounts; several large Malaysian companies that had taken foreign loans suffered large losses. Second, the continuous changes in the exchange rate were very destabilizing; traders and enterprises were unable to conduct business in a predictable way because the prices of imports and exports (in local currency terms) kept changing. Third, the prospect of continuous decline in the ringgit's rate contributed to a sharp fall in the value of shares in the stock market and the inflow of foreign portfolio funds in the stock market was reversed. One positive effect was that those involved in exports (including producers of commodities such as palm oil and petroleum) obtained higher incomes.

As a result of the serious adverse effects of currency depreciation, stabilizing the ringgit became perhaps the overriding concern of the policymakers during the crisis.

Another major effect on the economy was the very steep decline in the value of shares in the stock market. The Kuala Lumpur Stock Exchange (KLSE) index fell from a high of over 1000 in July 1997 to a low point of 262 in September 1998. This affected the creditworthiness of many companies and individuals that had used the value of their shares as collateral for loans; it thus also affected the banks. The fall also had a negative effect on consumer sentiment and spending as investors saw their wealth dwindling.

The third major concern was the prospect of large capital outflows as the confidence of foreigners and residents in the economy fell. This concern increased the more the values of the currency and shares in the stock market declined. The main form of short-term capital flows in Malaysia had been portfolio capital rather than credit. There was a large reversal of foreign portfolio capital flows at the early stage of the crisis. Net quarterly flow of portfolio capital turned negative in the second quarter of 1997 for the first time since 1991, and total net outflow in the first three quarters of the year was over US$11 billion (Athukorala 2001: 61).

The main mechanisms conveying the 'contagion effect' were financial in nature and were not factors located in the real economy of production or trade.

8.2.2 Initial Response: Orthodox Policy

Since the external debt situation was under control, Malaysia could choose whether or not to turn to the IMF for loans to boost the external reserves to a more comfortable level. The government decided from the start that it would not do so, because it was concerned that many of its existing policies (for example, regulation of foreign ownership, assistance to local companies, subsidies, price controls, and economic and social policies relating to ethnic communities) would be affected by IMF conditionality.

Nevertheless, for about the first year of the crisis (mid-1997 to mid-1998), Malaysia on its own accord followed an orthodox IMF-style approach in responding to the crisis. This included: (1) allowing the currency to float with minimal intervention; (2) maintaining an open capital account regime; (3) sharply increasing the interest rate; (4) tightening monetary policy; and (5) drastically reducing government budget expenditure.

On December 5 the then finance minister announced a set of policies that included an 18 percent reduction in government spending, postponement of several pending public sector investment projects, and the cutting of government ministers' pay by 10 percent. The central bank increased the inter-bank lending rate from the pre-crisis level of 7.6 percent to 8.7 percent in December 1997, 10 percent in January and 11 percent in February 1998 (Athukorala 2001: 65). The criterion for banks' non-performing loans was changed from six months in arrears to three months, which was meant to strengthen prudential supervision but had the effect of tightening credit flows.

However, Malaysia did not significantly change its policy toward foreign ownership in the same manner or degree as Thailand, Indonesia, and South Korea (although Malaysia did somewhat liberalize foreign investment policy in manufacturing). Malaysia also retained its socially-oriented policies on price controls for some essential items and subsidies.

The orthodox interest rate and fiscal and monetary policies were aimed at shoring up the confidence of the financial markets and investors. It was believed that if the investors were impressed that the government was serious in tackling the crisis by adhering to the IMF-style prescription, then the ringgit would stabilize, the stock market would recover, and there would not be serious capital outflows.

In some ways the Malaysian policies were even more stringent than the IMF policies prescribed for the other three countries. For example, the cut in government-budgeted expenditure by 18 percent was drastic indeed.

However, the orthodox policies did not set the economy on the road to recovery. On the contrary, the macroeconomic policies were contractionary and converted the initial financial problems into an economic recession. The jump in interest rates raised the debt servicing burden of local companies. Thus the microeconomic financial crisis spread from companies that had taken foreign loans to the far larger number of companies that had taken local currency loans. In turn the banking system was hit by an increase in non-performing loans and some banks came under stress. Consumer demand fell as interest rates on consumer loans (especially for houses and motor vehicles) rose. The deterioration in the companies' performance contributed to the depressed state of the stock market, and this in turn adversely affected the position of the companies, the banks, and the state of consumer demand.

The real economy was badly affected as real GDP growth turned from plus 7.7 percent in 1997 to minus 6.7 percent in 1998 (BNM 1998: 236).

The deterioration in the real economy in turn had a negative effect on investor confidence, on the value of the currency, on stock market performance and on capital outflows. Local citizens were channeling their savings abroad, attracted by higher deposit rates offered by banks in neighboring Singapore for bank accounts denominated in Malaysian ringgit.

8.2.3 Developing the Malaysian Alternative Strategy

As both the financial and the real economy deteriorated, the government decided to adopt a different economic strategy. This new strategy was not adopted all at once but stage by stage and part by part as developments unfolded.

First, on the institutional side, the National Economic Action Council (NEAC) was formed in January 1998 to take overall charge of economic crisis management. Previously the Finance Ministry had taken the lead in managing the crisis; in 1998 the decision-making center shifted to the Prime Minister's department which hosted the NEAC. The Council was chaired by the prime minister and comprised several federal ministers, the chief ministers of the state governments, several government agencies, and industry representatives. It had an executive committee led by the prime minister and included the deputy prime minister, finance minister, executive director of the NEAC secretariat, some key economics-related officials (including the central bank governor, the director general of the Economic Planning Unit and the Secretary General of the Treasury), and a few other individuals. A new NEAC secretariat was established in the Prime Minister's department, and an executive director and a full-time staff were drawn initially from the Economic Planning Unit (the country's main planning agency). The NEAC was also serviced by a working group of five individuals drawn from business and academia.

The establishment of this high-powered council with almost overriding authority to deal with the economic crisis on an emergency basis, was a central and structural aspect of the Malaysian model of crisis management. Eventually it was the NEAC that drew up an alternative medium-term strategy to deal with the crisis. But the NEAC also intensely monitored all aspects of the economy and made decisions on a day-to-day basis. The NEAC executive committee chaired by the prime minister met every day for several hours to receive feedback on the implementation and effects of policy decisions and to make decisions on new measures. The NEAC was also able to cut through the usual territorial compartmentalization of the various ministries and agencies and to make decisions in a coordinated way.

The evolution of the alternative Malaysian strategy occurred in several phases. After the NEAC's establishment in January 1998, its executive director, working group, and secretariat undertook an intensive consultation over several months with representatives of many economic, commercial, financial, and social sectors, along with some non-governmental organizations, to determine their problems and obtain their views and policy suggestions.

The National Economic Recovery Plan was then formulated and launched in July 1998. Its objectives were to stabilize the currency, restore market confidence, maintain financial market stability, strengthen economic fundamentals, continue the equity and socio-economic agenda, and revitalize affected sectors. The Plan constituted a new approach to fiscal and monetary policy. The Plan's implementation also covered structural and institutional issues, including recapitalization of the banking sector, strategies for dealing with the non-performing loans, and corporate debt restructuring (Economic Planning Unit 1998).

Various measures were taken from the beginning to the middle of 1998 to reverse the contractionary monetary and fiscal policies that had been introduced toward the end of 1997.

On September 1, 1998, measures were announced by then prime minister Dr. Mahathir Mohamad relating to the currency and the mobility of capital flows. They were aimed at stabilizing the level of the local currency (through fixing the exchange rate to the US dollar); at preventing overseas speculation on the value of the local currency and local shares (by banning the overseas trade in these); and reducing capital outflows (through selective capital controls). This set of measures was a watershed since until they were introduced it had been almost taboo for economists—let alone governments—to even discuss capital controls. By coincidence, a week earlier the American economist Paul Krugman, in an article in *Fortune* magazine, had broken the intellectual taboo by advocating that Asian countries should adopt exchange controls.

The Malaysian move involved measures to regulate the international trade in its local currency and regulate movements of foreign exchange, aimed at reducing the country's exposure to financial speculators and the growing global financial turmoil. The policy package included officially fixing the ringgit to the US dollar, deinternationalizing the trade in the ringgit, a one year moratorium on the outward transfer of foreign-owned funds invested in the local stock market, and strict limitations on the transfer of funds abroad by local residents.

The rationale for the move was explained by prime minister Mahathir in a television interview on the day the measures were announced. Asked whether the exchange control measures were regressive, he said they were not. Instead it was the present situation, where currency instability and manipulation was prevalent, which was regressive. He stated that when the world moved away from the Bretton Woods fixed exchange system, it thought the floating rate system was a better way to evaluate currencies, 'but the market is now abused by currency traders who regard currencies as commodities which they trade in. They buy and sell currencies according to their own system and make profits from it but they cause poverty and damage to whole nations. That is very regressive and the world is not moving ahead but backwards'. He added the Malaysian measures were a last resort:

We had asked the international agencies to regulate currency trading but they did not care, so we ourselves have to regulate our own currency. If the international community agrees to regulate currency trading and limit the range of currency fluctuations and enables countries to grow again, then we can return to the floating exchange rate system. But now we can see the damage this system has done throughout the world. It has destroyed the hard work of countries to cater to the interests of speculators as if their interests are so important that millions of people must suffer. This is regressive.

(*The New Straits Times* 1998; *The Star* 1998)

The prime minister added that the Malaysian measures were aimed at putting a 'spanner in the works of speculators', and at taking speculators out of the currency trade. He said

the period of highest economic growth was during the Bretton Woods fixed exchange system. But the free market system that followed the Bretton Woods system has failed because of abuses. There are signs that people are now losing faith in this free market system, but some countries benefit from the abuses, their people make more money, so they don't see why the abuses should be curbed.

8.3 Elements of the Malaysian Alternative Strategy

8.3.1 *General*

The Malaysian alternative strategy was composed of several aspects. They were not developed all at once, but stage by stage as a response to the developments in the crisis and as the initial policies proved inadequate.

The elements of the Malaysian strategy included the following:

- the core macroeconomic policies of interest rates, monetary policy, fiscal policy, and a financing plan, which were essential for preventing the real economy from further deteriorating and to get the recovery going;
- stabilizing the exchange rate, which was necessary for preventing further destabilization, to enable the macroeconomic policies to be implemented and avoid difficulties in servicing the external debt;
- closing down the overseas trade in the local currency and the local stock market in order to prevent overseas speculative activities;

- regulating capital flows, particularly short-term capital outflows by foreigners and local citizens;[4]

- maintaining financial stability through a policy of not closing down financial institutions facing difficulties and of announcing that the government would guarantee deposits placed in banks and finance companies;

- restructuring and recapitalizing the banking and corporate sectors in order to create a recovery in the micro economy;

- revitalizing the various economic sectors affected by the crisis; and

- maintaining certain key economic and social policies, in particular the regulation of foreign ownership of assets, subsidies and price controls, and policies relating to distribution and balance among local ethnic communities.

8.3.2 *The Core Macroeconomic Elements*

REDUCTION IN INTEREST RATES

During the initial year of the crisis, interest rates for loans had shot up to as high as 25 percent, which had choked business. The interest rate was brought down as a key component of the alternative strategy. The central bank three-month intervention rate was reduced from 11 percent at the end of July 1998 to 6 percent on May 3, 1999. According to the United Nations Conference on Trade and Development, 'after the introduction of capital controls, interest rates were reduced further throughout 1999, falling to some 3 percent in December, compared to 5 percent in Thailand, 6.7 percent in Korea and 13 percent in Indonesia' (UNCTAD 2000: 57). The base lending rate of banks was reduced from 12.3 percent in June 1998 to 7.75 percent in December 1999.

EXPANSIONARY MONETARY AND CREDIT POLICY

During the initial phase of the crisis, credit flow had slowed to a trickle. The alternative strategy was aggressive in its measures to increase liquidity in the system. The government took measures to increase liquidity in the banking system and then urged banks to increase credit to the private sector. The government reduced the statutory reserve requirements (the funds that banks are required to maintain with the central bank as a prudential measure) from 13.5 percent to 10 percent in February 1998, to 8 percent in July 1998, and to

---

[4] Such measures included an initial one-year moratorium on outflow of foreign portfolio capital and foreign-owned financial assets denominated in ringgit. Restrictions were placed on capital transfers by local citizens and companies. The restrictions did not apply to the flow of funds relating to foreign direct investment to trade.

4 percent in October 1998. This released significant liquidity to the banks. The government also set a target for the banks to increase their loans by 8 percent in 1999. To ease the pressure on the banks, the government also reverted to the original definition of non-performing loans as loans not serviced for six months (instead of the more stringent three-month criterion that had been introduced after the crisis broke out).

EXPANSIONARY FISCAL POLICY

The initial contractionary fiscal policy (which had planned to cut government expenditure by 18 percent in December 1997) was reversed. In July 1998 a fiscal stimulus package was announced, which mandated additional development expenditure of RM7 billion allocated to agriculture, housing, education, health and rural development. Also, a RM5 billion infrastructure development fund was set up to finance infrastructure projects. The federal government had a budget surplus equivalent to 0.8 percent of GNP in 1996, and this rose to 2.5 percent of GNP in 1997. Reflecting the expansionary measures, the fiscal position then turned into a budget deficit of 1.8 percent in 1998, which increased to 3.2 percent in 1999 and 5.5 percent in 2001 (Ministry of Finance, Malaysia 2001; BNM 2002).

8.3.3 *Stabilizing the Currency*

FIXING THE EXCHANGE RATE

Stabilizing the exchange rate became about the most important objective. The NEAC studied the experiences of many countries and decided to adopt a fixed exchange rate system, thereby fixing the ringgit to the US dollar. This would not be done through a currency board system (as adopted by some other countries) because in such a system the country's money supply would be linked to the level of the country's foreign reserves. In the Malaysian system, this linkage was not made. The exchange rate chosen was RM3.80 to US$1, which was the approximate rate at the time the prime minister announced the adoption of a fixed exchange rate system in September 1998. The central bank used this rate to exchange dollars with ringgit in its dealings with the commercial banks and other authorized financial institutions, which in turn were required to use this rate in their currency dealings with the public. The ringgit–dollar rate remained the same, until the government decided to discontinue the fixed exchange rate system in 2005. Until that decision in 2005, the government had announced several times its intention to stick to the same rate for as long as possible (i.e., if this does not cause the ringgit to be overvalued or undervalued, especially in relation to concerns for export competitiveness) so that there would be a high degree of predictability. There was no 'black market' or parallel trade with a different rate. The predictions, especially by international analysts (voiced when the Malaysian system was introduced), that a fixed exchange rate system would result in misalignment and a black market have not been borne out.

The fixing of the exchange rate was important for stabilizing the financial situation. Perhaps its most important role, however, was that it allowed the government to take monetary and fiscal policies on the basis of their own merit and to thereby avoid being constrained by fears of a fall in the value of the currency if the funds analysts did not approve of the measures. The exchange rate fixing also reduced the opportunity for speculation.

As stated by the prime minister when he introduced the measures in September 1998: 'With the introduction of exchange controls, it would be possible to cut the link between interest rate and the exchange rate. We can reduce interest rates without speculators devaluing our currency. Our companies can revive.' He added that the country would not be affected by external developments as much as Russia was during its crisis.

MEASURES TO PREVENT OVERSEAS SPECULATION AND TRADE IN THE RINGGIT

Measures were taken to reduce and eliminate the international trade in the ringgit and to repatriate back to the country a large amount of ringgit-denominated financial assets (such as cash and savings deposits) that were held abroad in overseas banks and other institutions. The measures mainly comprised the non-recognition or non-acceptance of such assets in the country after the expiry of a one-month period; in other words, local financial institutions were not allowed to accept the entry of such assets after the deadline. (Permission to repatriate after this deadline would, however, be given under certain conditions.)

This measure also effectively put an end to the offshore trade in the Malaysian ringgit and in assets denominated in ringgit (including the operation and holding of ringgit denominated bank accounts abroad). Dr. Mahathir explained the move to make the use of offshore ringgit invalid by pointing out that normally it was offshore ringgit that was used by speculators to manipulate the currency. The speculators held the ringgit in foreign banks abroad and had corresponding amounts in banks in Malaysia.

8.3.4 *Selective Capital Controls*

THE INITIAL MEASURES IN SEPTEMBER 1998

Several measures were introduced on September 1, 1998, to regulate the outflow of funds.

Measures aimed at foreigners and foreign-owned funds included the following:

- Non-residents holding shares in companies listed on the local stock exchange would have to retain the shares or the proceeds from the sale of shares for a minimum period of one year from the purchase date. The objectives of this measure were to discourage foreign speculative short-term trade in local shares and to prevent capital outflow for at least a one-year period.

- Domestic credit facilities to non-resident correspondent banks and non-resident stockbroking companies were no longer allowed (previously domestic credit up to RM5 million was allowed).

- Conditions were imposed on the operations and transfers of ringgit denominated funds in external accounts, including those held by non-residents. Transfers between external accounts held by non-resident corporations and individuals residing outside Malaysia would require prior approval for any amount (previously freely allowed). Transfers from external accounts to resident accounts would require approval after September 30 , 1998. Sources of funding external accounts were limited to proceeds from the sale of ringgit instruments and other assets in Malaysia: salaries, interest and dividends, and the sale of foreign currency.

Measures aimed at local residents included the following:

- Resident travelers were allowed to import ringgit notes only up to RM1,000 and any amount of foreign currencies, and to export only up to RM1,000 and foreign currencies only up to the equivalent of RM10,000.

- Except for payments for imports of goods and services, residents were freely allowed to make payments to non-residents only up to RM10,000 or its equivalent in foreign currency (the limit was previously set at RM100,000).

- Investments in any form made abroad by residents and payments under a guarantee for non-trade purposes would require approval.

- The prescribed manner of payment for exports would be in foreign currency only (previously such payments were allowed to be in foreign currency or ringgit from an external account).

- Residents would require prior approval to make payments to non-residents for purposes of investing abroad for amounts exceeding the equivalent of RM10,000 in foreign exchange.

- Residents were not allowed to obtain ringgit credit facilities from non-residents.

It should also be noted that the ruling, in existence before the outbreak of the crisis, prohibiting local companies from obtaining foreign currency denominated loans from abroad (unless these were for activities that earned foreign exchange remained in force).

The capital controls were selective in that they covered movements of funds in the capital account. In the case of foreigners, the controls covered mainly some aspects of portfolio investment. In general, the ringgit was still to be freely (or at least easily) convertible to foreign currencies for trade (export receipts and import payments), inward foreign direct investment (FDI), and repatriation of FDI-related capital and dividends by non-residents. In the case of local residents, the capital controls covered a wider range of activities, and in fact the aim of preventing the flight of locally owned capital was to be just as important as (if not more than) the controls imposed on foreign-owned funds. However, there was no control on currency convertibility by local residents for purposes of trade. Convertibility up to a certain limit was also allowed for certain other purposes, such as the financing of children's education abroad. But convertibility for autonomous capital movements for several purposes not directly related to trade was to be prohibited or limited.

SUBSEQUENT AMENDMENTS AND RELAXATION

The capital control measures were amended and, in effect, relaxed subsequent to their introduction on September 1, 1998.

The requirement that proceeds from the sale of ringgit assets be maintained by foreigners in the country for one year was replaced by an exit levy on assets owned by foreigners, that went into effect on February 15, 1999:

- For capital brought in before February 15, 1999, an exit levy was imposed on the principal. The rates were 30 percent for a maturity period of seven months, 20 percent for nine months, 10 percent for 12 months and zero levy for capital exceeding a 12-month maturity period.

- For capital brought in after February 15, 1999, an exit levy was imposed on the profits at the rates of 30 percent for a maturity period of less than 12 months and 10 percent for a maturity period of more than 12 months.

A further amendment was made on September 21, 1999. Irrespective of when the capital was brought in, an exit levy with a single rate of 10 percent was instituted on profits repatriated by foreigners. On May 1, 2001, this 10 percent exit levy was also abolished.

8.3.5 Stock Market Measures and Closure of Overseas Trade in Malaysian Securities

The Kuala Lumpur Stock Exchange (KLSE) established new measures that began on September 1, 1998. One major aim of the measures was to reduce possible capital leakage from the country through the stock market. Among these measures were:

- clearings in securities traded on the KLSE were to be undertaken only through the KLSE or a recognized stock exchange and through the KLSE trading system;

- new disclosure requirements, including the beneficiary owners of shares, must be identified in all dealings, and each Central Depository System account operated by a nominee must have only one beneficiary;

- stockbroking companies were to engage only in direct off-market dealings such as crossing and married deals; and

- all new issues of shares were to be made by crediting the securities into the Central Depository System accounts of securities holders.

The measures taken caused the closure of existing secondary markets abroad that conducted trade in stocks of companies listed on the KLSE since after the measures, trade would be limited only to the KLSE. A major aim of the measure was to prevent speculation or manipulation of KLSE share prices and transactions from outside the country and to prevent the outflow of capital through the sale of Malaysian shares outside the country. The shares of 112 companies listed on the KLSE had been traded since 1990 in the Central Limit Order Book International (CLOB) based in Singapore, which was in effect an offshore market for Malaysian securities. The CLOB market was also linked to the ringgit offshore market as CLOB shares were used as collateral by currency traders dealing in ringgit. On September 16, 1998, the Stock Exchange of Singapore discontinued the trading of Malaysian shares on CLOB and subsequently a deal was made between the two stock exchanges whereby the CLOB shares were released into the KLSE and the CLOB shareholders could again trade in those shares.

8.3.6 *Restructuring the Financial System and Corporate Debt*

GENERAL

A major threat posed by the crisis was the serious destabilizing effect on the banking and financial systems. As local companies and consumers faced difficulties in servicing their loans because of the initial raising of interest rates, the sharp currency depreciation and the recession in the real economy, the incidence of the banks' non-performing loans (NPLs) increased sharply. It was estimated by the NEAC that total NPLs in the banking system would be RM74 billion (15.5 percent of gross loans outstanding) by the end of 1998 and would rise to RM100 billion (19.7 percent) by the end of 1999.

As public confidence eroded, there was a need to restore confidence and prevent a run on the banks. Also, several banks that had come under pressure had to be recapitalized or face insolvency. Measures were taken to deal with these problems. First, measures to restore public confidence were taken through a government guarantee of deposits and a decision not to close down troubled institutions was made. Second, a set of three new agencies was created: Danaharta, an asset management company to manage NPLs; Danamodal, a special agency to recapitalise weak financial institutions; and the Corporate Debt Restructuring Committee (CDRC), a committee to restructure corporate debts. These three agencies worked together to try to resolve the interrelated problems in a coordinated way.

GOVERNMENT GUARANTEE OF DEPOSITORS' FUNDS

As a result of the erosion of public confidence in the local financial institutions, many depositors at the end of 1997 began to shift their assets from locally-owned to foreign-owned banks and abroad. To prevent a potential run on some of the banks or a run on the local banks in general, the government announced that it would guarantee depositors' funds in the commercial banks and licensed finance companies. This restored depositors' confidence.

DECISION NOT TO CLOSE DOWN FINANCIAL INSTITUTIONS IN TROUBLE

The government decided it would not order the closure of any commercial bank or licensed finance company that was suffering financial difficulties. Instead other measures would be taken to restore their viability. This also helped maintain public confidence in the financial system.

ESTABLISHMENT OF DANAHARTA

The government-owned company, Danaharta, was formed in June 1998 to buy or transfer NPLs from the banking system; to manage, restructure, or dispose of the acquired loans and the assets attached as collateral; and to maximize the recovery value of the acquired assets.[5]

Danaharta's initial funding of RM13.2 billion came mainly from bonds issued to the selling banking institutions (RM8.2 billion) and from government contributions (RM3 billion) and government loans (RM2 billion). By the end of 2000, Danaharta had taken over RM47.5 billion of NPLs at an average discount of 56 percent of the nominal loan value (Mahani 2002: 150). Viable loans were restructured; for non-viable loans, the assets attached as collateral were restructured (this involved the sale of the collateral or the business); and foreign loans were sold. At the end of 2000, Danaharta expected to collect recovery proceeds of RM23.8 billion.

Because of Danaharta's operations, the banking system's NPLs peaked at 13 percent of total loans in April 1999, which was far below the market expectations that NPLs would rise to the rate of 20 percent or 30 percent.

---

[5] See Mahani (2002: 147–57) for an account of the operations of Danaharta.

ESTABLISHMENT OF DANAMODAL

Danamodal was established in August 1998 as a subsidiary of the central bank. Its aim was to recapitalize financial institutions under financial stress from inadequate capitalization. Its functions were to assess recapitalization requirements of the banks, undertake the recapitalization exercise, restructure the affected institutions, and monitor performance. Danamodal raised RM10.7 billion of funds for its work (RM7.7 billion through issue of its bonds; and RM3 billion seed capital from the central bank). By mid-1999, Danamodal had injected RM7.59 billion to assist in recapitalizing ten financial institutions. The injected funds were all initially in the form of exchangeable subordinated capital loans (ESCLs). Of the RM7.59 billion, a total of RM3.9 billion had been repaid in 2002 and, by then, Danamodal funds remained in only three institutions. In these remaining institutions, the original ESCL loans had been transformed into preference and ordinary shares (RM2.6 billion); subordinated bonds (RM500 million); and the rest were retained as ESCL loans (RM1.1 billion) (Mahani 2002: 157–69).

Danamodal's work helped in recapitalizing and reviving several troubled institutions and prevented what could have been the closure of some of them. The amount of public funds used by Danamodal was relatively small since most of its financing was through its own bonds. Furthermore, over half of the loans have been repaid by the recapitalized financial institutions. Additionally, the rates of return for Danamodal's investments have been 7.5 percent for the ESCLs, 12 percent for shares owned, and 10 percent for subordinated loans (Mahani 2002: 165). These rates are relatively high.

ESTABLISHMENT OF THE CORPORATE DEBT RESTRUCTURING COMMITTEE (CDRC)

The CDRC was established in July 1998 to assist in resolving large corporate debts by creating a forum for creditors and borrowers for debt restructuring workout through voluntary agreement.[6] Its steering committee initially comprised finance ministry and central bank officials, and representatives from the legal, accounting, and banking professions. Later, representatives of the creditor banks joined the committee.

The restructuring process involved four phases: an initial debtor–creditors meeting to agree on a temporary informal standstill and to appoint a creditors' committee; appointment of consultants to review the company's status and recommend action; the making of a formal standstill agreement and agreement on restructuring plans; and the submission of creditors' committee progress reports to the steering committee.

The CDRC's work started slowly and faced some challenges, including the fact that (unlike Danaharta and Danamodal) it lacked statutory powers and

---

[6] See Mahani (2002: 170–4) for an account of the operations of the CDRC.

that the workout arrangements were of a voluntary nature. In its first few years, however, it was able to complete a significant number of cases. By mid-2001, 73 applications had been received by corporations for debt workout. Of these, 21 were withdrawn or rejected (mainly because they were unviable businesses) and 9 were transferred to Danaharta. The remaining 43 cases involved a total of RM38 billion in debts. Of these, 33 cases involving RM28 billion in debts had been completed, and another two cases involving RM1 billion had been resolved with Danaharta's assistance, leaving eight outstanding cases involving RM9 billion in debts. The CDRC was able to conduct debt workouts involving several large corporate debts. A limitation was that the CDRC only accepted applications from companies that it assessed to be still viable, and which had over RM50 million of debts. Thus, the CDRC dealt only with large companies with big debts, whereas small companies requiring a similar debt workout exercise were left out (Mahani 2002: 170–3).

8.3.7 *Maintaining Some Basic National Policies and Socioeconomic Goals*

A major part of the Malaysian alternative strategy was that it maintained several key aspects of the overall national development policies that had been in place before the crisis. Some of these policies had been part of the central tenets of Malaysian political and socioeconomic life, and some represented a compact among the various ethnic communities.

Malaysian political leaders were justifiably concerned that some of these policies would have to be jettisoned if the country had to turn to the IMF for loans and abide by IMF loan conditions. Asked by journalists if the IMF would be unhappy with the Malaysian exchange rate and capital control measures, Dr. Mahathir replied that the IMF's actions had benefited foreign companies but were not in the country's interests. 'They see our troubles as an opportunity for foreign companies to do business without any conditions. [The IMF] says it will give you money if you open up your economy, but doing so will cause all our banks, companies, and industries to belong to foreigners.'

Thus, an important component of the Malaysian strategy was to ensure that it would be able to maintain several of its national policies. For example:

- The country could retain its policy of regulating the entry and degree of participation of foreign companies and investors in the domestic economy. Malaysia has one of the most liberal policies toward foreign investment. However, it also has a complex and sophisticated set of policies regulating foreign participation. The Malaysian crisis response strategy did not involve a significant change in policies toward foreign ownership. Moreover, the exercise of restructuring financial institutions and local corporations mainly involved local institutions and players. This was unlike the situation of countries undergoing reforms with IMF assistance, where opening up to foreign participation was a major plank of IMF conditionality.

- The government was able to assist locally-owned companies and financial institutions that were facing financial difficulties or imminent insolvency. In countries undergoing IMF reforms, assistance to local institutions in economic difficulties was not allowed in many cases or was frowned upon. During the Asian financial crisis, there was heated debate about whether the state should come to the assistance of corporations and banks during a crisis, or whether they should be allowed to collapse. The debate was also heated in Malaysia, where there were accusations that in the corporate and banking rescue plans, the government favored certain businessmen associated with factions of the ruling party, especially in how it regarded the terms of debt settlement or asset restructuring. However, by not going to the IMF, the country had the option of determining its own policies on assistance to local institutions. The restructuring exercises had a fair rate of success.

- The government was able to maintain the policy of striving for balance in the distribution of assets and equity between locals and foreigners, as well as among the local communities (known in Malaysia as the New Economic Policy).

- The government was also able to maintain socially oriented policies such as controls on prices of some essential consumer items, and subsidies on a few consumer items as well as to farmers (for example, government fertilizer subsidies to rice farmers). In several countries receiving IMF loans, some price controls or subsidies were reduced or withdrawn, causing social unrest.

- Government policies on privatization remained in place, and so did the policies on the extent and rate of financial and trade liberalization.

8.4 Some Lessons and Conclusions

8.4.1 *Some Lessons from the Malaysian Experience*

There are some interesting lessons from the Malaysian policy response to the crisis.

1. *There are alternatives to the IMF conditionality package.* There are alternatives to the IMF's loan conditionality policy package that can be formulated and tried out. The Malaysian case shows that such an alternative approach exists and can be applied to achieve relatively successful results.

2. *Having policy space and flexibility is important to a developing country.* The Malaysian experience also shows that if a country is able to avoid turning to the IMF, it can also avoid the straightjacket of the IMF's mainly one-size-fits-all policies and can choose its own policies as well as change them if they are found to be unsuitable. Malaysia initially took on several elements of the IMF fiscal and monetary policies but when these damaged the real economy, the country was able to switch to a different approach.

3. *A coherent anti-crisis strategy should be seen as an integrated package of its elements and policies.* Policymakers often (even constantly) grapple with difficult policy decisions since the goals of policy are multiple. A policy instrument meant to achieve one goal may negatively affect other goals. In a situation where there are many complex trade-offs, it is useful to think outside the box and seek other policy tools.

In the Malaysian case, it is useful to analyze and appreciate the various policy elements as parts of an integrated approach and as parts of a whole policy package. Thus, each element should be considered not only on its own merits or for its own role in achieving a particular goal but also for its function of having an effect on another element or on another goal. A particular element or policy may not have the same successful intended effect, unless accompanied by or done in conjunction with some other element of policy. Thus, the interrelationship of the elements and the interaction with one another should be appreciated.

For example, lowering the interest rate was important for rescuing the microeconomy and reviving the real economy but doing so would have brought down the ringgit's exchange rate and threatened the country with a debt-default situation. The interest rate therefore had to be decoupled from the exchange rate. A new policy instrument, fixing the exchange rate, was thus introduced.[7]

However, this alone would have been insufficient since: (a) speculation on the currency could still take place in ringgit offshore markets; and (b) there was still the possibility of capital flight that could pose a threat to the foreign reserves position and also make maintenance of the exchange rate unsustainable. Thus, besides fixing the exchange rate to the dollar, stabilization of the currency also required two additional policy instruments: (a) ending the overseas speculation by banning the currency's trade abroad; and (b) introducing selective capital controls to regulate the outflows and inflows of funds. Thus, if we start with even one major

---

[7] It should be noted that a fixed exchange rate system of the type introduced by Malaysia does not imply that the rate at which the local currency is pegged (in this case to the US dollar) is permanent, as the policymakers can adjust the rate from time to time when deemed appropriate.

policy goal (reviving the local companies and the local economy) and a single policy tool (interest rate reduction), we end up with several other policy tools and goals.

4. *Financial openness poses serious dangers to developing countries and can be avoided.* Too much openness in the financial sector can make a developing country vulnerable to financial speculation, to sudden or large movements of foreign capital, and to volatile movements in the exchange rate. If a country were to maintain an open financial policy, it risks losing the ability to determine its own macroeconomic policies (or at least its flexibility to choose among macroeconomic policy options is seriously reduced). Thus, the country may find it desirable not to have such an open financial policy.

The Malaysian experience shows that if a developing country reaches such a policy conclusion, it is possible to adopt policies to limit financial openness through an array of policy tools. Such tools could include some capital controls, regulations to discourage or prevent speculation, and a fixed exchange rate system. Of course, 'one-size-does-not-fit-all' also applies here, and the policies that may have been appropriate for Malaysia may not be so for other countries that have different conditions (economic, political, institutional, etc.) or different goals.

8.4.2 Conclusions

How successful was the Malaysian alternative strategy? From 1999, after the adoption of the policies, the economy recovered rather well. Real GDP, which had fallen by 7.4 percent in 1998, grew again by 6.1 percent in 1999 and 8.3 percent in 2000. The growth rate slowed significantly to 0.4 percent in 2001 due to unfavorable world economic conditions, then recovered to 4.2 percent in 2002. The balance of payments current account, which had a RM15.8 billion deficit in 1997, turned around to surpluses of RM36.8 billion in 1998, RM47.9 billion in 1999, and RM32.2 billion in 2000. The central bank's international reserves had fallen from RM70 billion (US$27.7 billion) at the end of 1996 to RM59.1 billion (US$21.7 billion) at the end of 1997 during the onset of the crisis. It increased to RM99.4 billion or US$26.2 billion (1998), RM117.2 billion or US$30.9 billion (1999), and RM131.4 billion or US$34.6 billion (2002).

Total external debt had risen from RM97.8 billion (40 percent of GNP) in 1996 to RM170.8 billion (64 percent of GNP) in 1997. It then declined to RM162 billion (60 percent of GNP) in 1998 and to RM161 billion or US$42.3 billion in 2000 (51 percent of GNP) before rising again to RM185.3 billion or US$48.8 billion (55 percent of GNP) in 2002 (BNM various years). External debt service payments in 1998–2002 stayed within manageable levels, equivalent to 5.4 to 7.0 percent of the value of exports of goods and services. The rate of inflation had risen from 2.6 percent in 1997 to 5.2 percent in 1998, but declined to 2.8 percent in 1999 and to 1–2 percent in 2000–2 (BNM various years; Ministry of Finance Malaysia 2001).

Most of the banks recovered and the level of non-performing loans and risk-weighted capital ratios have come within internationally accepted standards. Some local corporations have not yet recovered fully to the pre-crisis conditions (and some may never do so), but many have remained economically viable.

UNCTAD's *Trade and Development Report 2000* assesses the effects of the Malaysian capital control measures and concludes:

The success of the measures taken was confirmed by the fact that when the controls were lifted in September 1999 there was an immediate outflow of only 5.2 billion ringgit, and another 3.1 billion in the rest of the year. In the first quarter of 2000 there was a net inflow of 8.5 billion, an amount roughly equal to what had flown out at the expiry of the controls. By May 2000 total official reserve assets were $32 billion, over six times short term debt. In December 1999 Malaysia's long term foreign currency rating was raised to BBB and more recently the country was returned to the Morgan Stanley Capital International emerging market securities benchmark indices, indicating a normalisation of relations with international capital markets. (UNCTAD 2000: 55)

Comparisons have been made between the recovery in Malaysia and in Thailand, South Korea, and Indonesia. It is true that in Thailand and South Korea, at least there was also recovery within a few years. Some analysts point out that the Malaysian policy example may have encouraged the IMF to relax its initial contractionary fiscal and interest rate policies in the three countries and thus that the Malaysian policies indirectly assisted the recovery in these countries. The controversies over the comparison between the performance of Malaysia and that of countries undergoing IMF policies will continue. However, it cannot be denied that the Malaysian experience shows that an alternative to the IMF policy package can and does exist and that it can produce results that are at least as successful.

Can the Malaysian strategy be replicated? As stated above, 'one-size-does-not-fit-all' also applies here, and the policies that may have been appropriate for Malaysia may not be so for other countries because they have different conditions or different goals. For example, Malaysia did not have a problem servicing its external debts, so it had a choice of whether to seek IMF assistance. Countries facing a debt default may not be in such a comfortable situation and if they turn to the IMF for assistance, then many of the options open to Malaysia may not be available to them—unless the IMF changes its approach.

In relation to capital controls, the policies Malaysia took were adapted to its own peculiar circumstances. The lesson is that countries can and should consider the use of capital controls as part of the array of policy tools available. There is a large range of capital controls that can be applied to inflows and outflows. It may be that to prevent a crisis, controls on inflows could be more efficient. In any case, the Malaysian regulation limiting foreign loans to local companies only in cases where the loans will yield foreign exchange earnings has proved to be very useful in safeguarding Malaysia from the excessive and rapid build-up of short-term foreign debt that was a major factor in the Thai, Indonesian, and South Korean crises.

The Malaysian capital controls were applied only to capital account out-flows and mainly to local residents. There were no restrictions on trade-related transactions or on transactions involving FDI. This was considered wise by the policymakers since Malaysia has an economy that is dependent both on trade and FDI; thus policymakers rejected the option of capital controls which could disrupt trade and FDI. Foreign funds and foreigners were affected mainly in relation to short-term portfolio investment in measures that were eventually relaxed and then abolished relatively rapidly. Countries facing a different situation could more appropriately choose to apply different controls over a different set of flows.

For a fixed exchange system and a system of capital controls to work, some degree of institutional capacity and administrative efficiency is required for successful implementation and the prevention of leakages or black markets. Malaysia has a relatively capable administrative machinery, which contributed to the successful implementation of the policies. Countries lacking this capacity may not be able to implement the same kind of policies so successfully. This point has often been made. However, a developing country need not be discouraged from instituting these policies simply because it does not have a very efficient administrative machinery. After all, there were many predictions (from the IMF, market analysts, and investment funds) that the Malaysian currency policy and capital controls would not work and would plunge the country into disaster, and yet the country was able to implement the policies successfully.

In its approach to core macroeconomic policies, the Malaysian strategy was intended to follow the basic Keynesian prescription that in a recessionary situation, a package of low interest rates and expansionary monetary and fiscal policies will help revive the economy. The Malaysian strategy was unique only because the IMF conditionality appears to prohibit recipient countries from following this prescription. Many developed countries, including the United States, follow the same strategy that Malaysia did. It remains strange to neutral observers why the IMF does not allow its developing country borrowers to adopt policies that the US, its most important creditor member, adopts but instead insists on contractionary macroeconomic policies that usually induce recessionary conditions.

References

Athukorala, P.-C. (2001). *Crisis and Recovery in Malaysia: The Role of Capital Controls*. Cheltenham: Edward Elgar. Bank Negara Malaysia (BNM) (1998). *Annual Report*. Kuala Lumpeur: BNM.

____ (2002). *Annual Report*. Kuala Lumpur: BNM.

____ (various other years). *Annual Report*. Kuala Lumpur: BNM.

Economic Planning Unit (1998). *National Economic Recovery Plan: Agenda for Action*. Kuala Lumpur: Prime Minister's Department.

Kaplan, T. and Rodrik, D. (2000). *Did the Malaysian Capital Controls Work?*

Khor, M. (1998a). 'Why Capital Controls and International Debt Restructuring Mechanisms are Necessary to Prevent and Manage Financial Crises'. Paper presented at the Seminar on the Financial Crisis, organized by the Asian Strategic and Leadership Institute, Kuala Lumpur, November.

____ (1998b). *The Economic Crisis in East Asia: Causes, Effects, Lessons*.

____ (2001). *Globalisation and the South*. Penang: Third World Network.

Lin, S. Y. (1998). 'Rebuiling ASEAN in the Wake of the Current Economic Crisis—Causes, Impact, Response and Lessons: A Malaysian Perspective'. Paper presented at the Roundtable Discussion on the Current Economic Crisis in ASEAN, Kuala Lumpur.

Mahani, Z. A. (2002). *Rewriting the Rules: The Malaysian Crisis Management Model*. Kuala Lumpur: Prentice Hall.

Ministry of Finance Malaysia (2001). *Economic Report 2001/2002*. Kuala Lumpur: Ministry of Finance Malaysia.

Mohamad, M. (2000). *The Malaysian Currency Crisis: How and Why It Happened*. Kuala Lumpur: Pelanduk Publications.

____ (2003). *Globalisation and the New Realities*. Kuala Lumpur: Pelanduk Publications.

The New Straits Times (1998). News report on Prime Minister's announcement of currency measures, Kuala Lumpur, September 2.

The Star (1998). News report on Prime Minister's announcement of currency measures, Kuala Lumpur, September 2.

UNCTAD (2000). *Trade and Development Report 2000*. Geneva: United Nations.

____ (various other years). *Trade and Development Report*. Geneva: United Nations.

9

Domestic Financial Regulations in Developing Countries: Can They Effectively Limit the Impact of Capital Account Volatility?

Liliana Rojas-Suarez[1]

9.1 Introduction

After more than a decade of financial sector liberalization, policymakers in many developing countries remain concerned about the effects that large and highly volatile capital flows have on their financial systems. This is not surprising, given the increasing evidence that, in sharp contrast to policy objectives, financial crises have become more frequent following financial liberalization. However, in spite of the tremendous costs associated with the resolution of crises and signs of discontent among the population with the outcome of some reforms, to date there is no significant evidence indicating a reversal of the reform process. With few exceptions (mostly of a temporary nature) developing countries have not returned to a regime of highly controlled domestic financial markets or closed capital accounts. While one could advance a number of hypotheses explaining this commitment to reforms, developing countries' decisions and actions seem to indicate that policymakers perceive capital inflows as a necessary component to achieve growth and development. Rather than severely restricting the movement of capital, many countries have intensified their attempts to strengthen their domestic economies, and especially their financial systems. The hope is that if only the right policies could be designed to insulate domestic financial

[1] I would like to thank José Antonio Ocampo and other members of the Capital Markets Liberalization Task Force, organized by Joseph Stiglitz's Initiative for Policy Dialogue, for their valuable comments, and Trond Augdal, Carlos Gallardo, and Sebastian Sotelo for excellent research assistant support. The errors that remain are, of course, my own.

sectors from the volatility of international capital flows, countries could enjoy the benefits of both additional foreign capital for growth and stable domestic financial systems.

In this regard, policy recommendations for dealing with domestic financial market problems generated by highly volatile capital flows have not been in short supply, and many of these recommendations have indeed been applied in a wide range of developing countries. While the policy menu is quite ample, analysts' emphasis on one set of recommendations rather than another greatly depends on what they view as the major cause of the problem. For those that believe that capital flow volatility is largely the result of a faulty international financial architecture that does not sufficiently take into account market imperfections and information asymmetries at the international level, appropriate policies include further official intervention, such as additional controls on the activities of the international capital markets, including regulation of hedge funds. For this group of analysts, capital controls are a desirable policy response by developing countries.

To others, the major cause of capital flow volatility experienced by developing countries resides in the domestic macroeconomic policies of the recipient countries. To this group, policy recommendations stress the avoidance of fiscal, monetary, and external imbalances, and the maintenance of a sustainable debt path. Yet, there is a third group of analysts that view domestic financial weaknesses as the key cause of major disruptions derived from capital flow volatility. Since a large proportion of capital inflows is intermediated through domestic financial markets, especially banks in developing countries, the central policy prescription for this group of analysts lies in strengthening domestic financial institutions through improved regulation and supervision. An additional policy recommendation deals with increasing the maturity of financial assets by encouraging the development of domestic capital markets.

Emphasis on one set of policy prescriptions does not mean, of course, total disregard of the others. Indeed, most analysts would agree that the disruptive effects of capital flow volatility on developing countries are the result of a combination of most of the factors mentioned above. For example, those that emphasize improvements in the regulatory and supervisory framework of developing countries also recognize that these policy tools can be effective only in a stable macroeconomic environment, and some analysts in this group would also support certain forms of capital controls.

In this connection, this chapter focuses on a particular aspect of the problem at hand and asks how appropriate prudential financial regulation should be designed to contain the risks resulting from liberalized financial systems facing high external capital volatility. In order to provide advice to developing countries on how to improve regulation and supervision of financial markets, it is first necessary to answer two questions. The first is whether commonly used regulatory tools have been effective in reducing the adverse effects of capital flow volatility on domestic financial markets. The second is whether appropriate regulatory and supervisory tools in developing countries need to be different from those that work in industrial countries and even differ between developing countries at different degrees of financial sector development.

To conduct this task, the chapter identifies two alternative forms of prudential regulation. The first set is formed by regulations that directly control financial aggregates, such as liquidity expansion and credit growth. An example is capital requirements as currently incorporated in internationally accepted standards; namely, capital requirements with risk categories used in industrial countries. The second set, which can be identified as the 'pricing-risk-right' approach, works by providing incentives to financial institutions to avoid excessive risk-taking activities. A key feature of this set of regulations is that they encourage financial institutions to internalize the costs associated with the particular risks of the environment where they operate. Regulations in this category include ex ante risk-based provisioning rules and capital requirements that take into account the risk features particular to developing countries. This category also includes incentives for enhancing market discipline as a way to differentiate risk-taking behavior between financial institutions.

The main conclusion of this paper is that the first set of regulations—the most commonly used in developing economies—have had limited success in helping countries contain the risks involved with more liberalized financial systems. The primary reason for this disappointing result is that the particular characteristics of financial markets in developing countries are not adequately considered, so these regulations cannot effectively control excessive risk-taking by financial institutions. Moreover, contrary to policy intentions, this set of prudential regulations can exacerbate rather than decrease financial sector fragility, especially in episodes of sudden reversal of capital flows.

In contrast, the second set of prudential regulations can go a long way in helping developing countries achieve their goals. This chapter proposes sequencing of implementation of these regulations for different groups of countries.

The rest of this chapter is organized as follows. Section 9.2 summarizes features of domestic financial markets in developing countries that exacerbate the effects of international capital flow volatility on the domestic economies. Section 9.3 assesses the experience of developing countries with the most commonly used prudential regulatory and supervisory tools for coping with the volatility of capital flows and explains why these policies have been of limited usefulness. Section 9.4 advances specific policy recommendations for prudential regulatory policies that might have a good chance of working effectively in developing countries. In doing so, the section identifies and analyzes features of prudential regulation used in industrial countries that would need to be modified to be effective in developing countries. Section 9.5 concludes the chapter.

9.2 Features of Financial Markets in Developing Countries that Exacerbate the Adverse Effects of Capital Flow Volatility

Sudden stops of capital inflows are the most feared characteristic of capital account volatility in developing countries because they create an abrupt and dramatic reduction in funding for growth and development. A drastic decrease in net capital inflows will bring about pressures on a number of financial variables. By reflecting a reduction in the overall demand for domestic assets, interest rates will increase and prices of assets—held either by locals or foreigners—will decrease. Pressures on the exchange rate and/or international reserves also will materialize.

The extent to which domestic financial systems in developing countries can manage the adverse impact of a sudden reversal of capital inflows is certainly influenced by the strength of the systems before such a shock.[2] For example, the damage to the value of banks' assets as a result of a sudden increase in interest rates will be minimized if the quality of their loan portfolio is high. This would imply that the banks' client base is able to generate liquidity to service its payments on a timely basis and that the ratio of non-performing loans to loans is low before the emergence of a shock. Likewise, the effect of a significant exchange rate depreciation on the quality of banks' balance sheets would be minimized if bank managers had either arranged adequate hedges on net foreign currency denominated bank liabilities or strictly limited these exposures in countries lacking liquid private sector markets to hedge foreign exchange positions.[3,4] The stronger the initial conditions of banks before the shock, the greater the confidence of depositors in the banks' capacity to

---

[2] As discussed in the introduction, there are also a number of other factors that will determine the impact of the shock on the domestic economy.

[3] In many developing countries, banks' risks from net foreign currency exposures go beyond the currency denomination of their assets and liabilities. Potential exchange rate risks also arise from lending in foreign currency to firms and individuals with revenues denominated in domestic currency. As will be discussed below, incentives for banks to adequately avoid excessive foreign exchange risk taking depends on the announced government policies.

[4] The importance for banks to limit their net foreign-currency liabilities cannot be overstressed. In most developing countries, currency futures markets are lacking. Moreover, in the few cases where these markets exist, they do not have sufficient depth and liquidity as to provide adequate hedge in times of high exchange rate volatility. For example, in late 1998 in Brazil, when expectations about exchange rate depreciation mounted, the only source of hedge came from the government who placed a large amount of dollar-linked government debt in banks' balance sheets. While this action insulated the banking system from the sharp devaluation in early 1999, it also transferred the exchange rate risk (and the associated fiscal costs) from the private sector to the government.

weather the shock and, therefore, the lower the probability that depositors will empty banks of their money when adverse international financial conditions arise.

Indeed, strong confidence in domestic financial systems is usually reflected in a: (1) high degree of financial intermediation; (2) stable deposit base; and (3) dynamic financial system that intermediates funds to the private sector on a sound basis.

These features of financial sector strength were not typical characteristics of developing countries in the 1980s. At the time, in most developing countries, depository institutions—banks and savings institutions issuing deposit-like liabilities—were the most important vehicles for institutional savings. However, with the exception of a few countries, in the 1980s deposit liabilities to the private sector of all banking institutions constituted a low percentage of GDP in developing countries relative to the corresponding ratio in major industrial countries. In other words, relatively few saving funds were held in financial intermediaries.

Not only were the banking sectors relatively shallow, but also the liabilities and assets of these institutions were of short maturity: bank deposits financed short-term loans, short-term government paper, and central bank securities. The combination of these two features reflected lack of depositors' confidence in domestic financial systems and made these systems highly vulnerable to capital flow volatility.

Recognition of the need to strengthen domestic financial systems led to comprehensive reforms in a number of developing countries during the late 1980s and 1990s. By attempting to improve the quality of financial intermediaries' portfolios, the policy objective was to improve investors' confidence in the financial systems and, therefore, to increase the resilience of domestic financial systems to capital flow volatility. Moreover, it was also expected that stronger financial systems would help lower the volatility of capital flows.

While it is difficult to argue against the advantages of stronger financial systems as a tool to help mitigate the adverse impact of capital flow volatility, efficient and effective implementation of reforms requires careful consideration of the appropriate pace, timing and sequencing of these reforms. After all, even in a number of industrial countries, financial liberalization occurred not until the 1970s and in some countries, like Norway, not until the early 1980s. A reform implemented in countries with the lowest level of financial development would most likely have a different effect than in countries with more developed financial systems.

The issue of reform-readiness, however, was not sufficiently taken into account in developing countries. Indeed, one can identify clusters of reforms over the last two decades that have been implemented in countries with dramatically different degrees of development. The first reform cluster included both liberalization of interest rates and dismantling of credit controls. These reforms proved to be destabilizing in the absence of appropriate supervision.[5] Indeed, this first round of reforms created incentives for increased risk-taking by banks. Competition for market share without appropriate rules of the game determining not only entry requirements into the banking systems, but also provisions for exit out of the system resulted in dramatic increases in the risk features of banks' portfolios that were fully exposed following the eruption of adverse shocks. The second cluster, therefore, focused on improving the regulatory and supervisory frameworks—including advances in the implementation of the recommendations of the Basel Committee.[6,7] Once again, however, these improvements were not sufficient to prevent the eruption of large financial crises that followed the reversal of capital inflows that started in the late 1990s and continued through 2002. Reasons for the less-than-satisfactory results of these reforms efforts will be discussed in the next sections.

While, generally speaking, developing countries around the world have followed similar clusters of reforms, not all regions or countries within a region have implemented reforms at the same time or with the same intensity. Abiad and Mody (2003)[8] found that, in spite of partial reversal in some regions at some times, there is a clear trend towards increased financial liberalization. Among regions of the developing world, East Asia's financial systems are the most liberalized and South Asia's, the least. Interestingly, because of continuous progress in liberalization by OECD countries, the financial liberalization gap between developing and industrial countries has not decreased significantly over time. An exception is in Latin America, where from the mid-1980s to the mid-1990s, countries undertook massive reforms and consequently did reduce the financial liberalization gap with industrial countries.

In addition to financial liberalization and improvements in regulatory and supervisory frameworks, developing countries have made significant efforts to attract foreign capital into their financial systems. In many cases, this was the

[5] See Diaz Alejandro (1985) for a recount of how financial liberalization without appropriate supervision resulted in severe financial crises in Latin America in the early 1980s.

[6] The Basel Committee provides a forum for regular cooperation on banking supervisory matters. Over recent years, it has developed increasingly into a standard setting body on all aspects of banking supervision. The Committee's members come from Belgium, Canada, France, Germany, Italy, Japan, Luxembourg, the Netherlands, Spain, Sweden, Switzerland, the United Kingdom, and the United States. Countries are represented by their central bank and also by the authority with formal responsibility for the prudential supervision of banking business where this is not the central bank (see www.bis.org/bcbs/index.htm).

[7] In a recent database constructed by Barth et al. (2001a), only 17 countries out of 110 surveyed responded that their minimum required capital-to-asset ratio did not conform to the Basel's guidelines.

[8] Abiad and Mody developed an index of financial liberalization formed by six components: (a) credit controls; (b) interest rate controls; (c) entry barriers, including limits on the participation of foreign banks; (d) privatization of the financial sector; and (e) restrictions on international financial transactions. The higher the value of the index, the higher the degree of financial liberalization. See Abiad and Mody (2003) for a detailed methodology.

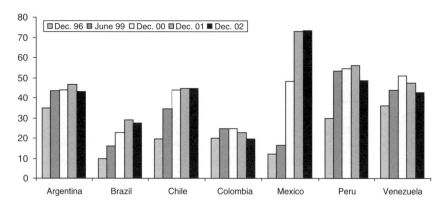

Figure 9.1. Main Latin American banking systems: foreign effective control, 1996–2002 (percent of total loans)

Source: Salomon Smith Barney: Foreign Financial Institutions in Latin America (2002).

result of deep banking crises that required huge injections of capital in order to restore financial solvency. In other cases, the increased participation of foreign banks in developing countries was the result of a combination of lower yields on investments in industrial countries and the expectation of higher yields on investments in developing countries as a result of the impetus from the structural reforms of the 1990s.[9] The trend toward internationalization of banking systems has been particularly notorious in Latin America, where in some countries, such as Mexico, the effective foreign control in banking systems reached more than 70 percent[10] in 2002 compared with slightly more than 10 percent in 1996 (see Figure 9.1).

After two decades of reforms, have the main weaknesses that characterized developing countries' financial markets in the early 1980s improved? Has the depth of financial intermediation increased during the late 1990s and early 2000s? Are there signals that investors' confidence in the strength of domestic financial systems has improved? An analysis of the data provides a mixed response. Consider first the degree of financial deepening Table 9.1 shows that for most countries (with countries in East Asia as an important exception) the depth of financial intermediation, measured by the ratio of deposits to GDP, has remained below 30 percent.[11] This contrasts with industrial countries where the ratio is above 50 percent in most cases.

The relative shallowness of financial systems in developing countries suggests that investors' confidence that financial assets will yield a positive and

---

[9] For an analysis of the role of foreign banks in Latin America, see Latin American Shadow Financial Regulatory Committee (2002).

[10] Measured as the ratio of loans to total loans in the banking system provided by banks that have at least 40 percent foreign ownership in local institutions.

[11] In some cases, most notably Venezuela, this ratio has declined significantly.

Table 9.1. Bank Deposits to GDP in Selected Countries

	Ratio			Coefficient of variation	
	1980–89	1990–2006*	2006*	1980–89	1990–2006*
Industrial countries:					
Australia	34.71	58.65	72.09	0.08	0.13
Canada	40.52	56.09	63.22	0.06	0.09
France	61.24	61.39	68.06	0.03	0.08
Norway	45.89	50.54	49.97	0.11	0.06
United States	69.05	63.55	68.24	0.04	0.07
Africa and Middle East:					
Gabon	15.18	12.20	12.91	0.14	0.13
Ghana	6.29	15.01	20.68	0.18	0.22
Niger	10.59	8.51	8.93	0.23	0.38
Nigeria	18.63	13.99	15.52	0.14	0.25
South Africa	47.57	45.50	53.27	0.03	0.20
Uganda	3.96	9.12	15.00	0.29	0.42
Turkey	20.26	29.47	40.90	0.06	0.34
Asia:					
Korea, Rep.	28.98	48.14	67.08	0.07	0.35
Indonesia	15.62	39.93	34.46	0.35	0.14
Malaysia	51.45	75.65	89.14	0.12	0.17
Thailand	44.04	78.64	80.03	0.19	0.15
Latin America:					
Argentina	9.94	18.91	21.41	0.15	0.34
Brazil	9.31	20.94	21.94	0.34	0.11
Chile	24.74	33.53	32.30	0.06	0.11
Colombia	11.31	16.69	24.20	0.31	0.34
Mexico	18.52	23.26	22.92	0.28	0.15
Peru	11.59	19.86	21.65	0.25	0.31
Venezuela, RB	29.39	17.42	15.14	0.12	0.23
Transition economies:					
Bulgaria	n.a.	37.27	40.58	n.a.	0.39
Poland	31.32	29.53	35.07	0.23	0.20
Romania	n.a.	18.62	24.10	n.a.	0.24
Kazakhstan	n.a.	8.96	18.68	n.a.	0.58
Russian Federation	n.a.	18.70	28.15	n.a.	0.32

Note: * Or as recent as data permit.

Source: IMF, International Financial Statistics (April 2007).

stable rate of return over an extended period of time has remained weak. Investors' concerns are reflected in the high degree of volatility in the ratio of deposits to GDP that persisted in developing countries during the 1990s. This is shown in the last two columns of Table 9.1 that presents the coefficient of variation during the 1980s and the 1990s to the early 2000s. Most developing countries not only displayed a much higher degree of volatility of deposits to GDP than did industrial countries, but volatility actually increased from the first to the second period in a number of developing countries.

The persistence of investors' concerns finds justification in Table 9.2, which presents real interest rates on deposits in selected industrial and developing countries over the last two decades. In contrast to the industrial countries,

Table 9.2. Real Interest Rates in Selected Countries

	Average			Standard deviation	
	1980–89	1990–2006*	2006*	1980–89	1990–2006*
Industrial countries:					
Australia	3.45	2.41	0.70	2.82	2.52
Canada	2.92	1.06	0.27	1.27	1.96
Japan	1.10	0.65	0.75	1.25	0.86
Norway	1.58	1.52	−3.53	3.81	2.46
United States	4.58	1.69	2.69	2.17	1.63
Middle East:					
Algeria	0.14	−0.48	−0.51	4.55	7.97
Egypt, Arab Rep.	−0.98	2.55	−5.37	5.09	4.70
Israel	−4.33	2.87	0.65	15.18	4.01
Turkey	−1.47	5.25	11.38	12.52	8.01
Africa:					
Central African Republic	6.25	4.48	−4.35	7.12	8.04
Gabon	3.00	4.82	−0.77	15.61	8.04
Malawi	1.55	5.53	6.96	9.96	14.92
Sierra Leone	−18.99	19.26	2.57	21.39	58.86
South Africa	−1.39	4.22	1.35	4.37	3.22
South Asia:					
Bangladesh	n.a.	2.48	2.88	n.a.	3.74
Sri Lanka	3.52	2.85	1.90	7.11	4.35
East Asia:					
Malaysia	3.62	2.23	0.26	3.06	1.27
Philippines	0.96	2.67	0.92	8.83	2.64
Singapore	3.43	1.03	−0.11	2.43	1.66
Thailand	6.38	2.95	1.05	4.85	3.14
Latin America:					
Argentina	−7.48	3.05	−3.06	16.36	7.69
Chile	10.86	4.53	2.54	11.25	3.02
Colombia	6.84	5.39	1.75	2.13	4.11
Ecuador	−10.07	−3.10	2.54	10.06	13.25
Mexico	−7.05	0.31	−0.64	11.94	3.55
Venezuela, RB	−5.68	8.66	10.96	9.72	10.81
Transition economies:					
Bulgaria	n.a.	−9.74	−2.30	n.a.	13.95
Czech Republic	n.a.	−0.47	−0.36	n.a.	1.49
Poland	−73.50	0.75	0.48	n.a.	9.71
Russian Federation	n.a.	−5.41	−4.28	n.a.	12.14

Note: * or as recent as data permit.
Source: IMF, International Financial Statistics (April 2007).

where real interest rates have remained mostly positive, at low levels, and quite stable (as measured by the values of the standard deviation), in developing countries real interest rates remained either negative for substantial periods of time or skyrocketed to unsustainably high levels. Times of extremely high real interest rates by no means indicated high levels of productivity. Instead, they reflected the elevated risk of liabilities issued by domestic borrowers as investors perceived a high probability of significant losses in the real value of their assets either through inflation, devaluation, controls, or outright default. With the exception of East Asian countries, interest rate volatility in developing countries has been much higher than in industrial countries and, in many countries, has even increased during the 1990s to early 2000s, relative to the 1980s.

An indicator of financial strength that is rarely analyzed is the share of government claims in bank assets. This indicator, however, is quite important because, after all, one of the objectives of financial liberalization and reforms was to reduce the massive transfer of resources from the private financial sector to the public sector, which in the 1970s and early 1980s had served to finance large fiscal deficits. Yet, in a number of cases, the results have been disappointing. While governments significantly reduced their interference in *direct* allocation of credit, a number of governments continued financing their deficits with resources from the domestic banking system. Whereas in the 1980s this was achieved by direct lending to governments or high reserve requirements, since the mid-1990s governments issued large amounts of debt that was purchased by banks and by the general public. Indeed, it is interesting to note that in addition to bank deposits, government paper constitutes the other major source of liquidity in developing countries. Absent liquid private capital markets, with some noteworthy exceptions including Chile and some Asian countries, investors in developing countries largely hold their financial wealth in bank deposits and government paper. As will be discussed in the next section, this development has had important consequences for the effectiveness of reserve requirements.

Figure 9.2 illustrates the evolution of government paper held by domestic banking systems in developing countries. The figure shows that the share of government paper in banks' balance sheets increased from the 1980–94 period to the 1995–2006 period in many developing countries (many countries are located to the right of the 45 degree line). This result is a sad irony: a significant component of the efforts of financial sector reform undertaken in the early to mid-1990s aimed at decreasing the share of banks' claims on government. It is important to note, of course, that the results in Figure 9.2 should not be entirely attributed to an inappropriate implementation of regulatory reform. In a number of countries, banking crises were resolved by replacing bad loans with government paper (Mexico and East Asian countries following the 1997 crisis are examples of this). Given the lack of access of emerging markets to international capital markets during crisis periods, it is very difficult to conceive alternative procedures for banking crisis resolution. To take this into account, banking crisis periods were eliminated from the sample, including *five years* after the crisis. The basic result did not change: many banking systems in developing countries held as much or more government paper in the most recent period relative to the 1980s.[12]

[12] The case of Argentina is particularly telling. During the early 1990s, following the implementation of the currency board, banks decreased their relative holding of government paper. After the banking crisis of 1995, there was an increase in holdings of government

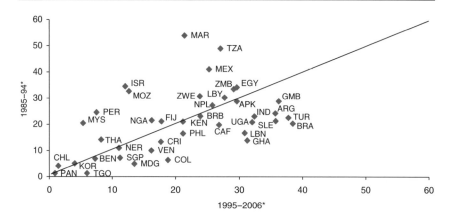

Figure 9.2. Claims on government as a percentage of total bank assets: selected developing countries, 1985–94 and 1995–2006*

Note: * Or as recent as data permit.

Source: IMF, International Financial Statistics (April 2007).

As Figure 9.2 shows, the ratio of claims on government as a percentage of deposits not only has increased for many countries, but is also very high. Large countries such as Argentina, Brazil, India, and Turkey display ratios above 30 percent. Among the sample of countries, those that can be identified as succeeding in reducing this ratio to a low level include Chile, Panama, and Korea.

These large and increasing stocks of government paper in the balance sheet of developing country financial systems have exacerbated the adverse effects of sudden stops of capital flows into the domestic economies, as demonstrated by the 2001 crisis in Argentina. As sudden stops in capital flow usually bring about a decline in the market value of government debt, banks' asset value deteriorates. Thus, a significant deterioration in the credit risk perception of sovereigns by international investors may translate into severe problems in domestic banking systems.

In sum, financial systems characterized by a large predominance of short term and highly volatile instruments are features of most developing countries that contribute to exacerbate the adverse effects of capital flow volatility on the stability of domestic systems. These features also constrain the effectiveness of policy instruments to deal with a sudden reversal of capital

paper that one can associate with the restructuring efforts of the financial sector, including improving the liquidity of the banks. However, for a long time after the crisis was completely resolved, banks continued to increase their claims on government. By the end of 2000, the share of bank claims on central and non-central government as a percentage of total assets reached 25 percent, a ratio close to the 27 percent observed in 1991 at the beginning of the currency board.

flows.[13] The evidence suggests that the reforms undertaken since the 1980s have not been able to substantially improve the destabilizing features of financial systems in most developing countries. The next section will assess two of the most common prudential regulatory policies implemented to deal with capital flow volatility.

9.3 Commonly Used Financial Regulatory Policies to Deal with the Adverse Effects of Capital Flow Volatility

While experience shows that reforms have not resulted in the desired increase in financial deepening in most developing countries, the question remains as to whether some forms of regulation may be more effective than others in dealing with the adverse effects of capital flow volatility on the currently shallow domestic financial markets.

Prudential regulatory policies to deal with capital flow volatility can be divided into two groups.[14] The first consists of regulations aimed at *directly* controlling financial aggregates, such as liquidity expansion and credit growth. Their purpose is to limit the expansion of balance sheets following a period of large capital inflows to minimize the adverse effects on the financial system if a sudden reversal of the inflows were to materialize. The best-known examples are the use of reserve requirements and capital requirements *as currently incorporated in international standards*, namely capital requirements that contain risk categories used in industrial countries.[15] Other policies in this category include the imposition of limits to the exposures of banks to real estate and equity and restrictions to the investment portfolios of domestic pension funds.

The second group, which can be identified as the 'pricing-risks-right' approach to regulation works by providing financial incentives to managers and owners of financial institutions to avoid excessive risk-taking activities. The main feature of this set of regulations is that they encourage financial institutions to internalize the costs associated with the particular risks of the environment where they operate. Policies in this group include ex ante risk-based provisioning rules and capital requirements that are designed to take

[13] Consider, for example, that following a sudden reversal of capital inflows policymakers decide to increase the short term policy rate in order to stabilize exchange rate movements. Because of the absence of a yield curve covering a large spectrum of maturities, the increase in the policy rate would bring about an increase in interest rates throughout the financial sector, imposing unwanted effects on the entire system.

[14] A similar, although not exactly equal, classification of regulation is discussed in Barth et al. (2001).

[15] As will be discussed below, capital standards designed to appropriately reflect the risk features of bank portfolios in developing countries would belong to the category of 'incentives-based' regulations.

into account the particular risk features of developing countries. As will be discussed below, these risk features may differ significantly from those faced by financial institutions in industrial countries. This category also includes the enforcement of market discipline mechanisms to encourage holders of financial sector liabilities to discriminate among financial institutions according to risk. By inducing financial institutions to internalize the costs of holding high risk assets, this regulatory approach also aims to minimize the social cost of financial sector disturbances.

Most efforts in developing countries have been concentrated on the first set of policies. This section will discuss and assess the effectiveness of two of the most common policy tools in this group, reserve or liquidity requirements and capital requirements as recommended by the Basel Committee, in controlling the adverse impact of volatile capital flows on the domestic financial systems. The next section will discuss whether the 'pricing-risk-right' approach to prudential regulation can do a better job than more commonly used policies.

9.3.1 *Can Reserve Requirements Play an Effective Prudential Role in Dealing with Capital Flow Volatility?*

The use of reserve requirements in developing countries has evolved significantly over the last quarter of a century. As mentioned in Section 9.2, high reserve requirements in the 1970s and 1980s were often used as a mechanism to finance fiscal deficits with banks' resources. Indeed, an important component of the first cluster of reforms was to reduce reserve requirements as a complement to the elimination of governments' credit controls. During the mid-1990s, after the severe banking crises that followed the exchange rate crisis in Mexico, reserve requirements, and more generally liquidity requirements were given a new role: this instrument could be used as a prudential device to limit the intermediation of large amounts of capital inflows through weak banking systems. An additional argument for high reserve requirements as a prudential regulatory tool is that they can act as a cushion to protect banks from sudden withdrawal of funds, especially in the context of a sudden reversal of capital inflows.[16] By ensuring the availability of liquidity to meet unusually large withdrawals of deposits, reserve requirements may contribute to the stability of the banking system.[17] This role could be particularly effective if the resources derived from the requirements are placed abroad in foreign currency denominated assets.

---

[16] For an analysis of the effects of reserve requirements on *real* variables such as output and the real exchange rate, see Reinhart and Reinhart (1997).

[17] When reserve requirements are remunerated, they are usually referred to as 'liquidity requirements'. In addition, in a number of cases, liquidity requirements include not only funds deposited in the Central Bank but also liquid funds that can be managed by the banks and invested in certain category of liquid assets previously defined by the Central Bank.

This chapter deals only with the role of reserve requirements in controlling the availability of liquid assets in the economy. It does not discuss the differentiation of reserve requirements on deposits denominated in domestic currency and deposits denominated in foreign currency.

Enthusiasm for the use of reserve requirements as a prudential tool grew strong in a number of developing countries after the events in Argentina during the banking crisis that ensued in early 1995, following the Tequila Crisis in Mexico. Before the crisis, during the period of large capital inflows (1991–94), the Argentinean authorities had imposed high reserve requirements. The funds generated by these requirements were invested in foreign currency liquid assets, such as bank deposits in large banks in New York or US Treasury Bills, either by the Argentinean banks themselves or by the Central Bank. Following the uncertainties in international capital markets that resulted from the Tequila Crisis, investors withdrew large amounts of deposits from Argentinean banks, especially from large banks owned by provinces and municipalities. More than 70 percent of the deposit loss was financed by a decline in liquid assets. The central bank accommodated the decline in assets by sharply reducing reserve requirements.[18] Hence, it can be argued that high reserve requirements allowed a number of banks in Argentina to withstand large deposit withdrawals following an unexpected reversal of capital inflows.

What made reserve requirements serve their designed purpose in the Argentinean case? In addition to a well managed system by the central bank, it is important to stress that a key reason for its success was that significant sources of liquidity in Argentina were limited to practically only cash and bank deposits.[19] The prudential role of reserve requirements to provide international liquidity to the financial system can be undermined if there are substantial amounts of short-term paper (issued by the private sector, the government, or the central bank) that are not held on the balance sheet of banks. If a sudden loss of confidence in the financial system causes investors holding this paper to attempt to flee the market at the same time as deposit holders are withdrawing their funds, international assets generated from placing reserve requirements on bank deposits may not be enough to cover the demand for international reserves generated by the combination of the sale of government or corporate short-term paper and the withdrawal of bank deposits.[20]

[18] For further details on this episode, see Rojas-Suarez and Weisbrod (1996).

[19] This changed substantially in Argentina in the late 1990s when the government's issue of domestic debt increased significantly providing an alternative source of liquidity.

[20] It could be argued that a flexible exchange rate system would avoid the problem of 'insufficient foreign exchange reserves'. However, if a sharp decline of confidence leads to a run on the financial system, a sharp depreciation of the exchange rate would have limited usefulness to contain the run as investors would be in search of foreign cash. Since a sharp depreciation of the currency cannot generate foreign funds 'quickly enough', the run would not be contained.

The discussion above indicates that for reserve requirements to be effective as a prudential regulatory tool in dealing with capital flow volatility it is necessary that: (1) bank deposits account for most liquid assets in the economy; and (2) reserve requirements be invested in liquid foreign denominated assets. Moreover, even if conditions (1) and (2) are satisfied, banks will have an incentive to avoid the requirements if they perceive that the requirements are *excessive* relative to the liquidity they would hold in the absence of the regulation. A well-known mechanism to avoid reserve requirements in developing countries has been the booking of domestic business in off-shore branches. In the 1990s, this was a common practice in Colombia, Costa Rica, and Malaysia. Banks can also borrow and lend short-term funds in other markets, often called *mesa de dinero* in Latin America, that do not appear on their balance sheets and are, therefore, not subject to reserve requirements.

Conditions (1) and (2) above provide a simple, yet meaningful way to assess the potential effectiveness of reserve requirements in developing countries. Consider first condition (1). Since reserve requirements are part of the monetary base, countries with high reserve requirements on bank deposits should display a low ratio of liquid financial assets to monetary base, unless non-deposit securities are a substantial component of liquid assets.[21]

Figure 9.3a shows the ratio of liquid assets to monetary base against average reserve requirements for a sample of developing countries in early 2003.[22] The major finding derived from the figure is that there is no straightforward relationship between the ratio of reserve requirements and the ratio of liquidity to base money. For example, in 2003, the ratio of liquidity to monetary base was the highest for countries with very different reserve requirements: Korea and Chile with low reserve requirements and Singapore and Brazil with very high reserve requirements. In these four countries, non-bank short-term securities, especially government paper, are important components of the domestic financial systems. In these countries, therefore, reserve requirements can have very limited capacity to contain the expansion of liquidity.

Turning to condition (2), even if bank deposits account for most liquid assets, reserve requirements can not provide protection against an unexpected reversal of capital inflow unless the funds generated by the requirements are, in fact, invested in international reserve assets. This condition is particular to developing countries and is a reflection of the high volatility of the real value of domestic financial assets discussed in Section 9.2.

---

[21] The sample used in Figures 9.3a and 9.3b includes only those countries that keep traditional reserve requirements. It excludes countries that have move to the broader concept of liquidity requirements. To exemplify this, Mexico is shown as having zero reserve requirements. This country, however, maintains regulations regarding liquidity requirements.

[22] Data on reserve requirements for Latin America is taken from López Valdés and Jiménez (2003). The rest is taken from the web pages of the corresponding Central Banks.

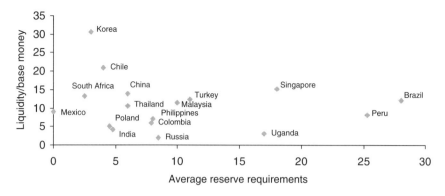

Figure 9.3a Liquidity to base money vs. average reserve requirements, 2003
Source: Web pages of respective Central Banks.

Figure 9.3b plots the ratio of liquidity to international reserves against reserve requirements for a sample of developing countries. As shown in the figure, taken together the countries in the sample do not display an inverse relationship between the level of reserve requirements and the ratio of liquid assets to international reserves. While Peru and South Africa conform to the inverse relationship, the rest of the countries show no clear relationship between the two indicators. For example, Mexico (with zero reserve requirements) and Chile, India, and Poland (with low reserve requirements) display a ratio of liquidity to international reserves similar to that of Singapore (with high reserve requirements). Moreover, Brazil, the country with the highest reserve requirements in the sample also has the highest ratio of liquidity to international reserves. This indicates that funds from the requirements often have not been invested in international reserves.

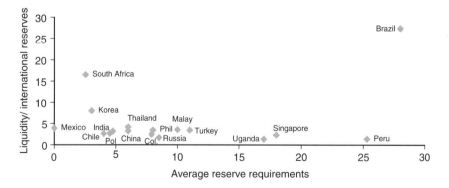

Figure 9.3b Liquidity to international reserves vs. average reserve requirements, 2003
Source: Web pages of respective Central Banks.

Thus, the analysis above raises caution about the effectiveness of reserve requirements as a prudential regulatory tool to face capital account volatility. While certainly there are some countries that satisfy both conditions (1) and (2), these conditions seem not to be met by many developing countries.

Moreover, even if reserve requirements are effective in providing liquidity to banks when needed, this policy has an important drawback: it is applied equally to weak and strong banks. Because strong banks are better positioned than weak banks to maintain liquidity by ensuring that its borrowers remain liquid, the tax imposed by reserve requirements penalize strong banks more severely than weak banks.

9.3.2 Have Capital Adequacy Ratios been Effective in Dealing with Capital Flow Volatility?

Capital requirements are an additional prudential tool to deal with the volatility of capital flows. The aim of this policy is to contain the expansion of excessive risk taking by banks. This is done by requiring banks to comply with a risk weighted capital to assets ratio determined by the regulators. At least at the conceptual level, riskier assets are assigned higher capital charges.

If capital requirements were, indeed, estimated to reflect the true risk features of banks' portfolios and could be effectively enforced, this supervisory tool would indeed be a powerful mechanism to deal with capital flow volatility. Moreover, under those conditions capital standards would have two important advantages over reserve requirements. First, the problem of evasion inherent to a high reserve requirements policy would be avoided. Second, banks with riskier portfolios would be required to hold more capital than banks with sounder portfolios. Thus, the tool would allow supervisors to focus on weaker banks since capital ratios would decline in those banks that increase their risk taking activities, hence providing an early warning signal for supervisors. In a period of large capital inflows, this policy would limit the risk taking of banks that intermediate the inflows.

Encouraged by the perceived success of capital requirements as a supervisory tool in industrial countries, developing countries were advised to adopt similar rules for capital adequacy. Consequently, during the 1990s many developing countries directed their financial reform efforts towards implementing the recommendations of the Basel Accord on capital requirements. However, albeit with quite diverse outcomes, the experience of banking problems in developing countries, especially in emerging markets, indicates that capital requirements as suggested by industrial country standards often have not performed their expected role as an effective supervisory tool, as the accumulation of capital in banks' balance sheets has not acted as a buffer to deal with unexpected adverse shocks to banks.

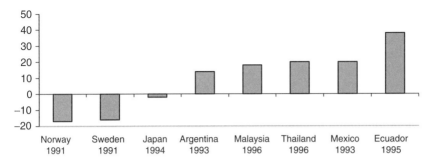

Figure 9.4 Real net equity growth in selected banking systems at the eve of a crisis (in percent)

Source: Rojas-Suarez and Weisbrod (1997); Rojas-Suarez (2001); Central Banks.

The evidence supports this observation. Figure 9.4 shows growth rates of banking systems' net equity during the year *prior* to the eruption of a major banking crisis. If equity capital were at all a good indicator of banking soundness (that is, insufficient or decreasing capital should be signaling banking weakness), banks in countries about to fall into major crisis should be facing difficulties in raising capital. This has indeed been the case prior to banking crises in industrial countries. As shown in Figure 9.4, during the year before the eruption of banking crises in Sweden, Norway, and Japan, net real equity growth became negative. In contrast, at the eve of disastrous crisis episodes in developing countries, real net equity growth was not only positive, but also reached very high levels. Cases in point are Thailand, Mexico, and Ecuador where, judging from the rapid accumulation of equity capital, this indicator did not serve well as a signal for major banking turbulence.

Further evidence that capital ratios have been largely meaningless in signaling banking problems in many developing countries is contained in Rojas-Suarez (2002a). The main result of that study is that, among traditional indicators used by supervisors as early warning indicators of banking problems, the capital–asset ratio has performed the worst. For example, in Mexico, a country that claimed to have adopted the capital standards recommendations of Basel just before the eruption of the 1994–5 banking crisis, the behavior of the risk-weighted-capital–asset ratio was useful in predicting problems accurately in only 7 percent of the banks that experienced severe crises. Indeed, according to the data provided by the Mexican Supervisory Authority, most banks in Mexico were in full compliance with capital requirements and held a ratio well above 8 percent.

The conclusion that can be derived from the above evidence is not that capital requirements can never be useful for supervisors in developing countries. As the discussion below demonstrates, the conclusion is that for the capital standards to be effective the standards need to take into account the specific risk features of developing countries. Just adopting standards that are based on the risk characteristics of industrial countries simply does not work.

Why haven't capital adequacy ratios been effective prudential tools in developing countries? The reasons for the disappointing performance of this instrument can be broadly organized into two groups. The first group relates to the specific structural features of financial markets in developing countries, including those discussed in Section 9.2 as well as those related to the concentration of ownership of financial and real assets. The second group relates to the particular characteristics of the Basel capital standard, the standard chosen by most developing countries. It is argued here and elsewhere (see Rojas-Suarez 2002a) that implementation of the specific risk weights for different categories of assets contained in the Basel capital standard might exacerbate rather than reduce the vulnerabilities of domestic financial markets to capital flow volatility.

A clarification is needed here. The discussion in the rest of this chapter mostly refers to the capital standard currently used by many developing countries, namely the 1988 Accord (Basel I). In June 2004, a new Accord (Basel II) was finalized by the Basel Committee on Banking Supervision for implementation beginning by the end of 2007 in some countries. While this chapter does not deal with Basel II, it is important to point out that the large majority of conclusions reached here, regarding the limited effectiveness of Basel I to control excessive risk taking activities by banks in developing countries, remain valid under Basel II. As will be discussed below, the explanations lie not only on the specifics of the regulation, but, most importantly, on the structural features of many developing economies.

Regarding the first set of reasons constraining the effectiveness of capital requirements and to determine the factors included in this group, we raise the following question: Assuming that banks' risks were appropriately estimated in the capital standards, what features in developing countries could prevent the standards from working properly? As is well known, compliance with adequate accounting and regulatory frameworks is necessary to make the capital adequacy standard work. Inappropriate accounting standards and reporting systems and improper classification of non-performing loans stand out as the best examples of inadequacies reducing the effectiveness of capital requirements. In addition, a deficient judicial framework that is unable to enforce supervisory actions when a bank's performance is deemed faulty seriously undermines the efficiency of bank ratios. Indeed, in spite of advances in reforms, these factors are also behind the lack of investors' confidence in the stability of domestic financial sectors discussed in Section 9.2.

But if these inadequacies were the only factors preventing capital standards from working, concerns about the appropriateness of the capital standard for developing countries would be exaggerated. All that would have to be done is setting priorities from the Basel Committee's *Core Principles for Effective*

Banking Supervision. This, in fact, is often done in practice. A more fundamental problem with the capital standards, however, goes beyond the establishment of rules and regulations into a feature particular to developing countries, namely the lack of deep and liquid capital markets. This factor implies that, even when accounting, reporting and legal frameworks are adequate, capitalization ratios will be less effective if liquid markets for bank shares, subordinated debt and other bank liabilities and assets are not available to validate the real value of bank capital (as distinct from its accounting value). Therefore, since these markets are typically either not available or not liquid in developing countries, changes in the market value of bank capital that provide supervisors in industrial countries information regarding the quality of reported capital are not an effective instrument in developing countries.

In contrast to industrial countries, asset ownership, both financial and real, is still highly concentrated in many developing countries, making the potential market for equity capital small and uncompetitive. In such an environment, the intent of the capital standard—to increase the proportion of uninsured funding (equity and subordinated debt) to insured funding (deposits) in order to reduce bank stockholders' incentive to take risks at the expense of existing public safety nets—can be easily subverted.[23] Shareholders' wealth may not really be at risk when they supply equity capital to a bank because shareholders can finance their stake with a loan from a related party, which could even be a non-financial corporation and hence outside the regulators' purview. Thus, concentration of wealth provides incentives for bank owners to supply low quality bank capital and, therefore, to undertake higher risks than bank shareholders in industrial countries would allow.

This suggests that it can be relatively easy for bank owners in several developing countries to raise large amounts of low quality equity capital relative to the bank's capital base in a short time. Indeed, this feature may explain the results shown in Figure 9.4: the rapid growth of net accounting equity displayed at the eve of banking crises in several developing countries reflects the low quality of capital in these economies. Lacking a market that assesses the quality of bank capital, capitalization ratios cannot serve as an effective supervisory tool.

Clearly, the severity of this problem varies widely across developing countries. For many countries, the constraints limiting the usefulness of capital requirements are extremely binding, and therefore beg the question: Is there an alternative to the use of capital standards for assessing the strengths of banks now, in the immediate future, when preconditions for the effectiveness of the capital standard are not in place? These questions will be addressed in Section 9.4.

---

[23] This point has been advanced by Rojas-Suarez and Weisbrod (1996) and Rojas-Suarez (2002a).

In some other countries, however, a continuous increase in the participation of foreign banks from industrial countries (as shown in Figure 9.1) is de facto reducing the degree of connected lending among financial institutions and between financial institutions and the real sector. Furthermore, in this (still small) group of countries, the accounting, regulatory and supervisory frameworks have improved drastically. Although there are very few developing countries with sufficiently deep and liquid capital markets,[24] the participation of foreign banks can provide an outside and independent source of capital in the pursuit of new wealth. The competition induced by the entry of new providers of wealth can indeed contribute to improving the usefulness of capitalization ratios.

For this group of countries, the relevant question becomes whether adopting the internationally accepted capital standards recommended by the Basel Committee is appropriate (both the current Accord and the recently published Basel II). Indeed, to determine the second group of factors explaining the observed inefficacies of capital requirements, we ask the following question: assuming that developing countries are structurally and institutionally ready to effectively implement capital standards, are the Basel Committee's standards adequate for developing countries? To answer this question we first assess whether the classification of assets according to risk in the current Basel Accord 'matches' risk features of bank assets in developing countries. Then, we quickly question whether a move towards Basel II could be the solution.

There is a poor match between the assessments of risks contained in the current accord recommendations and the actual risks in developing countries (Rojas-Suarez 2002a). Indeed, a straightforward application of the Basel I standard can actually weaken banking systems in developing markets as the standards create incentives for banks to increase the risk characteristics of their portfolios. Two features of the standards weakened rather than strengthened banks' balance sheets: the treatment of government claims held by banks and the treatment of inter-bank lending.

Regarding the treatment of bank credit to the government, under the current Basel Accord, loans to the public sector carry a zero percent risk weight if the country belongs to the OECD and 100 percent if the loan is to a non-OECD government. The idea, of course, is that claims on OECD governments can be considered safe assets. However, when applying the Basel recommendations to their domestic economies, most non-OECD countries attach a zero percent risk weight to their own government paper. That is, banks in developing countries treat paper issued by their own governments as a safe asset, an assumption far from reality if one takes into account the default history of emerging market governments, highlighted by the defaults

---

[24] Chile, Hong Kong, and Singapore may be the countries, among emerging markets, with the deepest financial sectors.

of Argentina, Russia, and Ecuador.[25] The problem with this practice is that by economizing on capital requirements, banks have a strong incentive to concentrate a significant portion of their asset holdings in government paper. This incentive not only gives a false impression of bank safety, but even more importantly, also contributes to weakening the franchise value of banks, which is rooted in their capacity to assess credit risk.

A thorough understanding of banks' decisions to hold public or private assets would require a more elaborate analysis. However, it is fair to argue that the regulatory treatment of government paper has played an important role in banks' decisions. Indeed, the increase of government paper as a share of total bank assets in many countries since the mid-1990s, as depicted in Figure 9.2, coincides with the adoption of the Basel capital adequacy recommendations in developing countries. This regulatory incentive also has important consequences during recessions as banks tend to magnify the downward trend in economic activity by shifting their portfolio further away from credit to the private sector and towards government paper as they seek to reduce capital costs.

The evidence above suggests that the regulatory treatment of banks' claims on government tends to reduce the soundness of banking systems in developing countries.[26] This concern, as obvious as it may look, is, however, not taken into account when International Financial Institutions (IFIs) assess country progress in strengthening financial systems. Indeed, developing countries attaching zero risk weight to domestic government liabilities will not receive a warning signal from IFIs even if the government is highly indebted as such a practice is not perceived as conflicting with the international standards.

Regarding the treatment of inter-bank lending, the Basel Accord attaches a risk weight of 100 percent to bank lending to non-OECD banks with a maturity of over one year, while lending to this group of banks with a maturity of one year or less carries a risk weight of just 20 percent. The obvious result has been a bias towards short-term cross-border lending towards developing countries banks. This, of course, exacerbates the volatility of flows to developing countries as any adverse news from developing countries quickly translates in a sharp reduction of cross-border lending.[27, 28]

---

[25] Argentina does not attach zero risk weight to government paper, but the risk weights still favor this kind of instrument.

[26] A counter case may be made by arguing that domestic government debt is safer than public external debt. However, given the long history of government induced domestic defaults, either in the form of straight confiscation of deposits or sharp devaluations and inflations that drastically reduced the real value of government paper held by residents, I find this argument simply unconvincing.

[27] This effect has also been discussed in Reisen (2001) and Griffith-Jones and Spratt (2001).

[28] The new Basel Accord aggravates this problem as the definition of short term has been reduced from 'one year maximum' to 'three months maximum'. Further discussion of the problems for Latin American countries associated with the plausible implementation of the

But problems for developing countries associated with the Basel Accord treatment of inter-bank lending go beyond increased volatility of capital flows as this regulatory provision also creates incentives to decrease the maturity of loans extended by domestic banks to the local economy. This is because to strengthen their banking systems, a number of developing countries have introduced regulations that reduce the maturity mismatch between banks' assets and liabilities. The shorter the maturity of international loans to banks in developing countries, the shorter the marginal maturity of loans extended by banks in developing countries to their local customers in order to prevent a maturity mismatch between banks' assets and liabilities. This, of course, adversely affects the vulnerability of economic activity to sources of funding.

Thus, a lesson from capital standards as a prudential tool to deal with capital flow volatility is that even if adequate accounting, supervisory, and judicial frameworks are in place, the current Basel Accord is not the appropriate capital standard for developing countries. One of its major shortcomings is that by incorrectly assessing the risk features of developing countries, it creates incentives for excessive risk taking by banks in these countries.

Would implementation of Basel II help solve the problems outlined above? The spirit of the recommendations, namely, an attempt to align regulatory capital with the true risk of banks portfolios, would help, but the actual prescriptions would not. For the purpose of this chapter, it is sufficient to point out that the only approach within Basel II that allows for an adequate measurement of risk is the advanced Internal Rating-Based approach (the IRB approach). The problem, however, is that most banks and supervisors in developing countries are simply not ready to implement this approach. Unfortunately, the other two approaches available under Basel II for calculating minimum capital requirements create a new set of problems that would have undesirable consequences for the stability of the financial systems of developing countries. See Rojas-Suarez (2002a) for a comprehensive discussion of these issues.[29]

9.4 Prudential Regulations that Work in Developing Countries: How Should They Differ from Policies in Industrial Countries?

9.4.1 *The Degree of Financial Development Matters a Lot*

The discussion above leads to two central conclusions. The first is that, very often, the implementation of traditional prudential regulations to deal with

Basel II Accord is contained in Latin American Shadow Financial Regulatory Committee (2001).

[29] For example, a major issue in the so-called 'standardized approach' relates to the reliance on credit rating agencies for the determination of 'risk weights' attached to loans in the calculation of minimum capital requirements.

capital account volatility in developing countries has not delivered the desired results. The second is that the identification of factors explaining inadequacies in prudential regulation constitutes a major step forward for improving the design of policies so that they work in developing countries.

With respect to necessary conditions for prudential regulations to work, Section 9.3 showed the importance of the degree of financial development. For example, in industrial countries, where deep and liquid capital markets validate the value of accounting capital, capital ratios have proven useful. It is interesting to note that in those industrial countries with well developed short term non-deposits liquid instruments, such as the United States, reserve requirements have lost their effectiveness to a large extent, and are little utilized. Thus, the development of liquid capital markets tends to increase the effectiveness of capital ratios and simultaneously decrease that of reserve requirements.

In contrast, for the least developed countries in the world, wealth concentration and the resulting absence of competitive capital markets severely hinders the usefulness of *any* bank capital standard, not only the ones recommended by the Basel Committee. In this group of countries, reserve requirements could help dealing with capital account volatility. Unfortunately, inadequacies in reporting and supervisory systems are also the worst in this group of countries and these deficiencies provide fertile ground for evasion of reserve requirements.

In between these two extremes, the industrial countries and the least developed countries, there is a group of developing countries, where the participation of foreign banks has improved the functioning of the markets. Moreover, the accounting, reporting and supervisory frameworks have improved significantly. In these countries, mostly classified as emerging markets, some form of capital adequacy requirements could be an effective supervisory tool. But as Section 9.3 has argued, outright application of the Basel Accord (I or II) is not the right path to follow for strengthening their banking systems.

9.4.2 *Prudential Policies that Work in Developing Countries*

In light of the experience discussed in Section 9.3, this section advances arguments supporting the need to develop regulatory and supervisory frameworks that better fit developing country needs. Because of the difficulties in obtaining desirable results from traditional regulatory policies, it is argued that policies that attempt to price developing countries' risk right may prove quite beneficial for strengthening financial sectors in these countries. As discussed above, the pricing-risk-right approach to regulation works by taking the particular financial features of countries into account in order to provide incentives for avoiding excessive risk taking activities by financial institutions.

In the case of industrial countries, the new Basel II proposal is based on this philosophy. The issue for developing countries is the identification of policies that would be able to provide the right incentives.

Because the degree of development matters, policy recommendations for the least developed countries need to differ from the most financially advanced developing countries. Based on a simple classification of countries into two groups according to their degree of financial development, the pricing-risk-right approach suggests that the following policy recommendations might be effective. The set of recommendations that follows is by no means complete or fully inclusive. They are simply examples of policies that are consistent with the objective of making prudential regulatory tools work.

For the first group, the financially least developed group, where traditional regulations, such as reserve requirements and any capital standards are largely ineffective, it is obvious that sustainable policies consist in removing the constraints to the effectiveness of prudential regulations. That is: (1) the implementation of appropriate accounting, reporting and judicial frameworks, that would prevent the evasion of reserve requirements; and (2) the development of markets that validate the accounting capital ratios.

Those policy reforms, however, often take a significant amount of time to implement.[30] In the transition to a more comprehensive reform, the pricing-risk-right approach suggests that it is still possible to identify and develop some indicators of banking problems that help to reveal the true riskiness of banks. For example, deposit markets have often been identified as markets that work in many developing countries in the sense that they have been able to provide effective early warning signals about the relative strength of banks (see Rojas-Suarez 2002a). Recommendations for policymakers in this set of countries, therefore, should focus on strengthening the role of market discipline. In other words, regulators should focus on developing tools that utilize information from markets that already work or that can be developed in a relatively short period of time. The central idea is that, if encouraged to do so, depositors and other holders of banks' liabilities can discriminate between sound and weak banks by pricing risks adequately by, for example, charging higher interest rates on deposits or withdrawing deposits from financial institutions perceived to be unsound.

The key for market discipline to work, however, is the elimination of distortions that encourage bank liability holders not to discriminate among banks. A typical example that 'kills' market discipline is a deposit insurance scheme that promises unlimited coverage to all depositors. It is important to

---

[30] Moreover, reducing concentration of financial and real assets could be a difficult task especially in countries where some political powers are 'captive' to the agenda of economically powerful groups.

stress that, as long as the institutions determining the effectiveness of prudential regulation remain weak, market discipline cannot work at its best. The recommendations that follow, therefore, can ease but not solve the problems associated with an inadequate regulatory framework.

With this in mind, specific recommendations that promote market discipline include: (1) encourage the public offering of uninsured certificates of deposits; (2) publish inter-bank bid and offer rates to improve the flow of information on bank quality; (3) develop credit bureaus that provide timely and relevant information about debtors' creditworthiness; (4) encourage the process of financial internationalization—through promotion of foreign banking—as adequate market depth can only be achieved if a diverse group of investors and users of capital enter the market, that is, if the market becomes less concentrated; (5) strengthen regulatory efforts on improving deposit insurance schemes to credibly limit the insurance while ensuring that the scheme is sufficiently funded to finance the closing or selling of financial institutions in severe difficulties; and (6) avoid excessive bank access to central bank liquidity to contain moral hazard problems associated with the existence of a lender of last resort.

The last two recommendations (avoid generous deposit insurance and excessive access to central bank liquidity) can be credibly implemented in cases where contagion within the domestic financial system is limited. Often, however, the failure of a large bank creates systemic problems that have led authorities to intervene in order to prevent the eruption of a major crisis. The policy recommendation, once recognizing the existence of contagion, is twofold. First, in order to avoid the eruption of systemic problems, improve the credibility of the safety net by establishing prompt corrective actions to minimize the expansion of incipient banking problems. Second, if in spite of preventive efforts, a systemic crisis nevertheless materializes, recognize that the solution of the problem should involve: (1) keeping the payments system alive; and (2) minimizing the fiscal cost of banking crisis resolution (see Rojas-Suarez 2004b).

Policy recommendations are quite different for the second group of developing countries, namely those with a sufficient degree of financial development to allow traditional prudential regulatory policies to be meaningful, but where their particular features such as limited access to international capital markets imply that strict application of industrial country regulation, such as the Basel Accord, may be of limited effectiveness. In this group of countries, the recommendations advanced for less financially developed countries have to a large extent already been implemented.

Following the pricing-risk-right approach, reserve requirements do not seem to be desirable tools not only because they lose their effectiveness as alternative sources of liquidity develop in the domestic markets, but also because they do not discriminate between different levels of bank quality. These arguments may explain Mexico's decision to eliminate reserve requirements and the low ratios observed in Chile.

Instead, the main recommendation for this group of countries is to design a transitional capital standard that appropriately reflects the risk of banks' assets because Basel (I or II) does not fit the bill in the short run. This chapter recommends that the standard should have two basic components. The first is the development of ex ante risk-based regulations in loan loss provisions. While this is widely recognized by the Basel Committee to be an essential complement to any capital standard, the proposal in this paper is one based on setting priorities. Given the high frequency of adverse shocks in developing countries, especially the sudden reversal of capital inflows, the expected probability of occurrence of these adverse outcomes is very high compared to industrial countries. In this environment, provisioning takes a role, at times, more important than capitalization. Ex ante risk-based provisioning would be a significant departure from current practices in almost all developing countries.[31, 32]

The second characteristic is the establishment of a reduced number of risk categories to classify assets, with the central qualification that the categories of risk should reflect the particular features of banks' assets in developing countries. If loan loss reserves are designed to reflect the expected losses in banks' assets, minimum capital requirements need to reflect unexpected losses. Issues that need to be considered in the design of appropriate risk categories include an adequate risk assessment of government paper and the introduction of distinct capital charges for borrowers in the tradable and non-tradable sectors.[33]

Problems associated with attaching risk weights to government paper that severely understates the risk features of those assets have already been discussed. It is, however, important to stress that as long as governments do not make the political decision to correctly price the risk of their own liabilities, banks will have an incentive to discriminate against credit to the private sector relative to the public sector. Moreover, this inadequacy has an important adverse consequence for the effects of the volatility of capital flows: at times of increased uncertainties in the international capital markets, governments will have an incentive to turn to their domestic banking sector to place additional debt. While this will have the short-term advantage of allowing governments to continue their fiscal plans, the policy increases the risk features of domestic bank portfolios and prevents market signals originating in the capital markets from inducing governments to undertake necessary fiscal adjustments. The 2001 crisis in Argentina is an excellent example of

[31] This point has been raised by Cavallo and Majnoni (2001).

[32] The use of ex ante provisioning as an effective counter-cyclical prudential regulation tool is discussed in Ocampo (2003).

[33] For a more comprehensive analysis of this proposal see Rojas-Suarez (2002a).

how banking systems can be weakened by the incorrect pricing of risk of government paper. While in the mid-1990s, the ratio of government paper held by banks was about 15 percent; this ratio had escalated to over 30 percent by 2001. Unsurprisingly, the international debt crisis at the end of 2001 also triggered a severe banking crisis. [34]

The need to distinguish risk features between tradable and non-tradable sectors when calculating capital requirement responds to the well-known fragility of the latter sector to adverse unexpected shocks, such as a sudden stop of international capital inflows. In developing countries, market risks—especially exchange rate risk—quickly translate into credit risk, especially for the non-tradable sector. While the need to distinguish risk characteristics between sectors can certainly help to strengthen domestic banking systems, the issues involved with this policy are quite complicated and cannot be resolved in this paper. The problem is that pricing risk right in this context could bring about a reduction in bank credit, from already depressed levels, to small enterprises or to producers in the agriculture sector. Thus, the social problems created from this policy could be larger than its potential contribution to the stability of the financial system. The only conclusion that can be made is that the risk features of different sectors should not be ignored when designing capital standards. Instead, additional and complementary policies would need to be in place to prevent the elimination of sources of funding to enterprises in the non-tradable sector.

Additional recommendations to allow these countries to deepen their financial systems and, hence, improve the effectiveness of accepted international prudential regulation include: (1) further enhancing the mechanisms of market discipline beyond the recommendations advanced for the least developed group of countries (an example is the use of the information in credit bureaus to estimate the probability distribution of loan losses and, therefore, to calculate adequate requirements for capital and provisioning, see Powell 2001); and (2) deepening the process of financial internationalization through the increased participation of foreign institutional investors, especially pension funds and insurance companies.

9.5 Concluding Remarks

This chapter has shown that traditional prudential regulatory policies used in industrial countries have had limited effectiveness in controling the

[34] Some analysts have argued that the interference of the government in Argentina's banking system, including the freezing of deposits, was the cause of the crises. Those measures, however, might have not been considered if bank assets were strong. With one-third of banks' asset invested in government paper of little value, the banks were in severe problems even if additional measures had not been taken.

adverse impacts of capital account volatility on financial systems in developing countries. The main reason for this disappointing result is that, by not taking into account the particular characteristics of financial markets in developing countries, these regulations cannot effectively control excessive risk taking by financial institutions. Moreover, the chapter shows that contrary to policy intentions, some of these regulations, such as the Basel Accord on capital requirements, can exacerbate rather than decrease financial sector fragility, especially in episodes of sudden reversal of capital flows.

Important features that distinguish financial markets in developing countries from those in industrial countries include the predominance of assets with short maturity and high volatility as well as the large concentration of financial and real assets. These features significantly decrease the effectiveness of traditional prudential regulatory instruments. For example, reserve requirements cannot be effective in developing countries with abundance of short term government paper because, in a highly volatile environment, holders of these instruments would tend to flee the markets at the same time depositors are withdrawing their funds, rendering insufficient the amount of foreign exchange reserves—generated from placing reserve requirements on deposits—to meet the demand for foreign currency.

Likewise, because assets in developing countries have different risk characteristics than assets in industrial countries, there is a poor match between the assessments of risks contained in the Basel I recommendations implemented in developing countries and the actual risks faced by banks in these countries. This implies that a straightforward application of Basel I can actually weaken banking systems in developing markets as the standards create incentives for banks to increase the risk characteristics of their portfolios. The chapter also points out that the implementation of the new accord for minimum capital requirements (Basel II) is not the solution for developing countries, at least in the short and medium term. The advanced approach for the calculation of capital requirements is simply out of limits for developing countries. Ironically, the method that could be implemented by a number of developing countries, the standardized approach would create a new set of problems with adverse consequences for the stability of developing countries' financial systems.

The shortcomings of traditional prudential regulations can be overcome to a significant extent by following a pricing-risks-right approach to regulation, whose main feature is to encourage financial institutions to internalize the costs associated with the particular risks of the environment where they operate. In doing so, the approach attempts to provide incentives to avoid excessive risk taking by financial institutions.

The pricing-risk-right approach recognizes that developing countries are not a uniform group of countries and, therefore, the same regulatory policy should not be implemented uniformly in all countries. The claim is that the degree of financial development matters and that policies should be implemented only after taking those differences into account.

By using a simple division of developing countries in two groups, the chapter advances policy recommendations that are consistent with the pricing-risk-right approach. For the least developed group of countries, where concentration of financial and real assets is high and where basic accounting and judicial standards are inappropriate, the challenge is to identify and develop indicators of banking problems that reveal the true riskiness of banks. These indicators can be found, at least partially, in markets that already work such as the deposit markets. Specifically, recommendations for policymakers in this group of countries focus on strengthening the role of market discipline, while working on removing the inadequacies of traditional prudential regulations. Recommendations include encouraging the public offering of uninsured certificates of deposits and publishing inter-bank bid and offering rates to improve the flow of information of bank quality. Equally important is the need to encourage the process of financial internationalization as market depth can only be achieved if a diverse group of investors and users of capital allow the market to become less concentrated.

For the second group of developing countries, the relatively more financially developed, the main recommendation is to design a capital standard that appropriately reflects the risk of banks' assets because Basel (I or II) does not fit the bill—at least in the immediate future. Among the policy recommendations advanced in this chapter, there are two that stand out for their importance. The first is for governments to adequately assess the risk features of their own liabilities when calculating capital requirements. Not doing so increases the vulnerability of banks to shocks in the international capital markets and induces banks to crowd out loans to the private sector in favor of the government. The second crucial recommendation is the development of risk-based regulations in loan loss provisioning. This would be a major deviation from current practices in a large majority of developing countries.

In sum, traditional prudential regulatory policies cannot effectively contain the problems associated with capital flow volatility because they do not adequately consider the particular risk features of financial sectors in developing countries. Eventually, it is hoped the financial development gap among countries will be significantly reduced, permitting the convergence of regulations throughout the world and, therefore, eliminating concerns about regulatory arbitrage. In the meantime, however, implementing policies that create incentives for financial institutions in developing countries to price right the risks inherent to the assets they hold might go a long way to mitigate the adverse effects from capital account volatility.

References

Abiad, A. and Mody, A. (2003). 'Financial Reform: What Shakes It? What Shapes It?' International Monetary Fund Working Paper No. 03/70 (April), Washington, DC.

Barth, J., Caprio Jr., G., and Levine, R. (2001a). 'Bank Regulation and Supervision: What Works Best?' World Bank Working Paper (August).

―― ―― ――(2001b). 'The Regulation and Supervision of Banks Around the World: A New Database', in R. E. Litan, and R. Herring (eds.), *Integrating Emerging Market Countries into the Global Financial System*. Brookings-Wharton Papers on Financial Services, Brooking Institution Press.

Cavallo, M. and Majnoni, G. (2001). 'Do Banks Provision for Bad Loans in Good Times'. Empirical Evidence and Policy Implications (June), World Bank.

Díaz-Alejandro, C. (1985). 'Good-Bye Financial Repression, Hello Financial Crash.' *Journal of Development Economics* (September/October), 19.

Griffith-Jones, S. and Spratt, S. (2001). 'Will the Proposed New Basel Capital Accord have a Net Negative Effect on Developing Countries?' Institute of Development Studies, University of Sussex. Mimeo.

Latin American Shadow Financial Regulatory Committee (2001). 'The New Basel Capital Accord and Financial Stability in Latin America'. Statement No. 2 (April), Caracas.

―― (2002). 'Foreign Banks: Do They Strengthen the Financial Systems of Latin America?' Statement No. 7 (November), Lima.

Lopez Valdes, J. M. and Jimenez, F. (2002). *La Regulación Bancaria en América Latina*. Santo Domingo: Asociación de Bancos Comerciales de la República Dominicana.

Ocampo, J. A. (2003). 'Capital Account and Counter-Cyclical Prudential Regulations in Developing Countries', in R. Ffrench-Davis and S. Griffith-Jones (eds.), *From Capital Surges to Drought: Seeking Stability for Emerging Markets*. London: Palgrave/MacMillan.

Powell, A. (2001). 'A Capital Accord for Emerging Economies?' (September). Universidad Torcuato Di Tella. Mimeo.

Reinhart, C. and Reinhart, V. (1999). 'On the Use of Reserve Requirements in Dealing with Capital Flows Problems'. *The International Journal of Finance and Economics* (January), 4/1: 17–54.

Reisen, H. (2001). 'Will Basel II Contribute to Convergence in International Capital Flows?' (May). OECD Development Center Mimeo.

Rojas-Suarez, L. (2002a). 'Can International Capital Standards Strengthen Banks in Emerging Markets?' *The Capco Institute Journal* (5th edn). Washington, DC: The World Bank. (Also in 'Institute for International Economics'. Working Paper WP01-10, Washington DC, November 2001.)

―― (2002b). 'Banking Crises in Latin America: Can Recurrence be Prevented?'. Paper presented for a World Bank Conference on Banking Supervision, Montevideo, March.

―― (2004a). 'Argentina and Uruguay: Two Contrasting Experiences of Banking Crisis Resolution'. Chicago: Federal Reserve Bank of Chicago.

―― (2004b). 'International Standards for Strengthening Financial Systems: Can Regional Development Banks Address Developing Countries Concerns', in N. Birdsall and L. Rojas-Suarez (eds.), *Financing Development: The Power of Regionalism.* Washington, DC: Center for Global Development.

―― and Weisbrod, S. (1996). 'Building Stability in Latin American Financial Markets'. Inter-American Development Bank Working paper series No. 320 (February), Washington, DC.

10

The Pro-Cyclical Impact of Basel II on Emerging Markets and its Political Economy

Stephany Griffith-Jones and Avinash Persaud[1]

10.1 Introduction

Over the last 25 years, there has been a slow realization that what matters for a successful economy, one that delivers rapidly improving living standards for all, is not only the exact calibration of the *instruments* of policy, but also the *institutions* of policy.

One of the most important institutional frameworks is the national and international regulatory regime for banking. The role of banks went through a period of neglect in the late 1990s, when storming equity markets provided much of the new money flowing to big business, especially in the developed economies. But, now as then, most businesses and entrepreneurs are too small to raise money on the stock market and most depend on bank finance. A well-functioning banking system is essential to economic growth. This is even more the case in developing countries with underdeveloped financial markets (see Singh 1997). Japan may have the second largest stock market in the world but a wrecked banking system has strangled economic growth. In industrial and emerging economies, stock markets are not substitutes for banks; we need them both.

The right regulatory regime for banks is critical to the economic vitality of nations and international markets. But when judged from the perspective of the main market failures that should be addressed by banking regulation,

[1] We are very grateful to Stephen Spratt and Miguel Segoviano for their invaluable cooperation. The views expressed here are those of the authors alone. We are particularly grateful to Ricardo Ffrench-Davis, José Antonio Ocampo, Ariel Buira, Otaviano Canuto, Gunther Held, Jonathan Ward, and Martin Wolf for insightful suggestions.

the new Basel Committee's Capital Accord (Basel II), published in June 2004, is not right: it is complex where it should be simple, it focuses on processes when it should be driven by credit outcomes, it is implicitly pro-cyclical, when it should be explicitly contra-cyclical, it relaxes the discipline on systemically important banks when it should tighten that discipline, it is supposed to more accurately align regulatory capital to the risks that banks face, yet in the case of lending to developing countries it ignores the proven benefits of diversification. One consequence of this will be an inappropriately large increase in the costs of such lending to developing countries, as well as a likely reduction in its volume. It is possible that this is just bad luck. It is more probable that it relates to the political economy of Basel II and the odd composition of the Basel Committee on Banking Supervision.

The Accord contains a number of important positive features, particularly in the standardized approach. From the perspective of developing countries, positive features of Basel II refer, for example, to the removal of the OECD/non-OECD distinction and the reduction of the excessive incentive towards short-term lending to lower rated borrowers.

However, a number of major concerns exist about the Internal Ratings Based (IRB) approach, and its negative impact on developing economies:

1. It would significantly overestimate the risk of international bank lending to developing countries, primarily because it would not appropriately reflect the clear benefits of international diversification which such lending has in terms of reducing risk. A further reason why at present the IRB approach would inappropriately discourage international bank lending to developing countries is because even large international banks lack the data on developing countries required for IRB modeling.

   The combination of these factors is likely to cause an excessive increase in regulatory capital requirements on international lending to developing economies, creating a risk that bank lending to them could be sharply reduced, and a significant part of the remaining lending could see its cost increased. This is contrary to the stated objective of G-10 governments to encourage private flows to developing countries, and use them as an engine for stimulating and funding growth. This is particularly the case at present as all capital flows to developing countries—and especially bank lending—have fallen sharply in the past six years, posing a constraint on growth.

2. It would accentuate the pro-cyclicality of bank lending, which is damaging for all economies, but particularly so for fragile developing ones, which are more vulnerable to strong cyclical fluctuations of financing.

The implementation of Basel II for European banks and investment houses will be done via the Capital Adequacy Directive (CAD) 3, which has been approved by the European Parliament, as legislation, based on the suggestions of the European Council. However, while Europeans will implement Basel II fully (not just for banks but also for investment houses), the United States will implement it 'à la carte', applying Basel II only or mainly to the largest and most international banks; the rest of US banks will stay on Basel I to avoid negative consequences of Basel II. Furthermore, where Basel II will be implemented in the US, it will be done so more slowly that in the original schedule.

In Section 10.2 we discuss alternative explanations for the final features of Basel II; this will focus on the political economy of the Basel Committee's decisions. In Section 10.3, we examine the likely impact of the new Accord on the cost and quantity of bank lending to developing countries. In Section 10.4, we consider whether these changes are justified objectively. In Section 10.5, we conclude and consider proposals for avoiding the potentially negative impact Basel II could have on the developing world.

10.2 If Not Justified, Then Why . . .

When the outcome of any major process is examined, one means of assessing the degree of influence wielded by the various players is to determine who wins and who loses. As we discuss in more detail below, the 'winners' from the Basel II process are clearly the most sophisticated banks and the large, highly rated corporations in developed countries. The former will see their overall level of regulatory capital decline as they move to the internal ratings based (IRB) approaches, particularly if their loan portfolio has a large proportion of highly rated borrowers. The latter will see the pricing and terms on which they are able to obtain bank loans improve considerably, as the level of regulatory capital that banks must put aside for such loans falls sharply. The 'losers' in the process are again clear: lower rated sovereign, corporate, and bank borrowers. Given that these belong disproportionately to developing countries, we can conclude that an unambiguous loser from the Basel process will be the developing world.

This likely outcome could be the result of one of two things: first, as the Basel Committee and its supporters argue, it could be the essentially unintended outcome of a more accurate measurement of risk; second, it could be the product of excessive influence of the financial and business sectors in the developed world.

Given that, as we show below, Basel II, in a number of key respects, does not provide an accurate measurement of risk (and in particular it does not reflect at all the international diversification benefits of lending to developing countries), we are forced to consider the second of these alternatives. However, the question remains: how could the large financial and business sectors in developed countries influence the Accord in this way? We suggest two factors that may shed light on this issue.

10.2.1 *Governance*

The Basel Banking Committee members are from Belgium, Canada, France, Germany, Italy, Japan, Luxembourg, the Netherlands, Spain, Sweden, Switzerland, the United Kingdom, and the United States (that is basically the G-10 plus Switzerland). Each of these countries is represented by their central bank, and by the authority responsible for banking supervision in that country, where this is not the Central Bank. The composition reflects the world political order in the middle of the twentieth century. In contrast with other Basel Committees, where at least some representation of developing countries has been introduced, there is *no* representation of developing nations on the Basel Banking Committee. Thus, the Basel Banking Committee is one of the international ad hoc bodies with the worst problem of representation of a large part of the world—the developing and emerging countries.

It is true that the Basel Banking Committee does liaise with a group of 13 non-G10 countries, including Russia and China, which meets every two months to review developments and comment on current work. However, this consultative group of developing and transition economies has no clear mechanisms of influence on Committee decisions. It is useful to be consulted, but it is no substitute to having a seat at the decision-making table. Indeed, we argue that Basel II appears to be the result of excess influence by the large financial institutions domiciled in the countries represented on the Committee. The new Accord is to their benefit and to the detriment of emerging market borrowers and developing countries not represented on the Committee. It will probably reduce flows to developing economies and make the remaining flows more expensive and susceptible to sudden stops.[2] However, while the new Accord is clearly to the benefit of large financial institutions in developed countries, by what mechanism has their influence been exerted? That is, how have the regulators that sit on the Basel Committee come to champion the interests of the very institutions they are supposed to be regulating?

10.2.2 *Influence by the Regulated on the Regulators: The Political Economy of Basel*

One of the most difficult tasks facing regulators of any industry is to avoid excessive influence against the public interest by those they are supposed to be regulating which is called regulatory capture. The heavier the regulation and the fewer the number of players in an industry the bigger the incentives are for

---

[2] For an early analysis on capital surges and abrupt stops in emerging markets see Ffrench-Davis and Griffith-Jones (1995).

the industry to try and influence the regulator. Banking is heavily regulated and a small number of large players invariably dominate banking systems. Just 12 banks dominate international banking worldwide.

Regulators are intelligent and hardworking. However, they are generally not as expert in the conduct of banking as the bankers. Furthermore, bankers have the resources and the incentive to pay for the studies that better inform their positions. Regulatory costs create a countervailing lobby against regulation. In the end, through superior expertise and information, regulators often become persuaded of the bankers' position. This is the most perfect and least visible form of influence—a capture of minds.

The principal way to observe the influence of minds is to step back from the detail and observe the mismatch between the points of regulation and the points of market failure that regulation should be addressing. Ideally, these points should meet, and the wider they miss each other, the more likely regulators and regulation have been subject to excessive influence.

In identifying the market failure that needs to be addressed by the international bank regulators, there are three characteristics about banks that we need to know.

SYSTEMIC RISKS, DISCIPLINE, AND LARGE BANKS

As is well discussed in the financial literature, banks pose systemic risks. Banks are leveraged: they lend several times their capital. They are in the *business* of mismatching duration and credit risks: they borrow cash short-term to lend to individuals and companies often on longer terms. As such, they play a key role in financing and supporting overall economic activity. They are at the center of the payments system: their loans are often used as collateral for other loans, so that if one large bank pulls its loan early, a whole pack of cards could come tumbling down. The bigger the bank, the bigger the systemic risks.

One of the consequences of the systemic implications of a failure of a big bank is that there is a loss of internal discipline as banks become too big to fail. Therefore, big banks are typically rescued, if their solvency is threatened, while smaller banks (e.g., Barings in the UK in 1995) are not, when the systemic risk is judged as minimal.

LOCAL KNOWLEDGE

A key point about banking is that it is part of the information industry. One of the most visible consequences of the collapse of information costs in society as a whole has been the disappearance of local branches: form filling in face-to-face meetings is no longer a cost effective way of gathering information when digital banking means every dollar or pound you spend or save can be monitored daily and fed through a computer program searching for patterns.

We have discussed the problem of the growing 'data divide' between developed and developing countries above. The increasingly quantified and depersonalized approach to banking in developed countries cannot be simply adopted in an internationally active bank's dealings with developing countries, however. The data is simply not yet available. This data took many years of painstaking collection in the US and Europe. The parameters of the models into which the data is fed have also been tested, retested and refined over a long period of time. However, this is not the only approach to the measurement of credit risk: local knowledge is essential. Indeed, the highly quantitative systems now common in the largest of banks could never have been constructed without this local knowledge of their own markets.[3]

UNCERTAINTY, HERDING, AND PRO-CYCLICAL BEHAVIOR

Banks exhibit herd behavior. Herding is a response to uncertainty.[4] Most banks can be characterized as thinking that others know something they do not know and then the best policy is to follow them. It is also a response to the institutional dangers of being wrong and alone. Being wrong and in company is not as uncomfortable as it should be. If you are wrong and in company, you cannot easily be singled out for punishment by the markets or courts, and if you and the crowd are so spectacularly wrong that you are in danger of bringing down the financial system, you may even get bailed out by the monetary or fiscal authorities.

Herding and uncertainty lead to pro-cyclical lending. If the economy starts to speed up, asset values rise and risks appear to fall, these developments may be just typical of a cycle that will shortly turn down, or they may be a result of some exciting permanent technological change or reform. It could be either. Opinion is evenly divided; risks are not.

If a bank extends more credit to the new sector, or region or country, it appears bold and part of the future. If the decision turns out to be a mistake, it is in respectable company. If instead it backs a narrow cyclical view of the world, resisting the new trend, it will appear hesitant and part of the past. If it sticks to this view and it turns out to be a mistake, it is wrong and alone, vulnerable to be punished by the financial markets.

These asymmetries in total risk mean that in the up cycle, bankers are biased to backing the new sector or new country. Indeed, the market begins to punish those seen to be slow to catch on, forcing the more reluctant

---

[3] The Grameen Bank in Bangladesh illustrates this point well, with an added twist. Grameen's success underscores an interesting distinction between sophistication and effectiveness of credit risk management. Grameen lends small amounts of cash to women engaged in cottage industries or small agribusinesses. Previously bankers did not lend to poor women, which meant that they did not have a credit history, nor did they have any collateral, yet Grameen's credit risk management was highly successful. Knowing your customers is key to good banking, precisely how you do it is less so.

[4] For more literature on herding see Shiller (2000).

to lend, too. Boldness is virtuous. At some point, however, the sector or country is smothered by over-lending and there may be a crash. In the crash, the earlier optimism is seen to be irresponsible; the bezzles associated with all booms are laid bare.[5] Prudence is the new virtue. The market now rewards banks, which are prepared to let opportunities go by if the risks are uncertain.

IMPLICATIONS FOR BANKING REGULATION

We have identified three aspects of banking that need to be addressed by regulation: first, the bigger the bank the more the systemic risk; second, good banking is about using superior, perhaps internal, information about local risks, and third, bank assessments of risk are inherently pro-cyclical. This suggests that good banking regulation should:

- place additional regulatory costs and scrutiny on the big, systemically important banks;
- encourage banks with superior local information; and
- use measures of inherent risk that, for example, do not chase booms and busts and emphasize the diversification and spread of risks.

Basel II does almost the precise opposite. This raises the suspicion that the Basel Accord has been excessively influenced by the large international banks that it is supposed to regulate. This is of course exactly what Basel II does look like. There is complexity where there should be simplicity. There is also a lower capital requirement (an implicit subsidy) to those with quantitative internal risk assessments, without much attention to whether or not these assessments work. Whether the Basel Committee has been excessively influenced by the large banks or not, we can never be sure. What is of concern is that the points of regulation do not meet the points of market failure, and they miss in a way that benefits those that regulation should be toughest on. Equally, or more seriously, the new regulation may inappropriately and unfairly harm developing countries, the weakest in the world economy.

The implications of this outcome are significant and harmful to financial stability. Use of models on their own does not keep banks away from bad lending. Moreover, *common* internal processes across financial institutions lead to financial instability. The principal implications of quantitative internal risk assessments are daily, price sensitive risk limits which require a bank to reduce its exposure to risk when the estimated probability of losses rise as a result of a decline in the price of an asset, or a rise in the volatility or correlation of asset prices. When a handful of banks use these systems, everyone may be better off. However, if every bank uses them, and they have

---

[5] See Galbraith (1997).

herded into similar positions, then when a price decline causes one bank to hit its risk limit, other banks hit theirs too. As many banks try to sell the same asset at the same time, prices plummet and volatility and correlation soar, causing the risk limits of more banks to be hit.[6]

As long as market participants herd, which they have been doing for as long as markets have existed, the spread of sophisticated risk systems based on the daily evolution of market prices may *spread* financial instability and will certainly promote pro-cyclicality. Basel II worsens each of the market failures it should be designed to correct.

Apart from the alignment of market failure with intervention, another measure of a system is how well it serves its most vulnerable members. If Basel II makes the flow of credit more unstable and pro-cyclical everywhere, as discussed above, this will have a bigger negative impact on developing countries, whose fragile economies and banking systems are more vulnerable to strong cyclical fluctuations of bank lending. Second, as shown above, Basel II is likely to inappropriately increase the cost—and reduce the supply of—bank lending to developing countries.

There has also been concern that the assumptions recommended for calculating the probability of default will excessively raise the regulatory cost of lending to small and medium enterprises (SMEs). This issue was of particular concern to German officials and bankers where bank lending to SMEs plays an important role for that sector and for the economy as a whole. In response to these concerns, and intense lobbying, the draft Accord was amended so that lending to borrowers with less than 50 million euros in annual sales received an average reduction in capital requirements of about 10 percent relative to large companies. It was argued that this was consistent with the principle of risk weighted capital requirements because the probability of default was less correlated amongst SMEs than large enterprises. A bank with a loan portfolio that is well diversified across a large number of SMEs will face lower overall risk at the portfolio level than one focused on a few larger borrowers. The result of the empirical work discussed in Section 10.3 suggests strongly that a similar modification is justified with respect to international diversification. *In order to accurately align regulatory capital with the actual risks a bank might face, the accord should take account of this portfolio level effect.* Given the changes already made to SME lending, as well as the fact that the changes we propose would seem to have at least as solid an empirical basis, there are no theoretical, empirical or practical reasons why changes should not be made to incorporate the benefits of international diversification. Of course, one key difference is that German SMEs had a representative on the Basel Committee and developing country borrowers did not.

---

[6] For a more detailed discussion see Persaud (2003).

Table 10.1. Estimates of Impact on Required Capital and Sovereign Spreads

Rating	Capital Required per £100	Estimated Spread Change*
A+	1.18	−42.65
A	1.89	−38.22
A−	1.89	−38.22
BBB+	2.96	−62.96
BBB	4.03	−49.68
BBB−	5.04	−36.97
BB+	5.61	−119.56
BB	7.76	−11.92
BB−	8.86	+43.24
B+	11.79	+331.38
B	19.08	+969.78
B−	21.31	+1165.00
CCC	31.33	+2041.13

Notes: * Estimates the change in spread needed to produce the risk-adjusted returns achieved under the existing Accord.
Source: Weder and Wedow (2002).

10.3 The Impact of Basel II on Developing Countries

One of the primary aims of the new Basel Capital Accord is to better align regulatory capital with actual risks. Critics of the 1988 accord have argued that the regulatory capital that is required is not sufficiently 'granular' to reflect the variable levels of risk associated with loans to different types of borrowers. In particular, it has been argued that the regulatory capital required for loans to the higher rated borrowers is too high. Consequently, one immediate effect of Basel II will be to reduce the required regulatory capital for loans to the highest rated borrowers. However, as the Basel Committee has also argued that the overall level of regulatory capital in the system should remain at the current 8 percent level, this can only be achieved by increasing the required capital for lower rated borrowers. The level of this increase will thus be most marked for the lowest rated borrowers. It is universally accepted, therefore, that an unavoidable impact of the IRB approach will be to increase regulatory capital requirements for lower rated borrowers, with the lowest rated borrowers seeing the sharpest increase. While this is accepted, there is no consensus as to the exact impact this will have on the pricing and terms of loans to such borrowers, although it is expected that pricing will generally improve for high rated borrowers and deteriorate for lower rated borrowers.

Table 10.1 gives estimates of the impact on the capital required per £100 for sovereigns of different ratings. In addition, it presents estimates of the impact on spreads, assuming: (1) constant returns to capital; and (2) binding capital requirements. Consequently, they should be viewed as the upper bound—or maximum possible—increase in spreads.

As can be seen from Table 10.1, the cut off point—where the change in spreads becomes positive, that is, there is an increase in costs—is at BB. After this point the change in spreads increases dramatically as the borrowers rating deteriorates.

The actual impact on the cost and quantity of bank lending to developing countries will clearly be determined by the extent to which regulatory capital requirements are a binding constraint. However, we can establish the upper and lower bounds: if, for example, changes in regulatory capital are passed on in a fully binding way, then the estimates of changes to spreads in Table 10.1 will correspond with changes in price. Thus, for countries rated B (B−)— such as Brazil—regulatory capital per US$100 lent would increase from the current figure of US$8 to US$21. Assuming the same risk-adjusted returns are demanded as under the existing Accord, this would equate to an increase in spreads of 1165 basis points. Similarly, for countries rated CCC, the increase in regulatory capital per £100 lent will be from US$8 to US$31. Again, assuming fully binding requirements and constant risk-adjusted returns, this would produce an increase in spreads of 2041 basis points. For unrated sovereigns with higher implied probabilities of default, the increases would, of course, be substantially higher than this figure. This obviously includes the great majority of countries in Sub-Saharan Africa, for example.

As shown in Table 10.2, the Basel Committee itself estimates that loans to corporates rated B− will require a capital increase from US$8 to US$20.8 for US$100 lent. This amounts to the requirement to set aside 20.8 percent of the loaned sum for loans to borrowers of this credit rating. For corporate borrowers rated CCC, the required regulatory capital would be approximately 29 percent. In contrast, a loan to a borrower rated AA− would require only 1.28 percent to be set aside as regulatory capital, relative to the current 8 percent.[7] Clearly, the estimates from the Basel Committee would imply similar maximum increases in spreads to that seen in Table 10.1, if the same assumptions are adopted.

As pointed out above, the estimates given in Tables 10.1 and 10.2 should be seen as maximum possible increases. Clearly, regulatory requirements are unlikely to be fully binding in practice, with the result that the increase in costs is likely to be lower than the maximum figures given. One factor that should be taken into account in this respect is the possibility that banks may choose to use off balance sheet transactions, and thereby bypass the regulatory requirements entirely.

The strongest—and most often used—argument against these changes being passed on, however, is that banks price loans on the basis of their own calculation of economic capital, rather than of regulatory capital.[8] Given that

[7] Similar estimates can be found in Powell (2002).
[8] Economic capital is the quantity of capital required to support the risk inherent in any banking activity—credit risk, market risk, or operational risk. It is thus closely related to

Table 10.2. Basel Committee's Estimates of Changes to Corporate Risk Weights

Rating	Probability of Default (PD)[1]	Approximate Corporate Risk Weights	Capital Required per £100*
AAA	0	—	—
AA+	0	—	—
AA	0	—	—
AA−	0.03	14.75%	£1.28
A+	0.02	—	—
A	0.05	20.03%	£1.60
A−	0.05%	20.03%	£1.60
BBB+	0.12%	30.20%	£2.42
BBB	0.22%	50.00%	£4.00
BBB−	0.35%	60.00%	£4.80
BB+	0.44%	67.00%	£5.36
BB	0.89%	90.00%	£7.20
BB−	1.33%	110.00%	£8.80
B+	2.91%	140.00%	£11.20
B	8.38%	210.00%	£16.80
B−	10.32%	260.00%	£20.80
CCC	21.32%	360.00%	£28.80

Notes: [1] S&P's one year average PD. The percentages given are relative to the current 8% capital requirement. Thus, a 200% estimate equates to a capital requirement of 16% of the loan value. * Relative to current figure of £8.

Source: The Basel Committee's CP3: 'Illustrative IRB Risk Weights'.

the aim of the Basel Committee is to bring regulatory capital requirements into line with economic capital requirement, it is argued that the reforms will have no impact on the pricing of loans. A study by the Bank of England (Hayes et al. 2002) argues, largely based on this assumption, that the Accord is likely to have only a minor impact on the pricing and/or quantity of loans to emerging markets. However, this argument presupposes that the use of economic capital is uniform across all major banks that are actively engaged with emerging and developing country borrowers.

A study by PriceWaterhouseCoopers[9] surveyed a cross-section of the most sophisticated European banks. They concluded that, far from being uniform, economic capital is only fully integrated into the business practice of less than half of those surveyed. This suggests strongly that, for at least more than 50 percent of European banks, pricing cannot be based on calculations of economic capital. We would therefore expect regulatory capital to have

Risk-Adjusted Return on Capital (RAROC) calculations. As a standardized measure, it allows a bank to compare directly the relative attractiveness, in terms of the risk/reward trade-off, of diverse potential opportunities. Regulatory capital is simply the quantity of capital that the regulatory authorities stipulate must be set aside for different banking activities. By making regulatory capital more risk sensitive, therefore, the new Accord will bring it more closely into line with banks' own economic capital assessments.

[9] Presented at the CBC Banking and Financial Services Symposium, London, June 25, 2003.

a strong impact on the pricing and terms of loans for these banks, thereby creating a significant average impact across the system.[10]

Second, there is both theoretical and empirical evidence that banks tend to keep a buffer of capital above the minimum required for regulatory purposes. As a result, if regulatory capital increases for a certain category of borrowers (e.g., those of a developing country) the capital that banks will allocate for lending to them will increase by the amount required plus the given mark-up.

Finally, the argument that regulatory capital does not influence banks' behavior is somewhat absurd, as precisely the aim of Basel II is to modify capital so it reflects risk more precisely, with a view to banks modifying their lending decisions.

10.4 Are the Increases of Regulatory Capital and Likely Cost of Credit Justified?

The Basel Committee, and supporters of the Basel II in general, argue that the increases in capital requirements for lower rated borrowers, that are an integral feature of the Accord, are entirely justified on the basis of a more accurate assessment of risk. They use the same argument to justify any increase in the cost of loans for lower rated borrowers, although they contend that a large increase is unlikely. Is this position valid?

From our perspective, there are two serious flaws in this argument. The first relates to the failure of Basel II to take account of the benefits of international diversification. The second problem concerns data problems in developing countries, which prevents an accurate assessment of the creditworthiness of borrowers, and leads to a tendency to 'assume the worst'. In combination, these factors are likely to create a situation where the regulatory capital requirements associated with loans to developing country borrowers will seriously *overestimate* the risks of such lending.

10.4.1 *Diversification*

It has long been argued that one of the major benefits of investing in developing and emerging economies is their relatively low correlation with mature markets. Recent empirical research has demonstrated that this is clearly the case (Griffith-Jones et al. 2003). Consequently, clear benefits—at the portfolio level—would accrue to banks with well diversified international portfolios. That is, a bank with a loan portfolio that is distributed widely across a range

---

[10] A study by a leading international risk management consultancy, Mercer Oliver Wyman (Garside and Peterson, 2003), concludes that the new Accord will produce: *an increase in credit spreads for higher risk segments such as mid-market lending, SMEs, low-rated sovereigns, and specialized lending.*

of relatively uncorrelated markets, is less likely to face simultaneous problems in all of those markets, than a bank with loans concentrated in a smaller number of relatively correlated markets. Therefore, in order to accurately align regulatory capital with the actual risks a bank might face, the Accord should take account of this portfolio level effect: the capital requirements for a bank with a well diversified international loan portfolio should reflect the lower total risk than for a more concentrated portfolio. The Accord contains no such considerations, however, suggesting that, in this area at least, capital requirements will not accurately reflect risk.

The argument of differential correlations between developed and developing markets has been extensively tested, first with specific regard to international bank lending and profitability and, second, in a macroeconomic sense (see Table 10.3). All our results offer strong, statistically significant, support for the validity of this position. The tests performed, using a variety of variables over a range of time periods, provide robust and unequivocal evidence in support of the diversification hypothesis.

In the case of spreads on syndicated bank loans, which are a proxy for the probability of default, they have had a greater tendency to rise and fall together *within* the developed regions than between developed and developing regions. Over the sample period (1993 to 2002), a bank with a loan portfolio that was well diversified across the major developed and developing regions would have enjoyed diversification benefits at the portfolio level. Similarly, over the same sample period, the profitability of banks in developed markets are correlated with each other, but negatively correlated with those in developing markets.

An analysis of macro variables tells the same tale. Consequently, if the incidence of non-performing loans (NPLs) in an economy is, at least partially, inversely related to the rate of GDP growth, then banks with a portfolio of loans diversified between developed and developing country borrowers would be less likely to experience a sharp increase in NPLs across the portfolio simultaneously. Similar implications can be drawn if we take movements in short-term interest rates as a proxy for the business cycle or long-term interest rates as a proxy for underlying inflation risks.

For many market practitioners, movements in government bond prices and yields are seen as strong indicators of both economic fundamentals and market views on the economic prospects of each country. The fact that developed country bond prices move in step to a far greater extent than do developed and developing country prices, suggests a closer correlation between both economic fundamentals in developed countries and market sentiment towards them. The evidence of lower correlation between developed and developing stock markets also supports this view.

These results are supported by additional recent research conducted at State Street. Using ten emerging and ten developed country equity markets we

Table 10.3. Correlation Coefficients of Financial and Macroeconomic Variables: Developed/Developed and Developed/Developing

Variable	Time-Period	Frequency	Developed/Developed Mean Correlation Coefficient	Developing/Developing Mean Correlation Coefficient	Test Statistic (H0:Mx=My) Critical Value of 0.05% one-tailed test in parentheses
Syndicated	1993–2002	Monthly	0.37	0.14	3.33 (3.29)
ROA	1988–2001	Annual	0.10	−0.08	4.40 (3.29)
ROC	1988–2001	Annual	0.14	−0.11	6.92 (3.29)
GDP	1985–2000	Six-monthly	0.44	0.02	9.08 (3.29)
GDP HP	1950–98	Annual	0.35	0.02	9.41 (3.29)
STIR	1985–2000	Six-monthly	0.72	0.23	11.09 (3.29)
STIRR	1985–2000	Six-monthly	0.66	0.22	10.93 (3.29)
GBI-EMBI	1991–2002	Daily	0.78	0.53	5.45 (3.29)
GBI-EMBI	1991–97	Daily	0.90	0.74	4.64 (3.29)
GBI-EMBI	1998–2002	Daily	0.42	0.09	5.87 (3.29)
IFCI-COMP	1990–2000	Daily	0.58	−0.15	7.83 (3.29)
IFCG-COMP	1990–2000	Daily	0.58	−0.17	8.06 (3.29)

Notes: Syndicated—Syndicated Loan Spreads; ROA—Return on Assets; ROC—Return on tier one capital; GDP—GDP Growth Rate; GDP HP—Hodrick-Prescott decomposition of GDP; STIR—Short term nominal interest rate; STIRR—Short term real interest rate; GBI—Global Bond Index; EMBI —Emerging Market Bond Index; EMBI+ —Emerging Market Bond Index Plus; IFC G—S&P International Finance Corporation (Global); IFC I—S&P International Finance Corporation (Investable); COMP—Developed countries composite stock indices. For further details see Appendix 10.1.

Table 10.4. Correlation Matrix Using Daily Correlations of Equity Returns Between Emerging Markets and Developed Markets, 1992–2002

	1 week returns		3 year returns	
	Emerging	Developed	Emerging	Developed
Emerging	0.0008	0.0003	0.4274	−0.0132
Developed	0.0003	0.0004	−0.0132	0.0745

Notes: (a) Countries included in analysis: developed—Australia, Canada, France, Germany, Italy, Japan, Norway, Switzerland, UK, and US. Emerging—Argentina, Brazil, Chile, Indonesia, Jordan, Korea, Mexico, Taiwan Thailand, and Turkey.
Source: Bloomberg, State.

find a similar result (see Table 10.4). Emerging markets are highly correlated with each other and for equity markets, more so than developed markets. This is even more apparent in periods of financial stress and it is this feature of emerging markets that has made many discount their diversification benefit. However, over both short and long periods (one week to three years) emerging equity markets are less correlated with developed markets than developed markets are with themselves. A bank with a portfolio of developed equity markets would have a less diversified investment or loan portfolio than if it were invested in companies from developed *and* emerging markets.

More recently, we have had the opportunity to access the data of one of the largest internationally diversified banks.[11] We obtained information on non-performing loans and provisions amounts. While the variables presented in Table 10.4 correspond to publicly available information, the data obtained from this bank is proprietary and has been collected with precise care. It is data that reflects in a more concise manner the riskiness of an internationally diversified portfolio. The results obtained are presented in Table 10.5.

Table 10.5. Average Correlation Coefficients and Statistical Tests for Proprietary Data from a Large Internationally Diversified Bank

Variable	Time period	Frequency	Developed/ developed mean correlation coefficient	Developing/ developing mean correlation coefficient	Test statistic ($H0:Mx=My$) critical value of 0.05% one-tailed test in parentheses
Non-Performing Loans:	1998–2002	Annual	0.71	−0.19	3.09 (1.86)
Provisions	1998–2002	Annual	0.55	−0.14	2.14 (1.86)

[11] We were asked to keep the source of the data confidential.

Table 10.6. Comparison of Globally Diversified and Globally Undiversified Portfolios

1. Diversified developed/developing Total Exposure = 117,625,333			2. Diversified developed Total Exposure = 117,625,333			Percentage difference
Percentile	Loss value	Unexpected loss (%)	Percentile	Loss value	Unexpected loss (%)	
99.8	22,595,312	19.21	99.8	27,869,349	23.69	+23.34

Let us recall that the null hypothesis to be tested was:

$$H_0 : M_x \text{ equals } M_y; H_1 : M_x \text{ different } M_y$$

We observe that the null hypothesis in both cases is rejected at the 5 percent significance level. The outcome is consistent with our previous results from independent datasets, which strongly suggest that a bank's loan portfolio that is diversified internationally between developed *and* developing country borrowers would benefit in terms of lower overall portfolio risk, relative to one focused exclusively on lending to developed countries. In order to test this hypothesis in the specific context of a bank's loan portfolio, we undertook a simulation exercise to assess the potential unexpected[12] loss resulting from a portfolio diversified within developed countries, and one diversified across developed and developing regions.

As can be seen from Table 10.6, the unexpected losses simulated for the portfolio focused on developed country borrowers are, on average, 23 percent higher than for the portfolio diversified across developed and developing countries.

Further simulations we have carried out (Griffith-Jones et al. 2004), using a dataset from Moody's for US banks showed again that capital requirements were significantly lower (in this case by 19 percent) if the benefits of diversification are incorporated into the IRB approach than if they are not. Furthermore, it is very interesting that if the benefits of diversification are incorporated, the simulations clearly show that the variance over time of capital requirements is significantly smaller than if these benefits are not incorporated. Therefore, introducing the benefits of geographical diversification significantly decreases, though it does not eliminate, the higher pro-cyclicality that the IRB approach will imply. This difference, though not preventing difficulties, may well be significant enough to prevent a 'credit crunch'.

---

[12] Expected losses are those that a bank estimates will experience on its portfolio over a given time period; they should ideally be covered by provisioning. Unexpected losses is the amount by which actual losses exceed expected losses; they could be covered by economic and/or regulatory capital.

A potentially significant issue, which has been raised in this regard, is the fact that correlations are not constant over time. The danger, of course, is that correlations within emerging markets increase dramatically in crises, as contagion spreads the crisis from one country or region to another. In this instance, it is possible that a portfolio diversified across a range of emerging and developing regions, might be hit simultaneously in all of the emerging market areas. In order to assess the validity of this argument, we extended our analysis to check what would happen to diversification effects during crises times in the three separate periods (see Appendix 10.2). Our results demonstrate that for each of the analyzed variables in each period concerned, the mean correlation between 'developed' and 'developing' countries is lower than the mean correlation between 'developed' and 'developed' countries. Given this evidence, we can conclude that the diversification benefits obtained through a well diversified portfolio of developed and emerging markets still hold in crises periods. As would be expected, the magnitude of the diversification benefits is lower in crisis periods than in non-crisis periods.

10.4.2 *The Growing 'Data Divide'*

An important issue that has received relatively little attention to date relates to the increasingly quantified approach to credit risk, and the reliance of this process on accurate data of sufficient historical length. It is likely that the new Basel Capital Accord will accelerate this process. Indeed, a number of commentators have argued that this acceleration is already well under way, as banks seek to upgrade their internal systems so as to be eligible for the IRB approaches.[13]

Under the Foundation[14] IRB framework a bank is required to provide its own estimates of probability of default (PD), with supervisory authorities providing estimates of loss given default (LGD), exposure at default (EAD), and maturity (M). Under the Advanced IRB approach, banks are required to provide estimates of all of these inputs, subject to meeting minimum standards. However, in order for a bank's estimate of PD to be acceptable as an input, 'the length of the underlying historical observation period used must be at least five years for at least one source.'[15, 16]

---

[13] In order to be eligible for the IRB approaches a bank must satisfy its national supervisory authorities that it meets minimum quantitative and qualitative criteria as set out in the Third Consultative Package (CP3) issued by the Basel Committee on Banking Supervision (2003).

[14] The Foundation IRB approach is the preparatory stage before a bank moves to the Advanced IRB approach. As such, supervisory authorities set a number of the key inputs in the earlier stage. Once a bank has demonstrated its ability to perform adequately under the Foundation approach, and established the robustness of the estimates required for the Advanced approach, it is able to proceed to the Advanced framework.

[15] As sources of data a bank is permitted to use: (1) their own internal data; (2) data from external sources such as ratings agencies; or (3) pooled data from the banking industry.

[16] Basel Committee on Banking Supervision (2003: para. 425).

For estimates of LGD: 'Estimates of LGD must be based on a minimum data observation period that should ideally cover at least one complete economic cycle but must in any case be no shorter than a period of seven years for at least one source'.[17]

For the most sophisticated internationally active banks, that have well developed systems of this sort, the historical data that underlies their estimates is derived from developed markets, and is integral to calculations of economic capital upon which they price their loans. As major banks have told us, the availability of these underlying data inputs in developing countries is far lower than in the developed markets. One consequence of this is that banks that wish to employ such systems in emerging markets must, in the absence of reliable data, make very conservative assumptions about potential borrowers; in effect, they 'assume the worst', and the pricing of loans reflects this. Thus, banks that employ quantitative systems of this sort in emerging markets have an inbuilt tendency to overestimate the risks involved in such lending, in the absence of data of comparable quality to that available in developed countries. It is noteworthy that these are the banks that have tended to withdraw from straight syndicated or bilateral lending to developing countries. The explanation for this retreat commonly stresses the fact that the spreads available are insufficient to compensate the banks for the risks they face in these markets. However, as discussed above, these 'risks'—while not illusory—may well appear greater than they actually are, due to the lack of reliable data. Therefore, although the spreads available may not compensate investors for the worst possible risks they might face—i.e., a 'conservative' assessment of risk, or 'assuming the worst'—they may well be appropriate for the likely real-world outcome.

However, the fact that spreads on syndicated lending are lower than those that these models produce suggests that the banks that are still involved in syndicated or bilateral lending are pricing these loans more generously than calculations of economic capital would imply, probably because their use of qualitative judgment makes them measure risk in those countries more realistically. Consequently, as the aim is to raise regulatory capital to levels compatible with economic capital for *all* major banks, then the banks that are currently pricing loans on a more realistic basis to economic capital—and are thus market-makers in the sense of determining the market price—will face regulatory capital requirements that will 'bite', thereby forcing them to increase the costs and/or decrease the supply of loans to these markets.

One accepted outcome of the Basel process is that banks, which previously had not, are investing significantly in quantitative systems compatible with the calculation of economic capital. The likely outcome of this will indeed be to increase the spreads required to persuade those banks to lend.

---

[17] Ibid. (para. 434).

Indeed, the Basel Committee has given explicit advice for banks estimating the inputs required for IRB calculations when data quality is poor. The following is typical of this advice:

In general, estimates of PDs, LGDs and EADs are likely to involve unpredictable errors. In order to avoid over-optimism, a bank must add to its estimates a margin of conservatism that is related to the likely range of errors. Where methods and data are less satisfactory and the likely range of errors is larger, the margin of conservatism must be larger.[18]

An alternative to this approach, of course, is for banks to simply cease lending to markets where the quality of data is insufficient to enable a robust IRB framework to be operated. Therefore, a bank operating under an IRB approach faces two options in relation to lending to developing countries: (1) withdraw from lending, which would reduce supply of loans; or (2) adopt a conservative approach to assigning borrowers to PD bands, which would increase cost, as banks will 'assume the worst' about those borrowers' creditworthiness. Furthermore, these factors are likely also to affect negatively the potential for future lending. Banks that are not currently engaged in lending to developing countries, and choose to adopt the IRB framework, will be effectively precluded from entering these markets in the future by the data limitations we have described.

10.5 Conclusion and Policy Proposals

It seems to be no coincidence that the critical stakeholder in the international banking system not represented on the Basel Committee—developing countries—receives the rawest deal from the new Basel Accord. It is no surprise that the one group that appears to have excessively influenced the Basel Committee are the most powerful financial institutions domiciled in countries represented on the Committee. Our four policy proposals are designed to address this issue, as well as the other key problems that have been identified above.

10.5.1 Governance

The outcome of Basel II seems to relate to the composition of the Committee. Given that the Basel Capital Accord is a global standard that is likely to have a very large impact on emerging economies, and that emerging markets are critical to the global economy, the composition of the Basel Committee needs to be changed. A more sensible composition would reflect global GDP. To

---

[18] Ibid. (para. 413).

include all the ten largest economies would bring in China, India, Brazil, and either Mexico or Russia to the Committee. The new countries are critical to the global economy and to cross-border bank lending. This new composition would have the virtue of powerful economic logic behind it, and would counter-balance the influence of the large international banks domiciled in developed countries.

Alternatively, the current membership could remain and India, China, and Brazil could be added. Additionally, one or two representatives of developing country regions (Asia, Latin America, and Africa) could be added for a four-year period. There could then be rotation for different countries to be represented (from each of the three regions). The principle would be similar to the one under which the Executive Boards of the IMF and World Bank operate. Particularly, but not only, if the latter formula is adopted, developing country representatives could be supported by a small permanent technical secretariat, that would contribute both expertise and continuity. In fact, the lack of such a secretariat at present is an important institutional gap.

Whatever the solution, concrete steps need to be taken as soon as possible to start changing the composition of the Committee to increase its legitimacy, especially in the light of the recent serious problems of Basel II. Indeed, we suggest that the Committee start meeting with a representative group from emerging countries (such as its own consultative group or members of the G-24 that represent developing countries at the IMF) to establish a process whereby emerging countries can quickly become full members of the Basel Banking Committee. This is urgent. The shortcomings of running the twenty-first century world economy, using the mid-twentieth century world order, are becoming greater over time. A Basel Committee with appropriate representation from the world economy would not just result in a fairer system, but also in a more financially stable system with welfare enhancing effects for all.

10.5.2 Diversification

Basel II does not explicitly take account of clear international diversification benefits of lending to developing countries, despite these being widely recognized and confirmed by our research described above. Capital requirements will—in this respect—not accurately reflect risk, and will unfairly and inappropriately penalize developing countries. It therefore seems important that as soon as possible, the Basel Committee incorporate the benefits of international diversification into the new Accord. The Committee has already recognized the impact of differential asset correlation on the appropriate level of capital requirements in its modification with respect to SMEs. Our empirical results strongly suggest that a similar modification is justified with respect to internationally diversified lending, especially when one considers the fact that our evidence is at least as strong as that used to support the modification with respect to SMEs.

We recognize the fact that SME lending has 'special characteristics' which justified the modification. However, our argument is precisely that lending to developing and emerging economies also has similar characteristics. López (2002) argues that large firms are more susceptible to systemic risk than are SMEs: the higher weight given to idiosyncratic factors in the latter thus justifies the modification. However, if one defines 'systemic risk' in a global sense as associated with global business cycles, then the fact that developing and emerging economies are less correlated with industrialized business cycles—as our results clearly show—demonstrates that these economies are also less susceptible to systemic risk. Furthermore, the life span of many SMEs is inevitably short, while that of most countries is intrinsically otherwise. This suggests that creditors have a greater chance of recovering their assets from the latter, thereby enhancing the diversification benefits yet further. Consequently, if a modification was justified with respect to SME lending, it is difficult to see why one is not justified in the case of developing and emerging economies.

The results of our simulation show that the unexpected losses for the portfolio focused on developed country borrowers are, on average, about 23 percent higher than for the portfolio diversified across developed and developing countries. As a specific proposal in this area, we would suggest an adjusting factor be incorporated into the Accord. This would be applied at the portfolio level, and could function in a tapered fashion. Our empirical results suggest that a fully diversified bank would qualify for a reduction of approximately 23 percent of required capital. This reduction would then decline as the level of diversification fell, reaching zero for an undiversified bank. Such a modification would be relatively straightforward to introduce, would not add to the complexity of the Accord, but would ensure a more accurate measurement of risk. Alternatively, the modification could be integrated into Pillar 1 of the Accord through the development of a separate developing country curve. This would be similar to the modification produced for SMEs and would be calibrated to produce a similarly tapered reduction in capital as in the adjusting factor described above.

As well as reducing the required capital for loans to borrowers in developing countries, in the context of an internationally diversified portfolio, such an adjusting factor or separate curve would also provide an incentive for banks to maintain or increase their level of international diversification, in response to an accurate measurement of risk.

One simple practical proposal to incorporate the benefits of international diversification is to introduce a correction coefficient to Basel II (that would increase as diversification grows), so that regulatory capital would be defined based on the one factor Basel II model multiplied by this coefficient.

Capital adjusted for diversification =

Capital defined by the one factor Basel II model $\times$ Correction coefficient

Thus, an internationally diversified bank would multiply its total regulatory capital by a coefficient to correct for international diversification. Such a correction coefficient has been calculated with real data by the Spanish bank BBVA (BBVA Risk Methodology 2004); it measures the error made when using a single factor model—such as that to be used in Basel II—when in fact there are two factors affecting diversification of portfolio (geographical areas, emerging vs. non emerging economies). The correction factor is estimated as the ratio between the capital calculated with the two factor model and the capital obtained with the single factor; as shown in BBVA Risk Methodology (2004) and Griffith-Jones et al. (2004), the correction factor increases as diversification grows.

Adoption of such a correction factor would: (1) produce a more accurate measure of risk and (2) prevent the current overestimation of risk in Basel II for international borrowers—particularly those in developing countries.

10.5.3 Dealing with Pro-Cyclicality

Introducing benefits of international diversification will not only lead to a more accurate measurement of risk. It will also reduce the pro-cyclicality of capital requirements through time, which will both allow smoothing of bank lending—and therefore some smoothing of economic cycles in both developed and developing countries. It should also help strengthen stability of banks, especially the large international ones, which is clearly a key economic objective and an absolutely central one for G-10 regulators.

It should be stressed that introducing the benefits of geographical diversification will reduce, but certainly not eliminate, the increase in pro-cyclicality that Basel II will bring. As a result, it would be highly desirable to introduce measures that would further compensate for this increased pro-cyclicality. Such measures could include *mandatory* forward-looking provisions for latent risks an approach already adopted by the Spanish authorities, as well as more discrete cycle-neutral prudential provisions (for an in-depth discussion see Ocampo and Chiappe 2003).

10.5.4 Overcoming the Data Divide by Allowing Long Transition Under Standardized Approach

The Basel Committee has recognized the problem of differential data quality in different jurisdictions. Although it is stated that:

Once a bank adopts the IRB approach for part of its holdings, it is expected to extend it across the entire banking group. This is subsequently qualified: once on IRB, data limitations may mean that banks can meet the standards for the use of own estimates for LGD and EAD for some but not all of their asset classes/business units at the same time.[19]

As a result, the Basel Committee concedes that: 'Supervisors may allow banks to adopt a phased roll-out of the IRB approach across the banking group'. However, this phased roll-out must be of a limited duration: 'A bank must produce an implementation plan, specifying to what extent and when it intends to roll-out IRB approaches across significant asset classes and business units over time. The plan should be exacting, but realistic, and must be agreed with the supervisor'.[20]

It is essential, if the negative impacts linked to data described above are to be avoided, that banks are given the time to accumulate data of sufficient quality and duration in different markets. That is, an internationally active bank should be free to employ the standardized approach in their lending to those developing countries where the data limitations are such to make adoption of the IRB approaches impractical. Furthermore, there should be no arbitrary limit set on the length of this period. Rather, the IRB approaches should not be adopted in lending to developing countries until it can be proved that the underlying data that are inputs into the framework are of sufficient quality and comprehensiveness. This transition period could also provide the space for more sophisticated full credit risk models to be developed, which could then make effective use of the better data available from developing countries. These models would, among other aspects, explicitly incorporate the benefits of international diversification.

These modifications would encourage a narrowing of the 'data divide' described above. In contrast, the Accord is more likely to encourage a widening and deepening of this divide.

Appendix 10.1   Data and Sources

Countries analyzed:

1. *Developing Countries*: Argentina, Brazil, Bulgaria, Chile, Ecuador, Indonesia, Korea, Malaysia, Mexico, Nigeria, Panama, Peru, Poland, Philippines, Russia, Thailand, South Africa, Venezuela.

2. *Developed Countries*: Canada, Germany, Japan, France, Italy, Spain, United Kingdom, US.

3. *Others*: Finland, Greece, Ireland, Portugal, Singapore.

---

[19] Ibid. (para. 225).   [20] Ibid. (para. 227).

Table 10A1.1. Variables Analyzed

Grouping	Code	Description	Time period	Frequency	Source
Financial Sector	ROA	Return on Assets (banks)	1988–2001	Annual	*The Banker*
Financial Sector	ROC	Return on tier one capital (banks)	1988–2001	Annual	*The Banker*
Financial Sector	Syndicated	Syndicated Loans Spreads	1993–2002	Monthly	BIS
Bonds	GBI[1]	Global Bond Index	1987–2002	Daily	JP Morgan/Reuters
Bonds	EMBI[2]	Emerging Market Bond Index	1987–2002	Daily	JP Morgan/Reuters
Bonds	EMBI+[3]	Emerging Market Bond Index Plus	1987–2002	Daily	JP Morgan/Reuters
Stocks	IFC G[4]	S&P International Finance Corporation (Global)	1990–2002	Daily	IFC/S&P
Stocks	IFC I[5]	S&P International Finance Corporation (Investable)	1990–2002	Daily	IFC/S&P
Stocks	COMP	Developed countries listed above: composite stock indexes	1990–2002	Daily	Reuters
Macro	GDP	GDP Growth Rate	1985–2000	Six monthly	IMF, World Bank, (author's own calculations)
Macro	GDP HP	Hodrick-Prescott decomposition of GDP	1950–1998	Annual	National Data (author's own calculations)
Macro	STIR	Short-term nominal interest rate	1985–2000	Six monthly	National Data (BIS) or IMF, IFS
Macro	STIRR	Short-term real interest rate	1985–2000	Six monthly	National Data (BIS) or IMF, IFS

Notes: [1] The GBI consists of regularly traded, fixed rate, domestic government bonds. The countries covered have liquid government debt markets, which are freely accessible to foreign investors. GBI excludes floating rate notes, perps, bonds with less than one year maturity, bonds targeted at the domestic markets for tax reasons and bonds with callable, puttable, or convertible features. [2] Included in the EMBI are US dollar denominated Brady bonds, Eurobonds, traded loans, and local debt market instruments issued by sovereign and quasi-sovereign entities. [3] EMBI+ is an extension of the EMBI. The index tracks all of the external currency denominated debt markets of the emerging markets. [4] IFC G (Global) is an emerging equity market index produced in conjunction with S&P. The index does not take into account restrictions on foreign ownership that limit the accessibility of certain markets and individual stocks. [5] IFC I (Investable) is adjusted to reflect restrictions on foreign investments in emerging markets. Consequently, it represents a more accurate picture of the actual universe available to investors.

Appendix 10.2   Correlations in Three Crisis Periods: Developed/Developed and Developed/Developing

Tables 10A2.1 to 10A2.3 demonstrate that for each of the analyzed variables, the mean correlation between 'developed' (deved) and 'developing' (deving) countries is lower than the mean correlation between 'developed' and 'developed' countries.

It is interesting to see from these results that, as would be expected in crisis periods, developing countries become relatively riskier in comparison to developed countries. This is illustrated in row 4, which measures the ratio of volatilities given by the

Table 10A2.1. Syndicated Loan Spreads Under Crises Periods

Row	SYNDICATED	Total Time Series	94-4 to 99-1	94-4 to 95-4	97-3 to 98-4
1	Mean correlation (deved/deving)	0.141	0.129	0.087	0.229
2	Mean correlation (deved/deved)	0.375	0.135	0.143	0.479
3	Ratio mean correlations	0.375	0.954	0.609	0.477
4	Ratio volatilities	1.739	2.771	4.300	2.514

Table 10A2.2. Global Bond Index-Emerging Market Bond Index Under Crises Periods

Row	GBI-EMBI+	Total Time Series	94-4 to 99-1	94-4 to 95-4
1	Mean correlation (deved/deving)	0.532	0.397	0.698
2	Mean correlation (deved/deved)	0.783	0.571	0.823
3	Ratio mean correlations	0.679	0.694	0.849
4	Ratio volatilities	1.656	2.400	1.716

Table 10A2.3. GDP Under Crises Periods

Row	GDP-HP	Total Time Series	94-4 to 99-1
1	Mean correlation (deved/deving)	0.020	0.114
2	Mean correlation (deved/deved)	0.351	0.409
3	Ratio mean correlations	0.056	0.279
4	Ratio volatilities	1.696	2.256

standard deviation of the developing countries divided by the standard deviation of the developed countries. We observe that this ratio increases in crisis periods.

Finally, we observe that the ratio given by the mean correlation of 'developed' and 'developing' divided by the mean correlation of 'developed' and 'developed' countries increases in crisis periods. This implies that diversification benefits are in fact aminorated in crisis periods, however, they still remain. This is observed by the fact that the ratio never reaches a value of 1 or greater.

References

BBVA Risk Methodology (2004). 'A Practical Proposal for Improving Diversification Treatment in Basel 2'. Madrid: Mimeo.

Basel Committee on Banking Supervision (2003). 'Third Consultative Package' (CP3). Basel: BCBS.

Ffrench-Davis, R. and Griffith-Jones, S. (eds.) (1995). *Coping with Capital Surges: The Return of Finance to Latin America*. Boulder, CO: Lynne Rienner Publishers.

Galbraith, J. K. (1997). *The Great Crash 1929*. New York: Mariner Books.

Garside, T. and Pederson, C. (2003). *The New Rules of the Game: Implications of the New Basel Capital Accord for the European Banking Industries*. London: Mercer Oliver Wyman.

Griffith-Jones, S., Segoviano, M., and Spratt, S. (2003). *Basel II and Developing Countries: Diversification and Portfolio Effects*. London: Institute of Development Studies. Available at: www.ids.ac.uk/intfinance/.

—— —— —— (2004). *Basel II and CAD 3: Response to the UK Treasury's Consultation Paper*. London: Institute of Development Studies. Available at: www.ids.ac.uk/intfinance/.

Hayes, S., Saporta, V., and Lodge, D. (2002). 'The Impact of the New Basel Accord on the Supply of Capital to Emerging Market Economies. *Financial Stability Review*, December 13.

López, J. A. (2002). 'The Empirical Relationship between Average Asset Correlation, Firm Probability of Default and Asset Size'. Paper presented at BIS Workshop Basel II: An Economic Assessment, May.

Ocampo, J. A. and Chiappe, M. L. (2003). *Counter-Cyclical Prudential and Capital Account Regulations in Developing Countries*. Sweden: EGDI.

Persaud, A. (2003). 'Liquidity Black Holes: and Why Modern Financial Regulation in Developed Countries is Making Short Term Capital Flows to Developing Countries Even More Volatile', in R. Ffrench-Davis and S. Griffith-Jones (eds.), *From Surges to Draught*. London: Macmillan Palgrave.

Powell, A. (2002). *A Capital Accord for Emerging Economies?* Buenos Aires: Universidad Torcuato Di Tella.

Shiller, R. J. (2000). *Irrational Exuberance*. Princeton, NJ: Princeton University Press.

Singh, A. (1997). 'The Stockmarket, the Financing of Corporate Growth and Indian Industrial Development'. *Journal of International Finance*.

Weder, B. and Wedow, M. (2002). 'Will Basel II Affect International Capital Flows to Emerging Markets?'. Technical Paper No. 199, OECD Development Centre.

11

Consequences of Liberalizing Derivatives Markets

Randall Dodd

11.1 Introduction

Derivatives are financial contracts whose price is *derived* from the value of an underlying item such as a commodity, security, rate, index, or event.[1] While derivatives markets have been in existence for a very long time, and by historical accounts they date back to at least 1700 BC, it has been their growth in the past 25 years that has made them one of the pillars of financial systems.[2] As of 2006, the outstanding amount of derivatives on global exchanges and over-the-counter (OTC) markets exceeds $485 trillion (Bank for International Settlements 2007; Dodd 2004b).

Derivatives markets are growing rapidly in developed as well as developing economies. Ranked by the number of futures and options contracts traded, derivatives exchanges in developing countries from Latin America and Asia now rank amongst the largest in the world. The world's largest derivative contract by trading volume is no longer that on the US Treasury Bond or Eurodollar interest rate, but now it is an option on the Korean stock index (data from FIA 2004 and discussed in Dodd 2004a). Foreign exchange trading volume in 24 developing countries, which includes spot, forwards, and foreign exchange swaps, doubled from 1998 to 2004 to reach $32.6 trillion.[3] Of the 11 developing countries, including Hong Kong and Singapore, that reported significant OTC derivatives activity, their trading volume rose from

---

[1] The term derivatives is used to mean financial instruments such as futures, forwards, swaps, options, and structured securities. For a more complete definition and description see Dodd (2000a, b).

[2] For an excellent history of derivatives see Swain (1993, 2000).

[3] Author's calculation from BIS Triennial survey for 2004—figures are for geographical distribution and not currency denomination, and data excludes Singapore and Hong Kong.

$0.5 trillion in 1998 to $3.6 trillion in 2004.[4] Section 11.2 below will provide some indicators of the size and growth of derivatives markets in developing economies. Despite the tremendous growth in the size and use of derivatives markets, their role in economic development and their regulatory treatment have received far less attention than that for banking and securities markets.

In a manner consistent with this neglect, the push to liberalize capital markets in developing countries in the 1990s showed no apparent concern for the potential dangers of unregulated derivatives markets. The need to address these dangers was most likely neglected for the following two reasons. One reason is that the push to liberalize financial markets focused largely on the elimination of controls, restrictions, taxes, and generally any regulation of capital flows. This focused attention on bank lending, securities issuances and trading, and foreign direct investment; and it focused attention away from introducing regulation on new areas of financial activity. The consequence was to overlook the fact that trading in derivative instruments is often closely related to transactions involving international capital flows.[5] The second reason stems from the theoretical economic framework that served as the foundation for capital market liberalization. This economic theory held that financial markets sufficiently disciplined themselves, and that they were more efficient than those distorted by government regulation. The theory concluded that the fewer the regulations, or the lower the degree of regulation, then the higher the degree of economic efficiency. The consequence was to build policy upon the sometimes unfounded assumptions of the theory and not upon the actual market conditions in developing countries.

In hindsight, this proved to be a costly error irrespective of whether it was due to an oversight or ideological over-confidence. If developing countries were imprudent to remove all capital controls and deregulate their banking sectors, then they were even more reckless in their treatment of derivatives.

In order to help rectify this omission in the future, this chapter provides a policy analysis that will lay out an analysis of the public interest concerns with derivatives trading in developing countries and suggest a set of regulatory measures to reduce derivatives-related financial sector vulnerability as well as to increase their efficiency.

While derivatives performed the economically useful purpose of risk shifting (hedging) and price discovery,[6] they also created new risks that were

---

[4] Author's calculation from BIS Triennial survey for 2004—figures are for geographical distribution and not currency denomination, and data excludes Singapore and Hong Kong.

[5] See Dodd (2002b) for a discussion of how the use of derivatives can shape capital flows to developing countries.

[6] Price discovery, which will be treated below, refers to the economic process of establishing prices in markets.

potentially destabilizing for developing economies. The following is an analysis of how derivatives played a constructive role in channeling capital from advanced capital markets to developing economies, and how at the same time they generated new levels of exposure to the stability of the financial system and the overall economies of developing countries.

The potential problem with derivatives can be broken down into two categories. The first category concerns issues that arise from the 'abuse or misuse' of derivatives. This includes fraud, manipulation, tax evasion or avoidance, and the distortion of information that is vital for the efficiency of the market. The second category pertains to the negative consequences from derivatives trading and derivatives markets. Whether or not derivatives are used or misused, improperly regulated derivatives markets can result in the creation of new risks, greater levels of market risk for a given amount of capital in the financial system, greater amounts of credit risk and in higher degrees of financial sector vulnerability. Section 11.3 below will address the many components of both categories of problems related to derivatives markets.

Taken together, these potential problems pose a substantial safety and soundness challenge to developing economies, and they therefore warrant immediate regulatory remedy. Towards this end, Section 11.4 of this chapter concludes with a policy proposal that is designed to curtail if not eliminate these problems while encouraging the use of derivatives for productive purposes.

11.2 Expanding the Definition of 'Capital Markets'

The usual definition of capital market liberalization, including both the policy principles and their implementation, needs to be broadened so as to encompass derivatives markets and their impact on economic stability. Establishing the notion of derivatives markets as an integral part of financial markets will help address the concerns that the inadequate regulatory treatment was due to their being overlooked.

A more complete view of capital markets is, by analogy, a four-legged table made up of securities markets (issuing and trading bonds and equity shares), banking industry (issuing loans and providing payment and settlement services), insurance and pension funds (providing future income and collateral for lending), and derivatives markets (risk management and price discovery). All four legs serve to support the table, and it is no more stable than its weakest leg.

It is perilous to focus exclusively on securities and banking even though that does describe the largest share of developing country financial market activities in the past. Derivatives have been growing rapidly in scope and scale, and they have already asserted themselves is financial crises.[7] Their presence was an important factor in the financial crises in Mexico, East Asia, Russia, and Turkey.

11.2.1 *The Presence of Derivatives in Developing Countries*

Worldwide, derivatives markets are huge, growing rapidly and expanding into developing countries. By some measures, derivatives markets are larger than those for securities, banking, and insurance. Although the exact size is unknown due to limited data collection efforts, the Bank for International Settlements (BIS) collects some aggregated data from the largest over-the-counter dealers and derivatives exchanges around the world. Their 2004 triennial survey of derivatives dealers shows that annual trading volume in OTC foreign exchanges derivatives for five Latin America countries (Brazil, Chile, Colombia, Mexico, and Peru) was $1,788 billion and for five East Asian countries (Indonesia, Korea, Malaysia, Philippines, and Thailand) it was $3,773 billion. The total figure for OTC foreign exchange derivatives trading in just these ten countries is $5,560 billion, compared with $448.2 trillion for the worldwide total. The figure for Hong Kong and Singapore—developing countries with especially sophisticated international financial markets—was $41,169 billion. The tremendous growth since 2004, especially in Latin America, would surely show even more remarkable growth.

Consider also the rise of derivatives exchanges in developing countries. The Futures Industry Association in the US makes an annual survey of futures trading activity around the world (see FIA 2004). Measured by the number of futures contracts traded, three of the largest futures exchange were in developing countries in 2003: Mexico's Merder is fifth, Brazilian BM&F is ranked sixth, and China's Dalian is ranked ninth. Other futures exchange from developing countries include the Korean Stock Exchange (eleventh), Shanghai Futures Exchange (thirteenth), National Stock Exchange of India (fourteenth), and South Africa's JSE Securities Exchange (twenty-third). Others in the top 40 include Paraguay, Malaysia, Hungary, and another Korean exchange. The exchanges in developing countries were also among the fastest growing, and so they will likely continue moving up the world ranking over the next few years.

Another way to look at this is by individual futures contracts. The FIA survey also shows that world's largest contract measured by trading volume is Korea's stock index option on the KOSPI 200 index. Mexico's TIIE 28 futures is the fourth largest.[8] Others in the top 20 include futures contracts on the KOSPI

---

[7] See Garber and Lal (1996), Garber (1998), Kregel (1998a, b), and Dodd (2002a), for discussions of the role of derivatives in the Mexican and East Asian financial crises of the 1990s.

[8] This 28 day interest rate on interbank loans is comparable to a LIBOR in pesos.

200 in Korea, soybean futures in China and an interest rate future in Brazil. These rankings are impressive in light of the fact that they are competing with other futures and options contracts that have been around for 25 years or more.

As a brief description, the Brazilian Mercantile and Futures Exchange (BM&F) trades a wide variety of futures, forwards, and options on interest rates, exchange rates, stock indexes, gold, foreign currency spreads, sovereign debt instruments, soybean, corn, sugar, coffee, live cattle, anhydrous alcohol fuel, and cotton. Trading occurs through the traditional open outcry methods and electronic traded platforms that use automated order matching systems. The BM&F also facilitates OTC derivatives trades. Through the BM&F alone, Brazil is trading over 235 million futures and options contracts in 2003 (this does not include the registration of OTC traded contracts).

Another example is Korea where the Korean Stock Exchange and the Korean Futures Exchange trade futures and options in interest rates, government securities, stock indexes, commodities, and foreign currency. Through these two exchanges, Korea traded over 2,975 million futures and options contracts in 2003.

Another part of the picture of these opaque markets concerns OTC options on emerging market debt. Gosain (1994) cites data from Paribas that trading volume in options on developing country sovereign debt rose from $1 billion in 1989, to $20 billion in 1991, and to $70 billion in 1993 (measured in notional value). The most popular options were on debt from Argentina, Brazil, Mexico, Venezuela, and Poland. The article contains at least one very alarming observation that because of lower costs of funding, local financial institutions in Mexico, Argentina, and Brazil were 'better buyers of call options' while their American and European counterparts were better sellers. The alarming feature is that developing countries, who were capital importers, were taking long derivatives positions on their own securities. That is not hedging because it does not reduce risk, rather it is taking on additional risk and is using OTC derivatives to speculate.

11.2.2 Derivatives and Growth in Capital Markets

Derivatives function in a way that is complementary with the economic functions of capital markets, and so it is not surprising to see them growing alongside each other. Derivatives markets emerged along with these forms of capital flows as part of an effort to better manage the risks of global investing. In doing so, derivatives facilitated the flow of capital by unbundling risk[9] in its component parts and redistributing risks away from investors who did not

---

[9] Unbundling refers to the practice of separating out the currency risk, interest rate risk, credit risk, and other types of risk associated with an investment and then treating them separately.

Table 11.1. Trading Volume

	1992	1993	1994	1995	1996	1997	1998	1999	2000	2001
Brady Bonds	248	1021	1684	1580	2690	2403	1541	771	712	573
Non-Brady	23	177	159	211	568	1335	1021	626	936	1255
Loans	229	274	244	175	249	305	213	69	99	37
Local Market	NA	NA	524	593	1274	1506	1176	599	993	1517
Derivatives	NA	57	142	179	471	367	223	119	106	102

Note: *US $billions, measured at year end.

Source: Data from EMTA.

want the exposure and towards those investors more willing and able to bear it. In the words of the annual report of the Emerging Markets Traders Association or EMTA (2001): 'Along with this increase in investment instruments, and in the development of their market place, has come greater liquidity and innovation in the use of derivative instruments, including non-deliverable currency forwards and various structured products'. Similarly, in Mathieson et al. (2004), co-author Anna Ilyina states: 'There is a broad consensus that the rapid expansion of derivatives products during the past 10 to 15 years was one of the key factors that facilitated the rise of global cross-border capital flows.'

As for empirical data, one survey that includes emerging market countries comes from the Emerging Market Traders Association (EMTA). Table 11.1 shows that from 1992 to 2001 the growth in derivatives trading volume grew and then contracted in parallel with trading in credit instruments.

A good illustration of the relationship between derivatives and capital markets is to identify the presence of derivatives features in some more conventional financial instruments. The convertible bond issued by corporations is comprised of a conventional bond plus a call option on the price of the corporation's stock (and implicitly contains a put option on the debt itself). This lowers the corporation's interest cost of issuing the debt instrument, and at the same time the call option can be inexpensively covered with unissued stock. The investor can gain if the stock price rises above the call's exercise price, or if the market interest rate rises so as to lower the present value of the bond's interest and principle payments.

Yet another illustrative example comes from an earlier period of development in North America. In the early 1860s, the Treasury of the Confederate States of America issued various types of bonds that were structured with a long call option position in currency and commodities. In one instance, a structured bond contained a long call option provision that granted the investor the right to be paid the principal and interest in either Confederate dollars or New Orleans Middling Grade Cotton. Another more creative Confederate issue was designed as a tri-valued call option that paid upon maturity the higher of 100 pounds sterling, 2,500 French francs, or 4,000 pounds of cotton.[10]

Another good illustration of how derivatives can facilitate capital formation is the callable bond. This instrument is comprised of a conventional bullet bond plus a short call option (usually with an exercise price equal to par or 100 percent of principal). This option allows the bond issuer to gain by recalling the bond if market interest rates decline sufficiently.

Similar structures have been used to enhance capital flows to developing countries. The IMF's Global Financial Stability Report (IMF 2002) shows that bonds and loans issued by sovereign borrowers in developing countries used a substantial number of features described as call options, put options, and structured notes. In 1997, for example, options were attached to $7.6 billion of the emerging market sovereign bonds and loans issued that year. This amounted to about 7.6 percent of total sovereign borrowing in that year.

In contrast, a bad example if this type of instrument is found in the put able bonds and bank loans used in capital flows to developing countries during the 1990s. These put options were in the form of 'hard' and 'soft' puts. Hard puts, usually attached to a note or bond, gave the lender the right to demand principal repayment after a certain date, e.g., a five year note might be put able after one year. Soft puts, usually attached to loans, gave lenders the right to reschedule the terms of their credit in the event of certain adverse 'events'. These attached put options facilitated lending by lowering interest costs to borrowers and by giving lenders greater assurance of recovering their principal. Putable debt is a bad example because it creates liquidity shortages in the event of a financial disruption, and it does so just at the time in which liquidity is crucial for the successful functioning of the financial sector. In sum, put able debt tends to increase indebtedness and does so in a manner that exacerbates financial disruptions.[11]

Most of the 'hard' put options were closer to the European rather than the American style option. In these cases, which are sometimes called 'Bermuda options', the lenders were granted the right to exercise the option only on specific days or perhaps semiannually; in only a very few cases were the options exercisable on a continuous basis like American options.

This put able debt instrument was used widely in the rapidly growing East Asian bond market. The IMF estimated in 1999, using available public databases, that there were $32 billion in debts put able through the end of 2000 for all emerging countries. Of the total is $23 billion from East Asian issuers,

---

[10] See Markham (1994) for this and other exemplary derivatives accounts.

[11] There is a limited but positive case than can be made for put options on local currency sovereign debt. See Neftci and Santos (2003).

Table 11.2. Putable Bonds Issued from East Asia Countries

$ million due in 1999 or 2000	
Hong Kong	2,642
Indonesia	963
Korea	3,986
Malaysia	1,730
Thailand	1,313
Total	10,634

Note: Involving the Private Sector in Forestalling and Resolving Financial Crises.
Source: IMF (1999).

and $8 billion was from Brazil (IMF 1999).[12] Of this $23 billion, $10.6 billion was in the form of bonds issued from the East Asian countries listed in Table 11.2. Of this East Asian debt putable through 2000, $11.5 billion are notes and bonds, and $12 billion is in loans. An estimated 90 percent of the total put able debt was issued by private, as opposed to government, borrowers. Similarly, Table 11.3 shows the case of put options on loan contracts.

According to an IMF memo written in the summer of 1997, there were instances of the use of *both* call and put options on bond principal and coupons in East Asia. The issuer held the call option in the event that interest rates fell, and the investor held the put option in the event of a decline in the credit rating of the issuer.[13] Of course, it is the short put position rather

Table 11.3. Loans with Put Options Issued From East Asia

$ million due in 1999 or 2000	
Hong Kong	1,549
Indonesia	2,876
Korea	3,263
Malaysia	547
Philippines	75
Singapore	532
Thailand	1,680
Total	10,522

Note: Involving the Private Sector in Forestalling and Resolving Financial Crises.
Source: IMF (1999).

[12] Note that the disaggregated figures in the tables do not add to $23 billion due to rounding and the exclusion of non-crisis countries such as Vietnam.
[13] IMF Office Memorandum on private market financing for emerging markets: developments for the second quarter of 1997, July 17, 1997.

Table 11.4. Emerging Market Sovereign Debt Issuance ($ million)

Putable Debt	3,052	4,064	2,543	1,295	2,062
Bonds	2,497	3,706	2,449	1,030	2,062
Loans	555	358	94	265	0
No. of issuances[1]	22	12	12	7	3
Total Debt Issuance	100,401	90,567	63,032	63,028	55,413
Percent putable	3.0%	4.5%	4.0%	2.1%	3.7%

Note: [1] Includes bonds and loans.

Source: IMF, Global Financial Stability Report, March 2002.

than the long call option position that poses potential problems to financial market stability in emerging economies.

The latest data on the issuance of putable debt comes from the IMF's Global Financial Stability Report from March 2002. This report contained a table reporting on the issuance of such debt for 1997 through 2001. This information is contained in Table 11.4 above.

The above discussion of how derivatives can enhance familiar capital vehicles[14] is but part of the whole picture. More generally, derivatives facilitate capital flows for reasons elaborated below in Section 11.3 on the useful economic functions of derivatives.

11.3 Use and Abuse of Derivatives

Derivatives markets provide at least two important benefits to the economy. One is that they facilitate risk shifting, which is also known as risk management or hedging. The other benefit is that they create price discovery—the process of determining the price level for a commodity, asset, index, rate, event, or other item.

The risk shifting function of derivatives facilitates capital flows by unbundling and then more efficiently reallocating the various sources of risk associated with traditional capital vehicles such as bank loans, equities, bonds, and direct foreign investment. Foreign currency loans expose the foreign investor to credit risk and the domestic borrower to exchange rate risk; a fixed interest rate loan exposes the foreign lender to interest rate risk and a variable rate loan exposes the domestic borrower to interest rate risk; and a long-term loan exposes the foreign lender to greater credit risk and a short-term loan exposes the domestic borrower to refunding risk (sometimes called liquidity risk). Equities expose the foreign investor to credit risk along with the market risk from changes in the exchange rate, market price of the stock, and the uncertain dividend payments. Notes and bonds expose the foreign investor to credit risk and market interest rate risk, and in the case

[14] That is, bank loans, equities, bonds, and direct foreign investment.

of hard currency bonds, expose the domestic borrower to exchange rate risk. The financial innovation of introducing derivatives to capital markets allows these traditional arrangements of risk to be redesigned so as to better meet the desired risk profiles of the issuers and holders of these capital instruments.[15]

Another economic benefit is price discovery; its importance, however, is not often reflected in public policy. One key exception can be found in US statutes governing derivatives regulation. Section 3 of the Commodity Exchange Act, entitled 'The Necessity of Regulation', stated—until being amended by the deregulatory Commodity Futures Modernization Act of 2002—the following prescient economic point.

'Futures' are affected with a national public interest. Such futures transactions are carried on in large volume by the public generally and by persons engaged in the business of buying and selling commodities and the products and byproducts thereof in interstate commerce. The prices involved in such transactions are generally quoted and disseminated throughout the United States and foreign countries as a basis for determining the prices to the producer and consumer of commodities and the products and by-products thereof and to facilitate the movements thereof in interstate commerce. Such transactions are utilized by shippers, dealers, millers, and others engaged in handling commodities . . . The transactions and prices of commodities on such boards of trade are susceptible to excessive speculation and can be manipulated, controlled, cornered or squeezed, to the detriment of the producer or the consumer and the persons handling commodities and products and byproducts thereof in interstate commerce, rendering regulation imperative for the protection of such commerce and the national public interest therein.

In other words, price discovery is so important for the efficient working of the economy that it is imperative that the integrity of prices be protected. In the case of the US law cited above, this includes statutory prohibitions on fraud and manipulation and regulatory oversight efforts to detect and deter manipulation before it occurs.

Derivatives can provide additional economic benefits by helping to complete otherwise imperfect commodity or securities markets, and they can help arbitrage between markets so that prices come to more efficiently reflect all the relevant information in the market.

While Section 11.2 addressed the problem of derivatives markets being ignored as part of financial markets, this section addresses the problem of the lack of a theoretical economic framework to analyze the private and social costs and benefits of derivatives and thereby to determine the most appropriate form of regulation for these markets.

While the risk shifting function of derivatives serves the useful role of hedging and thereby facilitating capital flows, and the price discovery process

---

[15] A good, short exposition of this point is made by John Chrystal (1996), and for a more complete discussion of this point see Dodd (2002b).

enhances the efficiency of financial as well as commodity markets, the enlarged presence of derivatives also raises concerns about the integrity, efficiency, and vulnerability of the financial system and economy as a whole.

The public interest concerns with derivatives in developing countries can be broken down into two categories. The first is best described as 'abuse of derivatives', and the second can be described as 'negative consequences' from the misuse of derivatives. The former pose a threat to the integrity of markets and the information content of prices. In other words, they increase capital costs due to lower trust and confidence in financial and commodity markets, and they reduce market efficiency by distorting, or posing a threat to the distortion of, market prices. The category of 'abuse' covers problems that arise from deliberate efforts to engage in destructive competition, such as fraud or market manipulation, deliberate efforts to engage in tax evasion or avoidance, and efforts—whether deliberate or not—that result in a distortion of information about a country's balance of payments (especially the capital account), a firm's income or balance sheet and expectations regarding the future depreciation of a developing country's currency.

The later category of 'misuse' poses a threat to the stability of the financial sector and the overall economy by increasing systemic risk, risk of contagion and possibly serving as a catalyst, or an accelerator, to financial disruption or crisis. The category of 'misuse' covers negative consequences that arise even if derivatives are being used primarily for hedging or risk management pursuits. The presence of poorly structured and improperly regulated derivatives markets can generate new risks, new levels of existing risk and create new economy-wide vulnerabilities. Even though individual firms and investors successfully hedge by shifting risk from those who can least bear it and towards those who are more willing and able to do so, the entire financial sector now includes new and greater risks from the presence of this trading activity and the resulting outstanding derivatives contracts.

This last point is not to argue that the cost of these negative consequences is a sufficient case for prohibiting the use of derivatives. Nor is the point simply that these costs must be less than the benefit of hedging in order to justify the presence of derivatives markets. Rather, the primary point is to identify and analyze the origin of the costs in order to assess whether they can be adequately reduced through appropriate regulatory measures.

The remainder of this section elaborates on the two basic categories of problems and breaks down each into its own relevant components.

11.3.1 *Abuse: Threats to Market Integrity and Efficiency*

FRAUD

In order to protect investors in their efforts to better manage risk through the use of derivatives, and therefore also to encourage more hedging and risk management activity so as to benefit from the improvements in economic welfare that it can generate, it is imperative that derivatives markets be protected from a form of destructive competition such as fraud and manipulation. It is an especially critical issue in derivatives markets, much like it is in securities markets, because the contracts invariably involve commitments over time. A cash-and-carry market is by comparison much more capable of self-policing. In contrast, the time dimension often results in the fraud not being noticed for some period of time, which allows the perpetrators to avoid detection or prosecution. In addition, time itself has value in financial terms and so this can further add to the magnitude of the loss.

Derivatives transactions also are susceptible to fraud because the parties— both the ultimate counterparties as well as intermediaries—are often in distant locations. Separated by space and time, derivatives transactions can be plagued by 'sharp', 'misleading', 'false promises of returns', or other 'boiler room' sales practices. Embezzlement is another type of problem arising from the differences in time and place. Additional unfair or fraudulent derivatives trading practices include 'fictitious trading', 'wash trades', misuse of market information, and 'front running' (trading ahead of customer orders). These activities can rob investors of part or all of the full value of their investment positions. Taken together, they can impose a substantial cost on risk management efforts and discourage firms and individuals from doing so.

As a matter of experience, the practice of fraud in derivatives trading is a major concern even in well established financial markets such as the US. There, the chief derivatives regulatory agency, the Commodity Futures Trading Commission, dedicates at least 29 percent of its resources to enforcement.[16] The US experience with fraudulent sales practices in derivatives, especially in the trading of options, has motivated periodic prohibitions on options trading and has resulted in a much higher supervisory and regulatory standard for options than futures or securities trading. This experience is applicable to developing countries if they adopt policy or programs such as the market-based recommendations by the World Bank's International Task Force on Commodity Risk Management in Developing Countries.[17]

MANIPULATION

Manipulation is not simply buying or selling for the purpose of driving prices up or down. In order to be successful, the manipulator must be able to profit from doing so. Simply buying or selling to move the market price will not necessarily allow the investor to profit because the act of selling at the

---

[16] CFTC budget request for fiscal year 2003 from letter of transmittal to Congressional Appropriations Committees, February 4, 2002.

[17] Summary of the Second ITF Meeting, May 3, 1999. The principal document is *Dealing with Commodity Price Volatility in Developing Countries: A Proposal for a Market Based Approach* (September 1999).

artificially high price will lower the price (or buying at the artificially low price will raise the price). The following is an overview of the basic types of market manipulation and the economic consequences of this form of destructive competition.

Known as information-based manipulation, this type of manipulation involves insider trading or making false reports on the market. An example of the former is the manner in which Enron executives made early moves to cash out their employee stock options and sell their Enron security holdings before the condition of the firm was known in the market. An example of the latter is a scandal in which stock analysts at Wall Street firms made 'buy' recommendations to their customers and the wider market so that their firms profit from securities underwriting and other business relationships. Derivatives facilitate this type of manipulation if they are excluded from reporting requirements (such as reporting the sale of equity shares by corporate executives.)

Action-based manipulation involves some deliberate activity that changes the actual or perceived value of a commodity or asset. This type of manipulation might occur when a firm's managers short sell the firm's stock and then announce to the public the loss of an important contract or the closing of a factory. After they profitably cover their short positions by buying at lower prices, they can capture further gains by announcing the negotiation of new contracts or opening new factories. Note that these two examples show that action-based manipulation can be combined with insider trading. Similarly, but without insider information, investors may take a position on the stock and then pursue legislation or regulatory changes that might change the value of the assets. Derivatives facilitate this type of manipulation by helping to capture the gains from such a price change and, in the case of OTC derivatives, by allowing the perpetrator to build up a position without the market or any one counterparty detecting the entire position.

The classic case of manipulation is trade-based and it involves either unexpectedly amassing a large position in the market, or more likely it entails using one market to capture the gains from creating a price distortion in another interrelated market. Derivatives are critical in this strategy. How does this work? In the latter case, a manipulator acquires a large long position in the derivatives market by entering forward or swap contracts for future delivery or future payments based on the future price. If the derivatives positions were transacted through the OTC market, then neither the government nor other market competitor would be able to observe the total position of the manipulator. Next the manipulator goes into the spot or cash market and amasses a large enough inventory (and also contracts to sell it to buyers who will not resell it) in order to push up the present price. This raises the value of the long derivatives positions so that they can be offset, exercised, or settled profitably. Then if the manipulator can sell off the amassed inventory without incurring substantial losses, the manipulation will be successful. This can work in a similar manner for a downward manipulation of market prices by building up a short position in derivatives and then engaging in sufficient selling or short selling in the cash or spot market to drive the price downwards.

What are the public interest concerns with fraud and manipulation? The prices established in derivatives markets are important because they are used not only by those directly involved in the market but also by producers and consumers throughout the economy. This economic meaning is expressed in the quote from the US Commodity Exchange Act in Section 11.3 above, and its economic significance is immense. Manipulation is thus a matter of public interest not just because it is a problem for those who incur losses as a result of another person's price manipulations, but also because it threatens the integrity of the price signals and market activity throughout the economy. The damages are not limited to the trading counterparties and thus cannot be remedied through a lawsuit by one counterparty against another.

Although not all derivatives markets result in price discovery, many of them do and many others can potentially serve this economic function. Price discovery pertains to not only the spot or cash market price of the underlying commodity or asset, but also its future prices and, in the case of options trading, the market value of the volatility of those prices. Price discovery certainly occurs in markets where derivatives are traded on exchanges. It also occurs in many OTC markets. However, in these dealer-based markets, the price discovery process is often not known by the entire market or the overall economy but is instead shared only among the major market participants. The fact that these prices are not known directly and immediately throughout the economy does not mean that price discovery does not occur; rather it poses a source of economic inefficiency due to the asymmetric distribution of this information.

Derivatives markets provide economically useful tools for hedging and risk management, and the extent of their use depends on investors' trust and confidence in the integrity of trading practices and market prices. If incidents of manipulation taint the public perception of derivatives markets, then market activity will suffer from lower trading volume—thus reducing liquidity—and possibly causing a higher risk premium to be priced into the bid–ask spread. Derivatives markets need a diversity of participants with varying market views because they depend upon people taking long as well as short positions. In contrast to a marketplace tainted by scandal, one that holds the public trust will provide the basis for the creation of more liquid and efficient markets.

Manipulation does not have to be grand in order to be destructive. Some manipulation cases involve only small changes in prices that generate large gains through large derivatives positions. Similarly, small distortions in prices can have a profound impact on living standards—especially if they affect major cash crops, commodity exports, or key consumer goods.

The famous copper price manipulation by Sumitomo Bank in 1995 and 1996 pushed prices above fair market value for an extended period of time. While some of the benefits likely fell upon exporters such as Chile and Zambia, the costs fell upon much of the developed and developing world. Similarly, oil price manipulation in the fall of 2001 by Arcadia (a British subsidiary of the Japanese firm Mitsui) affected the import costs of many developing economies. The 1989 soybean price manipulation by the Italian commodity firm Ferruzzi pushed up the cost of food and animal feed. All three of these instances involved the use of derivatives as part of a ploy to manipulate commodity prices that were crucial to developing economies.[18]

UNPRODUCTIVE ACTIVITIES

Investors sometimes abuse derivatives in order to manipulate accounting rules and financial reporting requirements, to dodge prudential market regulations, or to evade or avoid taxation.

Manipulate Accounting Rules: Accounting rules provide uniform standards for defining revenue, costs, and income, as well as for identifying assets and liabilities. In the face of these rules, which include even elaborate rules such as FAS 133 in the US, derivatives present powerful tools to transform incomes across time and national boundaries, fabricate revenue and income, and hide debt and other liabilities. The large corporate failures of Enron and others since December of 2001 have brought to light a host of these practices. So far the regulatory response has focused on corporate governance and has avoided reforming the accounting rules for reporting the use of derivatives. One reason is that accounting rules are difficult to change, and so it is very important that they are done right the first time. This is a valuable lesson for developing countries.

Outflank Prudential Regulations: Prudential regulations work by prohibiting, restricting, or discouraging certain types of activities. For example, commercial banks might be prohibited from holding equity shares on their balance sheets, they might be restricted from lending more than a specified percentage of their assets or capital to any one entity, and they might be assessed a higher capital requirement for some assets rather than others in order to discourage certain types of risk taking. The use of derivatives can allow banks to work around these restrictions. In the words of a former staff members of the IMF and European Commission, Steinherr (1998: 121): 'But derivatives allowed Mexican banks to circumvent national regulations and to build up a foreign exchange position outside of official statistics and unknown to policy-makers and a large of part of market participants. When the crisis arrived the surprise unfolded and turned a crisis into a catastrophe'. Again, he states (Steinherr

---

[18] For a longer discussion of these types and cases of market manipulation through the use of derivatives see Dodd and Hoody (2002).

1998: 278) what he describes as a fundamental proposition: 'Derivatives allow financial institutions to change the shape of financial instruments in such a way as to circumvent financial regulations in a fully legal way.'

The use of derivatives to circumvent or outflank prudential regulation has been acknowledged by the IMF, World Bank, and the OECD among others. The IMF's David Folkerts-Landau stated, 'Financial restrictions on such positions [domestic equity markets] are being circumvented through derivatives transactions' (quoted in Nussbaum 1997). The World Bank's Global Development Finance 2000 stated it in the following way: 'Brazil's complex system of prudential safeguards was easily circumvented by a well-developed financial market and over-the-counter derivatives'. The point was similarly stated in an OECD Economics Department Working Paper by Blondal and Christiansen (1999): 'The expansion of financial derivatives, which regulators have found difficult to control, has also seriously undermined prudential controls on currency exposure'.

The presence of derivatives markets pose a threat to a nation's tax system if it is not frequently updated in order to stay on top of new developments in those markets. This problem is doubly important for a developing economy whose tax base is not as well established, and where erosion of the tax base can threaten critical budgetary shortfalls that can lead to excess monetary expansion or greater foreign borrowing. Derivatives can restructure other financial transactions so that they appear to occur as capital gains instead of interest or dividend payments (or vice versa), or as long-term capital gains instead of short-term ones. In the US for example, an employee stock option program can transform compensation from salary income to capital gains and then get taxed at the lower long term capital gains rate.

In addition to raising funds to support government activities, some tax provisions are designed also to enhance regulatory safeguards by raising the relative costs of certain undesirable financial activities. For instance, short-term capital gains may be taxed at a higher rate than long-term gains in order to discourage short term speculation. Using derivatives, payments can be transformed from one type into another so as to evade the disincentives.

Distort Information: Although some of the issues in this subsection could also fit into some of the above categories, the importance of information in the smooth and efficient working of markets warrants special attention. The focus will be on three key locations: firm level financial reports on income and balance sheets; balance of payments or 'official statistics'; and false or misleading indicators of a currency devaluation.

Accounting rules are used to calculate profits and losses, designate assets and liabilities, and determine tax liabilities and capital requirements. Derivatives can distort the meaning of corporate income and balance sheets as the basis for measuring the profitability and risk profile of firms. Profitability can be distorted by fabricating income or revenue or moving it from one period to the next. Debt can be hidden through such derivatives as pre-paid forwards and swaps. Off-balance sheet positions, such as derivatives, can reverse, exaggerate, or dwarf the risk exposure indicated by items on the balance sheet. In short, derivatives can drive a wedge between total risk exposure and that reflected by a corporation's balance sheets.

For instance, a publicly traded corporation in Korea might report a balance sheet showing equal amounts of dollar assets and liabilities so as to reflect a neutral or balanced foreign exchange position. Yet it may have off-balance sheet derivatives positions that create substantially large short dollar positions. When Hong Kong-based Peregrine Securities failed in January of 1998, it drew attention to this distinction. The World Bank's Global Development Finance (1999: ch. 2) reported that its off-balance sheet liabilities were ten times what was reported on its balance sheet. The probable cause of this was an off-balance derivatives position that generated massive losses.

In the US, a recent survey of businesses reveals that 42 percent use derivatives primarily to 'manage reported earnings' such as by moving income from one period to another (cited in Woolley 1999). Another example drawn for the US experience involves the mortgage titans Fannie Mae and Freddie Mac, which are the world's largest hedgers, who filed financial reports which falsely understated the value of their derivatives positions by billions of dollars. The collapse of the energy merchant corporation Enron exposed their extensive use of derivatives for the purpose of fabricating income and revenue, hiding debt, as well as manipulating market prices. Although these examples are from a developed economy, they show that in an otherwise well regulated financial market derivatives misuse can lead to distorted market information.

In these ways the presence of derivatives can make it difficult for firms to make an accurate assessment of their counterparties' creditworthiness. Similarly, it makes it difficult for regulatory authorities to detect financial sector weaknesses, market manipulation and fraud. Although in some cases financial institutions are required to report on their credit exposure due to derivatives, that is not the case for their exposure to market risk. Thus, regulatory authorities cannot be fully informed. As a result, it is difficult for government regulators or supervisors to track the sensitivity of the economy to changes in certain key market variables such as interest rates and exchange rates. The former chief economist of the World Bank, Joseph Stiglitz (1998), put it this way, 'The increased use of derivatives [in developing economies] is increasingly making the full disclosure of relevant information, or at least the full interpretation of the disclosed information, even more difficult'.

This de-linking of risk exposure from balance sheets occurs not only with corporations but also in regards to a nation's balance sheet, and this applies to both their balance of payments accounts and fiscal accounts. A country's actual exposure to market risk was once reflected in the maturity and currency denomination of its foreign assets and liabilities as reported for its capital account in its balance of payments. Now those figures are less useful, if not misleading, because derivatives related currency exposures can add or subtract significantly from what is indicated by the capital or foreign investment positions. One notorious example can be found in Europe where several governments used derivatives to reduce their reported budget deficits in order to meet Maastricht Treaty restrictions on fiscal balances. In an introduction to a report on the incident by Benn Steil of the Council of Foreign Relations (Piga 2001): 'An actual market transaction documented by Piga indicates clearly that at least one euro zone country actively exploited ambiguity in accounting rules for swap transactions in order to mislead EU institutions, other EU national governments, and its own public as to the true size of its budget deficit.' The report's author, Gustavo Piga, concluded with the following warning: 'Window-dressing through derivatives might also be important in less-developed countries that have to implement ambitious fiscal stabilization programs'.

The currency denomination of assets and liabilities such as foreign loans can be changed with foreign exchange derivatives. Interest rate swaps can alter the interest rate exposure on assets and liabilities. Long-term loans can become short term ones if attached 'put' options are exercised. Even the form of capital or the investment vehicle can be transformed with derivatives. Total return swaps can make short term dollar loans (liabilities) appear as portfolio investments. Also, derivatives exposures can generate large, sudden cross-border transactions to meet margin calls or collateral calls, and the likelihood of these sudden flows would not otherwise be indicated by the amount of foreign debt and securities in a nation's balance of payments accounts. As a result, the balance of payments accounts no longer serve as well to assess country risk.

The use of derivatives by governments in the pursuit of public debt management poses similar dangers (Piga 2001). While some governments have used derivatives successfully to reduce their borrowing costs while encouraging the utmost in market liquidity in benchmark issues, only a few—and here only Sweden has been singled out as exemplary—have done so while maintaining market transparency.[19]

David Nussbaum (1997) explains that one of the 'main challenges facing the IMF due to the spread of derivatives is how to restructure the balance of payments accounting systems of its major member countries'. He paraphrases David Folkerts-Landau as saying that 'cross-country derivatives positions have

---

[19] According to Cassard and Folkerts-Landau (1997), countries setting up debt management agencies to pursue the goal of lowering borrowing costs include Austria, Belgium, Ireland, New Zealand, Portugal, and Sweden. They also mention that Colombia and Hungary were pursuing similar policies.

played havoc with the balance of payments data' and that 'one internal [IMF] estimate has off-balance positions potentially warping emerging market economic data by as much as 25%'. The report by Piga (2001), mentioned above, also draws attention to the need for public entities to conduct their use of derivatives in debt management practices with a high standard of transparency. Cassard and Folkerts-Landau (1997) also recommend transparency as a high policy priority.

Furthermore, the lack of transparency caused by off-balance sheet positions is also a problem for the public in their efforts to assess a central bank's ability to intervene in the foreign exchange market. The ability to intervene is critical in the context of a fixed exchange rate regime, but it is also important in the context of a floating rate system in order to stabilize the economy following a speculative attack or other financial market disruption. The problem arises when a central bank accurately reports the value of its foreign reserves, but does not report the amount they have contracted to sell in the future through foreign exchange forward and swap contracts.

The third type of information distortion concerns the price discovery process of derivatives markets in the context of fixed, and sometimes even floating, exchange rate regimes. Here the exchange rate or rates of primary concern are those between the local currency and the major world currencies such as the US dollar. In the developing country, the forward and swap market will create a market price[20] that will almost certainly indicate that the future value of the currency will be below the pegged spot rate. Relatively higher interest rates in the developing country together with interest rate parity will set a forward exchange rate higher than the spot rate and thus indicate a depreciation over the near term.[21]

In the context of a fixed exchange rate system, the higher forward or swap exchange rate will indicate a devaluation. This will regularly send the signal that the currency is going to move off the peg, and it will reflect the lack of confidence in the government's exchange rate policy. If, in the context of a fixed exchange rate system, the forward rate is not set according to interest rate parity conditions—and it makes sense that it might not because if the exchange rate peg holds then local currency sellers in the forward market continually lose as the fixed rate becomes in the future the spot rate—then the forward rate will be pricing the political viability of the exchange rate policy. In this case as well the derivatives markets is likely to pose a frustration to the government because currency appreciations are rare and so the forward rate will more likely be continually sending signals of a pending depreciation.

---

[20] The forward and swap exchange rates should be equivalent since the foreign exchange swap is just the combination of a spot and forward, or two forward, transactions.

[21] The exchange rate is defined as the local currency price of a unit of foreign currency so that a higher price, or a higher exchange rate, means that the local currency is worth less.

11.3.2 *Misuse: Vulnerability to Disruption and Crisis*

LEVERAGED RISK TAKING

One of the key features of derivatives contracts is that they provide leverage to hedgers and speculators alike. Leverage in this context means the quotient of the size of the price exposure, measured in notional value or the amount of underlying assets or commodities, divided by the amount of initial outlay required to enter the contract. Take, for example, the leverage provided by a futures contract on the Mexican peso traded on the Chicago Mercantile Exchange.[22] It has a notional value of 500,000 pesos, and the amount of initial margin (alternatively called collateral) required to open the position is $3250 for speculators and $2500 for hedgers and exchange members (who might otherwise be classified as speculators). The price exposure measured in dollars is about $45,500 (given that the peso is trading around 11 per US dollar), and so the leverage for speculators is 14 times the initial investment and for the hedgers it is 18.2. Similarly for the Brazilian real, the notional value is 100,000 reals, and the initial margin is $5600 for speculators and $4000 for hedgers and members. The rate of leverage is then 6.2 for speculators and 8.6 for hedgers and exchange members.[23]

This leverage for hedgers and speculators, whether using foreign exchange forwards, swaps, or options, lowers the costs of capital for taking the position (i.e., assuming the risk) and therefore raises the potential gain from such an undertaking. In addition to providing leverage, derivatives sometimes further lower the cost of taking on price exposure because of lower transaction costs and higher levels of liquidity. Together, these features facilitate greater risk-taking for a given amount of capital, and the extent of their use for risk-taking can result in greater overall levels of exposure to price risk for a given amount of capital in the financial system. This also has the consequence of encouraging greater amounts of currency speculation and empowering those who might mount a speculative attack on a country's currency regime.

The risk taking facilitated by derivatives can pose a problem even in the context of the Basel capital requirements. Consider an example of a developing country bank choosing between two investment strategies. One is to borrow abroad in US dollars and then make an outright purchase of 100 million pesos of a local corporate bond. The alternative is to enter a 100 million peso total return swap[24] in which the rate of return on the bond is swapped against LIBOR (plus a spread). Under Basel rules, the purchased securities would be treated as an asset on the bank's balance sheet and the bank would

---

[22] The exchange traded derivative is used as an example because its margin requirement is publicly known.

[23] Contract information is from the CME, and current exchange rates are from Bloomberg for December 2003.

[24] For a description of this type of derivative contract, see Dodd (2000a, 2002a).

be required to hold capital against those assets. At a capital requirement of 8 percent, this would require 8 million pesos in capital. Alternatively, the use of a total return swap would create the same investment position but would move it off-balance sheet. This off-balance sheet derivative would be treated as an asset and subject to capital requirements only to the extent that it had a positive present value (also called gross positive market value). This is because derivatives such as swaps are generally traded 'at the market' or 'par value' where their present value is zero. If there is no positive present value, then there is no capital requirement. Only if and to the extent that the swap were to 'move into the money'—perhaps as a result of falling LIBOR or local currency interest rates—would the bank be required to hold capital against the position. Even then, the swap would be cheaper in terms of capital costs because only the gain and not the entire notional principle would be assessed a capital charge of 8 percent.

This concern has come to the attention of the IMF report (1999: ch. 4, p. 119),

Third, the growing use of OTC derivatives and structured notes is increasing the ability of institutions to leverage up capital positions. The high levels of leverage may be creating financial systems that are capable of making costlier mistakes during periods of euphoria (exacerbating the boom) and that can magnify the adverse consequences of a negative shock or a reappraisal of risk.

Although alerted to this concern, it appears late for the purposes of the financial crises in Mexico, East Asia, Russia, and Brazil. And, although late, the IMF has never come forward with a specific policy response to this recognized problem. Although their reports often contain general statements about the need for prudential regulation, there is no apparent support for new measures of the type needed for derivatives. To the contrary, there are as many warnings and complaints about the dangers of any new regulation, such as in the *Global Financial Stability Report* (2003, March, ch. 4),

Whatever mix [regulation by government authority or a private self- regulatory organization] is decided upon, it is generally agreed that regulation and supervision should not be designed to stifle competition.

The main reasons for the underdevelopment of local derivatives markets are the underdevelopment of the underlying securities markets themselves, as well as tight regulations that restrict their use by banks and investors.

ILLIQUIDITY

The lack of liquidity, in other words the lack of active market trading, has adverse consequences for financial markets. It means that participants cannot adjust their positions, and it also means that there are no prices to serve as benchmark or reference prices for other related financial transactions.

Liquidity is especially critical in derivatives markets. While it is troublesome in securities markets because it hampers the ability of investors to adjust their positions and reduces price discovery, it is not as likely to leave investors with *new* levels of exposure. In derivatives markets, active trading is often a critical component of a risk management policy. Hedgers and speculators regularly trade in the market in order to dynamically manage their investment strategies. If that trading were to be interrupted, then it might prevent them from rolling over positions or offsetting positions or entering into new positions in derivatives, securities and other asset markets. This could leave investors with market risk exposures that they did not intend.

Liquidity is also important for derivatives markets because they depend critically on there being an equal number of those willing to take long and short positions. Illiquid derivatives markets can be the cause—as well as the effect—of one-sided markets. One possible consequence of this is to signal panic buying or selling or mania-based buying. To quote the IMF (2003), 'Problems arise when the [derivatives] market becomes one-sided as in Brazil's foreign exchange market by mid-2002, when the only supplier of foreign exchange hedge was the sovereign itself'.

OTC markets are much more prone to illiquidity problems. They are organized around dealers who act as multipoint market centers. However these dealers have no obligation to act as market makers—unlike their counterparts such as specialists on US stock exchanges or primary dealers in US OTC Treasury securities markets—and so they can and sometimes do withdraw from the market at critical times. Section 11.4 below addresses regulatory remedies to illiquidity under the heading, 'Orderly Market Rules'.

CYCLICAL EFFECT AND CRISIS ACCELERATOR

Derivatives help facilitate cross-border investments and thereby serve as a procyclical force in capital inflows. In the event of a downturn, devaluation, or financial disruption, they can play a stronger role to quicken the pace and deepen the impact of the crisis.

Derivatives transactions generally involve strict collateral or margin requirements. These require that a loss or decrease in the value of the position be matched by a commensurate amount of collateral—usually in the form of cash or government securities. Derivatives counterparties in developing countries, if they held some form of short dollar or other major currency position, would need to immediately post collateral in that currency following an adverse change in the market.

Consider the latter case of a Thai or Mexican bank entering a total rate of return swap in which they received the rate of return on a local security and paid US dollar LIBOR plus a spread. If the position moved against them, they would be required to post collateral in the form of US dollars or Treasury securities. A devaluation or broader financial crisis would then require the bank firm to immediately post US dollar assets to their derivatives counterparty. This would trigger an immediate outflow of the central bank's foreign currency reserves as local currency and other assets were exchanged into dollars in order to meet collateral requirements.

As an indication of the potential magnitude of these collateral outflows, Garber and Lall (1996) cite the IMF and 'industry sources' which reported that Mexican banks held $16 billion in tesabono total return swaps at the time of the devaluation of the Mexican peso. The authors calculated that the initial peso devaluation depressed the value of tesabonos by 15 percent, and that this would have required the delivery of $2.4 billion in collateral on the next day. This would explain about half of the $5 billion dollars of foreign reserves lost by the Mexican central bank the day after devaluation. In this way, collateral or margin calls on derivatives can accelerate the pace of a financial crisis, and the greater leverage that derivatives provide will similarly multiply the size of losses and thereby deepen the crisis.

CONDUIT FOR CONTAGION

The Bank of International Settlement's report known as the 'Lamfalussy Report' defined systemic risk as 'the risk that the illiquidity or failure of one institution, and its resulting inability to meet its obligations when due, will lead to the illiquidity or failure of other institutions' (BIS 1990). Similarly, contagion is the term established in the wake of the East Asian financial crisis of 1997—to replace the more colloquial term 'tequila effect' which was used to describe the spreading effects of the 1994 Mexican peso crisis—to describe the tendency of a financial crisis in one country to adversely affect the financial markets in other, and sometimes seemingly unrelated, economies. It is the notion of systemic risk taken to the level of national and international markets.

The presence of a large volume of derivatives transactions in an economy creates the possibility of a rapid expansion of counterparty credit risk during periods of economic stress. These credit risks might then become actual delinquent counterparty debts and obligations during an economic crisis. In his annual statement to investors, world renown investor Warren Buffett referred to this as 'daisy chain risk' and in the same letter he also called derivatives 'financial weapons of mass destruction'.[25]

The implication is that even if derivatives are used to reduce exposure to market risk, they might still lead to an increase in credit risk. For example, a bank lending through variable rate loans might decide to reduce its exposure to short-term interest rate variability, thus the volatility of its income, by

---

[25] Warren Buffett's letter to shareholders of Berkshire Hathaway in February 2003.

entering into an interest rate swap as the variable rate receiver. If short-term rates were to rise, then the fair market value of the bank's swap position would rise, and thus would increase the bank's gross counterparty credit exposure above that already associated with the loans which were being hedged.

The presence of derivatives can also increase the global financial system's exposure to contagion through two channels. Regarding the first, derivatives can spread the disturbance or crisis in one country to another because many derivatives involve cross-border counterparties and thus losses of market value and credit rating in one country will affect counterparties in other countries. The second channel of contagion, identified by Neftci (1998), comes from the practice of financial institutions responding to a downturn in one market by selling in another. One reason firms sell in other markets is because they need additional funds to purchase liquid G5 currency denominated assets to meet collateral or capital requirements. In order to obtain these assets, firms will make a portfolio shift and sell securities in other markets. This demand for collateral assets can be sudden and sizable when there are large swings in financial markets.

11.4 Policy Implications and Conclusion

This last section of the chapter will lay out a set of prudential financial market regulations designed to address the problems and potential pitfalls identified above in Section 11.3. They are intended to help make derivatives markets more transparent, more efficient, and less susceptible to disruptions and distortions. These policies should also encourage the use of derivatives for price discovery and risk management purposes while discouraging their misuse and abuse in unproductive pursuits.

These prudential regulatory measures are of three fundamental types. The first type relates to reporting and registration requirements; these requirements are designed to improve the transparency—and thus the pricing efficiency—and help prevent fraud and manipulation in the markets. Reporting requirements are especially useful to the government, and other market surveillance authorities such as derivatives exchanges, to better detect and deter fraud and manipulation.

The second type of prudential regulatory measures involves capital and collateral[26] requirements. Capital requirements function to provide both a buffer against the vicissitudes of the market and to act as a governor on the tendency of market competition to drive market participants to take on greater risks in

---

[26] Collateral, also known as margin, is an asset that is posted in order to assure performance on a derivatives contract. The higher the liquidity and the lower the price volatility, the best the asset is suited for this purpose.

the pursuit of higher return.[27] Collateral requirements have basically the same effect, although collateral requirements apply to transactions in particular and not entire financial institutions. Thus, non-financial corporations, as well as public entities, that would not otherwise be subject to capital requirements would be subject to collateral requirements on their derivatives transactions.

This is an especially critical issue because the current market practice for managing collateral, in so far as there is one, is dangerously inadequate. Many firms trade derivatives without collateral, a practice known as trading on capital. Those that do employ collateral nonetheless allow a threshold, sometimes set at a high level of exposure before the posting of collateral is required. Even when collateral is employed, some derivatives dealers engage in the dangerous practice of allowing illiquid assets to be used as collateral. Yet another dangerous practice in the employment of collateral to manage credit risk is to require that a counterparty become 'super-margined' if its credit rating drops substantially (especially if it drops below investment grade). This sudden change in collateralization requires that a derivatives counterparty post substantially greater amounts of collateral. This large and immediate demand for fresh capital would occur just at the time that the firm is experiencing problems with inadequate capital. This market practice thus amounts to a *crisis accelerator*.

The third type of prudential regulation falls under the rubric of orderly market provisions. These are measures, which have been tested over time in derivatives and securities markets around the world, that are designed to facilitate a liquid, efficient market with a minimum of disruptions.

While the following financial policy proposals are intended to apply to developing countries, it is not intended to imply that they are especially susceptible to derivatives abuse. Instead, it is to address the fact that they can ill afford it. Prudential regulations should apply to mature financial markets in developed countries as well as to developing countries. This is not to recommend a Procrustean or one-size-fits-all approach, but rather to merely recognize that derivative markets pose similar concerns to all financial systems.

It is worth noting that many of these measures are already present in the US and some other developed countries even though they are mostly applied to banking, securities markets, and derivatives exchanged for the trading of futures and options. Even the developed countries have not brought the OTC derivatives markets into the same realm of prudential regulation that they apply to other major types of financial transactions.

Another important facet of these measures is that they can be instituted and enforced independently by any nation. While such the regulation and

---

[27] John Eatwell (2001) has raised some serious concerns about the ability of capital held to meet capital requirements to successfully function as a buffer against such changes.

surveillance of transactions is better if conducted with international cooperation, it is not a necessary condition for applying prudential rules in one country. Moreover, insofar as these regulations are the same or similar as ones adopted in mature financial market economies, then there should be fewer objections by IMF, private financial firms, or other laissez-faire policy advocates.

11.4.1 Registration and Reporting Requirements

Derivatives dealers and brokers should be registered. Like their counterparts in securities, banking and insurance, these key market makers should be registered for the following reasons. Registration requirements for individuals establish a minimum competence level for the individuals (insofar as they are required to pass exams such as the Series 7 exam in the US), and they allow for background checks to detect fraud and theft convictions for salespeople and others with fiduciary responsibility. The registration of firms establishes minimum standards for capital (such as is the case with bank charters and securities brokers and dealers), management competence, and provides the basis for ongoing surveillance and reporting activities by and to the relevant public authority. In the US, the Securities and Exchange Commission is introducing registration and reporting requirements for hedge funds while the Commodity Futures Trading Commission already required such registration and reporting for hedge funds that pool investor funds or act as trading advisors for transactions on futures and options markets.

All derivatives transactions should be reported. The benefit is a more transparent marketplace which will, in turn, help produce a more efficient market and price discover process.

Reporting requirements should include information on price, volume, open interest, put-call volume and ratios, maturity, instrument, underlying item, amounts traded between other dealers and with end-users, and collateral arrangements. Publicly traded corporations should be required to report their derivatives activities in sufficient detail so as to convey the actual underlying economic properties and business purposes of business activities including any minority interests or special purpose entities. In order to bring off-balance sheet activities into the same light as balance sheets, derivatives should be reported by notional value (long and short), maturity, instrument, and collateral arrangements. This would enable investors to better determine whether the firm was under- or over-hedged, and whether they were primarily acting as a producer or wholesaler.

Large trader positions must be reported. Derivatives dealers and exchanges should report each entity that amasses a critical size of open positions in a market. The regulatory authority would compile this information from across dealers and markets in order to detect and deter market manipulation. This large trader reporting data has proven very useful by the Commodity Futures Trading Commission in the US for the purpose of market surveillance.

The proprietary nature of the information should be protected by the regulatory authority. Information would be compiled, aggregated and the non-proprietary data would be made available to the overall market so as to improve transparency. The level of aggregation would need to be sufficient to protect individual firms from exposing their trading strategies. The data of a proprietary nature would be retained by the regulator in order to detect and deter fraud, manipulation, and potential systemic breaks in the markets.

The ability to enforce reporting requirements can be enhanced by stipulating that any derivatives transaction that is not reported cannot be actionable in court for legal enforceability or bankruptcy claims. This provision will lead derivatives counterparties to thoroughly comply with reporting requirements in order to protect their interests in the contracts. Otherwise it amounts to giving a counterparty an option to legally abrogate the obligations of the contract.

This is not expensive, especially in the age of electronic communication, and it is information that firms should be tracking carefully in any case. When email-type messages are used to confirm derivatives trades between counterparties, as is already often the case, then reporting would be no more costly or burdensome than including the regulatory authority as a CC: on the confirmation message.[28]

11.4.2 Capital and Collateral Requirements

Capital requirements should be updated for all financial institutions, especially derivatives dealers that might not otherwise be registered as a financial institution, so that the capital is held in an amount that is commensurate with not only the exposure to credit loss, but also market exposure—since it has the potential to become credit exposure in the future—and value at risk (VAR).[29]

Capital requirements can be used to constrain the mismatch in currency composition or maturity on financial institutions assets and liabilities— measured to include both balance sheet and off-balance sheet positions. This will impose a prudential governor on firms' pursuit of higher rates of return by taking on greater amounts of market risk. It does not prevent risk taking, but merely limits it to the proportion of capital at risk.

---

[28] Most OTC derivatives transactions are traded through the ISDA Master Trading Agreement ('Master Agreement') which requires that the counterparties to the trades exchange confirmation messages to insure that all the key terms are understood.

[29] Examples from the US of non-financial firms acting as derivatives dealers include Enron, Williams, El Paso, and Duke energy corporations.

Capital requirements are critical to prevent the problems at one firm from becoming problems at another firm. This is especially important for dealers in financial markets because their failure can lead to market problems such as illiquidity (market freeze-up), meltdown or Lamfalussy type systemic failure.

Adequate and appropriate collateral (margin) should be posted and maintained on all derivatives transactions.[30] Collateral (margin) on transactions functions like capital does for financial institutions. It helps prevent the problems at one firm in one transaction from causing performance problems for other transactions and other firms. This reduces the likelihood of default or other credit-related losses, and it reduces the market's vulnerability to a freeze-up or meltdown.

The initial collateral rate should be adequate to cover short-term losses, and it should be adjusted frequently to account for growth of losses over time. A high standard for collateral practice can be found in most futures and options exchanges around the world, but no single rule need apply everywhere. Collateral should be in the form of cash or liquid government securities. Less liquid and more price volatile securities or assets should be discouraged if not prohibited. Alternatives such as performance bonds, letters of credit, or surety bonds should be discouraged, if not prohibited.

11.4.3 Orderly Market Rules

Strictly Prohibit Fraud and Manipulation and Make it Punishable by Civil and Criminal Penalties. In order to protect the integrity of market prices so that they encourage the widest possible market participation and do not signal distorting signals throughout the economy, fraud and manipulation should be strictly prohibited and punishable by civil and criminal penalties.

Require Derivatives Dealers to Act as Market Makers by Maintaining Binding Bid and Ask Quotes Through the Trading Day. This is a common financial policy for exchanges, and it is used in the OTC market for US Treasury securities.

Extend 'Know Thy Customer' Rules to All Financial Institutions Conducting Derivatives Transactions.[31] This provision will discourage fraud in the form of financial sharpsters 'blowing up' their customers. This regulatory provision already exists in some securities markets, and it should be extended to derivatives markets where there is even greater concern with asymmetric information or different levels of sophistication between market participants.

---

[30] For good background reading on collateral provision in OTC derivatives markets in the US, read C. A. Johnson (2002). *Over-The-Counter Derivatives: Documentation.* New York, NY: Bowne Publishing.

[31] For descriptions of these structured securities and how they are transacted, see Partnoy (1999) and Dodd (2002a).

Impose Position Limits in Derivatives Markets. These restrictions amount to explicit limitations on risk taking, but not hedging. This measure can be very effective in limiting the amount of carry trade or 'hot money' related transactions because they result in exchange rate exposure and sometimes interest rate exposure.

References

Bank for International Settlements (BIS) (1990). 'Report of the Committee on Inter-bank Netting Schemes of the Central Banks of the Group of Ten Countries'. Basel.

—— (1995, 1998, and 2001). 'Central Bank Survey of Foreign Exchange and Derivatives Market Activity'. Basel.

Blöndal, S. and Christiansen, H. (1999). 'The Recent Experience with Capital Flows to Emerging Market Economies'. OECD Working Paper No. 211 (February).

Brown, S., Goetzmann, J., and Park, J. (1998). 'Hedge Funds and the Asian Currency Crisis of 1997'. NBER Working Paper 6427 (February).

Cassard, M. and Folkerts-Landau, D. (1997). 'Sovereign Debt: Managing the Risks', in IMF-World Bank, *Finance & Development* (December). Washington, DC: IMF.

Chrystal, J. (1996). 'Using Derivative Products to Lower Borrowing Costs'. *Latin Finance, Latin Derivatives Supplement* (January/February).

Dodd, R. (2000a). 'Primer: Derivatives Instruments'. Available at: www.financialpolicy. org/dscinstruments.htm.

—— (2000b). 'Primer: Derivatives'. Available at: www.financialpolicy.org/dscprimer. htm.

—— (2002a). 'The Role of Derivatives in the East Asian Financial Crisis', in J. Eatwell and L. Taylor (eds.), *International Capital Markets: Systems in Transition.* New York: Oxford University Press.

—— (2002b). 'Derivatives, the Shape of International Capital Flows and the Virtues of Prudential Regulation'. UNU Wider Discussion Paper No. 2002/93. (Also in R. Ffrench-Davis and S. Griffith-Jones (eds.), *From Capital Surges to Drought.* New York, NY: Palgrave Macmillan Publishers, 2003.)

—— (2004a). 'Developing Countries Lead Growth in Global Derivatives Market'. Special Policy Brief 15, Financial Policy Forum. Available at: www.financialpolicy. org/dscbriefs.htm.

—— (2004b). 'Derivatives Use Surges By 30%'. Special Policy Brief 20, Financial Policy Forum. Available at: www.financialpolicy.org/dscbriefs.htm.

—— Hoody, J. (2002). 'Learning Our Lessons: A Short History of Market Manipulation'. Financial Policy Forum Special Policy Brief 3. Available at: www.financialpolicy. org/dscbriefs.htm.

Eatwell, J. (2001). 'The Challenges Facing International Financial Regulation'. Presented to the Western Economic Association, July. Available at: www.financialpolicy. org/dscconference.htm.

Futures Industry Association (FIA) (2004). 'FIA Annual Volume Survey: World Futures Volume'. *Futures Industry* (March/April).

Folkerts-Landau, D. and Garber, P. (1997). 'Derivative Markets and Financial System Soundness', in Enoch, C. and Green, J. (eds.), *Banking Soundness and Monetary Policy*. Washington, DC: IMF.

Garber, P. (1998). 'Derivatives in International Capital Flow'. NBER Working Paper No. 6623 (June).

_____ and Lall, S. (1996). 'Derivative Products in Exchange Rate Crises', in R. Glick (ed.), *Managing Capital Flows and Exchange Rates: Perspectives from the Pacific Basin*. Cambridge: Cambridge University Press. (Prepared for Federal Reserve Bank of San Francisco conference in 1996.)

_____ and Spencer, M. (1995). 'Foreign Exchange Hedging with Synthetic Options and the Interest Rate Defense of a Fixed Exchange Rate System'. (September) *IMF Staff Papers*, 42/3.

Gosain, V. (1994). 'Derivatives on Emerging Market Sovereign Debt Instruments', in R. A. Klein and J. Lederman (eds.), *Derivatives and Synthetics*. Chicago, IL: Probus Publishing.

International Monetary Fund (IMF) (1999). *International Capital Markets*. Washington, DC: IMF.

_____ (2002). *Global Financial Stability Report* (March). Washington, DC: IMF.

_____ (2003). *Global Financial Stability Report* (March), ch. 4: Washington, DC: IMF.

Kregel, J. A. (1998a). 'East Asia is Not Mexico: The Difference Between Balance of Payments Crises and Debt Deflations'. Jerome Levy Economics Institute Working Paper 235.

_____ (1998b). 'Derivatives and Global Capital Flows: Applications to Asia'. *Cambridge Journal of Economics* (November), 22/6: 677–92.

Lall, S. (1997). 'Speculative Attacks, Forward Market Intervention and the Classic Bear Squeeze'. IMF Working Paper (June).

McClintock, B. (1996). 'International Financial Instability and the Financial Derivatives Market'. *Journal of Economic Issues*, (March) 30/1.

Markham, J. W. (1994). ' "Confederate bonds," "General Custer," and the Regulation of Derivative Financial Instruments'. *Seton Hall Law Review*.

Mathieson, D. J., Roldos, J. E., Ramaswamy, R., and Ilyina, A. (2004). *Emerging Local Securities and Derivatives Markets: World Economic and Financial Surveys*. Washington, DC: IMF.

Neftci, S. N. (1998). 'FX Short Positions, Balance Sheets and Financial Turbulence: An Interpretation of the Asian Financial Crisis'. CEPA Working Paper No. 11 (October).

_____ and Santos, A. O. (2003). 'Putable and Extendible Bonds: Developing Interest Rate Derivatives for Emerging Markets'. IMF Working Paper WP/03/201.

Nussbaum, D. (1997). 'Seeing is Believing'. *Institutional Investor* (September).

Partnoy, F. (1999). *F.I.A.S.C.O.: The Inside Story of a Wall Street Trader*. New York: Penguin.

Piga, G. (2001). 'Derivatives and Public Debt Management'. A report by the Council of Foreign Relations and (commissioned by) International Securities Market Association, New York.

Schinasi, G., Craig, R. S., Drees, B., and Kramer, C. (2000). *Modern Banking and OTC Derivatives Markets*. IMF Occasional Paper 203.

Steinherr, A. (1998). *Derivatives: The Wild Beast of Finance*. West Sussex: John Wiley & Sons.

Stiglitz, J.E. (1998). 'Sound Finance and Sustainable Development in Asia'. Keynote address to the Asia Development Forum, Manila, (March 12).

Swain, E. J. (1993). *The Development of the Law of Financial Services*. London: Cavendish Publishing Ltd.

―――― (2000). *Building the Global Market: A 4000 Year History of Derivatives*. London: Kluwer Law International Ltd.

Woolley, S. (1999). 'Night Baseball Without Lights'. *Forbes*, November 1.

World Bank (1999). *Global Development Finance*. Washington, DC: The World Bank.

12

Do Global Standards and Codes Prevent Financial Crises?

Benu Schneider[1]

12.1 Introduction

The Standards and Codes (S&C) initiative has its genesis in its present form in the East Asian financial crisis in the late 1990s and the subsequent problems in Latin America and Russia.[2]

Standards and codes play a central role in the new international financial architecture being developed to promote greater financial stability following crises in Asia and elsewhere. The emphasis in Standards and Codes reflects a view that vulnerabilities are

[1] The views expressed are those of the author and do not necessarily express the views of the United Nations Financing for Development Office, Department of Economic and Social Affairs. The contributor thanks Palgrave Macmillan for permission to use some of the material from 'Implications of Implementing Standards and Codes: A Developing Country Perspective', published in *The Road to International Financial Stability: Are Key Financial Standards the Answer?* Benu Schneider (ed.) 2003. The author also thanks Cinthya Ramirez and Lynn Lynn Thway for excellent research assistance.

[2] Standards are not new. The international standard setting bodies have existed for a long time, but each was developing common codes and rules in isolation. There are various international and national organizations which, over the years, have made significant contribution to raising standards of soundness and risk awareness in financial systems. Some examples are the *Principles for the Supervision of Banks' Foreign Establishments* agreed to by the Basel Committee on Banking Supervision (BCBS) in 1983, and the *Framework for International Convergence of Capital Measurement and Capital Standards*, published in 1988. Work on some standards, such as those for data dissemination and fiscal transparency, existed prior to the outbreak of the East Asian crisis. The Special Data Dissemination Standard (SDDS), for example, was developed by the IMF in response to the deficiencies in major categories of economic data following the Mexican crisis in December 1994. The OECD countries adhere to standards defined by the OECD Codes of Liberalisation, and they have been subject to self-assessments with a peer review process. Other countries adhere to standards defined by their own national bodies and also international bodies. So, what is really new is the setting of an international forum for defining and redefining them, so that all countries in the world adhere to a global set of standards and rules.

reduced if transparency in the institutional and regulatory structures of the economic and financial sectors, and in the information these sectors provide to the public, reflects the good practices that many countries follow. (IMF 2000)

Seven years have elapsed since the initiative was launched in 1999. This chapter evaluates the progress made so far[3] and considers some of the basic assumptions and rationale of the S&C initiative and examines how far this initiative can be instrumental in preventing a financial crisis. It considers some issues that arise from a developing country perspective, and further explores issues related to surveillance mechanisms and the information generation system set up at the Bretton Woods Institutions (BWIs). In addition, it appraises the response of the private sector.

The chapter is organized as follows: the second section (12.2) presents the background for the present discussion. The third (12.3) analyzes the incentive structure for implementing the standards and codes exercise; it critically evaluates the sources and quality of information on compliance with the standards and examines the degree of compliance. The fourth section (12.4) critically evaluates the role of the BWIs in the standards and codes exercise and analyzes the private sector response. In Section 12.5, developing country issues are examined with respect to ownership, appropriateness, resource needs, the need for transition and the political economy of implementation and its role in determining the degree of compliance. The last section (12.6) concludes and makes policy suggestions for giving a new rigor and orientation to the standards and codes exercise which is better suited to the aspirations of developing countries.

12.2 Background

In the aftermath of the East Asian crisis, the international community has been engaged in reforming the international financial architecture to deal with some of the dangers inherent in globalization. The dynamic growth in capital markets following the liberalization of financial markets in many countries had occurred without taking fully into account domestic, economic and financial weaknesses, and regulatory and supervisory frameworks. A vital lesson that has been learned is that the health of both internal and external balance sheets is important in all sectors of the economy, be it the central bank, the government, or the private sector. Another important lesson concerns the role of information in the smooth functioning of international

---

[3] The analysis in this chapter is based on published and publicly available information.

financial markets, a lack of which often leads to contagion and herding by international investors.

The crisis highlighted that capital account liberalization in emerging markets is not without risks and in many cases has the potential for bringing about severely destabilizing effects not only in the countries of origin but also within the region and in other parts of the world. The limited attention given to policies towards capital movements in recent years as such is quite surprising. The crisis, in addition, revealed the lack of transparency on the part of international institutional investors and the inability of the international financial architecture to prevent and manage financial crises. The post-crisis international emphasis has been on strengthening players through stronger risk management, more prudent standards, and improved transparency. The establishment of the Financial Stability Forum (FSF) in February 1999 by the then G-7[4] finance ministers and Central Bank governors[5] was a new initiative in direct response to the East Asian crisis, and it reflects the importance given to globally coordinated financial and regulatory aspects of domestic policy and the need to rethink those regulations grouped together under the heading of S&C. This is the first attempt to develop a single set of international rules and principles for crucial areas of domestic policy in the financial and monetary spheres.

Seven years on there is also a surveillance machinery to assess compliance. The key instrument is the Report on the Observance of Standards and Codes (ROSC), prepared by the IMF as a part of Article IV consultations, or through joint missions with the World Bank on Financial Sector Assessment Program (FSAP). At the time of writing, there are ROSCs for 119 countries. There is also some self-assessment in the public domain, and some private sector activity.

Identifying standards is a complex task. Moreover, the dynamic nature of financial markets and their increasing sophistication mean that these standards will have to be flexible enough to incorporate processes of change. The FSF has identified seventy standards; and a set of standards (see Table 12.1) in the three areas of macro policy and data transparency, institutional market infrastructure, and financial regulation and supervision, was endorsed by the G-7 countries and the multilateral institutions as being necessary to ensure financial stability.

In practice, the classification of the standards and codes into these three categories is not very distinct. For example, macroeconomic policy can have

---

[4] Now the G-8.

[5] Its membership consists of representatives of the national authorities responsible for financial stability in selected OECD countries, Hong Kong (China), and Singapore, and of major international financial institutions, international supervisory and regulatory bodies, and central bank expert groupings.

Table 12.1. Key Standards for Financial Systems

Subject Area	Key Standard	Issuing Body
Monetary and financial policy transparency	Code of Good Practices on Transparency in Monetary and Financial policies	IMF
Fiscal policy transparency	Code of Good Practices in Fiscal Transparency	IMF
Data dissemination	Special Data Dissemination Standard (SDDS)/General Data Dissemination System (GDDS)	IMF
Institutional and market infrastructure		
Insolvency	Principles and Guidelines on Effective Insolvency and Creditor Rights System	World Bank
Corporate Governance	Principles of Corporate Governance	OECD
Accounting	International Accounting Standards (IAS)	International Accounting Standards Board (IASB)
Auditing	International Standards on Auditing (ISA)	International Federation of Accountants (IFAC)
Payment and settlement	Core Principles for Systematically Important Payment Systems	Committee on Payment and Settlement Systems (CPSS)
	Recommendations for Securities Settlements Systems	CPPS and International Organization of Securities Commissions (IOSCO)
Money Laundering	The Forty Recommendations/ 8 Special Recommendations Against Terrorist Financing	Financial Action Task Force (FATF)
Financial regulation and supervision		
Banking Supervision	Core Principles for Effective Banking Supervision	Basel Committee on Banking Supervision (BCBS)
Securities Regulation	Objectives and Principles of Securities Regulation	International Organization of Securities Commissions (IOSCO)
Insurance Supervision	Insurance Core Principles	International Association of Insurance (IAIS)

Source: Financial Stability Forum.

a crucial effect on financial stability through its impact on the values of financial firms' assets and liabilities as well as on the functioning of the payments and settlement system (which is at the heart of the infrastructure of financial markets). Effective financial regulation and supervision are related inextricably to accounting, auditing, and insolvency procedures.

Insurance products are frequently incorporated into, or sold in close conjunction with, investment products, thus increasing the channels through which disturbances affecting the market for one financial service can be transmitted between markets. And even such an apparently self-contained issue as money laundering has on occasion threatened the stability of financial firms (UNCTAD 2001). Still, the codes provide a body of 'best practice' pooled from different international standard-setting bodies and regulatory frameworks related to the legal, regulatory, and institutional framework for any financial system. Many of them are intended to serve as guidelines, but some, such as the standard on data dissemination, can be detailed and precise.

The implementation of Standards and Codes was announced to be voluntary and the implementation was to be different across countries and firms.[6] In order to discuss implementation of international best practices relating to the legal, regulatory, and institutional framework underpinning a financial system, a global overview of the present situation with regard to compliance would be desirable, but this is not readily available. In order to understand the motivation by countries to adopt (or not adopt) the Standards and Codes initiative, it is necessary clarify the incentive structures existing for each player of the game. The next section offers a critical point of view on these issues.

12.3 Incentives for Implementation, Sources of Information, and the Degree of Compliance

12.3.1 *The Incentive Structure of the Standards and Codes Initiative*

The FSF Task Force on the Implementation of Standards, established in September 1999, identified a blend of market and official incentives to encourage the implementation of standards and codes; the FSF follow-up group examined these in September 2000. Compliance rests either on countries being convinced of the usefulness of such standards and voluntary cooperation, or on pressures from the markets for their observance.

Compliance can in principle be based either on positive incentives or negative incentives (compulsions). Schneider (2001, 2005) catalogues market[7] and official,[8] positive and negative incentives. Examples for positive incentives are those that lie in the national self-interest, such as technical assistance and policy advice from international organizations. Examples for negative incentives are those dealing with higher costs of funds in the case of non-compliance, or banning from membership in international groupings.

---

[6] In practice, conditions for implementation of some of the codes are gradually creeping into Fund programs.

[7] The key requirements for these to be effective would be: (a) market familiarity with international standards; (b) their assessment of its relevance for assessments of market risk; (c) market access to information on compliance and the degree of compliance; and (d) use of information by the market in risk assessments.

[8] The period for assessing the effectiveness of market incentives is, admittedly, very short. Nevertheless, assessment of some codes in the literature points to the limited use of the market incentive. See, for example, Mosley (2001).

Incentives for compliance also differ between developed and developing countries. For instance, official incentives are not effective for the G-8/G-10 countries—as they no longer borrow from multilateral institutions. Market incentives also work asymmetrically in the case of industrialized and emerging market economies (EMEs). Although industrialized countries do borrow from private capital markets, the markets do not necessarily take the degree of these countries' adherence to international standards into account. For example, Germany only published its report on Fiscal Transparency (and most other codes) during late 2003, but this did not have a serious effect on its credit rating and ability to borrow, as would have been the case in an emerging market's economy.

A case for 'ownership' of the implementation of standards and codes can be made if countries can be persuaded that implementation is in their national interest in order to maintain domestic financial stability and hedge against external shocks. A crisis is a costly affair, and it is in a country's interest to avoid it. Moreover, a strong, healthy, financial sector is essential for the efficient allocation of resources and improved growth performance. Thus, self-interest is the best incentive.

An unsolved issue when considering the incentive structure for developing countries is whether—if the market does not assimilate information, as recent outreach activities and research suggests—negative official incentives such as conditionality can be put to use. This question will be taken up in more detail in the developing country issues section of this chapter.

12.3.2 The Sources of Information and Evidence on the Degree of Compliance

Once the incentives to comply with the standards are internalized, the next step is to analyze whether the corresponding convergence is brought about as expected. However, assessing the degree of compliance is a difficult task. The exercise is presently underway as a part of IMF Article IV consultations and FSAPs. Information is also available on different aspects covered by the codes in the public domain such as central bank reports. This information is then made available by the following sources: the Reports on the Observance of Standards and Codes (ROSCs) prepared by the IMF, countries' own self-assessments, and the information provided by a specific private sector initiative, the E-Standards Forum.[9]

---

[9] Other private sources include Credit Lyonnais, the assessment of corporate governance standard of Standard & Poor's and the opacity index of PriceWaterhouseCoopers. This paper analyzes ROSCs which are available in the public domain and the information produced by the E-Standards Forum.

ASSESSING ROSCs

The preparation of ROSCs started in the 1999 assessments, and publication is voluntary. Some of the ROSCs are part of the FSAP, run jointly by the IMF and the World Bank. ROSCs were (as of August 14, 2006) available for 119 countries. Major players, including some G-8 countries, published their first ROSCs very late in 2003 (Germany's first ROSC appeared in September 2003 while the United States' first and only one appeared in August 2003); many OECD countries have not published any ROSC at all. In addition, there are several problems regarding the quality of ROSCs:

- they use turgid language;
- they are dated;
- they do not provide a continuous stream of information;
- they are not standardized;
- there is no public schedule of announcements of country coverage and coverage of codes;
- there are problems in priority setting, in sequencing and follow-up action. For instance, there is very little link between the FIRST (Financial Sector Reform and Strengthening) Initiative that was set up to provide technical assistance and the recommendations on follow-up actions in FSAPs; and
- there is very limited information gained.

What is important to say is that if the goal is indeed international financial stability, then the IMF should be focusing on key players in financial markets.[10] The distribution of published ROSCs by regions in Table 12.2 indicates the priority which the surveillance mechanism has given to regions and codes. For fiscal and monetary transparency and banking supervision published ROSCs are the highest for transition economies, followed by advanced economies and Africa. For data dissemination, Africa is ahead of advanced countries. Banking supervision, which has been identified as a vital area which requires strengthening as countries open up their capital accounts, has a lower number of ROSCs for Western Hemisphere and Asia, regions in which financial vulnerability was a major problem in the late 1990s. Fiscal Transparency ROSCs for Russia, another country afflicted by financial problems, were published as late as September 2004.

This choice of regions and codes does not reflect the background that motivated the exercise—particularly the vulnerabilities in East Asia and Latin America. In one case, Argentina, which had the maximum number of ROSCs,

[10] The Fund may argue that the S&C exercise is a voluntary process. In practice, however, the Fund has enough room for maneuvers through Article IV consultations and through its programs with borrowing countries.

Table 12.2. Distribution of Countries with ROSCs Published by Region and Category[a] (As of August 14, 2006)

ROSCs published	Region						
	Africa	Asia	Western Hemisphere	Middle East	Transition[b]	Advanced	Total no. of countries
Data dissemination	17	10	13	3	22	13	78
Fiscal transparency	15	11	12	3	23	15	79
Monetary transparency	10	4	6	2	18	15	55
Banking supervision	11[c]	5	9	4	22	21	72
Securities regulation	5[c]	4	4	2	12	19	46
Insurance regulation	6[c]	3	2	1	13	18	43
Payments systems	6[c]	4	6	2	18	17	53
Corporate governance	1[c]	2	1[c]	0	4[c]	1[c]	9
Accounting and auditing	9	6	7	3	14	0	39
Insolvency	0	0	1	0	1	0	2
AML/CFT	4	2	4	2	6	14	32

Notes: Japan included in Advanced Countries; Hong Kong (China), Taiwan province of China, Mongolia, and the Republic of Korea classified under Asia. [a] Country classification according to World Economic Outlook, IMF. [b] Includes Central–Eastern Europe and Independent Countries. ROSCs for Barbados, Malta, Netherlands, Tunisia, and Uganda were included in our previous version based. [c] In March 2005 information available from IMF website. They are not shown in August 2006 IMF website. However, we included in the above updated table for consistency.

Source: Author's calculations based on information on the IMF website.

the information was not reflected in the country's assessments before the crisis. The distribution of ROSCs by codes indicates that fiscal transparency has been given the highest priority, followed by data dissemination, banking supervision, and monetary transparency. There is only a single ROSC (the Netherlands) for Corporate and Accounting standards for the advanced countries, which should have been given priority following the corporate accounting scandals in ENRON, WorldCom, and others.

Figure 12.1 shows available ROSCs classified into key players and non-key players in financial markets for each of the 12 codes. There have been more ROSCs conducted for non-key players in financial markets than for key players. The figures inside the bars indicate the proportion of key players that have a ROSC for a particular code to total key players in the market, and the proportion of non-key players that have a ROSC for a given code to total non-key players. The main finding is that there is not enough information on all of the key players in international financial markets.[11] And these are precisely the G-10 countries and top emerging markets, who are expected to affect global financial stability. In addition, there is no ROSC for any of the industrialized countries regarding corporate governance and accounting and auditing. Figures in the chart for corporate governance are only for emerging market economies.

[11] ROSCs for majority of the OECD countries have been published only very recently. There are no ROSCs available for Denmark.

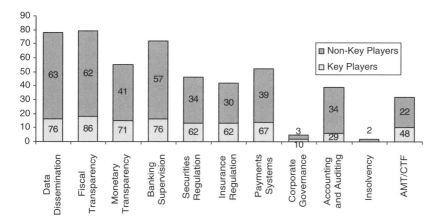

Figure 12.1. Number of ROSCs published by key and non-key financial players*

Note: * 21 Key players: G-10 (Canada, France, Germany, Italy, Japan, Sweden, Switzerland, UK, USA) and major EMEs (Argentina, Brazil, Hong Kong SAR, India, South Korea, Mexico, the Philippines, Poland, Russia, Singapore, South Africa, Turkey); 98 non-key players, for a total of 119 countries. Information as of August 2006. Figures in bars indicate the ratio of key players for which ROSC is available to total key players, and the ratio of non-key players for which ROSC is available to total non-key players.

There is a limitation to the number of ROSCs based on FSAPs. According to a recent evaluation by the IMF's independent evaluation office,[12] only 18 reports have been undertaken per fiscal year—counting those ongoing and planned for 2004 and 2005.[13]

If global financial stability is the objective function of the standards and codes exercise, then prioritization of the countries should ideally be on the basis of openness of the economies. Further data analysis provides evidence on prioritization of countries and whether it was in line with the degree of capital account liberalization.

Three approaches were adopted to gauge the degree of openness of an economy for this analysis. The first set of criteria is based on Summary Tables from the Fund's 1996–2004 Annual Reports on Exchange Arrangements and Exchange Restrictions.[14] The second looks at the actual financial account[15] to GDP as an indicator of openness and the third considers the ratio of foreign

[12] We refer to table published as Annex I, p. 18.
[13] See Appendix 12.3 for a list of published FSAP reports classified by the G-10, major emerging markets and non-key players in financial markets available in August 2004.
[14] A summary table on capital account restrictions from this source was kindly provided by Gian Maria Milesi-Ferretti, IMF.
[15] Since 1995 the presentation of the capital account data at the fund has changed. Two categories are reported now, financial account and capital account, the former reporting financial assets and the latter non-financial assets.

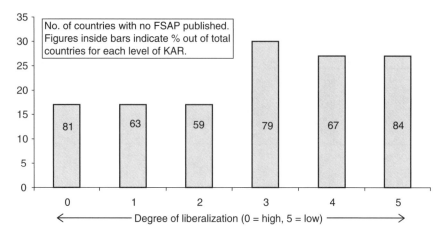

Figure 12.2. Capital account liberalization and FSAPs

Note: KAR measures degree of capital account liberalization. Information was available for 187 countries.

Source: Author's calculations based on IMF information as of 2004.

assets and liabilities to GDP, which is an indicator of the degree of financial integration.

Table 12.3 shows the number of ROSCs published for countries which have no restrictions on their capital account based on the information in the IMF's Annual Exchange Rate Arrangements. The figures inside the bars show that for 62 percent of the countries with fully open capital accounts, no data dissemination ROSC is available. The percentages of countries with no ROSCs and fully open capital accounts are also very high for all the other key standards. Further, Table 12.3 shows the non-availability of ROSCs for the top 50 net capital exporters and importers among IMF members. The financial account is averaged over the period 1999–2003 and the table indicates the link between high capital flows and the availability of ROSCs for key standards. The paucity in information for countries classified by the top 50 in terms of their financial account to GDP is very high for both net capital importers and net capital exporters. This shortcoming does not improve when looking at the number of countries without ROSCs for the top 25 ranked by the ratio of the sum of their assets and liabilities to GDP.

A similar analysis is carried out to establish the prioritization of countries by the Fund and the Bank for FSAPs conducted. In Figure 12.2, 81 percent of countries with zero restrictions had no FSAPs. The percentage remains high even when we go to progressively more restrictive capital accounts.

Table 12.3. Number of ROSCs by Code for Countries with Capital Account Openness

	Countries with capital account restrictions (KAR) = 0 and no ROSC	Percentage out of total countries with KAR = 0 (%)	Top 50 net capital exporters without ROSCs	Percentage out of top 50 net capital exporters without ROSCs (%)	Top 50 net capital importers without ROSCs	Percentage out of top 50 net capital importers without ROSCs (%)	Foreign assets+ liabilities/ GDP %: Top 25 countries without ROSCs	Percentage of top 25 Foreign assets+ liabilities/ GDP %: Top 25 countries without ROSCs
Data dissemination	13	62	34	68	33	66	19	76
Fiscal transparency	14	67	36	72	29	58	15	60
Monetary transparency	16	76	34	68	34	68	13	52
Banking supervision	15	71	31	62	30	60	9	40
Securities regulation	16	76	34	68	37	74	12	48
Insurance regulation	17	81	36	72	37	74	14	56
Payments systems	15	71	35	70	36	72	15	60
Corporate governance	19	90	48	96	45	90	23	92
Accounting and auditing	20	95	50	100	50	100	25	100
Insolvency	21	100	50	100	49	98	25	100
AML/CFT	16	76	42	84	44	88	19	76

The above assessment highlights the lack of emphasis on the degree of capital account liberalization in prioritizing the Codes. For further work at the Fund in this area, it is imperative to re-evaluate the purpose of the ROSC exercise and to prioritize the reports according to the objective function. This analysis is pinpointing that global financial stability was probably not the key criteria in selecting countries for the assessment of the standards and codes.

THE CASE OF THE ɛSTANDARDS FORUM

Self-assessments are not collected systematically by any international organization, and information about them is sometimes difficult to obtain. Private initiatives, such as the ɛStandards Forum website (www.estandardsforum. com), collate and provide information on the implementation of S&C from public sources for a large number of countries in the form of scores for compliance ranging from full compliance to zero compliance. This is to cater to the needs of market participants who prefer information in a simple format that can easily be quantified or used in a classification system that can be incorporated in tick boxes. However, implementation of S&C is a process and is not designed to meet fixed target deadlines for compliance, or to provide pass/fail tests. Such a process necessarily requires qualitative assessments.

Simplistic quantification and classification risk produces scoring systems capable of creating one-way expectations and bandwagon effects in the market. Moreover, the information can be quite misleading. Schneider (2005: 14–18) illustrates this point by using information provided by the ɛStandards forum. The author argues that a quantitative classification of country risk ends up giving the wrong message to markets (or no message at all), and this kind of treatment of the S&C exercise therefore needs to be revised. Compliance with the standards does not necessarily mean that timely information is available. If market participants are left to make their own discretionary judgments on a country's level of compliance, there is a better chance of a more reasoned assessment.

The burden of transparency has actually been on emerging market economies. Although the East Asian crisis was the trigger in highlighting problems with transparency and central bank balance sheets, the banking system and the corporate sector, implementation of international financial codes is a global issue. The idea that the crisis is an emerging market problem and that these countries had done something terribly wrong is not borne out by evidence, as the problem is widely prevalent.

In Table 12.4 an attempt is made to rank countries by the information available on compliance. The first column with scores gives equal weights

Table 12.4. Ranking of Key Players in Financial Markets

Rank	Country	Score with equal weights[a]	Country	Score with differential weights[b]	Country	Scores for full compliance and compliance in progress[c]
1	United States	78.46	United States	84.00	United States	26.15
2	United Kingdom	76.92	United Kingdom	80.00	Canada	21.54
3	Germany	72.31	Canada	79.00	Germany	18.46
4	Canada	70.77	Germany	79.00	United Kingdom	16.92
5	Hong Kong (China)	69.23	France	75.00	Switzerland	15.38
6	France	67.69	Hong Kong (China)	75.00	France	13.85
7	Korea, Rep. of	64.62	Sweden	67.00	Hong Kong (China)	13.85
8	Singapore	64.62	Korea, Rep. of	66.00	Italy	9.23
9	Sweden	61.54	Mexico	65.00	Korea, Rep. of	9.23
10	Switzerland	60.00	Poland	65.00	Singapore	9.23
11	Mexico	60.00	Singapore	65.00	Sweden	7.69
12	Poland	60.00	Italy	63.00	Poland	7.69
13	Italy	52.31	South Africa	60.00	South Africa	7.69
14	South Africa	52.31	Switzerland	59.00	Japan	6.15
15	Russia	50.77	Philippines	55.00	Brazil	6.15
16	Argentina	49.23	Argentina	54.00	Mexico	6.15
17	Philippines	46.15	Japan	52.00	Philippines	4.62
18	Japan	43.08	Russia	52.00	Turkey	4.62
19	India	43.08	India	50.00	India	3.08
20	Turkey	38.46	Turkey	47.00	Argentina	1.54
21	Brazil	32.31	Brazil	45.00	Russia	0.00

Notes: [a] All the thirteen codes covered by the *e*Standards Forum have been given equal weights to arrive at an overall. [b] The three standards relating to data dissemination, macro policy and fiscal transparency have been given the highest weight, followed by banking supervision and the other codes have been given the lowest weight. The choice of weights is based on the report of Fitch Sovereign ratings on which standards are useful for credit rating agencies. [c] Equal weights to full compliance and compliance in progress and for all other rankings zero.

Source: Author's calculations based on information on compliance at the *e*Standards Forum website.

to all the codes. This is the ranking which appears on the *e*Standards Forum website. In the second column of scores, transparency codes have been given the highest weight, followed by banking supervision and then all other codes were given equal weights. Both equal and differential weights indicate that many key players including Japan have low scores. In the last column on scores, ranking is calculated for countries with full compliance and compliance in progress for all the codes. Full compliance and compliance in progress are given a positive weight and the rest zero. The overall scores are very low beginning with the United States with a score of 26.15 and others even lower. Japan has a score as low as 6.15.

This analysis, which is based on the information summarized by *e*Standards Forum from publicly available information on compliance with standards and codes, shows that lack of compliance is an issue in the G-8 countries as well as emerging market economies.

12.4 The Links Between Bretton Woods Institutions and the Private Sector

Attempts by the Bretton Woods Institutions to involve the private sector in crisis prevention reflect their endeavour to deal with emerging issues consequential to the change in the profile of capital flows to developing countries, which brought with it many disruptions. This had significant knock on effects for the countries themselves, but also became a matter of great concern to other members of the international club.

In this section, we analyze whether the market incentive to implement standards has led to lower interest rate spreads for developing countries and if there is a relationship between credit ratings and compliance with the transparency standard. The section also explores whether new information is generated by some of the transparency exercises and if the private sector is making use of it.

12.4.1 *The Private Sector*

International organizations have put increasing emphasis on transparency in macroeconomic policy and data in order to ensure financial stability.[16] The rationale for greater transparency is based on the argument that: (1) it forces public and private institutions to be accountable; (2) it helps lenders and investors to evaluate risk; and (3) it prevents herding and contagion. Support for this view was voiced soon after the Mexican crisis and reinforced after the outbreak of the East Asian crisis. The G-7 finance ministers reported to the Cologne Summit that 'the availability of accurate and timely information is an essential ingredient for well-functioning financial markets and market economies' (Group of 7 1999).

The Group of 22 report on transparency points out that 'confidentiality may be warranted in some circumstances: for example, to encourage frank

---

[16] See the Code of Good Practices on Transparency in Monetary and Financial Policies at: www.imf.org/external/np/mae/mft and fiscal transparency at: www.imf.org/external/np/fad/trans.

internal policy deliberations. In determining the optimum degree of transparency, the benefits must be balanced against the costs (Group of 22 1998). Thus, although transparency is necessary, there is a question mark over how transparent developing countries should become.[17]

However, acknowledging some of the benefits, the private sector also acknowledges that the provision of information can backfire, since it might highlight faults that are shared by many countries but publicized by only a few. Persaud (2001) argues that, while transparency is a good thing, too much transparency may be self-defeating. His market research makes a convincing case for not making information on reserves available on a daily basis and so on.[18]

Transparency alone cannot avert a crisis or prevent contagion. Moreover, in a contagion situation there is a distinction between fully informed traders, who follow fundamentals, and less informed 'noise traders'. In the Keynesian 'beauty contest' world, informed traders anticipate irrational trading by noise traders since it is not a question of what one's own beliefs or knowledge are regarding fundamentals but rather that of the common perception. Information may help to ameliorate this situation but it is unlikely to eliminate it entirely (Persaud 2001). For example, while the Special Data Dissemination Standard (SDDS) was implemented before the crises in Turkey and Argentina, the new disclosure rules failed to serve as an effective warning system.[19]

Metcalfe and Persaud (2003) find that while stronger data standards will help market efficiency in general, they may not be the panacea that they are often assumed to be. There are some forms of disclosure that might even increase financial instability. Also, markets can sometimes turn 'a blind eye' to information during a bubble. And finally at its limit, if better disclosure ultimately reduces the diversity of investor opinion, this could actually contribute to greater financial instability.

---

[17] For example, many IMF members have been concerned about releasing data on foreign exchange reserves as they may reduce the effectiveness of market interventions. These data are therefore now provided following a one month lag. Similar points were made at the Overseas Development Institute conference in June 2000 (see ODI 2001, 2000).

[18] Persaud's study bases its argument on the following: (a) In the short run, there is compelling evidence to indicate that markets cannot distinguish between the good and the sustainable; (b) In a herding environment, tighter market sensitive risk management systems and more data transparency in fact make markets more prone to a crisis; (c) The growing fashion in risk management is to move away from discretionary judgments about risk to more quantitative and market sensitive approaches. Analysis is based on the daily earnings at risk. A rise in market volatility hits the daily earnings ratio (DEAR) limits of some banks, causing a hit in the DEAR limits of other banks. Several banks sell the same asset at the same time, leading to an increase in market volatility and higher correlations.

[19] The SDDS was launched in April 1996 and became operational in September 1998.

12.4.2 *Assessing Transparency*

In view of the arguments presented above, it is worth assessing the efforts towards increased transparency. The SDDS is one of the major tools for providing transparency. But only 60 out of the 184 IMF member countries are currently subscribers. This data cast some doubts about the role that both market and government responses are playing in favoring adherence to information disclosure projects. In fact this lack of subscription undermines the arguments favoring increased transparency.

The first line of argument put forth to promote SDDS subscription has been that compliance with the codes brings down spreads. The IMF has produced some research papers that emphasize the link. Although literature is rather scarce in testing the same hypothesis, research does not show conclusive results to confirm the role of SDDS subscription as a determinant of borrowing costs. In most cases, macroeconomic fundamentals are the main determinant of spreads. When not, the globalization of financial markets and liquidity conditions are found to be the significant determinants.[20] Table 12.5 summarizes the results of a simple econometric exercise undertaken on the role of SDDS in spreads determination. The finding is that, allowing for auto correlation and fixed effects,[21] SDDS is not significant.[22]

The studies by the IMF do not take into account the fact that spreads have been going down for all countries (thus, it is a global trend), not just for the countries that comply with the SDDS or the GDDS. Thus, the international environment and international liquidity have not been factored in those exercises. In addition, there is no economic proof that standards and codes

[20] Some research includes Ferrucci (2003), on determinants of emerging market sovereign bond spreads; Gelos and Wei (2002), on transparency and international investor behavior, and Kamin and von Kleist (1999), also on determinants of spreads.

[21] Fixed effects estimation is a method of estimating parameters from a panel data set. This approach is relevant when one expects that the averages of the dependant variable will be different for each cross-section unit, or each time period, but the average of the errors will not. In such a case random effects estimation would give inconsistent estimates of b in the model: $Y + Xb + e$.

[22] The exercise used time series/cross-section data for 11 countries for the period 1994 I to 2003 IV with a total of 250 observations. The explained variable, the logarithm of the spread, was calculated on the base of the JP Morgan's Emerging Market Bond Index Plus (EMBI+) with quarterly average data. The set of explanatory variables included in the regressions comprised: 'Annual GDP growth' in quarterly terms, 'long term interest rates' constructed by weighting Government Bond Yields of the United States, Japan, and the Euro Area; a series of variables to measure debt factors (debt service as a percent of exports and public external debt as a percent of exports); a dummy variable to measure SDDS: 1 after date of subscription; 0 otherwise. For the quarter in which subscription takes place, the dummy is given the value one if the subscription takes place in the first half of the quarter and zero if it is in the second half of the quarter. The estimation method is Generalized Least Squares (GLS). It assumes that residuals are cross-section heteroskedastic and contemporaneously uncorrelated. To correct the heteroskedasticity within each cross-section we used the White covariance estimator. To correct autocorrelation, a common $AR(1)$ term was included in the pool estimation.

Table 12.5. The Link Between Sovereign Spreads and SDDS: Econometric Results

Generalized least squares	log(Spread)			
	GLS	GLS with fixed effects	GLS with AR(1)	GLS with fixed effects and AR(1)
Constant	5.52[a]		5.75[a]	
GDP growth	−0.05[a]	−0.04[a]	−0.02[a]	−0.01[a]
Long term interest rate	−0.04	−0.11[b]	−0.37[a]	−0.48[a]
Public debt as a per cent of export	0.02[a]	0.02[b]	0.04[a]	0.02
SDDS	−0.13	−0.21[c]	−0.13	−0.19
AR(1)			0.92[a]	0.81[a]
Fixed effects test		62.11[a]		63.24[a]
R[2]	0.95	0.98	1.00	1.00
F	971[a]	666	24580[a]	2.E+11[a]
DW	0.29	0.58	.76	1.71
Total panel observations	250	250	239	239
Included observations	36	36	36	36
Period 94.1-02.4				

Notes: The estimation method is GLS (Cross section weights). [a] Denotes significant at the 1 percent level. [b] Denotes significant at the 5 percent level. [c] Denotes significant at the 10 percent level.
Source: Author's estimations based on quarterly data for the sample period 1994–2003.

are appropriate. There are a number of studies showing that there is no proof that this really works (see, for example, Sarr 2001; Mosley 2002; and Rojas-Suarez 2002).

Does subscription to SDDS and GDDS affect sovereign ratings? This is the second line of argument favoring SDDS/GDDS. Figure 12.3 shows countries classified into investment grade and speculative grade. For both categories there are countries that have subscribed neither to GDDS nor SDDS. This means that, in actual practice, a country can get a credit rating even if it does not comply with the SDDS and the GDDS. Thus, the view that market discipline (credit ratings responding to the availability of information based on a consistent data base) in the form of upgrades and downgrades of investor rating) is not really working in practice.

The view from the credit rating agency has been that standards and codes may—although there is no conclusive evidence—affect credit ratings; but there is no evidence on bond spreads:

Credit rating agencies looked favourably at countries that had published ROSCs although there is no conclusive evidence that the resulting upgrades in their assessments had led to lower spreads on international bond issues ... Credit rating agencies look mainly at the standards on data dissemination, banking supervision and the overall health of the financial sector, fiscal transparency, and transparency regarding monetary and financial policy. The provision of data on official reserves and international

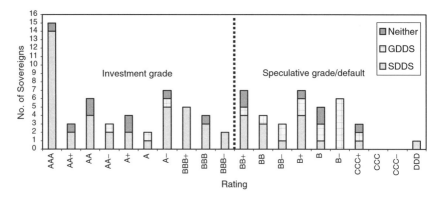

Figure 12.3. Sovereign ratings and SDDS/GDDS
Source: Fitch ratings.

investment positions were also seen to be helpful in ratings decisions. While the agencies recognize that issues such as corporate governance were important, these were considered less likely to be proximate causes of a sovereign default. (Price 2003)

Neither on the case of investment grade nor spreads does subscription to SDDS seem to radically benefit a country's situation. Summing up the private sector view, David Lubin argues that

since Standards and Codes is a public-sector driven initiative the private sector interest is a muted one... [Also,] the link between transparency and creditworthiness is not straightforward—the causality usually runs from creditworthiness to transparency— while some of the information is not crucial to risk assessments (and the value which the BWIs apply maybe too high). What the exercise should do is to assess the vulnerability of the foreign exchange balance sheet, as it was the weaknesses there that led to the crisis.[23]

Although the methodology to assess sovereign risk was changed after both the Mexican and Asian crises, the role played by information provided by the subscription to SDDS and/or the publication of ROSCs is rather a complementary one. After 1997, greater emphasis was put on off-budget and contingent liabilities, reserves adequacy, and detailed data regarding external debt (Bhatia 2002: 48). But greater emphasis does not mean that this information was not taken into account before; instead, a new look was given to already existing data.[24]

---

[23] David Lubin examines the reasons for the lack of interest by the private sector in standards and codes, and in this context discusses some underlying problems with the initiative. The document further examines other areas where steps need to be taken as a means of crisis prevention. His article is published in Schneider (2003: ch. 12).

[24] See Schneider (2005: annex 7, pp. 47–8) for one example of the marginal changes in risk rating methodologies undertaken in recent times.

Thus, the emphasis given to transparency in the current debate is overemphasized as indicated by these results. The links between compliance with data standards and spreads/credit ratings is weak.

12.4.3 *The BWIs: Monitoring and Surveillance*

The task of assessing the implementation of standards by countries is carried out jointly by the IMF and World Bank. These assessments are based on the World Bank and IMF FSAPs and IMF Article IV on surveillance, which includes progress in standards implementation among the subjects of surveillance under the heading of the strength of the financial sector more generally. The administrative capacity of the IMF is likely to be stretched by the Reports on Observance of Standards and Codes (ROSCs) conducted for a limited number of codes for some countries.

In addition, in the case of the IMF, it would be fair to make the evaluation of monitoring ROSCs independently of its other functions, such as lending.[25] Resources required for assessment and implementation are expected to be large. At the country level, the assessment exercises will often place an additional burden on a limited supply of supervisory capacity. Expanding this capacity takes considerable time. And countries are then faced with the prospect of the flight of human capital. A well-trained supervisor may be tempted by attractive alternative employment opportunities in the private sector, or even in the IMF or the World Bank, which themselves have recently been increasing the number of their staff with expertise in this area.

However, there remains a real danger that international assessment of countries' supervision will be at the expense of actual supervision on the ground (See UNCTAD 2001: ch. IV). A serious limitation of the monitoring process is that there is no public schedule with regard to the timing of future publications, and no information on the criteria followed in prioritizing one country or one code over another.[26]

One alternative to deal with the constraints faced by the BWIs serving as global monitors would be greater use of self-assessment combined with a peer review process. The Financial Action Task Force (FATF) is a useful

[25] As part of its monitoring task, the IMF has published and evaluation of progress in fiscal transparency ROSCs. The report publishes a cross-country comparison of progress in the form of 'check boxes' that end up by providing the private sector with pass/fail criteria. This exercise has the risk of putting the IMF in such a position of a credit risk agency, quantitatively 'rating' countries regarding to their progress on ROSC. See IMF (2003).

[26] In the case of human resources, for example, trained personnel for banking supervision are scarce. Technical assistance to train supervisors is a solution, but two drawbacks have to be considered: first, it takes time to train, and second, incentives exist for human capital flight due to competition between the demand for supervisors at local level supervision and those required for global monitoring, as was earlier mentioned.

example where self-assessment and mutual evaluation procedures are the primary instruments to monitor progress.[27] FATF is appealing because in its arrangements, members are strongly committed to the discipline of multilateral monitoring and peer review. Self-assessment is followed by a mutual evaluation process, each country is examined in turn by the FATF on the basis of an on-the-ground visit, conducted by a team of experts in the legal, financial, and law enforcement fields from other member governments. The result of the visit is a report that assesses the extent to which the evaluated member has progressed in implementing an effective system to counter money laundering and highlights areas that still need further progress. The process is enhanced by a policy to deal with members that are not in compliance. It represents a graduated approach aimed at reinforcing peer pressure on member governments to take action to tighten their anti-money-laundering systems.

The BWIs could be assigned an important role in coordinating the process and providing technical assistance to some countries in self-assessments and implementation. The BWIs could also play a useful role as depositories of information and links to sources of information at country level on self-assessment, thus facilitating the use of this information by market participants. This would also take care of the problems of resources and conflict of interest present in the BWIs.[28]

Moreover, identification of where different countries are with respect to their institutional, legal, and regulatory framework vis-à-vis the codes will also help to identify the real problems in applying a uniform rule across countries. The exercise will also be useful in defining the transition period needed for implementation. Another result of such an exercise will be in defining the areas in which a rule can be applied, and in which voluntary principles can best be utilized.

Thus, self-assessments backed by peer review of the type described offer the potential for ownership, independence, and rigor. If supported by technical assistance as needed, they can minimize both the extraordinary cost and difficulty of managing a centralized monitoring system. With these issues in mind, the next section will take a deeper view of the concerns relating to developing countries and the S&C initiative.

---

[27] See FATF's website: www1.oecd.org/fatf/AboutFATF_en.htm#What%20is for more details on these features.

[28] The first step forward may be country self-assessment available on the treasury website. The United States has set an example; the format is simple and may serve as one example for the simplifying of information. Among emerging markets, India has undertaken an exercise with the technical details of ten standards and posted their assessment on the Reserve Bank of India website (www.rbi.org.in/). Technical assistance for self-assessment of the kind India has undertaken may be a better way forward than the use of negative incentives for compliance.

12.5 Developing Countries

As it was a challenge to define standards, it is an even greater challenge to gain their global acceptance in order to ensure implementation.

There is an asymmetry in the incentive structure to implement standards, as industrialized countries do not borrow from the BWIs and therefore standards and codes are not binding for them. Many emerging markets have pre-paid to the Fund, but they need the IMF seal of approval for signals to the private sector. Since the codes are based on benchmarks appropriate to industrialized countries, their application is a potential source of comparative disadvantage for developing countries, especially in the financial sector. Other asymmetries are those in the resources required for implementation and transparency. The international community shies away from endorsing action requiring high-frequency disclosure of data on the large short-term positions in assets denominated in a country's currency held by foreign firms other than banks (a category including hedge funds), which several developing (and some developed) countries perceive as threats to the stability of their exchange rates and financial markets. Moreover, there is an asymmetry in jurisdiction.[29] The World Bank has no jurisdiction over Part I countries.[30] The asymmetry between developing and industrialized countries increases as we move away from using Standards and Codes solely as informing surveillance and creditors start to include compliance in their lending decisions.

Asymmetries must be taken into account when explaining the developing country perspective. Issues such as ownership, appropriateness, incentives, voluntariness, resources, and transition periods have to be considered.

12.5.1 'Ownership' Will Not Come Without the Representation of Developing Countries' Issues and Concerns

'OWNERSHIP' CANNOT BE IMPOSED FROM OUTSIDE

The effectiveness of Standards and Codes as a tool of global financial stability depends on the number of countries adopting them and the extent to which they are implemented. The latter is closely related to the way in which S&C are incorporated into the norms of business practice. In order to achieve effective implementation, country 'ownership' of these policies is crucial. In the case of developing countries, 'ownership' is not possible without representation and positive incentives for implementation. The most constructive incentive for implementation is the appropriateness and meaningfulness of standards in the national interest.

[29] See Mohammed (2003) for a discussion on this.

[30] Part I countries are contributors to the International Development Association (IDA) who make their donations in freely convertible currency.

'Ownership' of reforms in the domestic financial architecture cannot be achieved while the membership of the FSF[31] and other international organizations[32] involved in standard setting is so heavily dominated by the industrialized nations. Although developing countries were well represented in the formulation of some of the codes, such as those on transparency, their participation, and representation have been limited with respect to others.

The Financial Stability Forum is a very important initiative. To include members from developing countries as full members, and not just a few in working groups, will enhance its legitimacy and increase commitment. 'Ownership' is meaningless without representation.

12.5.2 'Ownership' Comes with Appropriateness

Appropriateness of the standards is another issue crucial to ensure implementation. The 'ownership' principle cannot work if national governments are not convinced about the appropriateness of some standards.

This is the 'one-size-fits-all' dilemma. In discussing the appropriateness of the selected standards, Rodrik (2000) points out that many rich countries have prospered by following different paths in corporate governance, where insiders and stakeholders have played a much more significant role, and in finance, where close links between governments have often been the rule rather than the exception. The Reserve Bank of India—perhaps the only country that evaluates the appropriateness and implementation issues and posts the information in the public domain—makes similar points.[33]

Although there is recognition in principle about the problems resulting from the varying stages of development and institutional capacities, real solutions are required. In the absence of appropriate institutions, developing countries' commitment to embracing standards and codes is not likely to

---

[31] At the time of writing, the FSF has a total of 40 members, comprising three representatives from each G-7 country (one each from the treasury, central bank, and supervisory agency); one each from Australia, Hong Kong (China), Singapore, and the Netherlands; six from international organizations (International Monetary Fund (two), World Bank (two), Bank for International Settlements (one) and Organisation for Economic Co-operation and Development (one); six from international regulatory and supervisory groupings (Basel Committee on Banking Supervision (two), International Organization of Securities Commissions (two) and International Association of Insurance Supervisors (two)), and two from Committees of Central Bank experts (Committee on the Global Financial System (one) and Committee on Payment and Settlement Systems (one), plus the Chairman). See Appendix 12.1.

[32] See Appendix 12.2 in this chapter for the countries represented in the various working groups of the FSF.

[33] The reports of the various committees are available on the Reserve Bank of India website: www.rbi.org.in/.

lead to the desired goals. Pistor (2000) examines this aspect with regard to legal rules, and argues that historical evidence supports the proposition that imported legal systems have in most cases not produced very efficient outcomes. The content of the rules is not as important as the existence of constituencies that demand these rules and the compatibility of the imported norms with pre-existing legal norms as well as pre-existing economic and political conditions.

Standardized rules are unlikely to be effective in countries where complementary laws exist only in part or not at all. For example, commercial law is a necessary prerequisite for the International Organization of Securities Commission (IOSCO) standards, and an independent judiciary is a prerequisite for defining and bringing into practice the code on insolvency. The issue of 'ownership' is also related closely to the 'incentives' a country has to implement standards, because at the end, self-interest is the best incentive.

12.5.3 'Adoption of Standards and Participation in External Assessments Should Be Voluntary' (FSF 2000: 10)

The Executive Board of the International Monetary Fund (January 29, 2001) has voiced similar sentiments. The Directors agreed that the adoption and assessment of internationally recognized standards will remain voluntary. They recognized that priorities for implementing standards would differ by country and over time, and that assessments would need to take into account differences in members' economic circumstances and stages of development (IMF 2001a). Although initial public statements have concentrated on the voluntary principle, a shift in focus is perceptible. In some cases, standards and codes are already a part of conditionality:

- Ecuador was required to publish the ROSC report on data dissemination in order to secure a stand-by agreement with the IMF;
- Uruguay's stand-by arrangement included recommendations of Fiscal ROSC;
- Ghana's arrangements for a fund program included recommendations of financial sector ROSCs; and
- Brazil's stand-by arrangement included recommendations of the Corporate Governance ROSC.[34]

---

[34] Implementation of standards and codes is a process. When the pressure to implement is tied to the period of an IMF program (Standby agreements take one year or 15–18 months), the period is too short to implement legal and institutional changes and progress can only be limited.

Developing countries have expressed concern that compliance with standards and codes should not become a part of conditionality; they believe compliance should be voluntary (see, for example, Reddy 2001a, b) because they are already overburdened with conditionality. Many, including Brazil (Gottschalk 2001: 16) and Russia (Granville 2001: 7) have also expressed the view that capacity building is more important than conditionality. While developing countries have been supportive of the need to observe certain minimum standards in areas relevant to the maintenance of the international monetary system, including greater transparency, there is less agreement on the design of some codes as being relevant and applicable in economies with different legal institutional set-ups and at different stages of development.[35]

Market incentive needs to be reviewed.[36] The international debate needs to focus greater attention on the possibilities of bad judgments by market participants. Market incentives have been brought into uncharted territory too early for single rules to be applied globally.

12.5.4 The Resources Required for the Implementation of Standards and Codes are Expected to be Enormous, and Many Countries Face Serious Practical Constraints

As discussed above, the resource constraint has been identified as the major problem in implementing standards and codes, and therefore the Bretton Woods Institutions, the Bank for International Settlements and the standard setting bodies are all supporting implementation through technical assistance. The government of the United Kingdom has taken the lead by setting up the Financial Sector Reform and Strengthening (FIRST) Initiative, a technical assistance program for implementation, in conjunction with other donors. In practice, the coordination between the World Bank and the FIRST Initiative is a weak one. Technical assistance is not geared to follow

[35] Mr Jin Liqun, Deputy Finance Minister of China, for example, voiced this at a conference organized by the IMF:

Developing countries are given to understand that they can pre-empt a financial crisis and achieve economic stability, providing they follow rigorously the international standards and codes. But there are two questions to answer: first, are the standards and codes suitable to developing countries at their stage of development; and second, do they have a minimum institutional capacity to apply these standards and codes at the same level as developed countries? (IMF 2001b).

[36] Axel Nawrath (Chairman of the Follow-Up Group on Incentives to Foster Implementation of Standards) to William McDonough (Chairman of the BCBS) (April 4, 2001): 'I am of the view that the new [Basel] Accord can provide incentives, albeit indirectly, to banks and other market practitioners to pay attention to Standards. This should in turn raise awareness among economies to the need to upgrade the implementation of Standards in their jurisdictions'.

up the recommendation in the FSAPS. Nor are the countries that receive technical assistance the same which were identified as weak in the FSAP reports.

12.5.5 The Goals of Financial Stability are Better Served If Some of the Limitations in Definition and Implementation As Well As Intrinsic Limits to the Codes Themselves are Recognized

Countries implementing standards and codes need to recognize that these are not static rules. Flexibility to take into account increasing sophistication in financial markets is important, and governments need to take care not to waste resources on standards that may already be outdated.

The political economy of implementing S&C should be considered carefully. International standards and codes are supposed to play a leading role in transforming financial regulatory governance in post-crisis East Asia. Walter (2003) argues that the main problem with this reform strategy is that it underestimates the likelihood of implementation failure in the reforming countries. Contrary to the intention of the standards and codes, the author shows that regulatory forbearance remains chronic in a number of East Asian countries. The result is that standards of prudential regulation lag behind the process of financial liberalization.

Implementing codes is a very recent exercise, and discussion of their effectiveness and limitations is therefore limited to a few specific codes which have been the subject of recent research. Some examples of the limitations are illustrated[37] in the carrying out of transparency codes (including SDSS and those on banking supervision and regulation), security listing and banking capital adequacy. In the case of SDDS, Mosley (2002) attributes the prohibitive costs of implementation or transition faced by governments as compared to the rather marginal/indirect use of the information by the private sector as grounds for the under-subscription to the SDDS. Transparency in the field of banking supervision and regulation can also be blurred because of off-balance sheet items in national accounts and corporate balance sheets. These cannot as yet be covered adequately by accounting rules and thus it may be difficult to assess exposure and its distinction between the short and long term. In some countries, the criteria for licensing of banks may have (usually proximate) relations to banking stability but cannot prevent serious banking instability or banking crises (UNCTAD 2001).

The discussion around Basel II has also illustrated that implementation is beset with problems in developing countries. Some even go as far as to argue that Basel II may increase pro-cyclicality of capital flows and the

---

[37] See Sarr (2001) for costs exceeding benefits of security list standards and Rojas-Suarez (2002) for limitations of capital adequacy standard in indicating a banking crisis.

cost of funds to developing countries (see, in this regard, Chapter 10, this volume).

A PricewaterhouseCoopers study (2004) for the European Commission of the macroeconomic and financial consequences of new rules for the capital of banks in the EU the National Institute of Economic and Social Research (NIESR) of the United Kingdom developed a taxonomy of characteristic features of financial crises, which can serve as a useful benchmark for reviewing the effectiveness of the key financial codes and standards in the prevention and management of such crises. Not all these features were of equal weight in all the historical instances studied.[38]

Many but not all features of financial crisis are covered by the codes and when they are covered, guidelines for policy making at both national and international levels are often missing, or at an early stage of development (see Cornford 2004: 14–16).

12.5.6 *If Globalization is Here to Stay, then the Challenge is to Prepare Developing Countries for a Highly Integrated World and Work Out Transition Periods*

The risk inherent in opening up capital markets requires a well thought out preparatory stage and hence the growing acceptance for gradualism. The principles behind Standards and Codes are also some of the preconditions identified for the opening up of the capital account. Capital account liberalization requires that central banks have effective regulatory, supervisory, enforcement, and informational structures in place. Liberalization must not be seen to require authorities to retreat from these essential functions. Priority setting and sequencing of the implementation exercise for standards and codes therefore need to be linked to the timing and sequencing of capital account opening in global capital market.

Research on country experiences needs to be collated in order to understand fully the implications of applying internationally defined codes to countries with divergent systems. The risks inherent in introducing codes without an understanding of the outcomes justify a gradual approach to implementation. The dire consequences of adopting a 'big bang' approach to capital account liberalization are well documented in the literature (see, for example, Schneider 2001). Gradualism also allows time for the inevitable learning curve in developing countries.

For official and financial incentives, an understanding of the transition period is crucial for the initiative to work to ensure financial stability. The

---

[38] In the interests of abbreviation and clarification the descriptions of features of financial crises which follow sometimes differ in minor ways from those of the NIESR.

IMF and World Bank can play an important role in helping member countries in this regard. The ROSC exercise may not provide information with respect to compliance in the form desired by the private sector, but it can be useful in identifying constraints in member countries and in working out transition periods.

12.6 Conclusion

12.6.1 *The Need for a Truly Global Initiative*

Although the initiative on S&C was taken in response to the financial crises of the 1990s in developing countries, difficulties with compliance and implementation also exist in the industrialized countries as recent events in the United States and other industrialized capital markets have illustrated. Despite this, the incentive structure for implementing standards and codes—other than those dealing with money laundering and terrorist financing—applies primarily to developing and transition countries that borrow from the private financial markets or from bilateral or multilateral official sources.

The standards and codes exercise is not the result of a participatory process jointly owned by all countries; rather, it is designed mainly by the G-8 and other industrialized countries.[39] This is why developing countries need a greater voice at the FSF. Issues as appropriateness and ownership, as well as the resources for implementation are a major concern.

12.6.2 *Re-Defining the Objective Function*

The objective of the standards and codes exercise is global financial stability. But the present prioritization of countries and codes for monitoring compliance by the BWIs indicate that global financial stability was not the main objective in choosing either the countries or codes. A better objective may be to utilize the standards to benchmark financial sector reforms while acknowledging that in the long-run financial sector reforms are likely to make an important contribution to global financial stability. The shift in emphasis on the rationale for this initiative will also result in a re-prioritization of resources and efforts in the standards and codes exercise and reduce the need for quantitative and simplified information by the private sector on an on-going basis; resources required to produce ROSCs can be re-allocated to a follow-up of the recommendations of the FSAP

---

[39] See Appendix 12.1 for countries' participation in standard setting bodies and Appendix 12.2 for membership of Financial Stability Forum working groups.

reports through technical assistance to developing countries. In addition, the emphasis on the standards and codes exercise is closely linked to the degree of international financial integration. Recent research has failed to confirm the link between financial sector liberalization and growth. The sequencing and prioritization of the standards and codes needs to be integrated into the discussion of the degree of financial sector liberalization and work out transition periods instead of instant assessments of compliance for developing countries.

12.6.3 *Alternatives to the IMF Monitoring Mechanism*

The shortcomings of the present monitoring mechanism through reports on the observance of standards and codes by the BWIs suggest that there maybe other alternatives to manage it. Self-assessments by countries, backed by a peer review process, offer the potential for independence, ownership, and rigor. It is a better way of dealing with ground realities and the appropriateness of standards. It also offers a constructive channel for feedback from countries across the world into the work at the Financial Stability Forum (FSF) to define codes that are flexible enough to cope with a dynamic and heterogeneous world.

12.6.4 *The Role of the IMF in the Information Generation Process and the Quality of Information*

A lot of emphasis was given to the provision of information to the private sector to enable them to make better assessment of risk and emerging vulnerabilities. Is it the role of the IMF to provide information to the private sector? It is assumed that more information will lead to better judgments and act as a tool of crisis prevention. Some, while accepting transparency is good, question if too much transparency may be bad by leading to a crisis or contagion.

The private sector response to the standards and codes exercise is a muted one. The origins of the exercise lay in the view that it was lack of transparency that led to misinformed judgments about economies that resulted in herding behavior and contagion. The subdued response weakens the market incentive as an incentive to comply with the codes.

There is also a tension between the information demanded by the market in a simplified quantitative format, and a time-consuming complex process of implementing the codes whose progress cannot be quantified in any reasonable form. In the face of the evidence of the limited use of this information by the private sector, is the exercise worthwhile?

Appendix 12.1

Table 12A1.1. Country Groups' Participation in Standard-Setting Bodies

	Monetary policy and financial policies:	Fiscal transparency:	Data dissemination:	Insolvency and creditor rights systems:	Corporate governance:	International accounting standards:	International auditing standards:	Systemically important payment systems:	Banking supervision:	Securities regulation:	Insurance core principles:
Organization	IMF (International Monetary Fund)	IMF (International Monetary Fund)	IMF (International Monetary Fund)	WB (World Bank)	OECD (Organization for Economic Cooperation and Development)	IASB (International Accounting Standards Board)	IFAC (International Federation of Accountants)	CPSS (Committee on Payment and Settlement Systems)	BCBS (Basel Committee)	IOSCO (International Organization for Securities Commissions)	IAIS (International Association of Insurance Supervisors)
Participation	184	184	184	184	30	This is not a membership organization	113	11	13	104	118
	G-10: 11 countries	*G-10:* 11 countries	*G-10:* 11 countries	*G-10:* 11 countries	*G-10:* 11 countries		*G-10:* 11 countries	*G-10:* 11 countries	*G-10:* 11 countries	*G-10:* 10 countries	*G-10:* 11 countries
	Other industrialized countries: 16 countries	*Other industrialized countries:* 16 countries	*Other industrialized countries:* 16 countries	*Other industrialized countries:* 16 countries	*Other industrialized countries:* 13 countries		*Other industrialized countries:* 18 countries		*Other industrialized countries:* 2 countries	*Other industrialized countries:* 17 countries	*Other industrialized countries:* 18 countries
	Other developing countries: 128 countries	*Other developing countries:* 128 countries	*Other developing countries:* 128 countries	*Other developing countries:* 128 countries	*Other developing countries:* 1 country		*Other developing countries:* 59 countries			*Other developing countries:* 54 countries	*Other developing countries:* 70 countries
	Transition economies: 29 countries	*Transition economies:* 29 countries	*Transition economies:* 29 countries	*Transition economies:* 29 countries	*Transition economies:* 5 countries		*Transition economies:* 25 countries			*Transition economies:* 23 countries	*Transition economies:* 19 countries

Note: Country grouping according to World Economic Outlook, IMF. The term 'country' also refers to territories or areas.

Source: Organizations' websites and Financial Stability Forum website.

Appendix 12.2

Table 12A2.1. Membership in FSF Working Groups

	Task force on Implementation of Standards	Incentives to Foster Implementation of Standards	Working Group on Capital Flows	Working Group on Offshore Centers	Working Group on Enhanced Disclosure	Working Group on Highly Leveraged Institutions	Working Group on Deposit Insurance
Established	September 1999	April 2000	April 1999	April 1999	June 1999	April 1999	April 2000
Ended	March 2000	September 2001	April 2000	April 2000	April 2001	April 2000	April 2001
TOR	To explore issues related to and consider a strategy for fostering the implementation of international standards for strengthening financial systems.	To monitor progress in implementing core standards and further raise market awareness of standards.	To evaluate measures in borrower and creditor countries that could reduce the volatility of capital flows and the risks to financial systems of excessive short-term external indebtedness.	To consider the significance of offshore financial centres for global financial stability.	To assess the feasibility and utility of enhanced public disclosure by financial intermediaries.	To recommend actions to reduce the destabilizing potential of institutions employing a high degree of leverage (HLIs) in the financial markets of developed and developing countries.	To review recent experience with deposit insurance schemes and consider the desirability and feasibility of setting out international guidance for such arrangements.
Final report	Issues of the task force on implementation of standards.	Final report of the follow-up group on incentives to foster implementations of standards.	Report of the working group on capital flows.	Report of the working group on offshore centres.	Multidisciplinary working group on enhanced disclosure final report.	Report of the working group on highly leveraged institutions.	Guidance for developing effective deposit insurance systems.
Member countries	G-10: Canada France Germany Italy Japan Netherlands Sweden United Kingdom United States *Other industrialized countries:* Australia Hong Kong (China)(Chair) *Other developing countries:* China India Mexico South Africa	G-10: Canada France Germany (Chair) Italy Japan United Kingdom United States *Other industrialized countries:* Australia Hong Kong (China) Singapore *Other developing countries:* Argentina India	G-10: Canada France Germany Italy (Chair) Japan United Kingdom United States *Other developing countries:* Brazil Chile Malaysia South Africa	G-10: Canada (Chair) France Germany Italy Japan Switzerland United Kingdom United States *Other industrialized countries:* Singapore *Other developing countries:* Thailand	G-10: Canada France Germany Japan Sweden United Kingdom United States *Other industrialized countries:* Australia *Other developing countries:* Mexico	G-10: Canada France Germany Italy Japan Netherlands United Kingdom (Chair) United States *Other industrialized countries:* Australia Hong Kong (China)	G-10: Canada (Chair) France Germany Italy Japan United States *Other developing countries:* Argentina Chile Jamaica Mexico Philippines *Transition economies:* Hungary

Source: Compiled from Financial Stability Forum website.

Appendix 12.3

Table 12A3.1. FSAP per fiscal year* (country groups)

	2000	2001	2002	2003	2004	2005	2006
Key players: G-10	Canada		Switzerland Sweden United Kingdom	Japan Germany	France	Italy	
Major EMEs	South Africa India	Poland Mexico	Philippines Korea	Hong Kong (China) Singapore Brazil Russia			
Non-key players:	Colombia Lebanon El Salvador Hungary Iran Kazakhstan Ireland Cameroon Estonia	Ghana Guatemala Armenia Israel Peru Yemen Senegal Slovenia Iceland Czech Republic Uganda Dominican Republic United Arab Emirates Latvia Tunisia Finland Croatia Georgia	Gabon Lithuania Luxemburg Costa Rica Bulgaria Sri Lanka Morocco Nigeria Slovak Republic Barbados Ukraine Egypt Zambia	Kyrgyz Republic Bangladesh Honduras Malta Mauritius Oman Mozambique Tanzania Romania Algeria Bolivia	Macedonia Jordan Kuwait New Zealand Kenya Ecuador Azerbaijan Austria Netherlands Nicaragua Chile Saudi Arabia Pakistan Moldova ECCU	Belarus Sudan Norway Belgium Paraguay Rwanda Serbia Albania Greece Trinidad and Tobago Bahrain Madagascar Mauritania	Jamaica Spain Namibia Uruguay Guyana Denmark Australia Bosnia and Herzegovina Brunei Darussalam Fiji Portugal Montenegro Turkey San Marino

(cont.)

Table 12A3.1. (*Continued*)

	2000	2001	2002	2003	2004	2005	2006
Total key players	3	2	7	4	1	1	0
Total non-key players	9	18	13	11	15	13	14
Total G-10	1	0	3	2	1	1	0
TOTAL	12	20	20	15	16	14	14
FSAP Updates		Lebanon	Hungary	Iceland	Ghana	Senegal	*Tunisia*
		South Africa			Slovenia	Colombia	*Guatemala*
					Kazakhstan	Uganda	*Georgia*
					El Salvador	Peru	*Poland*
						Armenia	*Ireland*
						Hungary	*Iran*
							Mexico
							21
TOTAL	12	22	21	16	20	20	
Average FSAP reports per year/only completed reports:	16						
Average FSAP reports per year completed and ongoing/planned reports:	19						

Note: *Countries in italics have on-going or planned FSAP.

Source: IMF, Independent Evaluation Office (2006). Report on the Evaluation of the Financial Sector Assessment Program's January, Appendix Table I, p. 124.

References

Acharya, S. (2001). 'New International Standards for Financial Stability: Desirable Regulatory Reform or Runaway Juggernaut?' in S. Griffith-Jones and A. Bhattacharya (eds.), *Developing Countries and the Global Financial System*. London: Commonwealth Secretariat.

Basel Committee on Banking Supervision (BCBS) (1983). *The Principles for the Supervision of Banks' Foreign Establishments*. Basel: Bank for International Settlements (BIS).

—— (1988). *Framework for International Convergence of Capital Measurement and Capital Standards*. Basel: BIS.

—— (2000*a*). *Report of the Working Group on Capital Flows*. Basel: BIS.

—— (2000*b*). *Report of the Working Group on Highly Leveraged Institutions*. Basel, BIS.

Beers, D. and Cavanaugh, M. (1997). *Sovereign Credit Ratings: A Primer*. New York: Standard & Poor's.

—— —— (2004). *Sovereign Credit Ratings: A Primer*. New York: Standard & Poor's.

Bhatia, A. V. (2002). 'Sovereign Credit Ratings Methodology: An Evaluation'. IMF Working Paper 02/170 (1 October). International Monetary Fund, Washington, DC.

Cady, J. (2004). 'Does SDDS Subscription Reduce Borrowing Costs for Emerging Market Economies?' IMF Working Paper 04/58 (1 April). International Monetary Fund, Washington, DC.

Charpentier, S. (2001). 'Nicaragua: Case Study on the Application of Priority Standards and Codes for International Financial Stability'. Unpublished.

Christofides, C., Mulder, C.B., and Tiffin, A.J. (2003). 'The Link Between Adherence to International Standards of Good Practice, Foreign Exchange Spreads, and Ratings'. IMF Working Paper 03/74 (1 April). International Monetary Fund, Washington, DC.

Clark, A. (2000). 'International Standards and Codes'. Remarks at a conference on the Role of Regulation in a Global Context, City University Business School and University of London.

Cornford, A. (2000a). 'Commentary on the Financial Stability Forum's Report on the Working Group on Capital Flows'. G-24 Discussion Paper Series, No. 7 (December). New York, NY and Geneva: United Nations Conference on Trade and Development and Center for International Development, Harvard University.

—— (2000b). 'The Basel Committee Proposal for Revised Capital Standards: Rationale, Design and Possible Incidence'. Geneva: United Nations Conference on Trade and Development. Unpublished.

—— (2001). 'The Basel Committee Proposal for Revised Capital Standards: Mark 2 and the State of Play.' UNCTAD Discussion Paper, No. 156 (August). United Nations Conference on Trade and Development, Geneva.

—— (2004). 'Key Financial Codes and Standards: Different Views of Their Role in a New Financial Architecture'. Paper prepared for the Multi-Stakeholder Consultations on Systemic Issues organized by the New Rules for Global Finance Coalition in cooperation with the United Nations Financing for Development Office. Unpublished.

Eichengreen, B. (1999). *Toward a New International Financial Architecture*. Washington, DC: Institute for International Economics.

—— (2001). 'Strengthening the International Financial Architecture: Open Issues, Asian Concerns'. Paper prepared for the IMF/KIEP Conference on Recovery from the Asian Crisis, Seoul, May.

Eichengreen, B. and Mody, A. (2000). 'Would Collective Action Clauses Raise Borrow-ing Costs?' NBER Working Paper No. 7458 (January). National Bureau of Economic Research, Cambridge, MA.

Ferrucci, G. (2003). 'Empirical Determinants of Emerging Market Economies' Sovereign Bond Spreads'. Working Paper, No. 205. Bank of England, London.

Financial Stability Forum (FSF) (2000). 'Report of the Follow-up Group on Incentives to Foster the Implementation of Standards'. Prepared for the Fourth Meeting of the Financial Stability Forum, Basel, September 7–8.

Gelos, R.G. and Wei S.-J. (2002). Transparency and International Investor Behavior'. NBER Working Papers No. 9260 (October). National Bureau of Economic Research, Cambridge, MA.

General Accounting Office (GAO) (2003). 'International Financial Crises: Challenges Remain in IMF's Ability to Anticipate, Prevent, and Resolve Financial Crises'. Report to the Chairman, Committee on Financial Services, and to the Vice Chairman, Joint Economic Committee, United States House of Representatives, Washington, DC, June.

Glennerster, R. and Shin, Y. (2003). 'Is Transparency Good for You, and Can the IMF Help?' IMF Working Paper 03/132. International Monetary Fund, Washington, DC.

Gottschalk, R. (2001). 'A Brazilian Perspective on Reform of the International Financial Architecture'. Report commissioned by the United Kingdom Department for International Development (DFID). Unpublished.

Granville, B. (2001). 'International Financial Architecture: Russia Case Study'. Report commissioned by the DFID. Royal Institute of International Affairs, London. Unpublished.

Griffith-Jones, S. and Spratt, S. (2001). 'Will the Proposed New Basel Capital Accord Have a Net Negative Effect on Developing Countries?' Institute of Development Studies, University of Sussex, Brighton. Mimeo.

Group of 7 (1999). 'Strengthening the International Financial Architecture'. Report of G7 Finance Ministers to the Cologne Economic Summit, June.

Group of 22 (1998). 'Report of the Working Group on Transparency and Accountability' (October). Washington, DC: Group of 22.

Gugiatti, M. and Richards, A. (2003). 'Do Collective Action Clauses Influence Bond Yields? New Evidence from Emerging Markets'. Research Discussion Paper, 2003–2 (March). Reserve Bank of Australia, Sydney.

Haldane, A.G. and Scheibe, J. (2004). 'IMF Lending and Creditor Moral Hazard'. Working Paper No. 216. Bank of England, London.

Hausmann, R. and Panizza, U. (2002). 'The Mystery of the Original Sin: The Case of the Missing Apple'. Paper prepared for the conference on Currency and Maturity Mismatching: Redeeming Debt from Original Sin, The Inter-American Development Bank Washington, DC, November 21–2.

Independent Evaluation Office (IEO) of the IMF (2004). 'Evaluation of the Financial Sector Assessment Program'. Issues Paper. Draft.

Institute of International Finance (IIF) (2002). *Does Subscription to the IMF's Special Data Dissemination Standard Lower a Country's Credit spread? IIF Action Plan Proposals and Dialogue with the Private Sector*, Appendix D. Washington, DC: Institute of International Finance.

International Monetary Fund (IMF) (2000a). 'IMF Outreach on Standards and Codes'. *IMF Survey*, 29/15.

—— (2000b). *Reform of International Financial Architecture: Armenia Case Study*. Washington, DC: International Monetary Fund.

—— (2001a). *Public Information Notice (PIN)*, No. 01/17/5 (March). Washington, DC: International Monetary Fund.

—— (2001b). *IMF Survey*, (April 2) 30/7:103.

—— (2003). *Assessing and Promoting Fiscal Transparency: A Report on Progress*. Washington, DC: International Monetary Fund.

Kamin, S.B. and von Kleist, K. (1999). 'The Evolution and Determinants of Emerging Market Credit Spreads in the 1990s'. *BIS Working Paper*, No. 68. Bank for International Settlements, Basel.

Kapur, D. and Webb, R. (2000). 'Governance-Related Conditionalities of the International Financial Institutions'. G-24 Discussion Paper Series, No. 6 (August). New York and Geneva: United Nations Conference on Trade and Development and Center for International Development, Harvard University.

Killick, T. (1995). *IMF Programmes in Developing Countries*. London: Routledge.

Lubin, D. (2003). 'Standards and Codes: Firing the Wrong Target?', in B. Schneider (ed.), *The Road to International Financial Stability: Are Key Financial Standards the Answer?* London: Palgrave Macmillan.

Metcalfe, M. and Persaud, A. (2003). 'Do We Need to Go Beyond Disclosure?' in B. Schneider (ed.), *The Road to International Financial Stability: Are Key Financial Standards the Answer?* London: Palgrave-Macmillan.

Mohammed, A. (2003). 'Implementing Standards and Codes through the BWIs: An Overview of the Developing Country Perspective', in B. Schneider, *The Road to International Financial Stability: Are Key Financial Standards the Answer?* London: Palgrave-Macmillan.

Mosley, L. (2001). 'Attempting Global Standards: National Governments, International Finance, and the IMF's Data Regime'. Unpublished.

—— (2002). *Financial Globalisation and Government Policymaking*. Cambridge, MA, and New York: Cambridge University Press.

Overseas Development Institute (ODI) (2000). *Conference Report*. Available at: www.odi.org.uk.

—— (2001). *Development Policy Review* (March), 19/1. Available at: www.odi.org.uk.

Persaud, A. (2001). 'The Disturbing Interactions Between the Madness of Crowds and the Risk Management of Banks in Developing Countries and the Global Financial System', in S. Griffith-Jones and A. Bhattacharya (eds.), *Developing Countries and the Global Financial System*. London: Commonwealth Secretariat.

Petrie, M. (2003). 'Promoting Fiscal Transparency: The Complementary Roles of the IMF, Financial Markets and Civil Society'. IMF Working Paper 03/9. International Monetary Fund, Washington, DC.

Pistor, K. (2000). 'The Standardization of Law and its Effect on Developing Economies'. G-24 Working Paper Series, No. 4 (June). UNCTAD and Center for International Development, Harvard University, New York and Geneva.

Price, L. (2003). 'Effects of Standards and Codes on Country Risk Ratings', in B. Schneider (ed.), *The Road to International Financial Stability: Are Key Financial Standards the Answer?* London: Palgrave Macmillan.

PriceWaterhouseCoopers (2004). *Study on the Financial and Macroeconomic Consequences of the Draft Proposed New Capital Requirements for Banks and Investment Firms in the EU.* Final Report MARKT/2003/02/F (8 April), pp. 133–137 and Appendix 6.

Reddy, Y. V. (2001a). 'Implementation of Financial Standards and Codes: Indian Perspective and Approach'. Speech at the Conference on International Standards and Codes organized by the IMF and World Bank, Washington, DC, March 7–8.

—— (2001b). 'Issues in Implementing International Financial Standards and Codes'. Speech at the Centre for Banking Studies of the Central Bank of Sri Lanka, Colombo, June 28.

Reisen, H. (2001). 'Will Basel II Contribute to Convergence in International Capital Flows?' Development Centre, Organisation for Economic Co-operation and Development. Paris. Unpublished.

Rodrik, D. (2000). *Exchange Rate Regimes and Institutional Arrangements in the Shadow of Capital Flows.* Cambridge, MA: Harvard University Press.

Rojas-Suarez, L. (2001). 'Can International Capital Standards Strengthen Banks in Emerging Markets?' IIE Working Paper 01–10. Institute for International Economics, Washington, DC.

—— (2002). 'International Standards for Strengthening Financial Systems: Can Regional Development Banks Address Developing Countries' Concerns?' Paper prepared for the Conference on Financing for Developing: Regional Challenges and the Regional Development Banks. Institute for International Economics, Washington, DC, February 19.

Sarr, A. (2001). 'Benefits of Compliance with Securities Listing Standards—Evidence from the Depository Receipt Markets'. IMF Working Paper 01/79 (June). International Monetary Fund, Washington, DC.

Schneider, B. (2001). 'Issues in Capital Account Liberalisation'. *Development Policy Review*, 19/1.

—— (ed.) (2003a). *The Road to International Financial Stability: Are Key Financial Standards the Answer?* London: Palgrave Macmillan.

—— (2003b). 'Implications of Implementing Standards and Codes: A Developing Country Perspective', in B. Schneider (ed.), *The Road to International Financial Stability: Are Key Financial Standards the Answer?* London: Palgrave Macmilan.

—— (2005). 'Do Global Standards and Codes Prevent Financial Crises? Some Proposals on Modifying the Standards-Based Approach'. UNCTAD Discussion Paper 177.

Speyer, B. (2001). 'Standards and Codes—Essential Tools for Crisis Prevention'. *Deutsche Bank Research Bulletin* (March). Malden, MA: Blackwell Publishing.

Tsatsaronis, K. (1999). 'The Effect of Collective Action Clauses on Sovereign Bond Yields'. *BIS Quarterly Review: International Banking and Financial Market Development* (November). Basel: Bank for International Settlements.

UNCTAD (2001). *Trade and Development Report, 2001.* United Nations publication, Sales No. E.01.II.D.10, New York and Geneva.

Walter, A. (2003). 'Implementation in East Asia', in B. Schneider (ed.), *The Road to International Financial Stability: Are Key Financial Standards the Answer?* London: Palgrave Macmillan.

Glossary

adverse selection
a situation caused by incomplete or asymmetric information wherein only "bad" agents enter into an agreement because "good" agents may not be interested, and the other party of the agreement cannot infer which agents are "good" or "bad". The canonical example is how health insurance is more useful to sick individuals than to healthy ones. As a result, healthy individuals may opt out of insurance, raising premiums for those who do get insured.

aggregate demand
the total demand for goods and services in the economy during a specific time period.

asset price bubbles
a situation where asset prices increase excessively, based more on the expectation that prices will be higher in the future than on actual returns yielded by the asset. The resulting price increase incorrectly confirms the belief and leads to an inflationary spiral that ultimately collapses.

assymetric information
a situation where parties to a transaction do not have identical information.

balance of payments
the accounting instrument of international transactions between one country and all others in a given period of time. Payments coming into the country, from exports of good and services, investments and obligations owed by foreigners are called credits and enter positively. Money leaving the country, through imports, investments abroad, and liabilities held by foreigners, are called debits and enter negatively. The BOP is the sum of its component parts: the current and capital accounts.

Bank for International Settlements (BIS)
an international organization that fosters international monetary and financial cooperation among central banks/monetary authorities. Among its other tasks, the BIS conducts research and drafts recommendations for bank regulation. This latter occurs under the auspices of the Basel Committee, and many of the recommendations form the basis for regulation in countries around the world.

The Basel Committee	a committee of the BIS formed by representatives from regulatory authorities of the G10 countries, plus Luxembourg and Spain, to discuss banking supervisory matters. Periodically, the committee drafts recommendations, known as the Basel Accords, for regulatory authorities. It has no authority to enforce these recommendations, but over 100 countries implement them, at least in part. However, since they are adopted on a country by country basis, they may differ from the draft recommendations in specific issues.
Basel Accords	a term for the collected recommendations of the Basel Committee regarding banking supervision. The original Basel Accord, issued in 1988, detailed regulations that would ensure financial institutions were able to operate despite unexpected losses. These regulations, including capital adequacy requirements, addressed credit risks, and in 1996 they were updated and extended to cover market risks. A second Basel Accord, known as Basel II, was published in 2004. It attempted to improve the alignment between regulatory capital requirements and the different underlying risks faced by financial institutions.
business cycle	movement of an economy from growth to recession and back to growth. It may also refer to the fluctuations of an economy around its long-term growth trend, but this may be is a misnomer since fluctuations may follow no predictable pattern.
capital	has many different meanings in economics including: (1) assets available for generating output, (2) the monetary value of such assets, and (3) liquid assets of economic agents.
capital inflows	the flow of funds for real or financial investment into a country as when a foreign firm brings funds to establish or finance a subsidiary or a financial investment brings money to buy bonds or stocks in the country.
capital outflows	the flow of funds out of a country for real or financial investment abroad, for example when domestic residents invest abroad or when foreign investors withdraw investments. Every time money flows from one country to another it is both an outflow and an inflow with the distinction depending on the destination.
capital account	also known as the financial account, refers to that part of the balance of payments that measures inflows and outflows of funds that are associated with the real or financial assets, and that results in changes in the foreign ownership of domestic assets or changes in the ownership of assets abroad by domestic agents.
capital account convertibility	a policy that allows for the exchange of local financial assets into foreign financial assets and vice versa, freely.

capital controls	a term used for all policies available to a country to regulate capital flows. Capital controls reduce capital account convertibility by driving a wedge between the demand and supply of domestic financial assets.
capital flight	a process wherein investors sell off their investments in a country and convert the proceeds into a different currency because they fear the assets will lose their value sharply. These fears often relate to exchange rate problems or expected regulatory changes. Capital flight is thus a large, sudden capital outflow.
capital movement	the flow of money or productive assets among countries.
capital adequacy requirements	a regulation that requires banks and some other financial agents to cover the normal risks of their operations. It is typically set as a portion of a bank's total assets, weighted by some evaluation of their risk.
conditionality	a condition attached to a loan or to debt relief forcing the borrower to adopt specific policies or meet specific targets. Frequently conditionality is used by international organizations like the IMF or the World Bank on loans to developing countries. Sometimes grouped under the label structural adjustments, conditionalities can be uncontroversial, as in anti-corruption measures, or highly controversial, as in fiscal austerity or privatization measures. A main criticism of conditionalities is that they subvert the democratic process by binding a country to policies that they have not chosen themselves.
contagion	a phenomenon where a financial crisis in one country spreads to other countries. It can also be applied domestically to refer to a situation in which a crisis in one sector or group of firms spreads to others.
contractionary monetary policy	any monetary policy that increases interest rates or reduces the size of the money supply
contractionary fiscal policy	a policy that reduces government spending or increases taxes to generate a reduction in aggregate demand.
counter-cyclical	a phrase used to describe an economic phenomenon or policy that follows the inverse of the business cycle. When the economy is in a boom, a counter-cyclical phenomenon would be in the trough of its cycle and vice versa.
crawling peg	an exchange rate system where the rate is periodically adjusted by the authorities, according to economic or market indicators, like inflation. The regular adjustment of the currency avoids larger movements of the exchange rate.
credit rationing	occurs when no lender will loan money to a borrower even if the borrower is willing to pay more than a comparable borrower who is receiving a loan. The situation arises

because of asymmetric information. Banks cannot determine which are good versus bad borrowers, and their response is to restrict lending and reduce their exposure.

currency appreciation (depreciation)	the increase (decrease) in value of a country's currency with respect to one or more foreign reference currencies. Many analysts use the term to refer only to variations in the exchange rate caused by market forces as opposed to direct intervention or correction by government.
currency board	public sector authority in charge of exchanging domestic for foreign currency at a rate set by law with no restriction.
currency convertibility	the aspect of capital account convertibility relating to currency. The term encompasses the regulations regarding the convertibility of domestic currency into foreign currency. A country with full currency convertibility allows its citizens to freely convert domestic to foreign currency at market rates.
current account	that part of the balance of payments that measures a country's international payments arising from trade in goods and services. It also includes financial transfers where ownership is not involved, as in aid or private donations.
debt ratio	in relation to external debt, it refers to the ratio of the liabilities of a country to GDP, exports or international reserves.
debt service	the scheduled interest and principal payments (amortization) due on outstanding obligations of a country or its residents.
debt sustainability	a characterization of whether or not a given debt level can be maintained without generating major disturbances. A debt level is sustainable if a debtor can meet current and future debt service obligations in full, without recourse to debt relief. Sometimes the concept is used to refer to an amount of debt that can be serviced without constraining economic growth.
Dollar/Euro-ization	abandonment of domestic currency in favor of the use of the US dollar or Euro in domestic transactions.
Dutch disease	the decline in some export and import-competing sectors that occurs when there is a boom of natural resource exports. The latter causes a significant real appreciation of the currency which reduces the international competitiveness of other industries. The name comes from the effects on manufacturing in the Netherlands after the discovery of natural gas. The concept is sometimes use for a similar phenomenon created by booming capital inflows.
expansionary fiscal policy	an increase in government spending or tax reduction aimed at expanding aggregate demand.
expansionary monetary policy	any monetary policy that reduces interest rates or increases the size of the money supply.

export-led growth	a growth strategy based on the dynamic growth of exports.
fiscal austerity	a catchphrase that indicates that a country is running a fiscal surplus, or has capped the size of permissible fiscal deficit to reduce aggregate demand (or, in other words, has adopted a contractionary fiscal policy).
fixed exchange rate	also known as a pegged exchange rate, this is an exchange rate regime where a currency's value is matched to the value of another currency, to a basket of other currencies, or to another measure of value, such as gold. The monetary authority must continually intervene in foreign exchange markets to ensure the exchange rate remains stable. A currency that uses a fixed exchange rate is known as a fixed currency.
floatng exchange rate	also known as a flexible exchange rate, this is an exchange rate regime where a currency's value is determined by the foreign exchange market. A currency that uses a floating exchange rate is known as a floating currency.
Group of 24 (G24)	a group of 24 developing countries that attempts to coordinate their positions on international monetary and financial issues. It also tries to ensure that the member country interests are adequately represented in the associated negotiations.
Group of 10 (G10)	a group of ten countries (Belgium, Canada, France, Germany, Italy, Japan, the Netherlands, Sweden Switzerland, the United Kingdom, and the United States) that came together to create and guide international finance. Its initiatives include the General Arrangements to Borrow, to provide additional funding to the IMF during crises, and the Basel Committee.
Group of 8 (G8)	an international forum for the governments of Canada, France, Germany, Italy, Japan, Russia, the United Kingdom and the United States that was formed to discuss global issues. The group has a rotating presidency which hosts an annual summit to discuss the prevailing issues of the day and consider policy responses. This group was known as the G-7 until Russia joined in 1997.
Group of 22 (G20)	a group of 22 developed and emerging market countries that met in 1998 to propose reforms of the international financial system to make it less susceptible to crises. It was a precursor of the G-20, which was created in 1999.
GINI index	measure of the inequality of a distribution, usually income or wealth. A higher value, in a scale of 0 to 1, indicates the distribution is less equal.

greenfield investment	A form of foreign direct investment where a parent company starts a new venture in a foreign country by constructing new operational facilities from the ground up.
hedging	refers to any process of reducing exposure to risk by holding offsetting positions (for instance, selling foreign exchange but at the same time buying it in the futures market).
hot money	a phrase that describes short-term speculative capital flows into a country. These funds often flow in to take advantage of an opportunity, such as a favorable interest rate, and can be pulled out at a moment's notice if conditions change.
Keynesian	an economist who believes in the economic theory developed by John Maynard Keynes. In Keynesian economics, recessions are caused by insufficient demand, so the government has a role to play in stimulating aggregate demand. This stands in contrast to neo classical, or laissez-faire, economics which are typified by assumptions of perfectly functioning markets and complete information.
margin call	buying on margin is borrowing money from the broker to purchase stock; the broker requires, however, that a minimum deposit be kept; if the price of the stocks falls below certain value, a request by the broker is made to either put some money into the deposit account or sell some of the assets.
monetary policy	any policy pursued by the government or its central bank/monetary authority to manage the supply of money or interest rates in order to achieve specific goals, such as specific inflation targets or faster economic growth.
moral hazard	also known as adverse incentive, this is a situation by which an agent engages in risky behavior that affects other agents that would bear part of the costs. One example is that individuals with car insurance may drive in a riskier manner because it knows that the insurance company will pay a large part of the costs of an eventual accident.
overshooting	a phenomenon where financial markets initially overreact to a shock, such as a change in money supply or other policy, before reaching a new short-term equilibrium. The term is most frequently applied to exchange rate movements.
Pareto efficient	a resource allocation is said to be Pareto efficient if there is no redistribution that can improve one individual's welfare without decreasing someone else's.
Ponzi scheme	another term for pyramid scheme, this is a fraudulent investment operation where returns paid to investors are not

generated by assets, rather they are generated by new investors joining. It is also used for a situation in which a debtor pays all debt service with new debt that exceeds its payment capacity.

portfolio investment — the practice whereby an individual invests in a collection of financial assets (stocks, bonds and more sophisticated instruments) that are managed by someone else.

price discovery — the process of determining the price of a given commodity or financial asset in the open market. In relation to new financial instruments, such as derivates, it refers to the capacity to find a price for a risk that otherwise will have no valuation (for example, the value of the risk that the exchange rate would depreciate).

price-based controls — in the context of capital controls, the use of taxes or subsidies to modify the amount of capital inflows or outflows. Contrast this with quantity-based controls.

primary surplus — the government budget surplus excluding interest payments on government debt.

privatization — the process of converting a state-owned enterprise into a privately owned entity, under the implicit assumption that private enterprises operate more efficiently.

progressive taxation — a term for a tax regime where the tax rate increases with the value of the thing being taxed. It is usually applied to income taxes where individuals with greater disposable income pay a higher percentage in taxes.

quantity-based controls — in relation to capital controls, the use of quotas or prohibitions to limit capital inflows or outflows.

real interest rate — the interest rate once inflation has been accounted for. If both the nominal interest rate and inflation are small, the real interest rate is approximately the nominal rate minus inflation.

relative prices — the price of one good in terms of another, or in terms of a basket of goods.

remittances — transfers of money from individuals working abroad back to their home country.

reserves (foreign exchange) — these are the accumulated holdings of foreign financial assets by central banks/monetary authorities. They are composed of foreign currency, bonds, gold, and occasionally Special Drawing Rights (SDRs) granted by the IMF.

reverse causality — a condition wherein the assumed direction of cause and effect is reversed. One example is that trade liberalization is argued to improve industrial productivity, but it could also

	be true that increased industrial productivity motivates the country to liberalize trade.
risk-weighted assets	one way of calculating the value of a portfolio of assets which accounts for each asset's underlying risk. For example, if two assets had equal payouts but one was riskier than the other, it would be worth less under a risk-weighting scheme.
speculative attack	in relation to foreign exchange markets, occurs when investors believes that a country will be forced to devalue its currency, and they sell off all their holdings of the country's currency or financial assets. In a fixed exchange rate regime, the central bank will be forced to sell foreign exchange at the fixed rate and will run down their reserves in the process.
shock	a sudden and unexpected event that can cause an acute change in a country's economy. Examples include large currency depreciations, commodity price declines and natural disasters. All of these are negative shocks which could impact employment, output, and price levels over a period of years.
speculation	refers to the practice of buying assets to produce returns from an expected short-term change in price rather than from the underlying performance of the asset. Speculation can occur on any financial asset and underlies some hot money flows and all speculative attacks.
stabilization program	a set of macroeconomic policies with the intended aim of reducing some form of economic volatility. That volatility can take many forms including price volatility (inflation), exchange rate volatility and strong business cycles.
sterilization	a monetary policy intervention in the domestic money market with the express aims of offsetting the monetary effect of the accumulation or reduction of foreign exchange reserves. Thus, when the central bank expands the money supply by buying foreign exchange, it could sell other domestic assets (particularly government bonds) it holds to absorb the additional money supply.
terms of trade	the ratio of the price index of a country's exports to the price index of its imports.
Tobin tax	a proposed tax on foreign exchange transactions named after its progenitor, James Tobin. The tax proposes to reduce exchange rate fluctuations by dissuading speculation.
trade balance	also known as net exports, this is an accounting measure of the difference between the value of exports and imports of goods and services of an economy for a given period of time. When

imports are larger (less) than exports, the country has a negative (positive) trade balance and is said to be running a trade deficit (surplus).

volatility (macroeconomic)

in general, this refers to the frequency of changes in given economic indicator such as the price level or GDP growth. It is used as shorthand for situations of great economic instability such as financial crises.

Acronyms

BWI	Bretton Woods Institutions: The World Bank and the International Monetary Fund, established in 1944
ADR	An American Depositary Receipt is how the stock of most foreign companies trades in United States stock markets
FDI	Foreign Direct Investment
PI	Portfolio Investment
OECD	Organization for Economic Cooperation and Development
GNP/GDP	Gross National Product/Gross Domestic Product
BNM	Bank Negara Malaysia
IFIs	International Financial Institutions
IMF	International Monetary Fund
IRB	Internal Rating-Based (approach)
LGD	Loss Given Default
EAD	Exposure At Default
OTC markets	Over-the-Counter Markets
LIBOR	London Interbank Offered Rate and is a daily reference rate based on the interest rates at which banks offer to lend unsecured funds to other banks in the London wholesale (or "interbank") money market.
S&C	Standards and Codes
ROSC	Reports on the Observance of Standards and Codes
FSAP	Financial Sector Assessment Programs
EME	Emerging Market Economy
SDDS	Special Data Dissemination Standards
GDDS	General Data Dissemination Standards
FATF	Financial Action Task Force
NIESR	National Institute of Economic and Social Research
FSF	Financial Stability Forum
NAFTA	North American Free Trade Agreement
ECLAC	Economic Commission for Latin America and the Caribbean

Index

Index

Brazil 78, 105, 114, 233, 244, 295, 341
Brazilian Mercantile and Futures Exchange (BM&F) 292
Bretton Woods Institutions (BWIs) 49, 320, 337–8
Brownbridge, M. 133
Budd, J. W. 129
Buffett, Warren 310
bureaucracy 157, 162, 164
business cycle 185

Calderon 121, 123
call option 295
callable bonds 294
Calvo, G. 5, 60, 68, 69, 102, 126, 132
Cambodia 134
capital:
  bargaining power 129–30
  economic 271–2, 279
  foreign-owned 106
  mobility 140
  portfolio 210
  ratios 253
  regulatory 235, 270–3, 274, 279
  requirements 258, 307–8, 310–12, 314–15
  short term 85, 91
  speculative 126
  standard 256
capital account:
  and current account 176–9
  evolution of 55–6
  instruments for restricting 55
  and interest rates 191
  liberalization 289, 327–30
  openness indicator 123
  volatility 16–18
capital account regulation:
  and capital flow composition 196–8
  evolution of 191–3
  macroeconomic effect 191–2
  nature of 180–3
  policy objectives 184–6
  and short term flows 183
  temporary effect 195, 201
capital adequacy ratios 246–52
capital controls 66, 140–1
  and crises 128
  defined 144
  dynamic 160–1, 163
  inflows and outflows 142, 155–6, 164
  Malaysia 217–19
  part of integrated policy package 228
capital flows 5, 145
  causes of volatility 231
  controls on 142, 155–6, 164
  and current account 202–3
  cycles 172–4

dynamics of 184, 201
and financial development 57
historical 49
magnitude of 186–90
need to manage 2
private 51–3
pro-cyclical 18–21, 82, 89, 126
restricted 65
short term 76, 183
capital management techniques 141–2
  achievements 164–5
  assessment 153, 157, 161–2
  China 159–61
  costs of 148–9, 154, 157–8, 162, 164–5
  India 155–7
  long run 163
  Malaysia 151–3
  static and dynamic 144–5
  types of 143–9
capital market liberalization:
  and crises 78, 127
  effect on developing countries 15–28
  and inequality 122–4
  limits policy options 78
  models 3–4, 77–8, 92–4, 95–8, 122
  potential collateral benefits 88
  and poverty 122–4
  see also financial globalization
capital markets:
  definition 290–1
  growth of 292–6
  regulation 30–3
  thin 12–15, 22, 34
Caplin, A. S. 5
Caprio, G. 61
capture of minds 266
Cardenas, M. 190
Cardoso, E. 163
Carlson, M. 20
Cassard, M. 305–6
Cavallo, M. 256
Central Limit Order Book International (CLOB) 220
Chamley, C. P. 5
Chang, H.-J. 146
Charlton, A. 27
Chiappe, M. L. 283
Chile 37, 244
  asset bubble 198
  capital account regulation 180–201
  domestic policies 105–6
  private capital inflows 186, 188
  real estate 198
China 128, 141, 145, 163–4, 180
  capital management techniques 159–61
  case study 158–63
  policy context 159